Contract Law in Ireland

Contract Law in Ireland

Cliona Kelly

This book was originally published as a monograph in the International Encyclopaedia of Laws/Contracts.

Founding Editor: Roger Blanpain
General Editor: Frank Hendrickx
Volume Editor: Jacques Herbots

Wolters Kluwer

Published by:
Kluwer Law International B.V.
PO Box 316
2400 AH Alphen aan den Rijn
The Netherlands
E-mail: international-sales@wolterskluwer.com
Website: lrus.wolterskluwer.com

Sold and distributed by:
Wolters Kluwer Legal & Regulatory U.S.
7201 McKinney Circle
Frederick, MD 21704
United States of America
Email: customer.service@wolterskluwer.com

ISBN 978-94-035-3113-7

e-Book: ISBN 978-94-035-3114-4
web-PDF: ISBN 978-94-035-3115-1

The Author

Cliona Kelly is an Assistant Professor of Law at the Sutherland School of Law, University College Dublin, having previously taught at Cardiff University and the National University of Ireland, Galway. She was the lead researcher for the Irish Law Reform Commission *Report on Privity of Contract and Third Party Rights* and has worked as a member of an Advisory Group on Consumer Law to the Irish Government. In 2011 she was appointed as the Internal Examiner in Contract Law for the Law Society of Ireland, a statutory position under the Solicitors Acts 1954–1994. She is a respected legal scholar and author of many authoritative articles and works in the fields of contract law and consumer law.

The Author

Table of Contents

List of Abbreviations

AC	Appeal Cases
All ER	All England Reports
B & Ald	Barnewall & Anderson
BLR	Building Law Review
Burr	Burrow
Ch App	Chancery Appeal
Ch D	Chancery Division
CJ	Chief Justice
CL	Common Law
CLR	Commonwealth Law Reports
Cmnd.	Command Paper
CMLR	Common Market Law Report
Comm Cas	Commercial Cases
DLR	Dominion Law Reports
E&B	Ellis and Blackburn
ECR	European Human Rights Reports
EHRR	European Community Reports
ELR	Employment Law Reports
Exch	Exchequer
HC	High Court
HL	House of Lords
IEHC	Irish High Court (neutral citation)
IESC	Irish Supreme Court (neutral citation)
ILR	Irish Law Reports 1838–1850
ILRM	Irish Law Reports Monthly
ILT	Irish Law Times
ILTR	Irish Law Times Reports
ILTSJ	Irish Law Times Solicitors Journal
IR	Irish Reports
IRCL	Irish Reports Common Law

List of Abbreviations

IREq	Irish Reports Equity
Ir CL Rep	Irish Common Law Reports
Ir Eq Rep	Irish Equity Reports
Ir Jur NS	Irish Jurist New Series
Ir Jur OS	Irish Jurist Old Series
Ir Jur Rep	Irish Jurist Report
J	Judge
KB	King's Bench
Lloyds Rep	Lloyds Report
M&W	Meeson and Welsby
NI	Northern Ireland
NZLR	New Zealand Law Reports
QB	Queen's Bench
QBD	Queen's Bench Division
SC	Supreme Court
s/ss	Section/sections
SGCA	Singapore Court of Appeal
SI	Statutory Instrument
Term Rep	Term Report
UKHL	United Kingdom House of Lords
Unrep	Unreported
VR	Victoria Reports
WLR	Weekly Law Reports

General Introduction

§1. THE GENERAL BACKGROUND OF THE COUNTRY

I. Population and Composition

1. The island of Ireland is divided into four Provinces – Ulster, Munster, Leinster and Connaught – and then subdivided into 32 counties. The Republic of Ireland consists of 26 of these counties, with the remaining 6 counties forming Northern Ireland, which is part of the United Kingdom of Great Britain and Northern Ireland. The population of the Republic, as per the latest census in 2016, was 4,761,865.[1] The population of Northern Ireland as per the latest census in 2011 was 1,810,863.[2]

2. The 2016 Census revealed that there were 535,475 non-Irish nationals living in the Republic of Ireland.[3] Polish nationals (122,515 people) made up the largest group, followed by the UK and Lithuania, with significant representation from countries such as Brazil, India, Lithuania, Latvia, Spain, Italy, Romania, France, Germany and America.[4] In terms of ethnic composition, the vast majority of residents (82%) identified as 'White Irish' in the last census. Travellers are now officially recognised in Ireland as an ethnic minority, and the 2016 Census showed that the number of Irish Travellers stood at 30,987, representing 0.7% of the general population.

3. Catholicism is still the largest religion, but the Census shows that numbers are falling, with 3,729,115 Catholics comprising 78.3% of the population as of April 2016, compared with 84.2% five years previously.[5] In addition, 481,388 persons stated that they had no religion (including atheists/agnostics), an increase of 204,151 (+73.6%) on five years previously.[6] The Census also revealed that there

1. Central Statistics Office https://www.cso.ie/en/census/census2016reports/.
2. Northern Ireland Statistics and Research Agency https://www.nisra.gov.uk/statistics/census/2011-census.
3. Central Statistics Office https://www.cso.ie/en/csolatestnews/presspages/2018/census2016-non-irishnationalitieslivinginireland/ and https://www.cso.ie/en/csolatestnews/pressreleases/2017pressreleases/pressstatementcensus2016resultsprofile7-migrationanddiversity/.
4. *Ibid.*
5. Central Statistics Office https://www.cso.ie/en/csolatestnews/pressreleases/2017pressreleases/pressstatementcensus2016resultsprofile8-irishtravellersethnicityandreligion/.
6. *Ibid.*

were 126,414 members of the Church of Ireland, 63,443 Muslims, 62,187 Orthodox Christians and 24,211 Presbyterians.[7]

4. The Constitution of the Republic of Ireland, *Bunreacht na hÉireann*, provides that the Irish language is the first official language, with the English language recognised as the second official language.[8] If the English and Irish texts of the Constitution or an Act conflict, the text in the Irish language shall prevail.[9] Official business in any part of the State may be conducted in Irish, and official forms are printed in English and Irish. The everyday use of the Irish language is largely confined to areas on the west coast of Ireland known as *Gaeltacht* areas, although a significant number of people in urban areas such as Dublin, Cork, Limerick and Galway would also speak Irish on a daily basis.[10] In the 2016 Census, 1,761,420 persons (aged 3 and over) stated that they could speak Irish, constituting 39.8% of the population.[11] However, 23.8% indicated that they never spoke it, and a further 31.7% indicated that they only spoke it within the education system.[12] The 2016 Census revealed that 612,018 residents spoke a language other than Irish or English at home, an increase of 19.1% since 2011. The top languages spoken were Polish (113,225), Lithuanian (30,502), Romanian (26,645) and Portuguese (16,737).

II. Outline of the Constitutional, Legal and Political History of Ireland

5. From the twelfth century, with the Norman Conquest of Ireland, the legal-constitutional history of Ireland has been inextricably linked with that of England.[13] Before the Conquest, the law which prevailed throughout the whole island of Ireland was Brehon law, an ancient customary legal system. Brehon law continued in force in large areas of Ireland outside the 'Pale'[14] long after King John formally ordained in the year 1210 that English laws should be in force in Ireland.[15] However, English law was gradually extended over the whole of Ireland, and by the early seventeenth century, Brehon law was superseded by English law. In addition, Irish judges and lawyers were thoroughly indoctrinated in the English common law system. The English influence has persisted even after independence as a highly persuasive factor in Irish decisions where the law in both jurisdictions has remained substantially similar, as is the case with the law of contract.

7. *Ibid.*
8. Article 8, *Bunreacht na hÉireann.*
9. Article 25.4.30, *Bunreacht na hÉireann.*
10. Central Statistics Office https://www.cso.ie/en/csolatestnews/pressreleases/2017pressreleases/pressstatementcensus2016resultsprofile10-educationskillsandtheirishlanguage/.
11. *Ibid.*
12. *Ibid.*
13. *See generally* Byrne, McCutcheon and Bruton, Gerard Coffey *The Irish Legal System* (6th ed., Bloomsbury, 2014) Chapter 2; Mhuirthile, O'Sullivan and Thornton, *Fundamentals of the Irish Legal System: Law, Policy and Politics* (Round Hall, 2016) Chapter 5, paras 5.53–5.57.
14. The Pale was an area around Dublin and a strip of territory along the east coast of Ireland.
15. Johnston, 'The First Adventure of the Common Law' (1920) 36 *Law Quarterly Review* 10.

6. The struggle for Irish Independence led to the Government of Ireland Act 1920 which partitioned Ireland and formally established a six-county Northern Ireland which excluded three of the counties (Cavan, Monaghan and Donegal) of the historic province of Ulster. The border between Northern and Southern Ireland was artificially drawn to provide Northern 'Unionists' with as much territory as they could safely control, and it was designed to ensure Unionist (overwhelmingly Protestants) supremacy over Nationalists (overwhelmingly Catholics).[16] The *Sinn Fein* nationalist movement in Ireland did not accept the Government of Ireland Act 1920. The military wing of *Sinn Fein* (the IRA) waged war against British rule in Ireland until a truce was agreed in July 1921 and negotiations produced Articles of Agreement (commonly called the Treaty) on 6 December 1921. This Treaty conferred dominion status, similar to Canada at that time, on the 26 Counties of Southern Ireland (the Irish Free State), and the boundary between Northern Ireland and the rest of Ireland was to be determined by a Boundary Commission.

7. After much debate, the elected representatives of Sinn Fein in the Dáil (which was not recognised formally by Britain) accepted the Treaty by a majority of 64 votes to 57 on 7 January 1922. A provisional government, established under the Treaty, was given the task of drafting a constitution for the new Irish Free State. However, the Treaty precipitated a bitter civil war between pro- and anti-Treaty supporters. The civil war continued in one form or another until April 1923, causing the death of some leading figures in the previously united independence movement including the charismatic Michael Collins. However, the provisional government survived, and the legislative and constitutional procedures in both Ireland and England were completed to permit the new Irish Free State to emerge in 1922. The 1922 Constitution of the Irish Free State in 1922 was eventually replaced by *Bunreacht na hÉireann*, the Constitution of Ireland, which was adopted in 1937. The new Constitution in Article 5 declared: 'Ireland is a sovereign, independent, democratic state.'[17] Both Constitutions contained clauses continuing the law in force. Article 50 of *Bunreacht na hÉireann* states:

> Subject to this Constitution and to the extent to which they are not inconsistent therewith, the laws in force in Saorstat Eireann immediately prior to the date of the coming into operation of this Constitution shall continue to be of full force and effect until the same or any of them shall have been repealed or amended by enactment of the Oireachtas.

Bunreacht na hÉireann – The Irish Constitution

---

16. Lee, *Ireland 1912–1985* (1989) p. 45.
17. The question whether Ireland had formally become a Republic after the 1937 Constitution remained controversial. The *Republic of Ireland Act* 1948 put the matter to rest.

8. *Bunreacht na hÉireann*, the Irish Constitution, is the fundamental law of the State.[18] Article 8 of the Constitution provides that the Irish language, as the national language, is the first official language of the State and recognises English as the second official language. The Constitution is written in both English and Irish; where a divergence occurs between both texts of the Constitution, the text in the Irish language will prevail.

9. The Constitution sets out the role and operation of institutions such as the Oireachtas (Parliament),[19] Government,[20] Courts[21] and the President.[22] Under the principle of the separation of powers, the 'sole and exclusive power of making laws for the State is … vested in the Oireachtas, and no other legislative authority has power to make laws for the State'.[23] However, the Oireachtas must not enact any law which is 'repugnant' to the Constitution, and any law which is unconstitutional may be declared invalid by the courts.[24] The upper chamber of the Oireachtas, the Dáil, is elected by direct vote on the system of proportional representation by means of the single transferable vote.[25] The lower chamber, the Seanad, consists of members nominated by the Taoiseach, members elected from University panels and members elected onto panels representing differing interests.[26] The executive power of the State is exercised by or on the authority of the Government.[27] The head of the Government is referred to as the Taoiseach.[28] In contrast to the Taoiseach, and despite being directly elected, the President is a formal figurehead, who is authorised to act mostly 'on advice of' the Government or Taoiseach.[29] This has resulted in controversy on occasions when the President has acted independently to the Government.[30] The President's formal roles include declaring the dissolution of the Dáil

18. For detailed analysis of the Irish Constitution, *see* Hogan, Whyte, Kenny and Walsh, *Kelly: The Irish Constitution* (2018); Oran Doyle and Eoin Carolan (eds), *The Irish Constitution: Governance and Values* (Thomson Round Hall, 2008); Carolan (ed.), *The Constitution of Ireland: Perspectives and Prospects* (Bloomsbury Professional, 2012); Forde and Leonard, *Constitutional Law of Ireland* (3rd ed., Bloomsbury Professional, 2016).
19. Articles 15–27.
20. Article 28.
21. Articles 34–37.
22. Articles 12–14.
23. Article 15.2.1°.
24. Article 4.
25. Article 16.2.5°.
26. Article 18. These panels are: National Language and Culture, Literature, Art, Education; Agriculture and Fisheries; Labour; Industry and Commerce; Public Administration and Social Services.
27. Article 28.2.
28. Article 28.5.1°.
29. *See* for example Article 13.11. *See* Coakley and Rafter, 'The President of Ireland: A Constitutional and Political Figurehead?' (2012) 27(4) Irish Political Studies 493; Coakley, 'An Ambiguous Office? The Position of Head of State in the Irish Constitution' (2012) 48(2) Irish Jurist 43.
30. *See* Mee, 'The Changing Nature of the Presidency: The President and the Government should be Friends' (1996) 14 Irish Law Times 2.

(on the advice of the Taoiseach),[31] signing acts of the Oireachtas into law[32] and referring to the Supreme Court any Bill for a decision as to whether the Bill is repugnant to the Constitution.[33]

10. The Constitution also sets out the fundamental rights of Irish citizens. This includes provision for fair trials in criminal cases, including the right to trial by jury.[34] As well as specific rights in relation to, for example, equality before the law,[35] freedom of expression,[36] freedom of religion,[37] personal liberty,[38] and rights to private property,[39] the Constitution contains a far-reaching guarantee of protection of personal rights in Article 40:

> The State guarantees in its laws to respect, and, as far as practicable, by its laws to defend and vindicate the personal rights of the citizen.
> The State shall, in particular, by its laws protect as best particular, by its laws protect as best it may from unjust attack and, in the case of injustice done, vindicate the life, person, good name, and property rights of every citizen. [40]

11. The Supreme Court has stated that this general guarantee extends to 'unenumerated rights', which are not expressly stated, such as the right to bodily integrity.[41] In *McGee v The Attorney General*[42] the Supreme Court found that under Article 40 there was a right to privacy in marital affairs, and thus legislation which at the time essentially banned the use of contraception was unconstitutional as it violated this right to privacy.

12. The Constitution also contains provisions recognising the 'family' 'as the natural primary and fundamental unit group of Society'[43] and guarantees to 'guard with special care the institution of Marriage' – although since a constitutional referendum on the issue, divorce is now available and provided for in the Constitution.[44] The Constitution also specifically recognises the rights of children,[45] including the right to education, the right to free primary education and the right to home educate.[46] However, after a controversial referendum in 2004, the automatic

31. Article 13.2.1°.
32. Article 13.3.1°.
33. Article 26.
34. Article 38.
35. Article 40.1.
36. Article 40.6. This right is subject to limitations set out in the Article.
37. Article 44.
38. Article 40.4, which sets out the procedure known as *habeas corpus* through which an individual may challenge the legality of their detention.
39. Article 43.
40. Article 40.3.
41. *Ryan v Attorney General* [1965] 1 IR 294.
42. [1973] IR 284.
43. Article 41.
44. Article 41.2. This was introduced by referendum under the Fifteenth Amendment of the Constitution Act 1995.
45. Article 42A.
46. Article 42.

right of citizenship to all children born in Ireland was removed, such right only now being available where one parent was a citizen, or entitled to citizenship.[47]

13. The Constitution can only be amended by means of a referendum.[48] High profile referendums in recent years have included the referendum to remove the constitutional barriers to provision of abortion in Ireland,[49] the referendum to allow same-sex marriage,[50] and the divorce referendum,[51] as well as referendums to approve entry into the European Community in 1973,[52] and all other treaties related to the European Union[53] and the Good Friday Agreement.[54]

Ireland and the European Union

14. Ireland became a member of the then European Economic Community on 1 January 1973, following a referendum. The Supreme Court has held that any subsequent revisions to the Treaties which involve a further ceding of sovereignty to the European Union must also be approved by referendum,[55] so Treaties such as the Lisbon Treaty have had to be approved by a referendum. Article 29.4.6 of the Constitution specifically provides for the supremacy of European Union law, the current version stating:

> No provision of this Constitution invalidates laws enacted, acts done or measures adopted by the State, before, on or after the entry into force of the Treaty of Lisbon, that are necessitated by the obligations of membership of the European Union … .

15. Under the terms of Article 29 of the Constitution, European Union law has the force of law in the State and cannot be declared invalid as being repugnant to the Constitution.

Ireland and the European Convention on Human Rights

---

47. Article 9, as inserted by the Twenty-Seventh Amendment of the Constitution Act 2004.
48. Articles 46–47.
49. Resulting in the Sixth Amendment of the Constitution Act 2018. The Thirty-Sixth Amendment repealed that part of Article 40 of the Constitution which protected the right to life of the 'unborn' (often referred to as the Eighth Amendment) and replaced it with a provision (Article 40.3) allowing the Oireachtas to regulate the termination of pregnancy.
50. Resulting in the Thirty-Fourth Amendment of the Constitution (Marriage Equality) Act 2015.
51. Resulting in the Fifteenth Amendment of the Constitution Act 1995, and, more recently, after a second referendum which approved a reduction in the waiting times before divorce, the Thirty-Eighth Amendment of the Constitution of Ireland Act 2019.
52. Resulting in the Third Amendment of the Constitution Act 1972.
53. *See*, for example, the referendum on the Lisbon Treaty, resulting in the Twenty-Eighth Amendment of the Constitution (Treaty of Lisbon) Act 2009, and the two referendums on the Nice Treaty, the first of which was rejected and the second of which, was approved and resulted in the Twenty-Sixth Amendment of the Constitution Act 2002.
54. Resulting in the Nineteenth Amendment of the Constitution Act 1998.
55. *Crotty v An Taoiseach* [1987] 1 IR 713.

16. In 1950, Ireland was among the first signatories to the European Convention on Human Rights. It was ratified by Ireland in February 1953 and came into force in September of the same year. Ireland was the first State to recognise the jurisdiction of the European Court of Human Rights under Article 46, and Ireland was also the respondent State in the first case heard by the European Court of Human Rights in 1959.[56] Cases which have been brought against Ireland include *Airey*,[57] in which the Strasbourg Court found that the lack of civil legal aid for a married woman seeking judicial separation from her husband was a violation of her right of access to the courts under Article 6(1); *Norris*,[58] in which it was held that the existence of legislation which criminalised certain sexual acts between consenting male adults, and which therefore in effect criminalised homosexuality, was a violation of the privacy right in Article 8; and *A, B and C v Ireland*,[59] in which the applicants claimed that the legal restrictions on abortion in Ireland at the time were contrary to their rights under the Convention.

17. However, Ireland's status as a dualist State[60] meant that the mere fact of ratification did not mean that the Convention could be directly relied upon by an individual in an Irish court, but rather domestic legislation was required to incorporate the Convention into national law.[61] In 2003, the European Convention on Human Rights Act 2003 was enacted to 'enable further effect to be given' to the Convention in Ireland. Under this Act it is not however possible to simply claim in court that one's Convention rights have been breached; nor is it possible to have legislation declared invalid on the basis that it breaches a Convention right. Section 2 provides for the interpretative obligation of the courts, whereby a court 'shall' interpret and apply any statutory provision or rule of law in a manner compatible with the State's obligations under the Convention provisions, 'in so far as is possible, subject to the rules of law relating to such interpretation and application'. If it is not possible to interpret a statutory provision or rule of law in a Convention-compatible manner under section 2, and if no other legal remedy is adequate and available, then under section 5 of the Act the court may make a 'declaration of incompatibility', i.e., a declaration that the statutory provision or rule of law is incompatible with the State's obligations under the Convention provisions. However, a declaration of incompatibility does not affect the 'validity, continuing operation or enforcement of the statutory provision or rule of law in respect of which it is made',[62] and it will not have any impact on the proceedings before the court or on the legal position of

56. *Lawless v Ireland* (1979–1980) 1 EHRR 1.
57. *Airey v Ireland* (1979) Series A, No. 32.
58. *Norris v Ireland* (1991) 13 EHRR186.
59. Application No. 25579/05, Judgment of 16 December 2010.
60. Article 29.6 of the Constitution states 'No international agreement shall be part of the domestic law of the State save as may be determined by the Oireachtas.' This means that international treaties entered into must be incorporated into domestic law by legislation before they are applicable within the State.
61. *Re Ó Laighléis* [1960] 1 IR 93; *Norris v Attorney General* [1984] IR 36.
62. Section 5(2)(a).

the applicant who sought the declaration. Nor does it give the applicant an entitlement to damages, although they may apply to the Government for an *ex gratia* payment of compensation.[63] Finally section 3(1) provides that every 'organ of the State' must perform its functions in a manner compatible with the State's obligations under the Convention. This is limited in two ways. First, it is 'subject to any statutory provision', so that where an organ of the State acts in accordance with legislation then the obligation under section 3(1) does not arise. Second, the definition of 'organ of the State' is limited and does not include the courts.

§2. Legal Family

18. Ireland has a common law legal system, which is English in origin, and indeed Ireland has been described as the 'first great adventure of the common law'.[64] Much of Irish law continues to be based on judge-made rules, and indeed most principles of contract law are derived from case law. Courts are often asked to interpret legislation, and the meaning of legislation is developed through cases. Where there is no legislation dealing with an area, the courts will develop their own principles which they apply. The development of principles through cases is an important part of the common law, and it is facilitated by a system of 'precedent'.

19. The relationship between the Irish and English legal systems is continuously changing and developing,[65] but it cannot be denied that the English common law has been a significant influence on Irish law. More than 1,200 pre-Independence Acts which were in force in Ireland on 6 December 1922 remained in force post-Independence unless they were repealed by the Irish Parliament (Oireachtas) or declared unconstitutional.[66] English judicial decisions prior to 1922 are of significant precedent value in Ireland, although the Irish courts are not bound to follow them. Although English decisions post-1922 are of persuasive value in the same way as decisions from other common law jurisdictions, the links and similarities between the two legal systems, as well as factors such as the familiarity of the format and language of decisions, the accessibility of the decisions and physical proximity, mean that Irish courts refer to decisions of the English courts much more frequently than to jurisdictions such as Australia, Canada and New Zealand.[67] However, with the departure of the United Kingdom from the European Union, it is likely that more divergences will emerge, particularly with regard to areas within

---

63. Section 5(4).
64. Johnston, 'The First Great Adventure of the Common Law' (1920) 36 *Law Quarterly Review* 9.
65. For a good summary of the development of the Irish legal system, *see* Byrne & McCutcheon, with Bruton and Coffey, *Byrne and McCutcheon on the Irish Legal System* (Bloomsbury Professional, Dublin, 5th ed., 2009) pp. 27—63.
66. *See* Article 73 of the 1922 Constitution of the Irish Free State and Article 50(1) *Bunreacht na hÉireann* 1937. The Statute Law Revision (pre-1922) Act 2005, and the Statute Law Revision Acts 2007 and 2009 repealed a significant number of pre-Independence statutes, although over 100 remain in force.
67. *See* Byrne & McCutcheon, with Bruton and Coffey *Byrne and McCutcheon on the Irish Legal System* (Bloomsbury Professional, Dublin, 5th ed., 2009) pp. 437–439.

the competence of the EU institutions, such as consumer protection.[68] If the UK is no longer bound by the CJEU, while Ireland remains so bound, it may no longer be possible to turn to UK cases for guidance on how to interpret and apply laws which have their origins in the EU. This would be a significant departure for the Irish legal profession.[69]

§3. PRIMACY OF LEGISLATION

20. Article 15.2.1.0 of the Irish Constitution *Bunreacht na hÉireann* provides:

> The sole and exclusive power of making laws for the State is hereby vested in the Oireachtas: no other legislative authority has power to make laws for the State.

21. In practice, all bills are promoted or supported by the government, which has majority support in the Dáil and in the Seanad.

22. The legislative competence of the Oireachtas is limited by the Constitution. Article 4 of *Bunreacht na hÉireann* provides:

> 1. The Oireachtas shall not enact any law which is in any respect repugnant to this Constitution or any provision thereof.
> 2. Every law enacted by the Oireachtas which is in any respect repugnant to this Constitution or to any provision thereof, shall, but to the extent only of such repugnancy, be invalid.[70]

23. This meant, for example, that while the Constitution expressly prohibited abortion except where the mother's life was at risk,[71] the Oireachtas was unable to legislate for abortion except in a very limited fashion.[72] A referendum was necessary to change the Constitution to allow the Oireachtas to legislate for abortion in wider circumstances.[73]

---

68. *See* Kelly, 'Consumer Reform in Ireland and the UK: Regulatory Divergence Before, After and Without Brexit' (2018) 47(1) *Common Law World Review* 53–76.
69. *Ibid.*
70. On the Constitution and constitutional law generally.
71. Article 40.3.3° stated: 'The State acknowledges the right to life of the unborn and, with due regard to the equal right to life of the mother, guarantees in its laws to respect, and, as far as practicable, by its laws to defend and vindicate that right.' This Article was added in 1983 after a referendum to amend the Constitution, and is often referred to as the 'Eighth Amendment'.
72. The Protection of Life During Pregnancy Act 2013 allowed for abortion under very limited circumstances, namely where there was 'a real and substantial risk of loss of the woman's life', and in practice abortion was unavailable in Ireland – *see A, B and C v Ireland* No. 25579/05 Judgment of December 16, 2010.
73. The Thirty-Sixth Amendment of the Constitution repealed Article 40.3.3 (the Eighth Amendment) and replaced it with wording which expressly allowed the Oireachtas to legislate for abortion. Abortion is now provided for in the Health (Regulation of Termination of Pregnancy) Act 2018, albeit subject to some limitations.

24. If legislation passed is unconstitutional, it can be declared invalid.[74] For example, in *McGee v Attorney General*[75] it was held that section 17 of the Criminal Law Amendment Act 1935, which made it unlawful for any person to sell or import into Ireland any contraceptive, was an unjustified invasion of the plaintiff's personal right to privacy in her marital affairs and was inconsistent with Article 40(3)(1) of the Constitution. As a result section 17 was struck down by the court. A recent example of this is *Bederev v Ireland*[76] in which section 2(2) of the Misuse of Drugs Act 1977 was held to be unconstitutional because it contravened the principle of separation of powers in Article 15.2.1 of the Constitution. The Act, which gave far-reaching powers to the Minister of Health to declare certain drugs illegal, purported to vest in the Government law-making powers which are in the exclusive authority of the Oireachtas.

25. In contrast, legislation which is constitutional but which is contrary to the European Convention of Human Rights cannot be struck down as invalid. The powers of review of the court are limited by Article 34.3.2° of the Constitution,[77] and a court cannot refuse to apply a statutory provision which is not unconstitutional.[78] The court can merely issue a declaration of incompatibility, which is essentially an acknowledgement of the breach of rights, and an invitation to the Oireachtas to remedy the situation.

§4. The Position of the Judiciary

I. The Judiciary

26. As a common law legal system, the judiciary sits at the apex of the Irish legal system[79] and have the power, *inter alia*, to decide cases both at first instance and on appeal. In addition, they can review legislation in terms of constitutionality and strike down legislation that they find repugnant to the constitution.

27. Members of the judiciary are to be independent in the exercise of their judicial functions[80] and are not eligible to be members of the Oireachtas or to hold any

74. *See* Hogan, Kenny and Walsh 'An Anthology of Declarations of Unconstitutionality' (2015) 54(1) Irish Jurist 1.
75. [1973] IR 284.
76. [2016] IESC 34.
77. 'Save as otherwise provided by this Article, the jurisdiction of the High Court shall extend to the question of the validity of any law having regard to the provisions of this Constitution, and no such question shall be raised (whether by pleading, argument or otherwise) in any Court established under this or any other Article of this Constitution other than the High Court or the Supreme Court.'
78. Constitution Review Group Report of May 1996, (Stationery Office, Dublin, Pn.2632) p. 191.
79. For general discussion, *see* Laura Cahillane, James Gallen, Tom Hickey (eds), *Judges, Politics and the Irish Constitution* (2017); Eoin Carolan (ed.), *Judicial Power in Ireland* (IPA, 2018); Hogan, Whyte, Kenny and Walsh, *Kelly: The Irish Constitution* (2018) Chapter 6.4.
80. Article 35.2, *Bunreacht na hÉireann.*

other office.[81] They retain office until the mandatory retirement age of 70.[82] Members of the Supreme Court, the Court of Appeal and the High Court cannot be removed from office save for stated misbehaviour, or incapacity, and then only upon resolutions passed by Dáil Éireann and by Seanad Éireann calling for their removal.[83] The independence of judges is further protected by a provision that remuneration of judges cannot be reduced during their term of office.[84] This caused difficulties during the economic crash, when judges were exempt from public expenditure cuts. As a result of constitutional amendment following a referendum, the remuneration of judges can now be reduced when the remuneration of other public servants has been reduced in the public interest, and any cuts to judicial pay must be proportionate to the reductions imposed on the public service generally.[85]

28. Judges are appointed by the government of the day, but under Part IV of the Courts and Court Officers Act 1995 an independent Judicial Appointments Advisory Board is required to advise the government prior to the appointment of any particular member of the judiciary.[86] To be appointed to the Supreme Court, Court of Appeal, or High Court, a candidate must be 'a practising barrister or practising solicitor of not less than 12 years standing who has practised as a barrister or a solicitor for a continuous period of not less than two years immediately before such appointment'.[87] A judge of the Circuit Court who has served for at least two years is also qualified for appointment to the Supreme Court, Court of Appeal or High Court. A barrister or solicitor who during the period of two years immediately before the appointment was a judge (or Advocate General) of the European Court of Justice, European Court of Human Rights, International Court of Justice or International Criminal Court may also be appointed. Anyone recommended by the Board to the Government for judicial appointment must not only hold the formal qualifications set out but must also display an appropriate 'degree of competence and probity' and be 'suitable on the grounds of character and temperament'.[88]

29. Section 19 of the Courts and Court Officers Act, 1995 provides that:

---

81. Article 35.3, *Bunreacht na hÉireann.*
82. Under the Courts and Court Officers Act 1995 the retirement age of ordinary judges of the Supreme Court was reduced from 72 years to 70 years.
83. Article 35.4, *Bunreacht na hÉireann.* The tenure of Circuit Court and District Court Judges is similarly protected by statute.
84. Article 35.5, *Bunreacht na hÉireann.*
85. Twenty-Ninth Amendment of the Constitution Act 2011. The remuneration of judges reduced according to this Article in the Financial Emergency Measures in the Public Interest Act 2011.
86. *See* Carroll 'You Be the Judge: The Politics and Processes of Judicial Appointments in Ireland' (2005) 10(6) The Bar Review 182.
87. Section 5 of the Courts (Supplemental Provisions) Act 1961, as amended by s. 4 of the Courts and Court Officers Act 2002, and s. 11 of the Court of Appeal Act 2014. Section 17(2) and s. 29(2) of the Courts (Supplemental Provisions) Act 1961 as amended provide that a practising barrister or solicitor of not less than ten years is qualified for appointment as judge of the Circuit Court or the District Court.
88. Section 16(7) of the Courts and Court Officers Act 1995.

> A person who wishes to be considered for appointment to Judicial office shall undertake to [The Judicial Appointments Advisory Board] his or her agreement, if appointed to Judicial Office, to take such course or courses of training or education, or both, as may be required by the Chief Justice or President of the Court to which that person is appointed.

30. Continuing education for the judiciary is facilitated by the Committee for Judicial Studies (previously the Judicial Studies Institute). However the Association of Judges of Ireland has noted that the Committee has 'extremely limited financial resources and is accordingly unable to provide the type of continuing training and education that is common in other jurisdictions'.[89]

II. The Modern Court System

31. Articles 34–38 of the Constitution provide for the system of courts in Ireland and the trial of offences. Article 34.1 provides:

> Justice shall be administered in courts established by law by judges appointed in the manner provided by this Constitution, and, save in such special and limited cases as may be prescribed by law, shall be administered in public.

32. The Constitution outlines the structure of the court system in Ireland. It establishes the Supreme Court as a court of final appeal in all matters of constitutional, civil and criminal law.[90] The decision of the Supreme Court is in all cases final and conclusive.[91]

33. Following a referendum the Thirty-Third Amendment of the Constitution Act 2013 amended the Constitution to allow for a Court of Appeal, which as the name suggests is an appellate court in matters of constitutional, civil and criminal law.[92] The Supreme Court has appellate jurisdiction from a decision of the Court of Appeal if it involves a matter of general public importance or if it is necessary in the interests of justice.[93]

34. The High Court is a court of first instance with full jurisdiction in all criminal and civil matters. When exercising its criminal jurisdiction, the High Court is known as the Central Criminal Court and has jurisdiction to try more serious offences. Criminal trials are held before a judge sitting with a jury. The Commercial Court is also a division of the High Court, which deals with business disputes worth more than 1 million. An appeal from the High Court may go to the Court of

89. https://aji.ie/supports/judicial-education/.
90. Article 34.5.
91. Article 34.5.6.
92. Article 34.4.
93. Article 34.5.3.

Appeal,[94] or directly to the Supreme Court if there are 'exceptional circumstances' warranting a direct appeal on matters of public importance or in the interests of justice.[95]

35. Provision is also made in Article 34.3.4 for the establishment of courts of local and limited jurisdiction, on the basis of which the Circuit Court and the District Court were established by statute. The Circuit Court has jurisdiction in civil matters where the claim exceeds the jurisdiction of the District Court but is not in excess of €75,000. The Circuit Court also has jurisdiction in family law matters (e.g., granting orders of divorce) and has jurisdiction to deal with criminal offences except those over which the Central Criminal Court has jurisdiction. The District Court has jurisdiction in civil matters where claims are not in excess of €15,000. In matters of family law, the District Court has jurisdiction in matters concerning maintenance, custody of, and access to, children and may make orders pertaining to domestic violence. In criminal matters, the District Court is a court of summary jurisdiction and deals with the non-jury trial of persons charged with minor offences. The Small Claims Court is also operated within the District Court, and deals with claims worth less than €2,000.

36. The Special Criminal Court was established under the terms of the Offences Against the State Act 1939. It deals with offences where the ordinary courts are inadequate to secure the effective administration of justice, such as organised crime or paramilitary actions, and sits with three judges and no jury.

§5. Distinction Between Public Law and Private Law ('Administrative Contracts')

37. There is no formal distinction between public and private law in Ireland. There is no separate system of public administrative jurisdiction and administrative law on the lines created by the French *Conseil d'Etat*. There is, however, a substantial body of administrative law and a number of administrative tribunals, and it is convenient to think of certain areas of the law dealing with central and local government, and even criminal law, as 'public law' as distinct from those matters which are of primary concern to the individual parties involved, and thus 'private law'. The whole area of contract, torts, property, company law, trusts, etc., are left to individuals to pursue their claims if they wish. The State facilitates private legal proceedings by providing courts, judges, sheriffs to enforce judgments, etc., but does not otherwise involve itself in the private litigation of citizens. The State itself of course may sue or be sued in contract or tort like any other defendant, and such a case is heard in the normal way in the normal courts.

---

94. Article 34.4.1.
95. Article 34.5.4.

§6. Distinction Between Civil Law and Commercial Law ('Commercial Contracts')

38. There is no formal distinction between the civil law and commercial law, or between contracts in general and commercial contracts. The term 'commercial law' is used as a matter of convenience, often for teaching purposes, to refer to contracts like sale of goods, hire purchase, agency, banking and insurance. Texts on commercial law define it as 'that branch of law which is concerned with rights and duties arising from the supply of goods and services in the way of trade'.[96] Lawyers who describe themselves as specialising in commercial law often take a broader interpretation of the term and may work in areas such as tax, intellectual property or company law, but again the label 'commercial law' is mostly a matter of convenience. One of the reasons commercial law is so difficult to define is that the Irish legal system has no commercial code. In other words, it has no set of rules or single piece of legislation which could be recognised as 'commercial law'.

39. The same general principles of the law of contract apply to special contracts. However, there is an acknowledgement, both in case law and statute, that different rules might be appropriate depending on the status and bargaining power of the parties. If a contract is entered into between two businesses of equal bargaining power, the law is primarily concerned with facilitating and giving effect to that transaction. In the words of Lord Goff:

> Our only desire is to give sensible commercial effect to the transaction. We are there to help businessmen, not to hinder them: we are there to give effect to their transactions, not to frustrate them: we are there to oil the wheels of commerce, not to put a spanner in the works or even grit in the oil.[97]

40. In commercial transactions, where the parties have met on equal terms, the principle of freedom of contract remains paramount and the courts will be slow to interfere with the agreement reached:

> It is not the function of a court to write a contract for parties who have met upon commercially equal terms; if such parties want to enter into unreasonable, unfair or even disastrous contracts that is their business, not the business of the courts.[98]

41. Similarly, legislation governing commercial transactions generally consists of default (optional) rules, rather than mandatory rules.[99]

96. Goode, *Commercial Law* (3rd ed., 2004), p. 8.
97. Lord Goff [1984] Lloyd's Maritime and Commercial Law Quarterly 382, 392.
98. *Tradax (Ireland) Ltd. v Irish Grain Board Ltd.* [1984] IR 1, 26.
99. There are some exceptions, and it should be noted that even default rules can be seen as a form of regulation.

42. This can be contrasted with the protective approach that is taken in relation to consumer contracts, and there is an increasing amount of statutory provisions to compensate for the weaker bargaining position of the consumer. The Sale of Goods Act 1893, for example, applies to all contracts of sale, but amendments introduced in 1980 introduced extra protections for consumers, in particular making the implied terms regarding the quality of goods mandatory in consumer contracts,[100] providing for additional consumer remedies of repair and replacement[101] and adding a new set of rules on the provision of services.[102] In addition, the European Union has introduced a large body of consumer protection measures, referred to as the *consumer acquis,* into Irish law.[103] Certain contract law doctrines were arguably influenced by the desire to protect consumers or weaker contracting parties, such as the judicial preference for the restriction of exclusion clauses which attempt to circumvent the implied terms in the Sale of Goods Act, even before the 1980 amendment,[104] or the rules on misrepresentation.

100. Section 22 of the Sale of Goods and Supply of Services Act 1980, amending s. 55 of the Sale of Goods Act 1893.
101. Section 21 of the Sale of Goods and Supply of Services Act 1980, amending s. 53 of the Sale of Goods Act 1893.
102. Sections 39 and 40 of the Sale of Goods and Supply of Services Act 1980.
103. *See* C Kelly 'The Impact of Europe on Irish Contract Law', in Devenney and Kenny (eds) *The Transformation of European Private Law* (Cambridge University Press, 2013).
104. *See* for example *Clayton Love v B&I Transport* (1970) 104 ILTR 157; *Wallis, Son and Wells v Pratt and Haynes* [1910] 2 KB 1003; *Andrews v Singer* [1934] 1 KB 17; *O'Connor v McCowen & Sons Ltd* (1943) 77 ILTR 64.

Introduction to the Law of Contracts

§1. Definition of Contract

43. The Irish courts have defined a contract on numerous occasions, saying for example that a contract is 'an agreement to which the law will give effect'[105] or 'an agreement made between two or more parties under which one promises or undertakes with the other the performance of some action'.[106]

44. Of course, this does not tell us *which* agreements the law will view as enforceable. In particular, it should be noted that in general there must be a mutual undertaking, and the law will not enforce gratuitous promises unless they are made under seal. Similarly, social and domestic agreements which are not intended to be legally binding will not be enforced by the courts. However, it may be less clear whether other types of promises made, such as 'letters of comfort', are enforceable,[107] and equitable doctrines such as promissory estoppel may be used in a limited fashion to prevent someone from going back on a promise made.[108] It is thus necessary to look at more detail at the principles surrounding formation of contract, as well as rules on, for example, public policy, to establish which contracts will be enforced by the court.

§2. Historical Background of the Law of Contract

45. The Anglo-Irish law of contract in its present form[109] is largely the product of nineteenth century case law. The body of rules developed during this period are the starting point for any discussion on the formation of a contract (agreement, consideration, intention to contract); the effect of vitiating factors such as mistake, misrepresentation, duress and undue influence; and the rules governing remedies for breach of contract.

---

105. *Conway v Smith* (1950) Ir. Jur. 3 at 5.
106. *Tansey v College of Occupational Therapists Ltd.*, Unreported, High Court, 27 August 1986.
107. *See* paras 134–137 below.
108. *See* paras 170 et seq. below.
109. For discussion of the development of contract law before this period, *see* Simpson, *A History of the Common Law of Contract* (Clarendon Press, 1975); Fifoot, *History and Sources of the Common Law: Tort and Contract* (Stevens and Sons Ltd., 1949); Salmond 'The History of Contract', in Holdsworth's *Select Essays in Anglo-American Legal History* Vol. 3 (Little, Brown & Co., 1968).

46. During the eighteenth and nineteenth centuries, the English courts adopted a 'laissez faire' or non-interventionist attitude to transactions. The courts would recognise the freedom of the parties to contract, and refused to question the adequacy of consideration or to intervene in contracts on the basis of fairness. In sales law, for example, the basic principle was *caveat emptor* – let the buyer beware. The seller did not warrant the quality of the goods; if the buyer was unsure, he should have made enquiries or obtained warranties from the seller. Around the middle of the nineteenth century, the principle of caveat emptor began to change slowly, as the courts began to imply certain undertakings into contracts. These were still very basic. For example, in a sales contract the seller would be deemed to have title to the goods being sold, and certain warranties as to the quality of goods were also implied into contracts but only if there was no express term in the contract to the contrary.

47. This period also saw an attempt to 'codify' the principles found in cases in certain discrete areas.[110] For example by the end of the nineteenth century, a substantial body of sale of goods law had been developed through case law. The law was complex and inaccessible, and it was decided to codify this body of common law rules into an Act governing the sale of goods. The result was the Sale of Goods Act 1893 which was described as 'An Act for codifying the law relating to sale of goods'. Other examples include the Partnership Act 1890, the Bills of Exchange Act 1882 and the Marine Insurance Act 1906.

48. The history of the Irish law of contract is essentially the same as the English law of contract, and the development of rules of contract in Ireland mirrored the situation in England. As mentioned above, pre-Independence Acts remained in force post-Independence unless they were repealed by the Oireachtas or declared unconstitutional.[111] As a result, key contract and commercial law statutes, including the Sale of Goods Act 1893, the Apportionment Act 1870, the Partnership Act 1890 and the Marine Insurance Act 1906 all still apply in Ireland, although some have been amended by subsequent legislation. In addition, Irish lawyers and courts continue to pay special attention to English case law, and English decisions, though no longer binding, are cited regularly in Irish contract cases as 'persuasive' authorities. Despite having a linked heritage, Irish contract law differs in a number of important respects from contract law in England and Wales, and there are also several differences in the legislative framework governing contract law, with the legislature in the United Kingdom being considerably more active than the Irish parliament.[112] For example, unlike the UK Ireland does not have any general legislation dealing with

110. *See* Ferguson 'Legal Ideology and Commercial Interests: The Social Origins of the Commercial Law Codes' (1977) 4 British Journal of Law & Society 18; Rodger 'The Codification of Commercial Law in Victorian Britain' (1992) 108 Law Quarterly Review 570; Bridge 'The Evolution of Modern Sales Law' [1991] Lloyd's Maritime and Commercial Law Quarterly 52.

111. *See* Article 73 of the 1922 Constitution of the Irish Free State and Article 50(1) *Bunreacht na hÉireann* 1937.

112. *See* Kelly 'The Impact of Europe on Irish Contract Law' in Devenney and Kenny (eds.) The Transformation of European Private Law (Cambridge University Press, 2013).

the fairness of exemption clauses[113] or the remedies for misrepresentation,[114] nor has there been legislation to deal with the effects of frustration of contract or to reform the rule of privity of contract.[115] In the case of the sale of goods, while Ireland inherited the Sale of Goods Act 1893 it has not been amended to the same extent as in the United Kingdom.

49. In recent years, Irish contract law has been increasingly influenced by measures emanating from the European Union, particularly in relation to consumer contracts but also in relation to areas such as commercial agency, which would have been relatively unknown to Ireland and the UK before this.[116] This has introduced, in a limited fashion, concepts such as 'good faith'[117] or 'conformity with the contract'[118] into Irish contract law. With the departure of the United Kingdom from the European Union, it is likely that more divergences will emerge between the Ireland and the United Kingdom over time.[119] It could also have the effect of emphasising the division between commercial contracts (which would still be primarily governed by common law principles and the Sale of Goods Act, and highly influenced by developments in the UK) and consumer contracts (which would be primarily governed by European directives, and thus impacted by decisions of the CJEU, with UK decisions not being of relevance).[120]

§3. CLASSIFICATION OF CONTRACTS

50. All contracts in Irish law are simple contracts or contracts under seal. Simple contracts may be oral, or in writing or by conduct or by a combination of these means. All simple contracts require agreement and consideration, and apart from some statutory exceptions,[121] no formalities such as writing are required to make a simple contract. The only relevant major theoretical classification of contracts in Irish law therefore is that of simple contracts and contracts under seal.

---

113. There are certain specific statutory restrictions on exemption clauses, for example, ss 55 and 40 of the Sale of Goods and Supply of Services Act 1980 restrict contract terms which attempt to waive or vary the rights of the buyer under ss 12–15 of the Sale of Goods Act 1893 (as amended).
114. Limited remedies in the context of contracts for the sale of goods and supply of services are set out in Part V of the Sale of Goods and Supply of Services Act 1980.
115. This is despite the reform recommendations, Law Reform Commission, *Report on Privity of Contract and Third Party Rights* (LRC 88-2008).
116. EU Council Directive 86/653/EEC on the Co-ordination of the Laws of Member States relating to Self-Employed Commercial Agents. *See* Kelly 'The Impact of Europe on Irish Contract Law' in Devenney and Kenny (eds) *The Transformation of European Private Law* (Cambridge University Press, 2013).
117. This is referred to, for example, in the Unfair Contract Terms Directive (93/13/EEC). *See* Guenther Teubner 'Legal Irritants: Good Faith in British Law or How Unifying Law Ends up in New Divergences' (1998) 61(1) Modern Law Review 11–32.
118. Found in the Consumer Sales Directive (Directive 1999/44/EC on certain aspects of the sale of consumer goods and associated guarantees).
119. *See* C Kelly 'Consumer Reform in Ireland and the UK: Regulatory Divergence Before, After and Without Brexit' (2018) 47(1) Common Law World Review 53–76.
120. *Ibid.*
121. *See below* paras 199 et seq.

51. It may of course be relevant for practical legal purposes to 'classify' a particular contract as, for example, a contract for 'the sale of goods' or a contract 'of hire purchase' or a contract 'for the sale of land' but these are merely 'internal' subclassifications of the major categories of 'simple' contracts or contracts under seal. The Irish common law contract system does not attach doctrinal significance to such civil law classifications of contracts as 'consensual', solemn', 'real', 'commutative', 'aleatory', 'nominate' or 'innominate'. In Irish law, the parties are free to make contracts as they wish (subject to the usual restraints of illegality public policy) and the court's primary approach to construction of a contract is to implement the intention of the parties to that contract. There is no necessity for the courts first to classify the contract into 'nominate' or 'innominate' and, if nominate, to assign it to some particular nominate contract which has standard incidents (in the absence of contrary intention).

§4. Contract and Tort

52. A tort is a civil wrong (other than a breach of contract or a breach of trust) for which the normal remedy is an action for unliquidated damages.[122] Liability in both contract and tort is civil, not criminal, and the same set of facts may give rise to liability in both; nevertheless the distinction between these two kinds of civil obligation is maintained quite clearly in Irish law. For example:

- Different limitation periods may still apply for tort and contract cases,[123] and the commencement of the periods differ. In contract, the period runs from the date of breach. In tort, as no cause of action arises until damage is suffered, the period runs from the date of occurrence of damage.[124]
- Traditionally, the object of awarding damages in contract was to put the injured party, so far as money can do it, in the same situation as if the contract had been performed.[125] In contrast, in a tort action, the traditional object of damages was to restore the injured party, in so far as money could do so, to the position he was in before the tort was committed.

53. The essence of contract is the voluntary assumption of obligations towards the other party to the contract and no liability in contract can arise in the absence of a voluntary contractual nexus between the parties. Liability in tort does not depend on the will of the parties involved but on community assessments of the standard of behaviour expected of all members of the community in particular relationships or circumstances. Clearly, no contract will normally exist between a motorist who injures another road user and the victim; nevertheless, if a driver does not exercise

122. For general discussion of tort law in Ireland, *see* McMahon and Binchy, *Law of Torts* (4th ed., Bloomsbury, 2013).
123. *See* Statute of Limitations 1957, s. 11.
124. *See O'Donnell v Kilsaran Concrete* [2001] IEHC 155; *Brandley v Deane* [2017] IESC 83.
125. *See* Parke, B. in *Robinson v Harmon* (1848) 1 Exch. 850.

the standard of reasonable care required of drivers, and as a result a person is injured, liability in tort arises and the prior relationship between the driver and their victim is not normally relevant.

54. Tort liability was greatly extended by the decision in *Donoghue v Stevenson*[126] in which it was established that the ultimate consumer of a product (who had no contract with the manufacturer) might sue the manufacturer in tort for negligence. Since that case, the tort of negligence has expanded to widen the categories of potential liability, for example, liability for negligent misrepresentations which cause financial loss.[127]

55. The relationship between contract and tort gave rise to a controversial development in English law in *Junior Books v Veitchi Co. Ltd.*,[128] which for a time at least appeared to move English law considerably towards an erosion of the differences between these distinct sources of liability. In that case, there was the major contract between the plaintiffs and a third party for the construction of a warehouse, and under that contract the plaintiffs were entitled to nominate a subcontractor for the flooring of the warehouse. They nominated the defendants who in due course entered into a separate contract with the third-party contractor. No direct contractual nexus existed between the plaintiff and the defendant subcontractor, and the rule of privity of contract meant that the plaintiff could not sue the defendant in contract. Nevertheless, the House of Lords held that the flooring subcontractors were liable *in tort* to the plaintiffs for the *financial* loss caused to them by the negligence of the subcontractors in installing a substandard floor in the warehouse. There was no question of physical injury or actual property damage to the plaintiffs (apart from the defect in the building which was the subject of the dispute) which might have given rise to a normal tort action for negligence against the subcontractors. This decision thus seriously eroded the distinction between contract and tort, and has since been rejected in England,[129] with the courts being of the view that 'financial losses are better regulated by terms of [contracts] that are specifically agreed in advance and that demarcate the parties' rights, duties and possible future liability'.[130]

56. In *Ward v McMaster*,[131] the Irish High Court approved the decision in *Junior Books*, but in *Glencar Exploration plc v Mayo County Council*[132] the Supreme Court refused to allow an action for pure economic loss on the facts, and Keane CJ expressly reserved for another occasion the question of whether *Junior Books*

126. [1932] AC 562.
127. *Hedley Byrne v Heller* [1964] AC 465; *Securities Trust Ltd. v Hugh Moore and Alexander* [1964] IR 417.
128. [1982] 2 All ER 201.
129. *See Murphy v Brentwood District Council* [1991] 1 AC 69; *D & F Estates Ltd v Church Commissioners* [1989] AC 117.
130. Healy *Principles of Irish Torts* (Clarus Press, 2006) at 123.
131. [1988] IR 337. *See also Siney v Corporation of Dublin* [1980] IR 400. Contrast *Colgan v Connolly Construction Co. (Ireland) Ltd.* [1980] ILRM 33.
132. [2002] 1 IR 84.

should be followed in Ireland.[133] The Court of Appeal has recently stated that '[a]s matters stand in this jurisdiction it is not clear whether a property owner can recover for pure economic loss of this kind' but commented that in *Glencar* judgment, Keane C.J. 'appeared to doubt the correctness of the expansive approach which had been taken in cases such as ... *Ward*.'[134]

Concurrent liability in contract and tort

57. Parties may have entered into a contractual relationship, e.g., solicitor and client, doctor and patient; builder and customer, etc., and as a result there may arise a concurrent liability in both contract and tort if a task is performed badly. In *Finlay v Murtagh*[135] the Irish Supreme Court held that a plaintiff might have a cause of action in both contract and tort, and can pursue whichever cause of action is most advantageous. Henchy J stated:

> The coincidence that the defendant's conduct amounts to a breach of contract cannot affect either the duty of care or the common-law liability for its breach, for it is the general relationship, and not any particular manifestation such as a contract, that gives rise to the tortious liability in such a case.[136]

58. Thus, where an action in contract is time-barred, it may still be possible to bring an action in tort.[137]

59. A difficulty can arise when establishing the exact parameters of this relationship, in particular whether the action in tort can be constrained by the contract itself. In the leading case of *Henderson v. Merrett Syndicates Ltd*,[138] which authoritatively accepted concurrent liability in English law, Lord Goff stated:

> [G]iven that the tortious duty is imposed by the general law, and the contractual duty is attributable to the will of the parties, I do not find it objectionable that the claimant may be able to take advantage of the remedy which is most advantageous to him, *subject only to ascertaining whether the tortious duty is so inconsistent with the applicable contract that, in accordance with ordinary principle, the parties must be taken to have agreed that the tortious remedy is to be limited or excluded.*[139]

60. This statement was endorsed in Ireland in *Kennedy v AIB*.[140] However, Hamilton CJ went on to state:

133. The Court similarly refused to discuss this issue in *Brandley v Deane* [2017] IESC 83.
134. *Paulson Investments Ltd v Jons Civil Engineering Ltd* [2016] IECA 169, para. 65.
135. *Finlay v Murtagh* [1979] IR 249. Applied in *Wall v Hegarty* [1980] ILRM 124.
136. [1979] IR 249, 257.
137. *O'Donnell v Kilsaran Concrete* [2001] IEHC 155.
138. [1995] 2 AC 145. For discussion, *see* Taylor 'Concurrent Duties' (2019) 82(1) Modern Law Review 17–45.
139. [1995] 2 AC 145, 194 (emphasis added).
140. [1998] 2 IR 48.

> The case clearly establishes that, when parties are in a contractual relationship, their mutual obligations arise from their contract and are to be found expressly or by necessary implication in the terms thereof and that obligations in tort which may arise from such a contractual relationship *cannot be greater* than those to be found expressly or by necessary implication in their contract.[141]

61. Although this latter statement caused some confusion and was criticised,[142] it is perhaps best viewed in light of the following statement of O'Flaherty J. in *Pat O'Donnell & Co. v Truck and Machinery Sales*:[143]

> The general duty of care in tort cannot be manipulated so as to override the contractual allocation of responsibility between the parties. Thus if, for instance, a contract provides – whether expressly or by necessarily implication – that the defendant is not liable for a particular risk, then the law of tort shall not be allowed to contradict it.

62. In a later Supreme Court case, *Wildgust,*[144] concerning negligent misstatement, the defendants sought to rely on Hamilton CJ's addendum in *Kennedy* – that the obligation in tort cannot be greater than that in contract. They argued that as the plaintiff's policy lapsed as a result of breach of contract, no duty of care in tort could impose a higher contractual duty than that expressly provided for in the contract. The Court expressly rejected this argument, stating that *Kennedy* is 'an authority for the proposition that, irrespective of the existence of a contract, a duty of care may still arise where a party undertakes to exercise a special skill to perform a particular task knowing that the party on whose behalf the task was being performed relied on that skill'. In relation to O'Flaherty J's statement in *Pat O'Donnell & Co. v Truck and Machinery Sales* the Court stated:

> It could not be clearer but that O'Flaherty J. was simply saying that if a contract provides, whether expressly or by necessary implication, that the defendant is not liable for a particular risk, then the law of tort should not, within the four corners of the contract, be allowed to contradict that.

---

141. Endorsing the earlier English Court of Appeal decision in *National Bank of Greece v Pinios Shipping (No.3)* [1988] 2 Lloyds Rep 126. Emphasis added.
142. *See*, for example, McMahon and Binchy who argue that 'That is exactly what Lord Goff denied in Henderson.' (McMahon and Binchy, *Law of Torts* (4th ed. 2013) para. 10.47). In contrast, Carey argues that the case is a 'clear recognition' of the decision in *Henderson*: Carey 'Concurrent Liability in Contract and Tort — Part I' (2001) 8(8) Commercial Law Practitioner 183–188; Carey 'Concurrent Liability in Contract and Tort — Part II' (2001) 8(9) Commercial Law Practitioner 214–220.
143. [1998] 4 IR 191.
144. *Wildgust v Norwich Union Life Insurance Society* [2006] IESC 16.

§5. CONTRACT AND QUASI-CONTRACT

63. Certain types of action – the action for money had and received, a claim of *quantum meruit* for the value of services rendered, the liability to account for profits gained by breach of fiduciary duty or breach of confidence and the action for money paid to the defendant's use, to name but a few – form part of the law of restitution or unjust enrichment. Historically these were considered as a category of 'quasi-contract', grouped in for procedural reasons with contract actions (under the form of action called *indebitatus assumpsit*). The connection of such cases with contract properly so-called was rather strained, resting, according to some judges, on an implied promise or agreement to pay for, or repay, a benefit wrongly or unjustly received.[145] However, in the *Fibrosa* case Lord Wright said:

> It is clear that any civilised system of law is bound to provide remedies for cases of what has been called unjust enrichment or unjust benefit, that is to prevent a man from retaining the money of or some benefit derived from another which it is against conscience that he should keep. Such remedies in English law are generally different from remedies in contract or in tort, and are now recognised to fall within a third category of the common law which has been called quasi-contract or restitution.[146]

64. For many years in England, however, aside from the dictum of Lord Wright in *Fibrosa*, the idea of a unified law of restitution was really only considered in academic writings,[147] and even then it was not universally accepted.[148] It was not until 1991, in *Lipkin Gorman v Karpnale Ltd*,[149] that the House of Lords recognised the principle of unjust enrichment as the true rationale of cases traditionally dealt with under the heading of quasi-contract.

65. It is important to remember, however, that the principle of 'unjust enrichment' does not give judges a *carte blanche* or unfettered discretion to allow the recovery of money just because it is fair or just to do so.[150] Rather 'recourse must be had to the decided cases to determine the prospects of success or failure of any

145. *Sinclair v Brougham* [1914] AC 398; *Leader v Leader* (1871) IRCL 20. Contrast the earlier view of Lord Mansfield that there was a natural law obligation to return an unjustly obtained benefit or enrichment: *Moses v Macferlan* (1760) 2 Burr 1005; 96 ER 120.

146. *Fibrosa Spolka Akcyjna v Fairbairn Lawson Combe Barbour Ltd* [1943] AC 32, 61.

147. *See* Goff and Jones *The Law of Restitution* (1st ed., 1966); Lord Wright *Legal Essays and Addresses* (1939).

148. *See*, for example, Atiyah's view in *The Rise and Fall of Freedom of Contract* (1979) p. 768; Hedley 'Unjust Enrichment as the Basis of Restitution – An Overworked Concept' (1985) 5 Legal Studies 56; Stoljar 'Unjust Enrichment and Unjust sacrifice' (1987) 50 Modern Law Review 603. *See also Orakpo v Manson Investments Ltd* [1978] AC 95, 104 where Lord Diplock stated that 'no general doctrine of unjust enrichment is recognised in English law'.

149. [1991] 2 AC 548. *See* Birks 'The English Recognition of Unjust Enrichment' [1991] Lloyd's Maritime and Commercial Law Quarterly 473; Mc Kendrick 'Restitution, Misdirected Funds and Change of Position' (1992) 55 Modern Law Review 377.

150. *See* the comments of Lord Goff in *Lipkin Gorman v Karpnale Ltd* [1991] 2 AC 548, 578.

particular claim'.[151] These actions have developed over time with specific and individual rules, definitions and concepts – it is now however accepted that unjust enrichment has long been the hidden principle guiding these rules and concepts.

66. The Irish High Court recently categorised the types of action which fall under unjust enrichment as follows:

(a) mistake, where an enrichment is conferred on the defendant by reason of the plaintiff's mistake;
(b) contracts discharged by breach, where the plaintiff seeks to recover a benefit that was conferred by him as part of his contractual performance, the contract itself having been discharged by breach of either the plaintiff or the defendant;
(c) contracts discharged by frustration, where the plaintiff seeks to recover a benefit that was conferred by him as part of his contractual performance, the contract itself having been discharged by frustration;
(d) legally recognised transactions which are void, voidable or otherwise ineffective where the plaintiff seeks to recover a benefit that was conferred by the plaintiff but where the transaction becomes unenforceable in law;
(e) claims for the recovery of money or the recovery of a non-money benefit and where the plaintiff has discharged the defendant's debt;
(f) restitution for 'wrongs'.[152]

67. It could legitimately be asked what difference it makes to individual restitutionary actions now that they are grouped together under the heading of unjust enrichment? The most obvious difference is the change in the approach of the courts, in the language used and the questions asked when faced with a restitutionary claim. Claims are now generally analysed in the language of unjust enrichment, rather than in terms of antiquated fictions such as the implied term theory. In *Corporation of Dublin v Building and Allied Trade Union*[153] the Supreme Court considered the following preconditions must be fulfilled by a plaintiff who claims for unjust enrichment:

(i) the enrichment of the defendant;
(ii) at the plaintiff's expense;
(iii) in circumstances in which the law requires restitution (the 'unjustness' of the enrichment); and
(iv) the absence of defences or other policies to deny restitution.

68. This structure has further helped the development of the law in this area by encouraging a general debate on the issues involved as opposed to isolated conclusions based on the peculiarities of individual actions. This is particularly noticeable

151. Goff and Jones *The Law of Restitution* (1st ed., 1966) p. 13.
152. *Vanguard Auto Finance Ltd v Browne & Ors* [2014] IEHC 465, para. 70.
153. [1996] 1 IR 468, 493. Cited in *Bank of Ireland Mortgage Bank v Murray* [2019] IEHC 234.

in the area of defences, which have been developed across the range of restitutionary remedies, often with reference to the principle of unjust enrichment. The principle defence available is the defence of change of position, where the recipient of the benefit has changed its position acted in good faith because of the receipt of the benefit.[154]

69. The law of restitution or unjust enrichment 'is an area of the law that has, in recent years, not featured prominently in Ireland'.[155] The existence of a unifying law of restitution was recognised by the Supreme Court in *East Cork Foods Ltd v O'Dwyer Steel Company*[156] and in *The Lord Mayor, Aldermen and Burgesses of the City of Dublin v Building and Allied Trade Union*[157] Keane J stated:

> It is clear that, under our law, a person can, in certain circumstances, be obliged to effect restitution of money or other property to another where it would be unjust for him to retain the money.[158]

70. The defence of change of position was recognised by the Irish Supreme Court in *Murphy v Attorney General.*[159] In the recent case of *Bank of Ireland Mortgage Bank v Murray*[160] the Court stated:

> I consider that a defendant does not need to show that he spent the money on something out of character or in a way he had never spent money before, but that he entered a transaction he would not have entered but for the enrichment, and that the balance of fairness means that the money is not to be restored..[161]

71. Specific examples of cases considered under the heading of the law of restitution are discussed in Part 2, Chapter 13.

§6. Contract and Trust

72. The law of contract originated, and was developed in, the courts of common law. The concept of the 'trust' and the law of trusts originated in the Court of the

154. *See* Jones 'Change of Circumstances in Quasi Contract' (1957) 73 Law Quarterly Review 48; Birks 'Change of Position: The Nature of the Defence and Its Relationship to Other Restitutionary Defences' in McInnes (ed.) *Restitution: Developments in Unjust Enrichment* (1996) p. 49; Denning 'The Recovery of Money' (1949) 65 Law Quarterly Review 37; Mc Kendrick 'Restitution, Misdirected Funds and Change of Position' (1992) 55 Modern Law Review 377.
155. Breslin & Breslin, 'Restitution Renaissance' (2019) 26(11) *Commercial Law Practitioner* 199, 199.
156. [1978] 1 IR 103.
157. [1996] 1 IR 468.
158. [1996] 1 IR 468, 483.
159. [1982] IR 241, 319.
160. [2019] IEHC 234.
161. [2019] IEHC 234, para. 172.

Chancellor and was developed in the courts of equity.[162] Equity (including trusts) as a system, influenced all areas of the common law, including contract, but there was, and is, a clear distinction between 'contract' and 'trust'. A contract is an agreement which will be enforced by the law. Under a trust, trustees are required to hold property of which they are the legal owners for the benefit of another (the beneficiary) and involves an obligation to exercise legal rights on behalf of the beneficiary.

73. There are several differences between trusts and contracts. For example while an agreement and consideration are necessary for a contract, in trusts questions of agreement[163] and consideration are irrelevant. However, the main difference is the type of relationship that exists between the parties. A trust creates a fiduciary relationship, that is 'one in which a person undertakes to act on behalf of or for the benefit of another, often as an intermediary with a discretion or power which affects the interest of the other who depends on the fiduciary for information and advice'.[164] The trustee owes special duties to the beneficiary, which are more onerous than a party's normal contractual duties.

74. The Irish High Court has explained the difference between a fiduciary relationship and a contractual relationship using the following example:

> While all who enter into contracts are obliged to discharge them honestly and in good faith, it cannot be supposed, for example, that a retailer is under a positive obligation to disclose to a customer that he or she is aware that exactly the same goods can be purchased for a lower price from a nearby outlet. That would, however, be the position in law if, for example, a retailer were held to be a fiduciary.[165]

75. The concept of the trust has been applied in some contract cases to circumvent the doctrine of privity of contract, as a third party can enforce a contract if a completely constituted trust was created in their favour by the contract.[166] However, the courts have rejected this approach, describing it as 'cumbrous fiction' in many cases,[167] and are reluctant to find that there is a trust unless it is clear that this was the intention of the parties.[168] This is not least because the obligations under a

162. On the law of equity, *see* Biehler, *Equity and the Law of Trusts in Ireland* (7th ed., Round Hall, 2020); Keane, *Equity and the Law of Trusts in Ireland* (3rd ed., Bloomsbury, 2017).
163. In fact, a constructive trust can exist simply from the circumstances and in the absence of any agreement: *Keech v Sandford* (1726) Sel Cas Ch 61. *See* Keane, *Equity and the Law of Trusts in Ireland* (3rd ed., Bloomsbury, 2017) Chapter 13
164. Law Commission of England and Wales, Report *Fiduciary Duties and Regulatory Rules* (Law Comm No. 236 1995).
165. *Irish Life and Permanent Plc v Financial Services Ombudsman & Ors* [2012] IEHC 367 (Irish High Court, Hogan J, 3 August 2012).
166. *Tomlinson v Gill* (1756) Amb 330; 27 ER 221; *Drimmie v Davies* [1899] 1 IR 176; *Kelly v Larkin* [1910] 2 IR 550.
167. Lord Wright (1939) 55 Law Quarterly Review 189, 208.
168. *See*, for example, *Cadbury (Ireland) Ltd v Kerry Co-op Creameries Ltd* [1982] ILRM 77; *Inspector of Taxes Association v Minister for the Public Service* High Court 24 March 1983.

trust are greater than that under contract.[169] In addition, converting the contract to a trust means that the parties cannot rescind or vary the agreement without the consent of the third-party beneficiary.[170]

§7. Contract and the Law of Property

76. The law of contract and the law of property are major separate divisions of Irish law, each with its own separate origin and line of development, and each with a large and complex set of rules and principles. However, many transactions involve elements of both and there is an inevitable connection between contract and 'property' in its widest general sense insofar as many contracts are designed to transfer ownership of property from one to another. This may occur immediately, as in many contracts for the sale of goods, or the contract may give a right to have property conveyed in due course.

77. Once a person becomes the 'owner' of property, under the law relating to property they acquire rights in rem, rights maintainable against all. However, a party to a contract has merely a personal right (right in personam) maintainable against the other party to the contract. All others are third parties (strangers to the contract) and cannot in principle sue or be sued upon that contract. While there are special requirements for some classes of contract, non-compliance with which may make the contract invalid or unenforceable, in general all contracts are subject to the same rules about formation and conditions of validity. Conveyances of property, on the other hand, are different for different types of property, and the law of real property relating to conveyancing is much more technical and more complicated than that applying to the making of contracts.[171]

78. Where relevant, the law on the effects of mistake, misrepresentation (fraudulent or innocent), duress, undue influence and illegality is the same for contract and conveyances of property.

§8. Good Faith and Fair Dealing

79. The principle that there is no general principle of good faith and fair dealing in Irish contract law was recently restated by the Irish Court of Appeal in *Flynn v Breccia*.[172] A duty to negotiate in good faith is 'inherently inconsistent with the

169. *See* Law Reform Commission, *Report on Privity of Contract and Third Party Rights* (LRC 88-2008)) para. 1.16.
170. *See Re Schebsman* [1944] Ch 83.
171. For the major works on Irish land law and Conveyancing, *see* Howlin and McGrath, *Lyall's Land Law in Ireland* (4th ed., Round Hall, 2018); Wylie, *Irish Land Law* (2013, 5th ed); JC Wylie & Una Woods *Irish Conveyancing Law* (2019).
172. [2017] IECA 74, [99] per Finlay Geoghegan J. On the Irish and UK position, *see* a series of articles by Gearóid Carey: 'Do Contractual Parties Have to Act in Good Faith?' (2013) 20(10) Commercial Law Practitioner 75; 'To Act (or even Negotiate) in Good Faith: The Irish Perspective' (2014) 21(3)

position of a negotiating party',[173] and while in the UK cases have suggested that it may be possible to have an implied term of good faith in performance of a contract,[174] this has not to date been followed in Ireland.[175] In the High Court in *Flynn v Breccia* Houghton J found that such a term was implied in a shareholders' agreement,[176] but this was overturned in the Court of Appeal.[177]

80. In place of a general principle of good faith, the common law of contract developed detailed rules (which included rules from equity) to deal with unfair and unconscionable conduct in the making and performance of contracts. The modern law of contract in Ireland therefore incorporates much of the substance of the natural law concept of 'good faith' in detailed rules on, for example, duress, misrepresentation, undue influence, promissory estoppel and unconscionable contracts. This is supplemented by legislative intervention such as regulation of exemption clauses, consumer protection measures and the regulation of particular kinds of contract such as employment contracts. These duties may be explicable on the basis of good faith, but these are still specific duties which are certain and clear, rather than simply being part of a general duty to act in good faith. There is also reference to 'good faith' in the Unfair Terms Directive, but even then good faith is used not as a general overriding duty but quite specifically as part of the test to determine whether a contract term is unfair, and guidance is provided as to the application of the test.[178] A more general duty to act in good faith might have been introduced by the Common European Sales Law, but this aspect of the proposal was controversial and the Common European Sales Law proposal itself was eventually abandoned.[179]

81. As was pointed out in *Flynn v Breccia*, there are 'certain types of agreements and contracts to which a duty of good faith applies, such as in a partnership

Commercial Law Practitioner 52; 'Further Developments in Contractual Good Faith' (2016) 23(1) Commercial Law Practitioner 3; Implied Good Faith: Appellate Developments (2017) 24(10) Commercial Law Practitioner 207.

173. *Walford v Miles* [1992] 2 AC 128, 138. Adopted in Ireland in *Triatic Ltd v Cork County Council* [2007] 3 IR 57; *Esso Ireland Ltd v Nine One One Retail Ltd* [2013] IEHC 514.
174. *Yam Seng Pte Ltd v International Trade Corp Ltd* [2013] EWHC 111 (QB). Leggatt J. stated (at para. 131): 'I doubt that English law has reached the stage, however, where it is ready to recognise a requirement of good faith as a duty implied by law, even as a default rule, into all commercial contracts. Nevertheless, there seems to me to be no difficulty, following the established methodology of English law for the implication of terms in fact, in implying such a duty in any ordinary commercial contract based on the presumed intention of the parties.' For analysis, *see* Severine Saintier 'The Elusive Notion of Good Faith in the Performance of a Contract, Why Still a Bete Noire for the Civil and the Common Law?' (2017) 6 Journal of Business Law 441–460.
175. The question of whether it should be followed in Ireland was expressly left undecided in *Flynn v Breccia* [2017] IECA 74, para. 102.
176. [2015] IEHC 547, para. 264.
177. [2017] IECA 74, para. 102.
178. Unfair Contract Terms Directive (93/13/EEC) as implemented in the Unfair Terms in Consumer Contracts Regulations 1995.
179. Proposal Regulation on a Common European Sales Law, COM(2011) 635 final. *See* Kelly, 'The Proposal for a Common European Sales Law: Looking Beyond the Merits of Optional Instruments' (2013) 7 Journal of Business Law 703; C Kelly & Paul Keane, 'A New Common European Sales Law?' (2012) 19(1) Commercial Law Practitioner 175 (Part 1), 195 (Part 2).

agreement or the principle of *uberrima fides* in insurance contracts'.[180] In the case of partnerships this is because the relationship is a fiduciary one, where there is a duty to disclose material facts to the other during negotiations.[181] The principle of *uberrima fides*, or 'utmost good faith', in insurance contracts, applies to ensure that an individual applying for insurance, who is in the best position to know the full facts concerning the risk being undertaken, is obliged to answer truthfully and disclose any material facts. Failure to do so may invalidate the policy,[182] particularly where the insurer includes a clause stating that the accuracy of all replies is 'the basis of the contract'.[183] However, cases such as *Keating v New Ireland Assurance Co Plc*[184] have limited this obligation to disclose to material facts of which the insured was in fact aware. In *Chariot Inns* the Supreme Court stated that the duty to disclose all material facts was to be assessed by reference to that 'which would reasonably influence the judgment of a prudent insurer in deciding whether he would take the risk and, if so, in determining the premium he would demand', and that the standard was objective, not subjective.[185] However, when insurance is provided 'over-the-counter' with minimal formality, full disclosure may not be a practical reality, and a lower standard will be held to apply.[186] Nonetheless, the standard of disclosure can be high, and the Law Reform Commission has recommended a relaxation of these rules in the context of consumers and small businesses.[187]

§9. Style of Drafting

82. The general approach for commercial contracts is to have lengthy, written contracts which attempt to foresee as much as possible and draft the contract as completely as possible.[188] Major commercial contracts and contracts for the sale or lease of land will normally be drafted by expert draftsmen in these areas and will often be in standard form (such as the standard Conditions of Sale contract issued by the Incorporated Law Society or a template developed within a law firm) which are comprehensively drafted and may be adapted as required.

---

180. [2017] IECA 74, [99] per Finlay Geoghegan J.
181. *Law v Law* [1905] Ch 140; *Dunbar v Tredennick* (1813) 2 Ball & B 304.
182. *See* the Marine Insurance Act 1906, s. 18(1).
183. *Keenan v Shield Insurance Co Ltd* [1987] IR 113; *Matthew Kirby v Friends First Life Assurance Company Ltd* [2018] IEHC 796; Clark (p. 431) notes that in the absence of such a clause the insurer will find it more difficult to avoid a policy concluded in good faith: *Manor Park Homebuilders Ltd v AIG Europe (Ireland) Ltd* [2008] IEHC 174.This case indicates that there may be a duty of enquiry on the insurer in certain circumstances, *see* Deirdre Ahern, 'The Formation of Insurance Contracts and the Duty of Insurers' (2009) 16(4) Commercial Law Practitioner 84.
184. [1990] ILRM 110. *See also Coleman v New Ireland Assurance plc* [2009] IEHC 173.
185. *Chariot Inns Ltd v Assicurazioni Generali SPA & Coyle Hamilton* [1981] ILRM 173.
186. *Aro Road and Land Vehicles Ltd v Insurance Corp of Ireland Ltd* [1986] IR 403. *See also Kelleher v Irish Life Assurance Co Ltd* [1993] ILRM 643.
187. Law Reform Commission, *Report on Consumer Insurance Contracts* (LRC 113-2015).
188. *See* generally Hill 'Why Contracts Are Written in Legalese' (2001–2002) 77 Chicago-Kent Law Rev. 59; Hill & King, 'How Do German Contracts Do as Much with Fewer Words?' (2004) 79 Chicago-Kent Law Review 889.

§10. Sources of the Law of Contract

83. The major sources of the principles and rules of the general law of contract are decisions of the courts (case law). Statutes have become a major source this century, and all of the most common types of contract (sale of goods, contracts of loan, employment contracts, sale of land, landlord and tenant contracts, etc.) are subject to special legislative rules. This includes European Union law, which is becoming an increasingly important formal source of the Irish law of contract. In addition, the constitution and constitutional law decisions may have some impact.[189] Trade customs and usages will be applied as implied terms where appropriate.[190]

84. As discussed above, Irish courts pay considerable respect to decisions on the law of contract given by common law courts in other jurisdictions and for obvious historical reasons, decisions of English courts are particularly 'persuasive'. English decisions are cited as a matter of course, either as the only 'authority' available on the particular point or in support of an argument based on Irish or Irish and English cases. However, there are many differences in principle and in detail between Irish and English contract law, and these divergences are likely to increase given the United Kingdom's exit from the European Union.

189. *Meskell v C.I.É.* [1973] IR 121; *Glover v BLN* [1973] IR 388.
190. *O'Reilly v Irish Press* (1937) ILTR 194; *O'Connail v The Gaelic Echo (1954) Ltd* (1958) 92 ILTR 156; *Carroll v Dublin Bus* [2005] IEHC 278.

Part I. General Principles of the Law of Contract

Chapter 1. Formation

85. The basic requirements for formation of contract under Irish law are: (i) that there is a final agreement on all the material terms; (ii) that the parties intended to create legal relations, (iii) that there is consideration; and (iv) that any relevant formal and evidential requirements are met. The Irish courts have been careful to separate the question of whether an agreement has been reached from the question of whether that agreement has been properly evidenced or recorded for the purposes of the rules on formalities. The first two parts of this chapter examine the Irish approach to formation of an agreement (§1) and any formal and evidential requirements that might apply (§2). A mix of statute law and common law principles governs this area, as well as equitable doctrines such as promissory estoppel and the doctrine of part performance.

86. The process of negotiating a contract can also raise issues regarding any pre-contractual liabilities, particularly in the event of negotiations breaking down. The final part of this chapter (§3) discusses how this is dealt with in the Irish context.

§1. Agreement and Quid Pro Quo (Reciprocity)

I. Offer and Acceptance

87. For parties to conclude a contract they must reach a final agreement on all the material terms. This is done by breaking down the sequence of events during negotiations, sometimes in an artificial fashion, in order to determine whether there was an unequivocal acceptance of a final offer.

88. Traditionally, Irish courts require a 'meeting of the minds', or a consensus *ad idem*, before deciding that a contract exists. An objective approach is taken, which focuses on what is said or done rather than on what may have been privately intended by any one contracting party. This approach can be seen in the classic statement of Blackburn J in *Smith v Hughes* that:

> if, whatever a man's real intention may be, he so conducts himself that a reasonable man would believe that he was assenting to the terms proposed by the other party, and that other party upon that belief enters into the contract with him, the man thus conducting himself would be equally bound as if he had intended to agree to the other party's terms.[191]

89. In the Irish context, this objective approach is also clearly favoured, as seen for example in the Supreme Court judgment in *Mespil Ltd v Capaldi*:

> Business relations would be thrown into undesirable uncertainty if a party to an agreement, who at the time gave no indication that he did not understand what he was doing, could later renounce the agreement on subjective considerations.[192]

90. However, subjective factors may become relevant if an apparent agreement is denied on grounds such as mistake or duress.[193] Indeed, this was an issue in *Mespil v Capaldi* itself, in which there was held to be a mutual mistake as to the nature of the agreement, meaning that there was not a true offer and acceptance (or *consensus ad idem*).

91. At this point it is worth noting the difference between a bilateral contract and a unilateral contract. In a bilateral contract, both parties make reciprocal promises and both parties are bound by the contract. In contrast, in a unilateral contract one party (A) states that they will do something if another party (B) performs a particular act. B is free to choose whether or not to perform the required act, but if B does so then A is bound to perform their part of the agreement. The unilateral nature of the contract consists in the fact that an obligation is (self) imposed only on the promisor, e.g., to pay the promised reward for the return of lost property. The classic example of this is the English case of *Carlill v Carbolic Smokeball Company,*[194] where the defendants stated that if you purchased the defendant's product (a smokeball) and caught influenza, the defendants would pay £100. This was a unilateral offer, as the defendants were bound by their promise, but it did not purport to 'bind' anybody who read the offer and/or bought the product.

A. *Offer*

92. An offer is defined by Clark as 'a clear and unambiguous statement of the terms upon which the offeror is willing to contract, should the person or persons to who the offer is addressed decide to accept'.[195]

---

191. (1871) LR 6 QB 597.
192. *Mespil Ltd v Capaldi* [1986] ILRM 373, 376.
193. On mistake, *see* paras 272 et seq. On duress, *see* paras 318 et seq.
194. [1893] 1 QB 256.
195. Clark, *Contract Law in Ireland* (Round Hall, 8th ed., 2016) p. 8.

93. It is important to distinguish an offer – which is capable of acceptance – from other statements which may be made during negotiations – which are not capable of acceptance. Certain statements made may just be made to provide information, without necessarily constituting an offer. An 'invitation to treat' is a statement which is not itself an offer, but is essentially an invitation to make an offer, which can then be accepted or rejected. For example, an advertisement to sell a car is not normally an offer, but merely seeks to attract others to make an offer which the seller is then free to accept or reject. However this is not an absolute rule, and in some circumstances an advertisement may clearly indicate that the advertiser intended to make an offer.[196]

1. Advertisements

94. An advertisement is generally construed as an invitation to treat and not an offer.[197] If this were not the case, a person who placed an advertisement in a newspaper, for example to sell a car, could be liable to each and every individual who purported to 'accept' the offer.

95. This is not an absolute rule, however, and the court may find that there is an offer if the wording or circumstances of the advertisement, objectively construed, clearly indicate that the advertiser intended to make an offer. The classic case on this is *Carlill v Carbolic Smokeball Company,*[198] where an advertisement claimed that if you purchased the defendant's product (a smokeball) and caught influenza, that that the defendants would pay you £100. This was held to be a binding offer, despite the fact that it was open to a mass audience ('the world at large') and not directed at any one individual. Similar reasoning can be found in Irish cases such as *Kennedy v London Express Newspapers,*[199] in which a newspaper offered free accident insurance to individuals who became registered readers of the paper, and *Billings v Arnott,*[200] in which an employer posted a notice offering any of their employees who joined the Defence Forces one half of their salaries up to the sum of £2 per week. It can be seen that these cases tend to concern unilateral offers. Thus while the person who reads the offer is not obliged to do anything – be that buying the smokeball, registering for the paper, or joining the Defence Forces – if they do so then the other party is bound.

96. Some attempts to rely on the *Carlill* case have been less successful, for example where no reasonable person would believe that a serious offer was being

196. *Carlill v Carbolic Smoke Ball Co.* [1893] 1 QB 256.
197. *Partridge v Crittenden* [1968] 1 WLR 1204 (Eng.) *Harris v Nickerson* (1873) LR 8 QB 286 (Eng.).

198. [1893] 1 QB 256.
199. [1931] IR 532.
200. (1945) 80 ILTR 50.

made,[201] or where the purported offer was in fact closer to a statement of information,[202] or where the source of the information was an unauthorised newspaper report rather than a communication from the defendant.[203]

2. Display of Goods

97. The display of goods in a shop window or on the shelves of supermarkets is not viewed as an offer to sell the goods, but as an invitation to treat.[204] The offer in that situation is usually made if a customer presents the goods at a cash point with the intention of buying them, and the seller may accept or reject the offer. This protects shops, in particular by avoiding any difficulties that might arise from a previous agreement to sell the goods in question or from incorrect indications of price. However, while a customer cannot insist that the shop sell an item on display at a particular price, the shop might be open to criminal prosecution under consumer protection legislation such as the Consumer Protection Act 2007, which prohibits misleading commercial practices.[205]

98. It is important to remember that this is only a general rule, which could be departed from in particular situations. For example, a shop which offered to sell specific goods at a discount price to the first customer into the store on the first morning of the January sales, or who complied with some other special requirement, could find it difficult to claim that this was merely an invitation to treat and not an offer.[206]

3. Quotations and Statements of Price

99. Quotations and statements of price will normally be regarded as invitations to treat. For example, in *Boyers & Co v Duke*[207] the defendants responded to a query about the price of canvas, stating that the lowest price was 4 5/8 d per yard, and the plaintiffs then purported to accept this 'offer'. There was held to be no binding contract, as the statement as to price was merely a quotation and not an offer capable of acceptance. The result in this case can however be contrasted with that in *Dooley*

---

201. Such as the US case of *Leonard v Pepsi Co*, Unreported, 4 August 1999, US District Court for the Southern District of New York, discussed in McDermott 'Litigating for the Pepsi Generation' (2000) 5 *Bar Review* 443.
202. *Tansey v The College of Occupational Therapists Ltd*, Unreported, High Court, 27 August 1986.
203. *Wilson v Belfast Corporation* (1921) 55 ILTR 205.
204. *Minister for Industry and Commerce v Pim* [1966] IR 154.
205. *See* ss 42–52. The consumer might also be entitled to damages under s. 74 of the Act. The Consumer Protection Act 2007 implements Directive 2005/29/EC of the European Parliament and of the Council of 11 May 2005 concerning unfair business-to-consumer commercial practices in the internal market.
206. Clark, *Contract Law in Ireland* (Round Hall, 8th ed., 2016) p. 11, citing the US case, of *Lefkowitz v Great Minneapolis Surplus Store* 86 N.W. 2d 689 (1957).
207. [1905] 2 IR 617. *See also Harvey v Facey* [1893] AC 552.

v T.L. Egan & Co. Ltd,[208] where the quotation included the statement 'all quotations are made for immediate acceptance only and are subject to change without notice'. It was held that this quotation was an offer, subject to immediate acceptance.

4. Auctions

100. Auctions are dealt with by section 58 of the Sale of Goods Act 1893, which provides that where goods are sold in an auction in lots, each lot is a separate contract of sale.[209] The auctioneer putting up property for sale is inviting offers. The 'offer' occurs when the bidder bids, with acceptance of the highest bid occurring when the auctioneer announces completion by the fall of the hammer, or 'in other customary manner'.[210] Until that point of acceptance the bidder can retract his bid, and the auctioneer can withdraw the property for sale. The owner (or his agent) cannot bid for his own goods at an auction, unless he expressly reserves the right to do so.[211]

101. An announcement that an auction will take place 'without reserve' means the auctioneer *must* sell to the highest bona fide bidder and may be liable for breach of contract if they refuse to accept the highest bid or withdraw the item from sale. There is thus a secondary contract, alongside the main contract of sale: the statement that the sale will be 'without reserve' constitutes an offer by the auctioneer (to sell the item to the highest bidder) which is then accepted by the bidder placing a bid on that item. The bid is thus both an offer (to buy) and an acceptance (of the auctioneer's offer to sell 'without reserve'). This principle was upheld by the Irish Supreme Court in *Tully* v *Irish Land Commission.*[212] An auctioneer who is found liable to pay damages for refusing to accept the highest bid may be indemnified where the refusal was caused by the owner changing his mind.[213]

5. Tenders

102. The traditional analysis of the tender process provides that advertisements inviting tenders to supply goods or services are invitations to treat.[214] When the contractor returns the tender form, it is regarded as an offer which the other party is free to accept or reject. Hence, there is only one substantive contract. However, this analysis of the tender process gives a lot of power to the party seeking tenders, and thus it has been mitigated somewhat by express and implied rules which regulate the process itself. This approach recognises that the advertisement inviting tenders

---

208. (1938) 72 ILTR 155.
209. Section 58(1).
210. Section 58(2).
211. Section 58(3).
212. (1961) 97 ILTR 174.
213. Clark, *Contract Law in Ireland* (Round Hall, 8th ed., 2016) p. 9.
214. *Spencer v Harding* (1870) LR 5 CP 561.

is not always 'merely' an invitation to treat, but can in fact give rise itself to obligations on the party seeking tenders. For example, there may be an obligation to consider all tenders which are submitted in accordance with the invitation.[215] It may also be implied that failure to comply with conditions, for example by submitting a referential bid, will invalidate the tender-offer – see *Harvela Investments v Royal Trust of Canada.*[216] This is particularly important for other parties who might wish to object to a non-compliant tender being accepted. The exact obligations which will be imposed depends on the exact wording of the advertisement inviting tenders.

103. The approach of the Irish courts to the tender process has been somewhat inconsistent. In *Howberry Lane v Telecom Éireann, RTE and NTL*[217] a tender document supplied to potential bidders included a statement that there was no obligation to accept the highest bid offered or any bid at all, and the sellers reserved the right to sell 'to any person at any time'. The plaintiffs submitted a bid of £410 million, but NTL submitted a formula (referential) bid, stating that it would pay 15% more than the highest bid. The plaintiffs sought a declaration that NTL's formula bid was invalid, and should have been disregarded, meaning the plaintiffs would have won the tender at that stage of the process. However, the court refused to grant an interlocutory injunction application. It was held that a term requiring the shareholders to complete the transaction with the highest bidder could not be implied because it was not necessary and would be inconsistent with the express wording of the contract.

104. However, more recently in *Smart Telecom v RTE*[218] Kelly J in the Commercial Court held that referential bids would not be allowed, even in the absence of an express provision in the tender advertisement. In this case RTE (the national broadcaster) opened a tender competition to four interested parties inviting them to submit their best offer in a sealed bid for sponsorship of the weather forecast. The tender email stated that the contract would be awarded to the highest bidder. Smart Telecom submitted a tender offering 5% above the highest priced bid received. However RTE accepted a bid from Glanbia, for almost €1.6 million per annum. Smart Telecom considered itself to be the highest bidder and sought to enforce the contract, but their action was dismissed. The terms of the email seeking tenders, when properly construed, did not permit the making of a referential bid. This approach would appear to strike the correct balance between the importance of maintaining fair procedures and commercial sense in the tender process while respecting the freedom of contract of the parties involved.

105. A further issue that arises in relation to contract formation and tenders is the point at which there is a 'formal' enforceable contract. Although commercial practice would indicate that the parties would not consider themselves bound at this point, and would in practice enter into further negotiations, it would seem to depend

215. *Fylde Aero Club v Blackpool Borough Council* [1990] 3 All ER 25. It should be noted that only nominal damages were awarded here.
216. [1987] 2 All ER 966.
217. [1999] 2 ILRM 232. *See* P. Mc Dermott 'The ABC of Tendering' (2000) 7(5) Commercial Law Practitioner 121.
218. [2006] IEHC 176.

on the exact wording of the invitation to tender. In *Guardians of Kells Union v Smith*[219] the invitation to tender stated that a formal contract for the supply of goods would be entered into on a particular date with the successful tenderer. The defendant was informed that his tender (offer) was successful, but he refused to conclude the formal contract to supply the goods. While the court agreed that no contract to supply the goods had been formed, it was held that the defendant was in breach of a collateral contract based on the invitation to tender and his acceptance of the conditions specified in that invitation.

B. Termination of an Offer

106. If an offer is terminated it cannot be then accepted. An offer may be terminated if it is revoked, rejected by the offeree, or after lapse of time.

1. Revocation

107. An offer may be revoked at any time before acceptance, even if the offer is expressed to be open for acceptance for a certain time.[220] Knowledge of the revocation must actually be communicated to the offeree, and for the purposes of revocation it is not enough to merely post a letter; it must be received.[221]

108. These rules are modified somewhat in the case of unilateral offers, where acceptance may take the form of performance. If the offer is validly revoked before performance commences there is no difficulty. But if performance has commenced, a strict application of the rules on revocation of an offer could lead to injustice to an offeree who has perhaps substantially performed the required act but not fully completed performance before the offer is revoked. In this situation, the court may hold that offeror may not revoke offer or prevent completion of a performance which has commenced.[222]

219. (1917) 52 ILTR 65 (H.C.).
220. *Walker v Glass* [1979] NI 129 (Northern Ireland High Court).
221. *Byrne v Van Tienhoven* (1880) 5 CRD 344. *See* however *Dickinson v Dodds* (1876) 2 ChD 463 where revocation of an offer was communicated via an unauthorised third party.
222. *See Daulia Ltd. v Four Millbank Nominees Ltd.* [1978] Ch 231 (Eng.).

2. Rejection of Offer

109. Rejection of an offer terminates it. Even if the offeree changes his mind and decides to accept it after all, the offer is no longer open for acceptance.[223] A counter-offer operates as a rejection and similarly terminates the offer.[224] The court may construe an apparent counter-offer as a request for more information about the offer, rather than a rejection of the original offer, in which case the offer is not terminated.[225]

3. Lapse of Time

110. If an offer is expressed to be open for acceptance for a limited time it will automatically expire at the end of that time. However, as mentioned above, in the absence of a legally binding promise to keep the offer open for the time stated, it may still be revoked before that time expires.[226] Where there is no time limit specified, an offer will remain open for acceptance for a reasonable time.[227] What is a reasonable time will depend in each case on all the circumstances of the offer such as the nature of the goods, the attitude of the parties to the transaction in hand, normal market practices, etc. An offer made 'for immediate acceptance only' must be accepted immediately or it will lapse.[228] The method to be used for immediate acceptance will again depend on the circumstances of the offer.

4. The Effect of Death

111. The effect of the death of either the offeror or offeree on the offer is not clearly established in Irish law. If the offer requires personal performance by the offeree, e.g., to paint a portrait or to act in a play, death of the offeree terminates the offer. Where an obligation could be discharged out of the estate of the offeror, the position is less clear, and there is a lack of significant case law on the issue.

223. *Hyde v Wrench* (1840) 3 Beav 334.
224. *Ibid.*
225. *Stevenson, Jacques & Co. v McClean* (1880) 5 QBD 346.
226. *Walker v Glass* [1979] NI 129 (Northern Ireland High Court).
227. *Ramsgate Hotel Co. v Montefiore* (1866) LR 1 Exch. 109; *Commane v Walsh*, Unreported, High Court, 3 May 1983.
228. *Dooley v Egan* (1938) 72 ILTR 155.

C. *Acceptance*

1. The Fact of Acceptance

112. Acceptance of an offer creates a contract if the other conditions required for validity exist. To constitute an acceptance, there must be an unconditional indication of assent to the exact terms of the offer.

113. A reply purporting to accept an offer but introducing a new term is not a valid acceptance but a 'counter-offer' which may in turn be accepted or rejected by the original offeror.[229] A counter-offer also acts as a rejection of the original offer. The court will, if necessary, distinguish between a counter-offer and superfluous statements relating to the offer. In *Harris' Case*[230] an offer was made to buy shares in a company, with payment for the shares to be made immediately. This offer was accepted, but the acceptor added that if payment was not made immediately, interest would be charged on outstanding amounts. This was held to be a valid acceptance, not a counter-offer. Similarly, a mere request for further information will not be regarded as a counter-offer.[231] In such a case, the original offer remains open for acceptance.

114. It is not easy to dissect the negotiations and correspondence between the parties to decipher at what point (if any) there has been 'acceptance' of a clear 'offer', with the parties *ad idem*. In a situation where each party seeks to conclude the contract on the basis of their own standard terms, it may be difficult to establish from negotiations conducted by an exchange of forms whether and on what basis there has been an offer and acceptance.[232] In other situations, the commercial reality of the process of negotiation simply does not fit the offer-acceptance analysis. The policy of common law courts is however to uphold contracts if at all possible. Irish cases on contract formation seem to emphasise whether there has been an agreement on material terms, rather than attempting to artificially break down negotiations into a single 'offer' and 'acceptance' per se. This issue of agreement on all material terms (or certainty of terms) is discussed in the section below.

115. It is sometimes said that silence or inaction cannot be acceptance. What is meant by this is that active acceptance is required and a contract cannot be imposed

229. *Ibid.*
230. *Harris' Case* (1872) LR 7 Ch Rep 587.
231. *Stevenson v McLean* 1880 5 QBD 346.
232. This is sometimes referred to as the 'battle of the forms', *see Butler Machine Tool Co. Ltd. v Ex-Cell-O Corporation* [1979] 1 All ER 965.

on the offeree by requiring them to refuse the offer.[233] The practice of 'inertia-selling', i.e., sending unsolicited goods with a requirement to return them or, in the event of failing to so do, pay the stipulated price, is dealt with by section 47 of the Sale of Goods and Supply of Services Act 1980.[234] The recipient of such goods, by complying with the requirements of this section, may treat the goods as if they were an unconditional gift.

116. In the case of unilateral contracts, it is possible to comply with the terms of an offer in ignorance of the fact that the offer has been made, e.g., by giving information for which a reward has been offered, but without awareness that there is a reward. There is little authority on the matter but again the weight of opinion appears to be against holding that a contract exists in this situation as the 'acceptance' is not made in response to an offer.[235] Conscious knowledge of the offer at the time of acceptance appears to be the essential requirement.

2. Communication of Acceptance

117. Acceptance must be communicated to the offeror or his agent, except where the offeror has waived the need to communicate acceptance. In such cases, there must be some overt act of acceptance, such as performing the required act in a unilateral contract[236] or accepting goods delivered in accordance with the terms of an offer.[237]

118. The contract is made at the place where the acceptance is received and is binding from the point it is received by the offeror.[238] Thus if X (in London) accepts an offer made by Y (in Dublin) over the phone, the contract is formed in Dublin, when Y hears ('receives') the acceptance.

119. An exception to this rule occurs when the parties intend that the ordinary postal service be used for acceptance, in which case acceptance is valid when and where the letter of acceptance is posted.[239] The postal rule will not apply where the

---

233. *Felthouse v Bindley* (1862) 11 CBNS 869; *Russell & Baird Ltd. v Hoban* [1922] 2 IR 159.
234. Section 47(1)–(5) apply to commercial transactions, but where the 'buyer' is a consumer s. 47(1)–(5) no longer applies. This is a result of S.I. No. 484/2013 – European Union (Consumer Information, Cancellation and Other Rights) Regulations 2013, which introduced a new s. 47 (7)–(10). This provides that the consumer is not deemed to have consented to and is not obliged to pay consideration for unsolicited goods or services, and may treat the unsolicited goods as an unconditional gift. These Regulations give effect to Directive 2011/83/EU of the European Parliament and of the Council on Consumer Rights.
235. *R. v Clarke* (1927) 40 CLR 227 (Australia).
236. *Carlill v Carbolic Smoke Ball Co.* [1893] 1 QB 256; *Billings v Arnott* (1945) 80 ILTR 50.
237. *Brogden v Metropolitan Railway Co.* (1877) 2 App Cas 666.
238. *Dooley v Egan* (1938) 72 ILTR 155.
239. *Adams v Lindsell* (1818) 1 B & Aid. 681; 106 ER 250. *Kelly v Cruise Catering* [1994] 2 ILRM 394; *Sanderson v Cunningham* [1919] 2 IR 234.

offeror specifies that the acceptance must be received,[240] or where 'its application would produce manifest inconvenience and absurdity',[241] or where it would cause an injustice.[242]

120. It is unlikely that emails come under the 'postal rule', and are best viewed as a form of instantaneous communication, meaning that acceptance occurs when the email is received. However, difficulties could feasibly arise as to whether an email acceptance is said to be 'received' by the offeror when it is in their 'Inbox', or when they have actually read it. This is arguably similar to a situation where a message is left on a voicemail or phone answering machine, although email has the added advantage of having facilities such as 'Out of office' settings, or the possibility of requesting confirmation that an email has been received ('read receipts'). There is unlikely to be a single answer to this question, and the answer on a given set of facts will most likely be resolved 'by reference to the intention of the parties, by sound business practice and in some cases by a judgment where the risks should lie'.[243]

D. The Need for Certainty and Agreement on Material Terms

121. It must be clear what has been agreed or an apparent agreement might be void for uncertainty. For example in *Mackie v Wilde and Longin*[244] an agreement to issue twenty-five annual fishing permits and 'a few' day tickets was held to be too uncertain to be enforceable, and in *Central Meat Products v Carney*[245] there was no agreement as there had been no agreement on important issues such as price variation clauses and insurance. In *Donnelly v Woods*[246] an arrangement for professional services was held not to be a contract as the court was 'left uncertain as to the nature of the professional services provided by the plaintiff; what exactly this consisted of; how many hours were involved; and what the hourly rate of charge would be'.[247] In this case, the court emphasised that although not every single issue needs to be agreed, certain matters will be essential:

> The essential aspect of a contract is that the parties come together and agree what their obligations are. Not every single issue as to liability and performance needs to be foreseen and provided for. To dismiss a contractual claim on the basis of a missing term would be to undermine the business efficacy which the courts are obliged to give to commercial transactions on the basis that reasonable people will conclude a contract where what is essential to their obligations is defined and agreed. Certain matters will be essential. This

240. *Holwell Securities Ltd. v Hughes* [1914] 1 All ER 161.
241. *Ibid.*
242. *Kelly v Cruise Catering* [1994] 2 ILRM 394.
243. *Brinkibon v Stahag Stahl und Stahlwarenhandelsgesellschaft* m.b.H. [1983] 2 AC 34.
244. [1998] 2 IR 578.
245. (1944) 10 Ir Jur Rep 34.
246. [2012] IEHC 26.
247. *Ibid.*, para. 9.

> depends on the nature of the obligations being undertaken through contract by the parties. … what is essential is that the parties to an agreement should not be left in doubt as to the substance of what they are to do in discharge of the obligation created by the contract.[248]

122. The courts give 'business efficacy' to commercial arrangements with gaps by means of tools such as implied terms or contractual interpretation.[249]

123. There is a strong line of Irish authority on the idea that there must be agreement on 'material' terms for there to be a contract. These cases often arise in the context of formalities requirements, particularly where the court is asked to grant specific performance of a contract for the sale of land. Before the court will turn to ask whether there has been a sufficient written evidence (note or memorandum) of the contract, they will ask whether there was an agreement in the first place:

> However, before one comes to the question of a note or memorandum it is necessary to see if an entire contract was concluded … for it is only in that event that the statutory note or memorandum would be required. If the negotiations between the parties had not ripened into the fullness of an entire contract, the plaintiff's claim for specific performance would fail, not for want of the statutory evidence necessary for the enforcement of a contract for the sale of lands, but simply in default of the existence of any such contract. There would be no contract to be specifically enforced. … [250]

124. The corollary of this is that a court might find that 'a binding and enforceable contract has come to existence even where the parties expressly contemplate that the oral agreement will later be formalised into a written contract'.[251] This can be seen in *Danbywiske v Donegal Investment Group Plc*[252] where heads of an agreement drafted by lay people with all essential terms were held to constitute a binding agreement, even though there was intended to be formal documents later.[253]

125. The starting point in these cases is whether there was agreement on all the material terms of the contract. In a contract for the disposal of an interest in land, the material terms are referred to as the 'Three P's',[254] namely the parties, the property and the price.[255] Failure to agree on these may mean there is no agreement, or

248. [2012] IEHC 26, para. 8 per Charleton J.
249. On implied terms, *see* paras 425 et seq. On contract interpretation, *see* paras 494 et seq.
250. *Lynch v O'Meara* (Unreported, Supreme Court, 8 May 1975. *See also Supermac's Ireland Ltd v Katesan (Naas) Ltd* [2000] 4 IR 273.
251. *Keena v Coughlan & Others* [2019] IEHC 12 [112] per Quinn J. *See also Greenband Investments v Bruton & Ors* [2009] IEHC 67.
252. [2015] IEHC 126.
253. *See also* the UK Supreme Court case of *RTS Flexible Systems Ltd v Molkerei Alois Muller GmbH* [2010] UKSC 14.
254. *Godley v Power* (1961) 95 ILTR 135; *Black v Grealy* [1977] IEHC 145; *Keena v Coughlan & Others* [2019] IEHC 12 [114] per Quinn J.
255. *See*, for example, on the price (or consideration): *Maloney v O'Connor & Dunne* [2015] IEHC 678.

that any apparent agreement is void for uncertainty. In the recent case of *Keena v Coughlan & ors,*[256] for example, there was no clear agreement on who the purchaser of the property was to be, and in *Sheridan & Quinn v Gaynor* [257] the precise piece of land which was the subject of an apparent agreement could not be identified. In the case of a lease it is usually stated that there must also be agreement on the term of the lease,[258] commencement date[259] and the rent.[260]

126. However, the concept is not limited to these terms, but also includes any other terms which the parties themselves viewed as essential. In simple terms, there 'cannot be a concluded agreement unless everything intended to be covered by the agreement has been either expressly or impliedly agreed'.[261] For example in *Globe Entertainment & Anor v Pub Pool Ltd & Ors*[262] the failure to agree on a closing date meant that there was no concluded agreement – not because there is a rule that you must agree on a closing date, but rather because the parties themselves viewed this as an essential term on which there had to be agreement:

> The question as to whether a term is material and must be agreed in order that a concluded agreement has come into existence depends upon a subjective assessment of the facts with particular regard being had to what the parties themselves considered to be material terms requiring express agreement.[263]

127. Similarly in *Shirley Engineering Ltd v Irish Telecommunications Investments plc*[264] and *Boyle v Lee and Goyns*[265] it was held that no concluded oral agreement had been reached because the parties had failed to agree on a deposit. In contrast, in *Supermac's Ireland Ltd v Katesan (Naas) Ltd*[266] there was still a concluded agreement where the question of the deposit had been left to the solicitors to deal with. On the facts of this case, the parties did not consider the question of the deposit as a 'material' aspect of the contract, but rather as a formality, and would have considered there to be a completed agreement. In this case the Supreme Court outlined that there could be a concluded agreement in the following circumstances:

> (2) That having regard to the nature of the transaction in this case … it was not intended that there be a deposit.

256. [2019] IEHC 12.
257. [2009] IEHC 421.
258. *Crane v Naughten* [1912] 2 IR 318.
259. *O'Flaherty v Arvan Properties Ltd*, Unreported, Supreme Court, 21 July 1977.
260. *Cosmoline Trading v DH Burke and Son Ltd* [2006] IEHC 38, citing *Shannon v Bradstreet* (1803) 1 Schoales & Le Froy 52.
261. *Supermac's Ireland Ltd v Katesan (Naas) Ltd* [2000] 4 IR 273, 288 per Geoghegan J [2000] 4 IR 273.
262. [2016] IECA 272.
263. [2016] IECA 272 [44].
264. Unreported, High Court, 2 December 1999. *See* Stack (2000) 5 Conveyancing and Property Law Journal 6.
265. [1992] 1 IR 555.
266. [2000] 4 IR 273.

(3) That in all the circumstances of the case there would have been an implied term that a reasonable deposit would be paid.
(4) That in all the circumstances there was an implied term that the standard deposit normally payable in transactions of this kind would be paid.
(5) That it would never have occurred to any of the parties that there would be a problem about the deposit and that a concluded agreement was reached ignoring it with the assumption that the solicitors when drawing up formal contracts would agree a deposit.[267]

128. Of course, in some cases the agreement simply contains too many gaps and uncertainties to be enforceable. In *An Cumann Peile Boitheimeach Teoranta v Albion Properties Ltd*[268] the court emphasised that 'the more numerous and significant the areas in respect of which the parties have failed to reach agreement, the slower a court should be to conclude' that there was an agreement. It was said to be 'a matter of fact and degree in each case whether the gap left by the parties is simply too wide to be filled' by the court. In this case the 'complexity of the outstanding issues' and the absence of any 'mechanism or formula or agreed standard' by which to resolve them meant that there was no concluded agreement between the parties.[269] Similarly in *McGill Construction v McKeown*[270] there was agreement on the price for land, but not on related matters such as disposal of a show house, deposit and closing date, meaning that there was no agreement in place. Clark comments that 'critically the matter was complicated ... and the evidence indicated that such matters might have gone on for some time'.[271] However, it should be noted that in commercial agreements the courts will assume that the parties intended to create legal relations, and may look to the course of dealing of the parties to incorporate associated documents in order to find a completed agreement.[272]

II. Intention to Create Legal Relations

129. It is arguable that at common law the presence or absence of consideration determines the enforceability of an agreement, and there is no need or room for an additional requirement of intention to create legal relations.[273] Nonetheless, it is possible to have a situation where there is an agreement, with consideration, but the parties never intended for that agreement to be an enforceable contract, and there are cases which are only explicable on the basis of a lack of legal intent. The classic example of this is in relation to arrangements between close family members, where there is a presumption that any agreements were not intended to create legally binding contracts. This is however a presumption only and may be rebutted. In contrast,

267. [2000] 4 IR 273, 290.
268. [2008] IEHC 447.
269. Although proprietary estoppel was applied in this case, and it was held that the plaintiffs held the land in question upon a constructive trust for the benefit of the plaintiffs.
270. [2005] IEHC 88.
271. Clark p. 18.
272. *See McCabe Builders (Dublin) Ltd v Sagamu Developments* [2009] IESC 31.
273. *See* Clark pp. 117–118; *Keogh v Gibbons* [2016] IEHC 319, para. 13.

in commercial arrangements, provided the other criteria are met, there is a presumption that any agreement is intended to be legally binding.[274] However, certain forms of commercial agreements, such as letters of comfort, are recognised to not be legally binding.

A. *Family Arrangements*

130. The general rule in relation to family arrangements is that there is a presumption that they are not binding – however, this may apply as between close family members only, such as spouses or as between a parent and child. In *Leahy v Rawson* the presumption did not apply to an agreement between the plaintiff and her partner's brother,[275] in *Horan v Reilly* an informal lottery syndicate between five friends nonetheless had legal effect,[276] and *Courtney v Courtney* indicates that no such presumption arises where a married couple is separated.[277] It is also clear that this is only a presumption, meaning that the onus is on the party seeking to enforce the contract to show that there was legal intent. The court will take into account factors such as the degree of closeness between the parties,[278] whether one party has acted in reliance on a promise,[279] and whether the promise was vague or made in general terms,[280] or, in contrast, certain and reduced to writing.[281]

131. This issue can arise before the courts when an individual gives money to another, and the question arises as to whether this was a loan, meant to be legally enforceable, or simply a gift which is not repayable. In *Keogh v Gibbons*,[282] for example, the plaintiff claimed the return of money which she had lent to the defendant over a six-year period, while they were in a relationship. The court found that these were contractual dealings, and moneys were lent with a view to repayment, remarking that 'there was perhaps a more commercial hue to arrangements between them than one might expect to find' in a relationship.[283] Similarly in *Kerrigan v Keenaghan* the defendants were found to have accepted a 'loan' rather than a 'gift' of €280,000 from a former friend and were ordered to repay the moneys lent.[284]

274. *See McCabe Builders (Dublin) Ltd v Sagamu Developments* [2009] IESC 31, paras 43–44.
275. Unreported, High Court, 14 January 2003.
276. [2008] IESC 65. It was held on the facts that the plaintiff was not a member of the syndicate at the time that it won a substantial amount of money.
277. (1923) 57 ILTR 42.
278. *Keogh v Gibbons* [2016] IEHC 319, para. 13.
279. *Ibid. McCarron v McCarron*, Unreported, Supreme Court, 13 February 1997.
280. *Rogers v Smith*, Unreported, Supreme Court, 16 July 1970. *See* however *Horan v Reilly* where an informal arrangement made in general terms and not written down nonetheless had 'indisputable legal consequences'. [2008] IESC 65, para. 4.
281. *See* Clark, *Contract Law in Ireland* p. 120.
282. [2016] IEHC 319.
283. [2016] IEHC 319, para. 16.
284. [2019] IEHC 5. *See* 'Couple ordered to repay EUR 280,000 loan after claiming it was a gift' *The Irish Times* 29 January 2019.

132. Of course, even in a situation where money is given as gift, it is possible for the court to use other techniques to allow recovery of the money, such as the concept of an unconscionable bargain.[285] The court in *Kerrigan* held that even if the money lent *had* been a gift, it would 'have set the gift aside as being an improvident transaction' which would have been unconscionable for them to retain.[286]

B. *Commercial Arrangements*

133. Commercial arrangements are presumed to have been intended to have legal effect.[287] In a commercial agreement 'the onus is on the party who asserts that no legal effect was intended, and the onus is a heavy one'.[288]

134. The presumption may be rebutted, for example where there is an express exclusion of legal enforceability,[289] or where on a correct interpretation, statements made involve at best 'a commitment to enter into honest negotiations' rather than a binding promise.[290]

135. In the commercial context, this issue can arise in relation to 'letters of comfort' which might be given by a parent company or government body in relation to a subsidiary, in lieu of a formal guarantee. Their legal effect depends on the intention of the parties, as determined from the wording used, and the circumstances as whole.[291] In *Kleinwort Benson v Malaysia Mining Corp*[292] the plaintiff bank had entered into negotiations with defendant to make a loan facility available to a subsidiary of the defendants. The defendants issued a comfort letter which stated, *inter alia*, 'It is our policy to ensure that the business of [the subsidiary] is at all times in a position to meet its liabilities to you under the above arrangements.' It was held that this letter was not intended to be legally binding and it was relevant that in fact the defendants had refused to offer a formal (binding) guarantee prior to this. In addition, the letter was merely a statement of the *current* policy of the defendant but not an undertaking not to change that policy in the future.

136. In Ireland, a case concerning letters of comfort was settled outside court when Aer Lingus, the national airline, issued letters of comfort to employees of a subsidiary, offering them re-engagement with the parent company should they lose their employment with the subsidiary. The purpose of the letter was to encourage

---

285. *Bourke*.
286. [2019] IEHC 5, para. 102.
287. *See The Commodity Broking Co Ltd v Meehan* [1985] IR 12; *McCabe Builders (Dublin) Ltd v Sagamu Developments* [2009] IESC 31, paras 43–44.
288. *O'Rourke v Talbot Ireland* [1984] ILRM 587, 593, citing *Edwards v Skyways Ltd* [1964] 1 WLR 349, 355.
289. *Rose and Frank v Compton* [1925] AC 445.
290. *Cadbury Ireland Ltd v Kerry Co-Op Creameries* [1982] ILRM 77. An agreement to enter into negotiations is itself unenforceable: *see* para. 254.
291. It may also be difficult to show consideration for the assurance given.
292. [1989] 1 All ER 785 (Eng.).

employees to leave the parent company and start work in the subsidiary company. Subsequently, the subsidiary ran into financial difficulties, and the employees sought to exercise the offer under the letters of comfort. The parent company denied that they had any legal effect. A court case commenced but was withdrawn following a satisfactory resolution through the industrial relation machinery.[293]

C. Collective Agreements

137. Collective agreements between an employer and a group of employees may be enforceable in the courts. This was confirmed by the Supreme Court in *Goulding Chemicals Ltd v Bolger*,[294] in which a redundancy agreement between an employer and a trade union was held to be binding. There must still however be an intention to create legal relations, and in many cases the parties will be held not have intended the agreement to be enforceable. In *Holland v Athlone Institute of Technology*[295] Hogan J stated:

> While the question of whether a collective agreement between employers and employees is legally enforceable remains something of a vexed one, in my view there is no *a priori* rule in the matter. … such agreement will only be binding if there is an intention to make the agreements binding in law between the parties, or it is apparent from the face of the agreement that it is to be so binding.[296]

138. It may be easier to show legal intent when an agreement appears to be 'a business-like document' which has 'all the appearances of being intended to create legal relations'[297] as opposed to an agreement 'composed largely of optimistic aspirations, presenting grave practical problems of enforcement'.[298] In other cases collective agreements have been unenforceable because of uncertainty of terms.[299]

139. In *O'Rourke v Talbot Ireland*[300] the plaintiffs were foremen who were given an assurance in writing from the defendant company, their employer, that compulsory redundancy would not be introduced. When the plaintiffs later argued that there had been a breach of this agreement, the defendant argued that there had never been any intention to create legal relations. However, it was held that the agreement was enforceable: while the company may not have intended by the agreements to create legal relations, they had not made this known to the plaintiffs; the plaintiffs had sought a legally binding agreement and the company knew this; in the circumstances there was a presumption that the parties intended to create legal relations;

293. *See The Irish Times* 'Guarantees spelled out in letters to staff' 26 May 1998.
294. [1977] IR 211.
295. [2011] IEHC 414
296. *Ibid.*, para. 23.
297. *Gouldings Chemicals Ltd v Bolger* [1977] IR 211, 231.
298. *Ford Motor Company v Amalgamated Union of Engineering Workers* [1969] 2 QB 303, 330.
299. *Ardmore Studies v Lynch* [1965] IR 1; Clark, *Contract Law in Ireland* p. 136.
300. [1984] ILRM 587.

and the company had not rebutted that presumption. This case emphasises that what is important is the *objective* intentions of the parties; not their own private or subjective beliefs as to the enforceability of the agreement.

140. In contrast, *Holland v Athlone Institute of Technology*[301] concerned the enforceability of the 'Croke Park Agreement'. The Croke Park Agreement was the Public Service Agreement 2010-2014, agreed between the Irish Congress of Trade Unions (and Gardaí and Defence Force Associations) and the Irish Government, under which costs and the number of people working the Public Service were reduced in return for various government commitments, such as no further reductions in pay rates and no new compulsory redundancies as long as public servants were flexible about redeployment. The issue which arose was whether this Agreement was binding 'merely at a political and industrial relations level' or whether it was 'intended to create justiciable rights enforceable at law'.[302] The court held that the agreement would pose difficulties regarding judicial enforcement – for example it would be difficult for a court to determine whether public sector unions had been 'sufficiently flexible' on redeployment issues – and that it was never intended to be enforceable at the hands of individual public sector employees.[303] Similarly in *Irish Pharmaceutical Union v Minister for Health and Children*[304] it was agreed by both parties that an agreement between the Minister of Health and the Pharmaceutical Union was not intended to be legally binding, and was thus not enforceable. In *McGowan v Labour Court*[305] the Supreme Court emphasised that this is often a preferable situation for the parties involved:

> In general collective agreements are considered not to be legally enforceable either by the parties thereto, or the persons represented by the parties to any such agreement. Indeed in general the fact that collective agreements exist outside a precise legal framework and are not enforceable by either the civil or criminal law, is normally seen as a desirable feature in industrial relations.

141. In this case, Part III of the Industrial Relations Act 1946, which provided for the registration of certain types of collective agreements with the Labour Court and their contractual and criminal enforcement as against 'every worker of the class, type or group to which it is expressed to apply, and his employer', even if they were not party to the agreement, or even in existence at the time, was held to be unconstitutional, and thus invalid.

---

301. [2011] IEHC 414.
302. [2011] IEHC 414, para. 25.
303. *Ibid.*, para. 27.
304. [2010] IESC 23.
305. [2013] IESC 21, para. 9.

III. Consideration

A. *The Requirement of Consideration in Irish Contract Law*

142. To have a valid contract, there must be 'consideration'. Consideration has been defined as 'the price for which the promise of the other is bought'.[306] In essence, this means that the agreement must have some element of reciprocity, exchange or quid pro quo.

143. This can take the form of an instantaneous exchange, such as when you purchase an item in a shop and pay for it immediately. In this situation the consideration is said to have been 'executed'. It can take the form of the exchange of promises – for example, if you hire a builder to construct a building, with payment to take place at an agreed future time. This is referred to as 'executory' consideration, and is sufficient to form a valid, enforceable contract even though nothing has yet changed hands. Consideration may take the form of forbearance, i.e., agreeing to *not* do something. An example of this would be agreeing to not sell a piece of land to a third party for a set period of time (in exchange for something of value, such as a sum of money), or agreeing not to bring proceedings.[307]

144. The corollary of a requirement of consideration is that a gratuitous promise is not enforceable as a contract. If there has been no reciprocal, agreed-upon act or promise in return for that promise, then it is not enforceable. This means for example that a simple gift, or promise of a gift, is not enforceable as a contract. There might be a 'moral' obligation to keep to one's word, but this is not enough to enforce a contract in court.[308]

145. There are, however, some notable exceptions to the general requirement of consideration. First, in the absence of consideration, an agreement might be enforceable if it is in the form of a 'deed under seal'. Second, equitable doctrines such as promissory estoppel and proprietary estoppel may operate in certain, limited circumstances to provide a remedy where a promise has been made and failure to uphold it would result in an injustice. Third, when a promise is made by a public body, there may be a legitimate expectation that this promise will be upheld. These are examined in more detail below.

306. *Dunlop v Selfridge* [1915] AC 847.
307. *The Commodity Broking Company Limited v Meehan* [1985] IR 12; *Harrahill v Swaine* [2014] IEHC 94.
308. *Eastwood v Kenyon* (1840) 113 ER 482. *Ferrar v Costelloe* (1841) 4 ILR 425 (Exch.).

1. What Counts as Consideration?

146. There is no requirement that the consideration that is provided by both parties be of equal value, or even proportionate.[309] The courts might of course treat with suspicion a contract where there is a gross disparity in the values of the exchange, and examine whether there was fraud, duress or undue influence, but these are vitiating factors, and the basic requirement of consideration will have been met.

147. This also means that there is somewhat of an anomaly in the law, in that a nominal consideration can suffice as consideration. Hence if a party wishes to bind themselves by a gratuitous promise, such as a promise to make a gift of property, they may do so by promising in exchange for a purely nominal consideration. There are examples in case law of nominal payments such £1 a year for accommodation,[310] or even pieces of paper[311] or chocolate wrappers,[312] counting as valid consideration. The consideration does have to have at least *tangible* value, or be something 'of value in the eyes of law', meaning that for example, natural love or affection are not legally sufficient consideration.

148. In some cases, a court's finding that there is an absence of consideration is in fact motivated by other concerns. The Northern Ireland case of *O'Neill v Murphy*[313] is often cited as authority for the idea that the saying of prayers will not suffice as consideration. However, this case is better explained as a case where there was undue influence over a parishioner who agreed to do building work on a church in return for prayers; the result of the finding of no agreed consideration meant that the builder in fact got paid money for work done on a *quantum meruit* basis, whereas if the contract had defined his pay he would not have been paid (or been 'paid' in the form of prayers). In reality, unless the contract states that the consideration is the saying of prayers with the intention of guaranteeing a particular result (which cannot be proven),[314] the saying of prayers is no different to the recital of a poem or story, or the singing of a song, and could in theory constitute valid consideration.

149. The case of *Keefe v Ryanair Holdings*[315] illustrates the wide view taken into consideration. In this case, Ms Keefe was the millionth passenger with Ryanair. She was asked if she would take part in a publicity event, with photographs being taken, in return for unlimited travel on Ryanair flights for herself and her nominee for the remainder of her life. She agreed, and took part in the publicity event, which

309. *Grogan v Cooke* (1812) 2 B&B 230, 234, Per Manners LC states: 'If there be a fair and bona fide consideration, the court will not enter minutely into it, and *see* that it is full and ample.'
310. *Thomas v Thomas* (1842) 2 QB 851.
311. *Haigh v Brooks* (1839) 113 ER 119.
312. *Chappell v Nestle* [1960] AC 87.
313. *O'Neill v Murphy* [1936] NI 16.
314. *See Pando v Fernandez* (1984) 485 NYS 2d 162.
315. [2002] 3 IR 228.

gathered a significant amount of attention in the media at the time. However, a number of years later she was told she would be limited to one flight per year, with restrictions in place. When she argued that this was breach of contract, Ryanair said that the 'free flights for life' was only a gift, and that she had not provided any consideration to make it an enforceable contract. This argument was rejected by the court, which found that the 'surrender by the plaintiff of her anonymity and privacy and her active participation in the generation of the publicity that was created on the day in question … amounted to a real consideration and sufficient to support a valid contract.'

2. Consideration Must Move from the Promisee

150. The rule that consideration must move from the promisee is closely related to the rule of privity of contract, although it is distinct from it. [316] The rule is well illustrated by the case of *McCoubray v Thompson.*[317] Here, a third party G owned a farm, worth £196, which he wished to divide equally between the plaintiff (McCoubray) and defendant (Thompson). It was agreed that the farm would be transferred to Thompson, who promised to pay the McCoubray £98. The land was duly transferred, but Thompson refused to pay McCoubray. As no consideration had moved from McCoubray to support the promise, (i.e., McCoubray had not promised to do anything) he was unable to sue on this promise. Although intended to be the beneficiary of a gift, McCoubray had no legal right in relation to the property and therefore had not surrendered any right 'in consideration' of Thompson's promise to both him and the owner of the property.[318]

151. It is likely that *McCoubray v Thompson* would not be followed in situations where there are joint promisees, with consideration being provided by one or the other, such as in the opening and operation of a joint bank account.[319]

3. The Rule Against Past Consideration

152. A promise given in return for a consideration which has already been supplied, i.e., one which is not given as part of the present bargain, is not a contractual promise and cannot be enforced. The 'rule against past consideration' prevents enforcement of a promise made in gratitude for an act already performed for the benefit of the promisor.[320] It also means that warranties given after the contract is formed may not form part of the consideration.[321]

---

316. *Dunlop v Selfridge* [1915] AC 847.
317. (1868) 2 IRCL 226.
318. Contrast *Barry v Barry* (1891) 28 LR (Ir) 45 where the plaintiff *had* rights against the land, an interest in a farm which he gave up in return for the promise that the defendant would pay personally. This constituted consideration.
319. *McEvoy v Belfast Banking Co.* [1935] AC 24.
320. *Re Mc Ardle* [1951] Ch 669 (Eng.).
321. *Roscarla v Thomas* (1842) 3 QB 234.

153. In *Provincial Bank of Ireland v Donnell,*[322] for example, a woman agreed to provide security for her husband's overdraft, in consideration of 'advances heretofore made or that may hereafter be made'. There was held to be no consideration here, as 'advances which had already been made' were past consideration (and that 'may hereafter be made' was illusory). Similar arguments have been made in recent years. In *AIB v Maguire,*[323] for example, the defendants had an arguable case that guarantees they had provided were not supported by any consideration since the money in question had been advanced a number of years prior to the execution of the guarantees, and no further money was advanced thereafter. In *ACC Bank Plc v Dillon*[324] Charleton J stated that what is relevant is whether any money was actually advanced and 'the mere recitation in a document of guarantee that the guarantee was given for consideration for "advances to be made" by the person to whom the guarantee was given will not, by itself be sufficient to support the guarantee if the evidence demonstrates that no such advances were, or were intended to be, made'.[325]

154. The issue of past consideration – or the absence of any fresh consideration – has also arisen in relation to other financial arrangements with banks. In *AIB v O'Brien*[326] a couple's debt to a bank had been restructured, and they were sued on the basis of a facility granted in 2010; however it was argued that this agreement was void for lack of consideration as no new funds had been advanced. It was held that there was at least an arguable case here that there was no consideration; however somewhat bizarrely the bank did not seek to rely on forbearance as a form of consideration, (i.e., the fact that they did not call in repayment of moneys due), and the court noted that this could possibly constitute consideration if pleaded. Such an argument succeeded in *AIB v Gormley*[327] where there was said to be consideration in the form of an 'implicit forbearance' by the bank from suing the defendants. In *ACC Bank v Dillon*[328] the question was whether the debtor had provided consideration for the extension of loans whose term had expired. There was said to be a 'series of different transactions each of which could be supported by a continued promise by the company to pay back the loan within a new term' but that these 'alterations could also be supported by a different rate of interest or could require some different form of security'.[329]

155. It may be possible to show that the act in question was performed at the request of the defendant in circumstances which implied that some payment would be made for performance of the act.[330] In such a case:

---

322. *Provincial Bank of Ireland v Donnell* (1932) 67 ILTR 142.
323. [2018] IEHC 561.
324. [2012] IEHC 474.
325. Quoting the Supreme Court of Victoria in *McKay and Another v National Australia Bank Ltd* [1998] 1 VR 173.
326. [2018] IEHC 408.
327. [2018] IEHC 744.
328. [2012] IEHC 474.
329. [2012] IEHC 474, para. 4.4.
330. *Lampleigh v Brathwait* (1615) Hof 105, 72 ER 960; *Bradford v Raulston* (1858) 8 IRCL 468.

The act must have been done at the promisors' request; the parties must have understood that the act was to be remunerated either by payment or the conferment of some other benefit and payment or the conferment of a benefit must have been legally enforceable had it been promised in advance.[331]

156. This can be seen in cases such as *AIB v Gormley*,[332] mentioned above, where there was said to be consideration in the form of an 'implicit forbearance'. In *Eirebus Limited v McConn*[333] it was argued that shares transferred to Eirebus prior to an agreement could not constitute valid consideration; this argument was rejected as the relevant shares were only issued after the agreement. In addition, it was held that even if the relevant shares had been subscribed for prior to entering into the agreement, that it would fall under this exception to the rule against past consideration, 'whereby the fact of a past service raises an implication that at the time it was rendered it was to be the subject of a reciprocal commitment, such that it can be sufficient consideration for a subsequent promise to perform that commitment'.[334] Here, it was clear that Eirebus subscribed for shares at the defendant's request, that the parties understood at the time that the defendant was to arrange for the transfer of the relevant bus licence to Flybus in exchange for the provision of those subscriptions; and that the defendant would have been able to enforce the agreement to make those subscriptions had he arranged the transfer of the bus route licence to Flybus in advance of their being made.[335]

4. Agreements to Compromise a Legal Claim as Consideration

157. An agreement to compromise and settle a legal claim for less than the amount originally claimed is a valid agreement with legally sufficient consideration. This is the case even if it transpires that the prosecution of the original claim could not possibly have been successful and in that sense the consideration for the agreement was worthless.[336] However, the original claim must have been a reasonable one, which the plaintiff believed bona fide could succeed. In *O'Donnell v O'Sullivan*[337] the compromise agreement concerned a gambling debt which both parties knew could not be legally enforced;[338] hence the court refused to enforce the agreement. In addition, the plaintiff must not have concealed facts about the original claim which would have revealed to the defendant that it could not succeed.[339]

331. *Pao On v Lau Yiu Long* [1979] 3 All ER 65 at 74 per Lord Scarman.
332. [2018] IEHC 744.
333. [2015] IEHC 869.
334. [2015] IEHC 869.
335. *Ibid.*, para. 45.
336. *Miles v New Zealand Afford Estate* (1886) 32 Ch D 266.
337. [1913] 47 ILTR 253.
338. *See* discussion below at para. 378 and paras 673 et seq.
339. *Leonard v Leonard* (1812) 2 Ball & B 171.

158. It is not necessary for parties to make a formal agreement not to sue or prosecute a claim. It is sufficient if there is a request, express or implied, to forbear from bringing proceedings which induces some forbearance.[340]

5. Performance of an Existing Duty under General Law

159. The performance or promise of performance of a duty which is already imposed by the general law (common law or statute) is not legally sufficient consideration, as the promisor is not doing anything that they are not already required to do by law. However anything which can be construed as performance above or beyond the strict limits required by the law will be accepted as providing sufficient consideration. Hence in *Glasbrook Bros. v Glamorgan County Council*[341] and *Harris v Sheffield United Football Club*[342] the provision of extra police protection during strikes (*Glasbrook Bros*) or football matches (*Harris*), over and above the normal duties of the police, constituted consideration.

6. Performance of Existing Contractual Obligation

160. The performance or promise of performance of a duty which is already contractually owed to the other party is not legally sufficient consideration.

161. Old cases in England[343] and Ireland[344] concerning extra wages promised to seamen in the course of a voyage applied this rule. In *Stilk v Myrick*[345] the crew of a ship were promised extra pay for continuing with a voyage and taking on extra duties after the desertion of two of the seamen, but this was unenforceable. The seamen were obliged to carry out these duties regardless and were giving nothing extra in return for the promise of extra pay. In the Irish case of the *Christiana*[346] it was held that the owners of a vessel are bound by a promise by the captain to give extra wages to crew who agree to navigate a ship home in a leaking and unseaworthy condition *only* if the crew can be regarded as released from their original contract.

162. This rule can cause difficulties when it comes to the modification of contracts. In the absence of fresh consideration, any agreement to pay extra money is prima facie unenforceable. However, the English Court of Appeal in *Williams v Roffey Bros*[347] provided a different approach to the question of consideration in such

340. *Barry v Barry* (1891) 28 LR (Ir) 45; *Commodity Broking Co. v Meehan* [1985] IR 12.
341. [1925] AC 270.
342. [1987] 2 All ER 838.
343. *Stilk v Myrick.* Cf., *Hartley v Ponsonby* (1791) Peake 102.
344. *The 'Christiana'* 5 Ir Jur NS 63 (Admir).
345. (1809) 2 Camp 317.
346. 5 Ir Jur NS 63 (Admir). *See also The Sansone* 3 IR Jur OS 258 (Admir) the crew of a salvage vessel were released from their original contract and thus entitled to extra wages for additional labour.
347. [1990] 1 All ER 512.

cases. In this case, a carpenter working on a subcontract encountered difficulties in completing his work on time. The main contractor was concerned about his own liabilities under the main contract if performance was delayed, and promised an extra sum of money to the carpenter to ensure that he completed on time. When the carpenter sued for this extra sum of money, the question arose as to what the fresh consideration for this extra sum was – the carpenter was not doing anything for this sum other than what he had originally promised to do. In this case, the Court of Appeal found that there *was* consideration, focusing on the additional 'practical benefit' to the defendant contractor rather than on whether the subcontractor was actually doing anything new. Glidewell LJ set out the test as follows:

(i) If A enters into a contract with B to do work for B in return for payment;
(ii) At some point before A has fully completed, B has doubts as to whether he will be able to complete;
(iii) B promises A extra money in return for A's promise to complete on time;
(iv) As a result B gets a benefit, or avoids a detriment; and
(v) B's promise is not the result of economic duress or fraud; then
(vi) The benefit to B is consideration for B's promise to pay more so will be binding.

163. This relaxes the requirement of consideration in this type of situation, as there will almost *always* be some sort of 'practical benefit', meaning that the consideration requirement is going to automatically be met.[348] Glidewell LJ's fifth point – the requirement that the promise is not the result of economic duress or fraud – then takes on an important role, and shifts 'the burden of regulating price re-negotiation on to the doctrine of duress'.[349] While this is not necessarily a bad thing – duress is arguably a better tool with which to decide which promises to enforce in this context – it is a pity that the Court of Appeal was forced to retain the formality of a consideration requirement, albeit one which is set at a very low threshold. In contrast, the New Zealand courts preferred to explicitly endorse an approach based on the intentions of the parties rather than on any artificial interpretation of the consideration requirement –under this approach if parties who had already made clear the intention to be bound acted upon an agreement to a variation, they would be bound by their agreement, in the absence of policy reasons to the contrary.[350]

348. *See* Giancaspro 'Practical Benefit: An English Anomaly or a Growing Force in Contract Law?' (2013) 30 Journal of Contract Law 12.
349. J Adams and R Brownsword 'Contract, Consideration and the Critical Path' (1990) 53 Modern Law Review 536.
350. *Antons Trawling Co v Smith* [2003] 2 NZLR 23. For analysis, *see* Coote 'Consideration and the Variation of Contracts' [2003] NZ Law Review 361.

7. A Promise by a Creditor to Accept a Lesser Sum than the Amount Due in Full Satisfaction of a Debt Due

164. Often referred to as 'the rule in *Pinnel's case*',[351] a promise by a creditor to accept a lesser sum than the amount due to them in full satisfaction of the debt due is not legally enforceable. To give a simple example: X has a contractual obligation to pay Y €200, but Y says that if X pays €100 then Y will forgive the rest of the sum due. The difficulty here is that X has given nothing, or promised nothing, in return for Y's promise not to sue for the rest of the sum due. Y's promise not to sue for the full sum is not enforceable as it is not supported by consideration. Although it dates from the early seventeenth century, this rule was upheld by the House of Lords in *Foakes v Beer*[352] in 1884, and applied in Ireland in *Drogheda Corporation v Fairtlough*[353] in 1858.

165. In the aftermath of the decision in *Williams v Roffey Brothers*, it was suggested that the principle contained therein (that a modification to the original contract is enforceable where there is a 'practical benefit' to the promisor) could be extended to the rule in *Pinnel's Case*. However, in *Re Selectmove*[354] this argument was rejected by the English Court of Appeal:

> [I]f the principle of the *Williams* case is to be extended to an obligation to make payment, it would in effect leave the principle in *Foakes v Beer* without any application. When a creditor and a debtor who are at arm's length reach agreement on the payment of the debt by instalments to accommodate the debtor, the creditor will no doubt always see a practical benefit to himself in so doing. In the absence of authority there would be much to be said for the enforceability of such a contract. But that was a matter expressly considered in *Foakes v Beer* yet held not to constitute good consideration in law.[355]

166. The rule in *Pinnel's Case* was also confirmed in Ireland in *Truck and Machinery Sales v Marubeni Komatsu*,[356] in which Keane J refused to depart from the authority of *Pinnel's Case,* and instead took the same approach as the UK Court of Appeal in *Re Selectmove.* More recently in *Barge Inn v Quinn* Laffoy J refused to depart from the rule, stating that it is 'beyond question that the rule in *Pinnel's*

351. (1602) 5 Co Rep 117a; 77 ER 237.
352. (1884) 9 App Cas 605.
353. (1858) 8 IrCLR 98 (Q.B.).
354. [1995] 2 All ER 531. *See also Collier v P&M J Wright Holdings Ltd* [2007] EWCA 1329, although on which *see* R Austen-Baker 'A Strange Sort of Survival for Pinnel's Case: Collier v P & M J Wright (Holdings) Limited' (2008) 71(4) Modern Law Review 611–620.
355. (1884) 9 App Cas 605.
356. [1996] 1 IR 12.

Case still represents the law in Ireland and this Court is bound by it'[357] and in *Harrahill v Swaine*[358] the Court of Appeal reached the same conclusion.

167. The rule can be circumvented if X can be said to offer some consideration in return for the promise, such as promising payment before the due date or, at the request of the creditor, payment in a place or in a manner not required in the original contract, or by adding something to the payment, even if of trivial value: 'the law will allow the payment of a smaller sum to be a satisfaction of a greater liquidated sum, if there be, along with the payment of the smaller sum, any collateral advantage, however small, attending the transaction'.[359] It is clear, however, that this collateral advantage must be a *new* advantage, and not merely confirmation of an already existing advantage.[360]

168. There are also long-established specific exceptions to the rule. First, where there are multiple creditors, there may be a composite agreement where all the creditors agree to accept some percentage payment of the total amount of the sum due to them. Such an agreement is binding,[361] on the basis that to permit any one of the creditors to abandon the agreement and sue for the outstanding balance of his debt would be a fraud on all the other creditors. Second, where a lesser sum is paid by a third party on behalf of a debtor on the agreement of the creditor that it will be accepted in full satisfaction of the debt, the creditor is not permitted to sue the debtor for the balance of the debt as this would be a fraud vis-à-vis the third party.[362] The rule would also not apply in a situation where the amount owed was in dispute – *see John K Rogers t/a John Rogers Engineering v Iaralco Ltd.*[363]

169. A more general exception arises under the doctrine of promissory estoppel, which in the proper case 'may obviate an inequitable outcome to which the application of the rule in Pinnel's *Case* would otherwise give rise'.[364] However, as discussed below this is subject to strict criteria and will not always be available in this situation.

---

357. *The Barge Inn Ltd v Quinn Hospitality Ireland Operations 3 Ltd* [2013] IEHC 387, para. 62. For criticism, *see* James Kane, 'The Rule in Pinnel's Case: The Case for Repeal, a Mistaken Preponderance and Finding Consideration in Debt Renegotiations' (2014) 37(1) Dublin University Law Journal 79.
358. [2015] IECA 36. *See also NALM v Kelleher* [2015] IEHC 169; *Gladney and others v P O'M* [2015] IEHC 718; *AIB Mortgage Bank v Reginald Hayes and Teresa Hayes [2017] IEHC 615; Neil Healy v Ulster Bank* [2018] IEHC 12.
359. *Drogheda Corporation v Fairtlough* 8 Ir CLR 98, 110 per Lefroy CJ, as cited by Laffoy J in *Barge Inn*, para. 58.
360. *See AIB Mortgage Bank v Reginald Hayes and Teresa Hayes* [2017] IEHC 615, para. 8.
361. *Morans v Armstrong* (1840) Arm Mac. Og. 25 (Exch.).
362. *Lawden v Peyton* (1877) 11 IRCL 41 (Ch).
363. [2007] IEHC 130.
364. *The Barge Inn Ltd v Quinn Hospitality Ireland Operations 3 Ltd* [2013] IEHC 387, para. 62 per Laffoy J. *See also Collier v P&M J Wright Holdings Ltd* [2007] EWCA 1329.

B. The Doctrine of Promissory Estoppel

170. Promissory estoppel is an equitable doctrine which supplements the common law dealing with variations of legal rights. As discussed above, at common law it is necessary to have fresh consideration to support a promise to vary an agreement. However, in the absence of consideration, promissory estoppel can be used to provide a remedy. Promissory estoppel is based on the idea that when one party makes a representation that they will not rely on their strict legal rights, and the other party relies on that representation, then the first party will be prevented (estopped) from going back on their word.

171. The modern development of promissory estoppel usually has as its starting point the *High Trees* case.[365] In this case, a landlord stated to his tenant that he would reduce the rent for a flat in London for the duration of World War II. Lord Denning stated *obiter* that even though there was no consideration for this promise to reduce the rent, the landlord would be bound by it. The tenants had relied on the promise not to look for the full rent by remaining on the premises. Hence, if the landlord looked for the full rent and sued for it, he would be estopped (prevented) from claiming it. However, this promise only suspended the landlord's right to claim the rent for the duration of the war, and did not extinguish it entirely; hence the landlord was entitled to restore the higher rate of rent once the war came to an end. Lord Denning gave a broad formulation for the operation of promissory estoppel, stating that 'a promise intended to be binding, intended to be acted on, and in fact acted on, is binding so far as its terms properly apply'.[366] However, this is not in fact an accurate representation of the law – if it were, the requirement for consideration would be all but done away with – and subsequent cases have shown that strict criteria will apply. In *Barge Inn Ltd v Quinn Hospitality*[367] Laffoy J set out the key ingredients of promissory estoppel in Irish law:

(a) the pre-existing legal relationship between the parties;
(b) an unambiguous representation;
(c) reliance by the promisee (and possible detriment);
(d) some element of unfairness and unconscionability;
(e) that the estoppel is being used not as a cause of action, but as a defence; and
(f) that the remedy is a matter for the court.[368]

172. The facts of this case were not dissimilar to those in *High Trees*. A landlord promised to accept a reduced rent from a tenant, owing to a change in the economic circumstances (namely, the recession in Ireland), but then later attempted to renege on that promise. There was no consideration for the promise to accept a lower rent, nor was the promise formalised in a deed under seal. However, it was held that on the facts it would be inequitable to allow the landlord to go back on their promise

365. [1947] KB 130. *See also Hughes v Metropolitan Railway Co* (1877) 2 App. Cas. 439.
366. Cited with approval in *Kenny v Kelly* [1988] IR 457, at 463 by Barron J.
367. *The Barge Inn Ltd v Quinn Hospitality Ireland Operations 3 Ltd* [2013] IEHC 387.
368. *Ibid.*, para. 68

and insist on the full rent payable, and thus they were estopped from doing so, at least for as long as the premises remained 'adversely affected by prevailing economic circumstances'.[369]

1. Pre-existing Legal Relationship Between the Parties

173. Although Lord Denning refers to a 'promise intended to be binding' in general terms, promissory estoppel in fact only applies in relation to promises made in the context of an existing contractual relationship between the parties. Some cases have cast doubt on the exact parameters of this principle,[370] but at a minimum the parties must have some form of relationship which give rights to legal rights and obligations. Given that the premise of promissory estoppel is that one party makes a representation that they will not rely on their strict legal rights against the other, there must be some legal rights in existence in the first place. (Such as in *High Trees* where the landlord had a contractual right to the full rent, but represented that he would not seek to rely on that right and would instead accept a lower rent during the war.) Promissory estoppel cases tend to arise in the context of a variation of existing contractual rights, and the doctrine is not concerned with the creation of new contractual rights or new contractual relationships.

174. One difficulty arises regarding a situation where a relationship has not yet come into existence. In *Revenue Commissioners v Moroney* where Kenny J stated that there was no need for a *pre-existing* contractual relationship in a situation where such rights would come into existence between the parties in the future.[371] However, more recently it was stated that 'an estoppel cannot operate until legal rights have been established' and hence 'the doctrine of promissory estoppel has no application to pre-contract negotiations in advance of the creation of any legal rights'.[372]

2. An Unambiguous Representation

175. There must be a clear and unambiguous representation[373] that the promisor is giving up his strict legal rights. In *Bennett Construction v Greene*[374] the plaintiff purchased a site from the defendants with an outline planning permission, which was based on a site plan which showed a drain for the disposal of sewage from the house across a portion of land retained by the sellers. The seller later said that he was not prepared to allow the drain to cross his land. The buyer claimed that the defendant had made a clear and unambiguous representation that the drain would

369. *Ibid.*, para. 86.
370. *Revenue Commissioners v Moroney* [1972] IR 372.
371. [1972] IR 372. *See also AIB v Counihan* High Court, 21 December 2016.
372. *Allied Irish Banks Plc v William Kennedy and Tim O'Keeffe* [2018] IEHC 38, para. 16.
373. Where the parties act on the basis of an assumed state of fact or law, rather than on a representation, this concerns 'estoppel by convention' rather than promissory estoppel: *See National Asset Loan Management v Downes* [2014] IEHC 71.
374. Unreported, Supreme Court, 25 February 2004.

cross his land and was estopped from reneging on that promise. However, it was held in the Supreme Court that there was no clear and unambiguous promise or assurance regarding the drain, and so the argument based on estoppel could not succeed. This requirement of 'a clear unequivocal promise or representation' was recently restated by the Supreme Court in *Furey v Lurgan-ville Construction Co. Ltd.*[375] In *Hoare v AIB*[376] in the context of a loan agreement which was in default, the defendants argued that the bank should be bound by certain statements it had made that it would hold off on its strict legal rights. However, it was held that the statements made were 'imprecise' and 'there would have to be an unequivocal representation whereby the plaintiffs, as customers of the defendant bank, act in such a way that it would be unfair to allow backtracking'.[377]

3. Reliance

176. Promissory estoppel is an equitable doctrine which is based on the idea that because the promisee has relied on the promise made to them it would be inequitable to allow the other party to renege to that promise. In a situation where the promisee has not in fact relied on the promise, it is difficult to see how it could be unconscionable for the promisor to go back on their word. This point was emphasised by the Supreme Court in the case of *Daly v Minister for the Marine*[378]

> It is the fact that it would be unconscionable for one party to be permitted to depart from a position, statement or representation upon which the other party has acted to his detriment that justifies the courts in intervening to restrain him from doing so. If the recipient of a promise or representation is to be dispensed from any obligation to demonstrate reliance, the doctrine would be more than exceptionally generous. It would be a virtually ungovernable new force affecting potentially not only equity but the laws of contract and property and, as here, the exercise of administrative powers.[379]

177. In this case, the claim of promissory estoppel failed as there had been no reliance.

178. The question that arises in this context is the extent to which that party must have changed their position in reliance on the promise, in particular whether it must be *detrimental* reliance. Although some cases have taken a wide view of the concept of reliance,[380] the Supreme Court's stance in *Daly* implies that the reliance

375. [2012] IESC 38, para. 5.3 per Clarke J.
376. [2014] IEHC 221. *See also NALM v Kelleher* [2015] IEHC 169.
377. *Ibid.*
378. [2001] 3 IR 513.
379. [2001] 3 IR 513 at 529, per Fennelly J.
380. *Revenue Commissioners v Moroney* [1972] IR 372.

must at least be detrimental enough to warrant a finding that it would be unconscionable to allow the promisor to renege on their promise.[381] In *McGuinness v McGuinness* it was stated that the detrimental reliance:

> must be substantial although not necessarily confined to monetary considerations. It must be tested against the principle that it would be unjust or inequitable to allow the assurance to be disregarded.[382]

179. While it is possible to embark on lengthy debates about whether what is required is a 'detriment' or 'reliance', or both, what is clear is that 'there must be conduct on the part of the party seeking to raise a promissory estoppel such as to render it unconscionable for their counterparty to resile from representations purportedly altering the state of legal relations between them'.[383]

180. In some cases the claim of promissory estoppel failed as the defendants could not show that they had in any way altered their positions to their detriment,[384] and in fact arguably any change of position was 'to their … betterment'.[385] This seems to be a relatively frequent occurrence in cases arising before the courts as a result of the downturn in economic circumstances in Ireland in the early twenty-first century. Debtors resisted claims for the repayment of large commercial loans on the basis of *inter alia* promissory estoppel, but were often unable to show that they had altered their position to their detriment.[386]

4. Some Element of Unfairness and Unconscionability

181. Because this is an equitable doctrine, the court will only estop the promisor from going back on their promise if the contrary result is unconscionable or inequitable.[387] This is a significant reason why in many cases promissory estoppel cannot be used as a means of avoiding the rule in *Pinnel's Case* – it is often difficult to show how it is inequitable for the promisor to seek to rely on their contractual right to payment of the full contractual sum owed.[388] In *Zurich Bank v McConnon* Birmingham J emphasised the importance of this requirement, and indicated that promissory estoppel would not automatically override the rule in *Pinnel's Case*:

---

381. *See also McCambridge v Winters*, Unreported, High Court, 28 May 1984.
382. *McGuinness v McGuinness*, Unreported, High Court, 19 March 2002, p. 7.
383. *Bank of Scotland v Kennedy* [2013] IEHC 420, para. 19 per McGovern J.
384. *Healy v Ulster Bank Ireland Ltd* [2018] IEHC 12, paras 51–58; *AIB Mortgage Bank v Reginald Hayes and Teresa Hayes* [2017] IEHC 615, para. 16.
385. *Clones Credit Union v Strain and ors* [2018] IEHC 241, para. 3.
386. As in *Healy v Ulster Bank Ireland Ltd* [2018] IEHC 12; *Clones Credit Union v Strain and ors* [2018] IEHC 241; *Bank of Scotland v Kennedy* [2013] IEHC 420. *AIB Mortgage Bank v Reginald Hayes and Teresa Hayes* [2017] IEHC 615.
387. *Daly v Minister for the Marine* [2001] 3 IR 513, 529. (Supreme Court).
388. Although *see* R Austen-Baker 'A Strange Sort of Survival for Pinnel's Case: Collier v P & M J Wright (Holdings) Limited' (2008) 71(4) *Modern Law Review* 611–620.

At the heart of the doctrine of estoppel is the requirement that there would be an element of unfairness or unconsionability in permitting the promissor to welch on what he has offered. ... I can find nothing unfair or inequitable or unconscionable in a party that has lent money seeking to be repaid.[389]

182. This is particularly the case where the promisee has failed to pay sums due or co-operate with the promisor,[390] or where there has been threat or illegitimate pressure on the promisor to make the promise in the first place.[391] Of course, in some cases it *will* be inequitable to simply apply the rule in *Pinnel's Case,* and in this situation promissory estoppel can circumvent the harsher effects of the rule.[392]

183. A further result of this being an equitable doctrine, is that equitable maxims, such as 'He who comes to equity must come with clean hands', apply. This was emphasised by Barret J in *Healy v Ulster Bank*, when it appeared that the party seeking to rely on promissory estoppel had been contemplating how to defeat their creditors:

[F]or an estoppel to operate it must be an estoppel which relates to a *bona fide* intention, and when it comes to the reliance which yields the estoppel, that reliance must be for a proper purpose. Equity counters injustice that the law, un-tempered, might otherwise yield; it does not exist to obviate obligations that the law justly imposes.[393]

5. Estoppel Is Not a Cause of Action

184. Promissory estoppel does not give rise to new contractual rights and can only be used as a defence to an action where the promisor attempts to enforce their strict legal rights. It is thus sometimes described as a 'shield' as opposed to a 'sword'.[394] This is an important limitation on promissory estoppel, and was quickly reasserted after the *High Trees* case, after concern that Lord Denning's wide definition of promissory estoppel in that case would create a new cause of action to enforce any promises made and relied upon. Indeed Lord Denning himself sought to clarify his statement:

Much as I am inclined to favour the principle of the High Trees case, it is important that it should not be stretched too far lest it should be endangered. It does not create new causes of action where none existed before. It only prevents a party from insisting on his strict legal rights when it would be unjust to allow him to do so, having regard to the dealings which have taken place

389. *Zurich Bank v Jim McConnon* [2011] IEHC 75. On the facts of this case, there was also no clear representation on which the defendant could rely.
390. *Re Selectmove* [1995] 2 All ER 531(Eng.).
391. *D & C Builders Ltd v Rees* [1966] 2 QB 617 (Eng.).
392. *See Collier v P&M J Wright (Holdings) Ltd* [2008] 1 WLR 643 (Eng.).
393. *Neil Healy v Ulster Bank* [2018] IEHC 12, para. 5, Mr. Justice Max Barrett.
394. *Chartered Trust Ireland Ltd v Healy*, Unreported, High Court, 10 December 1985.

> between the parties ... Seeing that the principle never stands alone as giving a cause of action in itself, it can never do away with the necessity of consideration when that is an essential part of the cause of action. The doctrine of consideration is too firmly fixed to be overthrown by a side-wind. Its ill effects have been largely mitigated of late, but it still remains a cardinal necessity of the formation of a contract, although not of its modification or discharge.[395]

185. A difficulty arises however in that in some cases it appears as though promissory estoppel is being used by the plaintiff in proceedings, i.e., by the party bringing the action. This is appropriate, provided that the plaintiff has an existing cause of action. The rule does not prohibit a plaintiff from using promissory estoppel, but rather prohibits it being used as a cause of action. For example, in *M'Neill v Millen*[396] the plaintiff was suing for misrepresentation, and was able to use promissory estoppel to prevent the defendant from reneging on a representation they had made. It can also be used as part of a cause of action to prevent a defendant from raising a defence which he has promised he will not plead.[397]

186. Other cases are less easy to understand. For example, in *Kenny v Kelly*[398] a student was assured by University College Dublin that she had a right to defer her place at the university until the following year, and the University was estopped from going back on its promise. In this case, it appears that promissory estoppel was used as a cause of action. However, it is likely that this would today be categorised as case of where a public body creates a legitimate expectation that a promise made will be kept, and dealt with under administrative law principles which *do* allow such promises to be enforced as a cause of action.

187. Further confusion can be caused by the fact that a different form of estoppel, proprietary estoppel, can form the basis of a cause of action. Although it is not always easy to distinguish between the two,[399] proprietary estoppel only arises when the promise concerns real property (i.e., land). Although the Australian courts have abandoned this distinction,[400] the Irish courts have not, and they are still viewed as distinct doctrines. However, there is still confusion between the two – in the recent case of *Naylor v Maher,*[401] for example, the court refers to 'promissory estoppel' in awarding a claim to the transfer of a piece of land, when the case clearly should have been dealt with under the doctrine of proprietary estoppel.

---

395. *Coombe v Coombe* [1951] 2 KB 215, per Lord Denning.
396. [1907] 2 IR 328
397. *Traynor v Fegan* [1985] IR 586.
398. [1988] IR 457.
399. *See In the Matter of JR* [1999] ILRM 657.
400. *Walton Stores v Maher* (1988) 164 CLR 387; *Giumelli v Giumelli* (1999) 161 ALR 437.
401. *Naylor v Maher* [2018] IECA 32.

6. The Remedy Is a Matter for the Court

188. The remedy which is available is said to be a matter for the court. Promissory estoppel is allowed to be used as a defence to a cause of action, and if successful it will prevent a party from denying or going back on a representation made. In some cases this is easy to apply – for example, in *High Trees* the landlord could not claim the higher rent for the duration of the war. In other cases, it is more difficult to apply this, and the courts have shown some flexibility in fashioning a remedy. A good example is provided by *In the Matter of JR.*[402] Here, a woman had moved out of her home to move in with a man, in reliance on an assurance that he would look after her, and that she would be sure of a home for the rest of her life. When faced with eviction from the home, she was entitled to rely on promissory estoppel as a defence – she was said to have an equity which entitled her to stay in the house rent free for as long as she wished. The court then had to decide how that equity might be satisfied. Usually this could be done by refusing to evict, or refusing an order of sale, however here the house was in a dilapidated state, and would cost a substantial amount to repair. It was held that the equity could be satisfied by selling the house and buying another smaller house suitable for her needs. This house was to be purchased in the man's name, but the woman would have a right to reside in it for as long as she wished.

7. Suspension of Rights

189. Promissory estoppel merely suspends the promisor's existing legal rights and does not extinguish them entirely. It is sometimes said that promissory estoppel is 'temporary' in nature, rather than permanent.[403] For example, in *High Trees* the landlord's right to ask for the full rent was only suspended for the duration of the war and he was entitled to claim full rent again once the war was over. However, it must be remembered that the wording of the representation made is key here – the estoppel is subject to the terms of the promise, so in *High Trees* the promise to reduce rent was only made with respect to the duration of the war. In some cases no such time limitation will be placed on the promise, meaning that it might be possible to resile from the promise upon giving of reasonable notice,[404] but this will not always be possible. In *Barge Inns* Laffoy J stated:

> In my view, it is that, if the Court can make a finding as to the terms on which there was consensus between the promisor and the promisee as to when the concession would cease, the promisor is entitled to withdraw the condition in accordance with those terms; otherwise, the concession may be withdrawn on giving reasonable notice, unless the promisee can demonstrate that he cannot

402. [1999] ILRM 657.
403. *Healy v Ulster Bank Ireland Ltd* [2018] IEHC 12, para. 57.
404. *Hughes v Metropolitan Railway Co* (1877) 2 App Cas 439 where a promise not to evict the tenant during negotiations regarding purchase only suspended the landlord's right to evict. *See also Ken Tyrrell v David Wright and Rope Walk Car Park Limited* [2017] IEHC 92, para. 77.

resume his former position. It would hardly be consonant with fairness and equity, if the promisor could ignore the terms, express or implied, as to the duration of the concession, and terminate it at will or on notice, even on reasonable notice.[405]

190. In this case, the promisor made a representation to accept lower rent owing to economic circumstances (i.e., the recession in Ireland) and was estopped from reneging on his promise while those economic circumstances prevailed.[406]

C. The Doctrine of Proprietary Estoppel

191. In cases of proprietary estoppel, an owner of land will be prevented from asserting their rights where another has exercised rights (e.g., erecting a building, or effecting improvements) over the land, having been actively encouraged to do so by the owner or perhaps mistakenly believing he had the right to so, and the owner stands idly by allowing him to proceed. The owner, as plaintiff, will be estopped as a matter of equity from asserting his undoubted legal rights and in a suitable case, as defendant, may be forced to formally recognise the situation which has been created and convey the property or grant the relevant legal interest in the land in question.[407] An expansive discussion of proprietary estoppel is beyond the scope of this text, but is dealt with extensively elsewhere.[408]

D. Legitimate Expectation

192. Although full discussion is better placed in an administrative or equity text,[409] it is worth briefly noting the doctrine of legitimate expectation. This doctrine allows the enforcement of a promise made by a public authority, even in the absence of consideration *or* reliance. The modern formulation of the doctrine was set out in *Webb v Ireland*,[410] in which an individual who found 'the Derrynaflan

405. *The Barge Inn Ltd v Quinn Hospitality Ireland Operations 3 Ltd* [2013] IEHC 387, para. 74 per Laffoy J.
406. *Ibid.*, para. 86.
407. *Cullen v Cullen* [1962] IR 268; *McMahon v Kerry County Council* [1981] ILRM 419; *Smith v Ireland* [1983] ILRM 300; *An Cumann Peile Boitheimeach Teoranta v Albion Properties Ltd* [2008] IEHC 447.
408. Howlin and McGrath, *Lyall's Land Law in Ireland* (4th ed., Round Hall, 2018) pp. 498–529; Keane, *Equity and the law of Trusts in Ireland* (3rd ed., Bloomsbury, 2017) paras 27.29–27.72.
409. *See*, for example, Hogan, Gwynn Morgan and Daly *Administrative Law in Ireland* Chapter 19; Browne, *The Law of Local Government* (1st ed., 2014) Chapter 7 Section D. *See also* Biehler, 'Legitimate Expectation: An Odyssey' (2013) 50(2) The Irish Jurist 40; Delany, 'Legitimate Expectations and Substantive Effect: Recent Developments' (2007) 29(1) Dublin University Law Journal 413.
410. [1988] ILRM 565.

Hoard' (an ancient chalice and other religious objects)[411] was promised by the National Museum that they would be 'honourably treated' when they handed over their find. It was held in the Supreme Court that while the hoard belonged to the State,[412] the plaintiffs were entitled to rely on a legitimate expectation that the State would give them a reasonable reward. Even though there was no consideration for the promise, or reliance on it, it would be inequitable to allow the State to repudiate that assurance.[413] It was said in this case that legitimate expectation was 'but an aspect of the well-recognised equitable concept of promissory estoppel'.[414] However, it is clear that the two doctrines operate in different contexts and according to different criteria, as later confirmed by Fennelly J in the Supreme Court:

> I would accept that there is a distinction between the doctrine of legitimate expectations and promissory estoppel. Legitimate expectations constitutes an accepted part of the principles of administrative law applied by our courts through the vehicle of Judicial Review. It is concerned essentially to see that administrative powers are not used unfairly. An expectation may be legitimate and cognisable by the courts even in the absence of the sort of action to the claimant's detriment that forms part of the law of estoppel.[415]

193. Although now firmly rooted in administrative law, legitimate expectation can be seen to be relied upon in contractual situations, where one party is a public body. In *Triatic Ltd v Cork County Council*[416] the doctrine of legitimate expectation was relied upon in circumstances where the parties were in negotiations concerning the development of a piece of land known as Fort Camden, but there was no contract in place. The plaintiff claimed that as a result of these negotiations that they had a legitimate expectation the defendant would continue to deal exclusively with the plaintiff until a contract was concluded. However, the plaintiff was unable to show on the facts that any representation to this effect had ever been made; moreover, even if any such representation had been made, the court expressed doubts as to how it could enforce such a representation:

> If the plaintiff had pursued its claim for injunctive relief and the court were to order that the defendant could not withdraw from its dealings with the plaintiff, what would that achieve? I think the answer is nothing. In reality, a court cannot effectively order litigants or negotiating parties to agree the terms of a complex property development and acquisition transaction.

---

411. The chalice is still on view in the National Museum, *see* https://www.museum.ie/Archaeology/Exhibitions/Current-Exhibitions/The-Treasury/Gallery-1-Iron-Age-to-12th-Century/Derrynaflan-Chalice-(1).
412. Under the common law principle of 'the prerogative of treasure trove', which was said to be an inherent attribute of a sovereign State.
413. Contrast *Re La Lavia* [1996] 1 ILRM 194, where the plaintiffs could not be said to have such a legitimate expectation as they had never recognised any entitlement of the State.
414. [1988] ILRM 565, 594.
415. *Daly v Minister for the Marine* [2001] 3 IR 513, 528.
416. [2006] IEHC 111.

194. The court also questioned whether legitimate expectation should apply to a situation such as this, involving normal commercial risks, merely because one party happened to be a public body.

IV. Modifications of the Contract

195. Any modification of the contract[417] must be done by mutual agreement.[418] *Horan v Reilly*[419] provides a good illustration of this requirement. The case concerned a small, local lottery syndicate whereby one individual would collect money weekly from the members of the syndicate to purchase lottery tickets, and any winnings would be shared equally between the members of the syndicate. The plaintiff was in arrears when the syndicate won a large sum of money, but 'it was not part of that agreement that individual members could pay in arrear and, nonetheless, remain a member of the syndicate'.[420] The question which then arose whether the parties had varied their original agreement such that the plaintiff could remain in the syndicate and claim a proportionate share in any winnings, even though he was in arrears. It was held that any such variation would have had to have been agreed by all members of the syndicate, but no such agreement was made.[421]

196. In addition, any modification of the contract must be accompanied by fresh consideration.[422] Thus, for example, an extension on a loan would need to be supported by fresh consideration.[423] This rule was discussed above, where it was noted that although *Williams v Roffey*[424] weakens the threshold of what constitutes consideration in the case of a variation of contract, there is still such a requirement. Moreover, the reasoning in that case does not change the rule in *Pinnel's Case*, and fresh consideration is still needed for any promise by a creditor to accept a lesser sum than the amount due to them in full satisfaction of the debt due. Where there is a variation to a contract without supporting consideration, but one party has relied on that variation, it may be unconscionable to refuse to give effect to the variation, and the courts will give effect to it within the confines of promissory estoppel in

---

417. A separate issue is that if an executed contractual document is unilaterally altered by one party after it is executed it could constitute fraud, or even a forgery under the Criminal Justice (Theft and Fraud Offences) Act 2001. *See Anglo Irish Bank Corp Ltd v Collins* [2011] IEHC 385.
418. *Clarke v Kilternan Motor Co Ltd* (Unreported, High Court, 10 December 1996) (no 'sufficient meeting of minds to vary the terms of the original agreement'); *Whelan Frozen Foods Ltd v Dunnes Stores* [2006] IEHC 171 (injunction granted restraining the defendant from proceeding with a unilateral variation of contracts); *Reilly v Drogheda Borough Council* [2009] 20 ELR 1 (employment contract could not be varied by a collective agreement without the consent of the employee) and *Finnegan v J & E Davy* [2007] 18 ELR xviii (changes to employment contract had to be fairly and reasonably brought to employee's attention before employee could be said to have acquiesced to them).
419. [2008] IESC 65.
420. [2008] IESC 65, para. 30.
421. [2008] IESC 65, para. 36.
422. [2008] IESC 65, para. 27.
423. *ACC Bank v Dillon* [2012] IEHC 474.
424. [1990] 1 All ER 512.

equity: *see Barge Inn Ltd v Quinn Hospitality*[425] and other cases, discussed above. However, even at common law, certain gratuitous promises to waive strict legal rights were enforced as waivers. Waiver or forbearance could occur in relation to, for example, the contractual date for delivery of goods, and where the seller consents to delay delivery at the request of the buyer, there is authority for the proposition that he is bound by his waiver,[426] and likewise the buyer is bound, so that he cannot claim that the seller is in breach of the contractual date for delivery when the seller delivers 'late' in implementing the waiver.[427] Similarly, a buyer who pushes for delivery of goods past the agreed date for delivery cannot simply terminate the contract without giving reasonable notice of a new date for delivery.[428]

197. One issue that arises is whether the variation to the contract can be oral, or whether it has to be in writing. In general an oral variation is sufficient.[429] If there is a statutory requirement that the original contract be evidenced in a note or memorandum, and the parties intend for that written document to constitute the agreement, then any oral variation must also be evidenced by a note or memorandum in writing.[430] However, 'where the oral agreement is intended to be the contract, evidence may be given of an agreed variation even if there is a memorandum or note of the contract but not of the variation'.[431]

198. The original contract may itself restrict the parties' ability to vary the contract. The UK Supreme Court in *MWB Business Exchange Centres Ltd v Rock Advertising Ltd*[432] recently ruled that an 'anti-oral variation clause', i.e., clause in a contract which requires modifications to that contract to be in writing, invalidates a subsequent oral agreement to vary the contract.[433]

§2. Formal and Evidential Requirements

I. Formal Requirements

199. In general, once there is an agreement, consideration and intention to create legal relations, an oral contract is binding, and there are no further formal requirements. However, there are exceptions to this rule.

425. *The Barge Inn Ltd v Quinn Hospitality Ireland Operations 3 Ltd* [2013] IEHC 387.
426. *Panoutsos v Raymond Hadley Corporation of New York* [1917] 2 KB 473.
427. *Ogle v Earl Vane* (1868) LR 3 QB.272; *Hickman v Haynes* (1875) LR 10 CP 598. *See*, in relation to a sale of land, *McKillop v McMullen* [1979] NI 85.
428. *Charles Rickards Ltd v Oppenheim* [1950] 1 KB 616.
429. R Clark, *Contract Law in Ireland* p. 666.
430. *McQuaid v Lynam* [1965] IR 564.
431. *Ibid.*, 573.
432. [2018] UKSC 24.
433. On the effect of similar provisions commonly found in construction contracts, *see* Hughes, '"No Oral Modification", "Confirmation of Written Instruction" and "Confirmation of Verbal Instruction" Clauses in Contracts' (2019) 37(5) Irish Law Times 73.

200. First, while not quite an exception, if there is no consideration then the contract must be made 'under seal'.

201. Second, some statutes require that particular contracts must be made in writing, e.g., bills of exchange, bills of sale, promissory notes, assignments of copyright, transfer of shares in a limited company. Other contracts, although they may be made orally, are not *enforceable* unless there is a sufficient written note or memorandum of the terms of the contract. This requirement dates back to the Statute of Frauds 1695, section 2 of which provides a list of contracts which must be evidenced in writing. This section has been replaced in part by the Sale of Goods Act 1893 and the Land Law and Conveyance Reform Act 2009, but still applies to other contracts. However, even where there is no note or memorandum in place, the contract may still be given effect under the doctrine of part performance.

202. Finally, there is now an extensive corpus on consumer protection legislation that requires that consumers are entitled to written confirmation of their contracts.

A. *Contracts under Seal*

203. Where a person makes a promise in writing by deed 'under seal' the promise is binding and there is no need for consideration.[434] In modern law the formality of sealing was easily satisfied by printed circles marked LS or by red plastic stick-on seals, or red stickers.[435]

204. Section 64 of the Land and Conveyancing Law Reform Act 2009 abolished 'any rule of law' which requires 'a seal for the valid execution of a deed by an individual'. Instead an instrument is a deed if it is described as such,[436] or made clear that it is intended to act as a deed, executed in the manner set out in section 64(2) – which, in the case of individuals, is essentially a witnessed signature, and in the case of a company is by affixing its official seal or stamp to the deed – and 'delivered as a deed' by the person executing it or someone authorised by them.[437] The language of the Statute is not however entirely clear, as acknowledged by the Supreme Court in *McGuinness & Mulligan v Ulster Bank Ireland Limited.*[438]

434. *Drimmie v Davies* [1899] 2 IR 176.
435. Clark p. 63.
436. Or indeed if it is described 'Assignment', 'Conveyance', 'Charge', 'Indenture', 'Lease', 'Mortgage', 'Surrender' or 'other heading appropriate to the deed in question' (s. 64(2)(a)).
437. *See* Woods 'The Demise of the Seal and the Validity of Certain deeds' (2014) 53 Irish Jurist 190.
438. *See McGuinness & Mulligan v Ulster Bank Ireland Limited* [2019] IESC 20. *See also AIB v Maguire* [2018] IEHC 561 where the defendants argued that a signature block on a guarantee, where each guarantor signed his name alongside the words 'signed and sealed by' were not enough to constitute making a deed under seal. No additional mark or impression was made on the letters to act as the seal.

B. Statutory Requirements to Have Evidence of Contract in Writing

205. The Statute of Frauds 1695 aimed to reduce the instances of fraud occurring in certain transactions, particularly the conveyance of real property. It sets out a list of contracts that are unenforceable unless there is a memorandum or note in writing, signed by the party to be charged (i.e., the defendant) or someone authorised by them.[439]

1. Contracts of Guarantee

206. Section 2 of the Statute of Frauds 1695 refers to 'any special promise to answer for the debt, default or miscarriage of another person'. In modern terminology, this relates to the guarantee of the liability of another.[440] A guarantee must be distinguished from an indemnity: with a guarantee, the primary obligation rests on the other (the principal debtor) and the guarantor is only liable if that principal debtor defaults; whereas an indemnity is an undertaking to be liable regardless of whether the other person is in default. The Statute only applies to guarantees, which are therefore unenforceable unless in writing or evidenced by writing, whereas oral indemnities are enforceable.[441] The distinction has been criticised, being described as 'both difficult to apply and at times arbitrary in its consequences'; nonetheless it has not yet been repealed.[442]

207. A guarantee requires the existence of a principal debtor who is primarily legally liable, the guarantor assuming a secondary or collateral liability on his promise. It follows that if the principal debtor is not in fact legally liable (e.g., if they are a minor) the guarantee may be either a nullity or interpreted as the assumption of a primary liability on the part of the promisor, that is, an indemnity, and therefore enforceable even if made orally.

2. Contracts for the Sale of Land, or of Any Interest in or Concerning Land

208. The rule that contracts relating to the disposition of land must be evidenced in writing still applies in Ireland, but this rule is now found in section 51 of the Land Law and Conveyancing Reform Act 2009, which states:

> [No] action shall be brought to enforce any contract for the sale or other disposition of land unless the agreement on which such action is brought, or some

439. In addition to the contracts discussed, contracts in consideration of marriage had to be in writing, but these are not relevant today. The action for breach of promise to marry was abolished by the Family Law Act 1981. *See* however *The Goods of Leslie Good, deceased*, Unreported, High Court, 14 July 1986, in which it was applied.

440. This can include liability in tort; *see Kirkham v Marter* (1819) 2 B& Ald 613.

441. *Fennel v Mulcahy* (1845) 8 Ir LR 434 (Exch.).

442. Clark *Contract Law in Ireland* p. 145.

memorandum or note of it, is in writing and signed by the person against whom the action is brought or that person's authorised agent.

209. It has been noted that this wording 'is so closely analogous to the Statute of Frauds, it is extremely unlikely there will be any significant deviation from the existing case law on writing requirements'.[443]

210. The provision applies to different forms of interest in land, including leases and the sale of things attached to the land. For example, in *Mackey v Wilde and Longin*[444] an agreement regarding fishing rights on a river was required to be in writing for the purposes of the Statute. However, in *Yolanda* it was held that a loan agreement intended to facilitate a property development project, involving the construction of apartments, was not a contract for the sale of an interest in land:

> The agreement did not directly envisage or provide for the passing of any estate or interest in the lands the subject matter of the development project to the lender. No estate was in fact passed and there was no mortgage, legal or equitable, created in the course of the transaction. Rather the transaction in its essentials involved little more than a loan agreement whereby monies were advanced in consideration of a commitment to repay them with interest following sales of the apartments under development and the repayment of certain other borrowings.[445]

211. It will be seen from the discussion below that this is the most important provision regarding evidential requirements, and most of the case law on the evidential requirements and the doctrine of part performance relate to contracts for the sale or disposition of land.

3. Contracts That Are Not to Be Performed Within One Year from the Making of the Contract

212. Where a contract is not intended to be performed within one year, for example, a contract to work for another for four years,[446] it cannot be enforced in the absence of a memorandum.

213. The court will not divide the contract into a separate enforceable period of one year and hold the remainder unenforceable.[447] It may however be possible to claim for work done on a *quantum meruit* basis.[448]

443. Buckley, Conroy and O'Neill, *Specific Performance in Ireland*, p. 60, approved in *Keena v Coughlan & Ors* [2019] IEHC 12 [123].
444. [1998] 2 IR 578.
445. *D & L Properties Limited v Yolanda Limited* [2017] IECA 11 [80].
446. *Naughton v Limestone Land Co. Ltd.* (1952) Ir Jur Rep 19.
447. *Ibid.*
448. *Savage v Canning* (1867) IR 1 CL 432.

214. If however the parties *intended* to perform the contract within one year, even if it did not in fact occur, then the Statute will not apply.[449] The mere possibility that an agreement might be performed by one party will not convert a contract which is not intended to be performed within a year into one which is to be performed within a year, and it will be unenforceable in the absence of a written memorandum.[450]

215. In the recent case in *Yolanda* monies were advanced on the basis that the borrower would pay interest to the lender 'of 20% per annum on sums drawn down for a period of 12 months and, thereafter, would pay a rate of 2% monthly on sums drawn down and remaining outstanding'. The court held that it was 'clearly envisaged that the contract was not to be performed within one year'[451] and section 2 of the Statute of Frauds would apply.

4. Contracts for the Sale of Goods in Excess of £10

216. Section 13 of the Statute of Frauds provided that certain contracts of sale be evidenced in writing. This was replaced by section 4 of the Sale of Goods Act 1893, which provides that a contract for the sale of goods of the value of £10 (€12) or more is not enforceable unless:

(i) the buyer accepts, and actually receives, part of the goods sold; or
(ii) the buyer has made part payment; or
(iii) the buyer gives something in earnest to bind the contract; or
(iv) there is a note or memorandum in writing of the contract, signed by the party 'to be charged'.[452]

217. In *Hopton v McCarthy*[453] an oral agreement for the sale of goods was not enforceable. An argument that there had been acceptance failed, as there had only been delivery to a third party (a rail carrier), who was not authorised to accept the goods. In contrast, in *Tradax (Ireland) v Irish Grain Board*[454] acceptance of 1,871 tonnes of grain out of a total of 12,000 tonnes was 'acceptance and receipt' so the contract was enforceable. The Supreme Court held that part acceptance would suffice.[455]

---

449. *Hynes v Hynes* [1984] IEHC 48.
450. *Farrington v Donoghue* (1866) IR 1 CL 675.
451. *D & L Properties Limited v Yolanda Limited* [2017] IECA 11 [82].
452. 'A contract for the sale of any goods of the value of ten pounds or upwards shall not be enforceable by action unless the buyer shall accept part of the goods so sold, and actually receive the same, or give something in earnest to bind the contract, or in part payment, or unless some note or memorandum in writing of the contract be made and signed by the party to be charged or his agent in that behalf.'
453. (1882) 10 LR (Ir) 266.
454. [1984] IR 1.
455. There was in fact a memorandum in writing in this case, but even if there had not been, the receipt of the goods would have sufficed for the purpose of s. 4.

218. Part payment or full payment will make the contract enforceable. In *Scully v Corboy*[456] it was held that an oral contract for the letting of a crop of 'meadowing' to be cut and removed from the land was a contract for the sale of goods, as opposed to sale of land, and was enforceable despite the lack of a written memorandum, because there had been part payment of the price. However, payment must be accepted and not merely tendered. In *Kirwan v Price*[457] the buyer of a horse wrote a cheque for £300, and claimed that this evidenced the contract as it constituted part payment. However, the seller returned the cheque, saying that the price was £350. The court held there was no part payment by the buyer, because the payment had not been accepted by the seller.

219. It is not altogether clear what is meant by 'giving something in earnest', particularly as 'part payment' is already mentioned by the section. It has been suggested that this requirement could be met by giving a business card or a credit card number over the phone.[458] However, as with payment, it would have to be accepted by the seller.[459]

220. Finally, the contract of sale can be evidenced in writing. However, unlike cases relating to the sale of land (discussed below), in commercial cases for the sale of goods the courts are more willing to uphold apparent agreements and to find that the contract has been evidenced in writing. For example, in *Tradax (Ireland) v Irish Grain Board*[460] it was held that there was a memorandum even though no price was mentioned, and moreover the court was willing to combine a number of documents together to find there was a memorandum, and to treat the company solicitor who signed the letter as agent for the seller.

221. Section 4 of the Sale of Goods Act 1893 has been repealed in the United Kingdom.[461] Its retention in Ireland has been criticised, with Clark describing it as a 'technical and unmeritorious defence to executory contracts'.[462] There is no such requirement for contracts for the supply of service, (or 'work and materials') meaning that it has historically been quite important to know what category a particular contract fell into.[463] Ní Shúilleabháin has suggested that some of the cases on the distinction between a contract for the sale of goods and contract for services / 'work and materials' can be explained on the basis that the court, in finding that there was a contract for services, was attempting to exclude the formalities rules which would

456. [1950] IR 140.
457. [1958] Ir Jur 56.
458. Clark *Contract Law in Ireland*, p. 149.
459. *Kirwan v Price* [1958] Ir Jur Rep 56.
460. [1984] IR 1.
461. Law Reform (Enforcement of Contracts) Act 1954.
462. Clark, *Contract Law in Ireland*, p. 150.
463. The distinction between goods and services can also be important for the standard of liability which is imposed (strict liability versus duty to take reasonable care) and the extent to which it is possible to exclude that liability in consumer contracts, *see*, for example, *Carroll v An Post National Lottery Co* [1996] 1 IR 443.

otherwise have defeated a legitimate claim.[464] The requirement in section 4 is also clearly out of date – requiring written evidence of sales of goods over £10 / €12 may have been intended to protect those entering commercial agreements in the nineteenth century, but owing to inflation it now places an evidential requirement on small sales which were never intended to be within the scope of the section. The Sales Law Review Group, in its 2011 report, stated that reform of this provision was 'long overdue'.[465] The Group recommended repeal of the provision in its entirety rather than increasing the threshold amount or broadening the ways in which it is possible to evidence the contract.[466] No such reform has yet occurred, but is likely to occur as part of a planned review of Sales law over the next decade.

C. What Is Required to Evidence the Contract?

222. There is a large body of case law on what is required in the note or memorandum to evidence the contract. This section focuses on contracts for the sale of land – as noted above, contracts for the sale of goods are subject to different requirements, which tend to be more lenient than those applied in relation to the sale of land.

223. In cases relating to the sale of land, there are usually two distinct questions to be asked:

(1) Is there a concluded oral agreement?
(2) Is there a sufficient written note or memorandum to evidence the contract?[467]

224. Thus the question of whether there is a sufficient note or memorandum to satisfy the Statute of Frauds or the 2009 Act 'only becomes relevant if there is a concluded agreement in the first place'.[468] The question of whether there has been a concluded agreement is discussed above.[469] In cases where the courts finds that there simply was no contract to begin with, any comments as to the evidential requirements are *obiter* only, although nonetheless important.[470]

225. The memorandum does not have to have been specifically drafted, and can be a letter from a solicitor or estate agent, or even cheques for deposits or

464. M Ní Shúilleabháin, 'Formalities of Contracting: A Cost-Benefit Analysis of Requirements that Contracts be Evidenced in Writing', (2005) DULJ 113,117. *See*, for example, *Robinson v Graves* [1935] 1 KB 579.
465. Sales Law Review Group, *Report on the Legislation governing the Sale of Goods and Supply of Services* (2011) para. 13.
466. *Ibid.*, para. 3.22.
467. *See Supermac's Ireland Ltd v Katesan (Naas) Ltd* [2000] 4 IR 273.
468. *Silver Wraith v Siúicre Eireann* (Unreported, High Court, 8 June 1989); *Keena v Coughlan* [2019] IEHC 12 [120].
469. *See* paras 123 et seq.
470. *See*, for example, *Shirley Engineering Ltd v Irish Telecommunications Investments plc* (Unreported, High Court, 2 December 1999).

receipts.[471] There need not be an intention that this document evidence the agreement, once it in fact does evidence it. In one case, an email in which it was *recommended* that an offer be accepted was not held to be evidence of an agreement to sell.[472]

226. It is possible to have a 'joinder of documents', i.e., to piece several documents together and produce as one memorandum to evidence the agreement, but the signature must be on the final document,[473] or at least be sufficiently contemporaneous,[474] and this final document must also expressly or impliedly refer to the other documents.[475] The court is prepared to examine chains of emails to see whether they could constitute a memorandum.[476] In *McGreal v Whyte*[477] it was noted that the plaintiff would have to show that the documents purported to constitute a memorandum, which were 'unstructured, informal, handwritten and extremely difficult to follow', were 'obviously connected with the same transaction'.[478] This task was further complicated by the fact that the relevant signature appeared only on one such document a piece of hotel notepaper, 'in what can only be described as a highly unconventional position'.[479] Despite these likely difficulties, the court was not prepared to dismiss the possibility that this might constitute a memorandum, stating that it would need 'careful legal analysis' at a full hearing.[480]

227. The memorandum must contain the '3 Ps' – the parties, the price, the property – as well as any other material terms which the parties considered to be essential and the signature of the defendant or their agent. [481] Not everything which is necessary for there to be an agreement in place must be contained in the memorandum.[482] Only terms thought to be 'material' by the parties must be included in the memorandum, provided that the 3 Ps are present.[483] For example, in *Guardian Builders v Kelly*[484] the defendant seller argued that there was no memorandum to evidence a sale of land, as the purported memorandum did not properly identify either the property or the parties, and it failed to refer to an alleged agreement as to possession. It was held that the parties were identified (even though the name of the

471. Clark, *Contract Law in Ireland*, p. 150.
472. *Globe Entertainments Ltd v The Pub Pool (In receivership)* [2015] IEHC 65.
473. *McQuaid v Lynam* [1965] IR 564.
474. *Keena v Coughlan* [2019] IEHC 12 [131].
475. *Kelly v Ross & Ross*, Unreported, High Court, 29 April 1980.
476. *Globe Entertainments Ltd v The Pub Pool (in receivership)* [2015] IEHC 115; *Keena v Coughlan* [2019] IEHC 12.
477. [2016] IECA 365.
478. [2016] IECA 365 [39].
479. *Ibid.*
480. [2016] IECA 356 [40].
481. *Godley v Power* (1961) ILTR 135.
482. *Shirley Engineering Ltd v Irish Telecommunications Investments plc* (Unreported, High Court, 2 December 1999); *Supermac's Ireland Ltd v Katesan (Naas) Ltd* [2000] 4 IR 273.
483. *Black v Kavanagh* (1978) 108 ILTR 91. *See*, however, the wide approach taken in *Maloney v O'Connor* [2015] IEHC 678 which seems to apply this test to the '3 Ps' also, although on the facts the 3 Ps were to be found on a document constituting the memorandum.
484. Unreported, High Court, 31 March 1981.

plaintiff company was misstated) and the property was identified through a combination of a map and letter. In addition, possession was not a term of the agreement; nor, if it had been, was it a material term which had to be included in the memorandum. Hence, there was sufficient memorandum of the agreement in this case. In *Godley v Power*[485] the Supreme Court considered whether there was a memorandum for a contract for the sale of a public house plus stock in trade. The purported memorandum failed to make reference to the terms of the contract for the sale of stock in trade, but the Supreme Court held that this was in fact part of a collateral contract, which did not have to be included in the memorandum, and the contract for the sale of the pub was thus enforceable.

228. The courts have taken a wide interpretation of the requirement of a signature in this context, holding in one case that a letter typed on headed notepaper constituted a signature, even if not technically signed, as it indicated an intention to authenticate the memorandum.[486] In contrast, a signature or initials added as a point of information or incidentally, rather than to authenticate a document, it may not be valid.[487] In *Maloney v O'Connor*[488] the signature 'Ger' – the short form of 'Geraldine' – was accepted, and an email signature would likely be accepted also.[489]

229. The memorandum must recognise the existence of the contract, meaning any purported memorandum which has the phrase 'subject to contract' included on it cannot satisfy the Statute of Frauds or the 2009 Act: *Boyle and Boyle v Lee and Goyns.*[490] However, the Supreme Court has suggested that the meaning of the phrase 'subject to contract' might be different depending on where it is placed on the document; being effective to deny the contract when at the head of the document but being open to interpretation if used in the text.[491] The phrase 'subject to contract / contract denied' might also not preclude the court from utilising the doctrine of proprietary estoppel in a case where a representation is made and relied upon – in such a case the person who inserted the phrase might be estopped from denying the existence of a contract on the basis that it would be unconscionable were they to do so.[492]

485. (1961) 95 ILTR 135.
486. *Casey v Irish Intercontinental Bank* [1979] IR 364. This case may not be good law, however, *see Boyle and Boyle v Lee and Goyns* [1992] ILRM 65.
487. *McQuaid v Lynam* [1965] IR 564.
488. [2015] IEHC 678.
489. *See* Clark, *Contract Law in Ireland*, p. 156.
490. [1992] 1 IR 155. *See*, for example, *Liberty Asset Management Ltd v Gannon* [2009] IEHC 468, approved at [2017] IESC 70.
491. *Jodifern Ltd v Fitzgerald* [2000] 4 IR 273.
492. *See*, for example, *Danny Prunty v Anne Crowley as Legal Representative of the Estate of Frank Crowley (deceased) and CFO Construction Limited* [2016] IEHC 293.

D. The Doctrine of Part Performance

230. If a contract fails to satisfy the formal requirements in the Statute of Frauds or section 51 of the Land Law and Conveyancing Reform Act 2009, it may nonetheless be enforceable under the doctrine of part performance. This equitable doctrine recognises that the Statute should not be used to *cause* a fraud, and certain acts of part performance raise an equity which the courts should enforce. In *Lowry v Reid* Andrews LJ stated:

> The question in each case is, whether the plaintiff has an equity arising from part performance which is so affixed upon the conscience of the defendant that it would amount to fraud on his part to take advantage of the fact that the contract is not in writing.[493]

231. In *Mackie v Wilde and Longin*[494] Barron J set out the requirements of the doctrine:

> Ultimately what is essential is that:
>
> (1) there was a concluded oral contract;
> (2) that the plaintiff acted in such a way that showed an intention to perform that contract;
> (3) that the defendant induced such acts or stood by while they were being performed; and
> (4) it would be unconscionable and a breach of good faith to allow the defendant to rely upon the terms of the Statute of Frauds to prevent performance of the contract.[495]

232. The classic example of part performance is taking possession of the land, or carrying out work on the land, with the agreement or acquiescence of the defendant.[496] Traditionally the payment of money could not constitute an act of part performance, however in *Steadman v Steadman*[497] the House of Lords stated that if the payment is referable to a contract and is accepted by the defendant (e.g., by cashing a cheque) then it might suffice, and this has been approved in Ireland.[498] However, it is clear that payment of a deposit by cheque will not suffice where the cheque is not in fact lodged.[499]

---

493. [1927] NI 142, 154.
494. [1998] 1 ILRM 449.
495. [1998] 1 ILRM 449, 458.
496. *Starling Securities v Woods*, Unreported, High Court, 24 May 1977; *WP McCarter & Co v Roughan* [1986] ILRM 447; *McCarron v McCarron*, Unreported, Supreme Court, 13 February 1997; *Liberty Asset Management Ltd v Gannon* [2009] IEHC 468, approved at [2017] IESC 70; *McGreal v Whyte* [2016] IECA 365.
497. [1976] AC 536.
498. *Howlin v Power* (1978), Unreported, High Court, 5 May 1978; *Re Irish Commercial Society*, Unreported, High Court, 12 February 1987.
499. *Keena v Coughlan* [2019] IEHC 112.

233. One issue that is arisen is the extent to which the act of part performance must evidence the contract. Although some early cases focused on the *evidential* aspect of the doctrine – meaning that the act of part performance had to clearly and unequivocally evidence the contract – this was a very high standard, and not in keeping with the underlying principle that the doctrine was based on whether the plaintiff has an equity arising from part performance. Under a more recent formulation, it will be sufficient if 'on the balance of probabilities, the acts of part performance have been carried out by the person alleging that the contract is not enforceable and that these acts of part performance are consistent with a contract for the sale of land'.[500]

234. Although court-made rather than based on statute, the doctrine of part performance was retained by section 51(2) of the Land Law and Conveyancing Law Reform Act 2009, which states that the requirement of writing in section 51(1) 'does not affect the law relating to part performance or other equitable doctrines'. In *Keena v Coughlan* the plaintiff attempted to rely on the doctrine of part performance when there was insufficient memorandum for the purpose of section 51 of the 2009 Act. However, in this case there was no complete contract, and thus any acts of part performance were irrelevant. The court stated:

> [I]f the facts justify application of the doctrine of part performance, this will cure the absence of an adequate note or memorandum. It will not cure the absence of a concluded contract containing the essential terms. That is the end of the matter.[501]

235. This is in line with the statement of Barron J in *Mackie v Wilde and Longin* that 'in the absence of a concluded agreement there is no point in seeking to finds acts of part performance'.[502]

236. It is unclear whether the doctrine of part performance can apply in contexts other than contracts for the sale of an interest in land. Palles CB in *Crowley v O'Sullivan*[503] refused to so restrict the doctrine, but in *Mackey v. Wilde (No. 2)* Barron J noted that in 'all the earlier cases, it was assumed that the acts of part performance must necessarily relate to and affect land'.[504] In *Dakota* the Supreme Court declined the opportunity to clarify the position,[505] and in *Yolanda* the Court of Appeal stated that it was at least capable of being argued in other contexts – in this case, in relation to a contract not to be performed within one year.[506] The Court also noted here that '[t]he law is also far from clear on whether the possibility of

500. Clark, *Contract Law in Ireland*, p. 162, citing *Re Gonin* [1977] 3 WLR 379. *See also Silver Wraith Ltd. v Siúicre Eireann*, Unreported, High Court, 8 June 1989.
501. [2019] IEHC 112 [135].
502. [1998] 2 IR 578. *See also Allied Irish Banks plc v Moloney* [2016] IEHC 346.
503. [1900] 2 IR 477.
504. [1998] 2 IR 578, 587.
505. *Dakota Packaging ltd v Wyeth Medica Ireland / AHP Manufacturing BV* [2004] IESC 102; [2005] 2 IR 54.
506. *D & L Properties Limited v Yolanda Limited* [2017] IECA 11 [95].

relying on part performance is to be confined to only those cases where the contract is capable of specific performance'.[507]

237. The doctrine of part performance is not the only equitable remedy that is available in the absence of a note or memorandum. In *Liberty Asset Management Ltd v Gannon* for example, it was held that if the doctrine of part performance had not been available, equity would have afforded relief to the plaintiff by virtue of estoppel.[508]

E. Consumer Contracts

238. Certain categories of consumer contracts must be in writing to be enforceable against the consumer. For example, the EU (Consumer Information, Cancellation and Other Rights) Regulations 2013, which implement the 2011 Consumer Rights Directive,[509] oblige businesses to provide consumers with certain pre-contractual information when entering into contracts. The kind of information which must be provided depends on whether the contract is an 'on-premises contract',[510] an 'off-premises contract'[511] or a 'distance contract'.[512] Post-contract formation, the trader is obliged to provide the consumer with a copy of the signed contract or with confirmation of the contract, on paper or another durable medium.[513] Failure to do so can result in the issuing of a Fixed Payment Notice – for example, in 2016, the Commission for Communications Regulation (ComReg) ordered Virgin Media Ireland to pay a €255,000 penalty after an investigation found that Virgin failed to provide 26,046 of its customers with a contract in a durable form.[514]

507. *Ibid.*, [96].
508. *Liberty Asset Management Ltd v Gannon* [2009] IEHC 468.
509. Directive 2011/83/EC of the European Parliament and of the Council of 25 October 2011.
510. An 'on-premises contract' is a 'contract between a trader and a consumer which is not a distance contract or an off-premises contract' (Regulation 2(1)).
511. An 'off-premises contract' is (a) a contract concluded in the simultaneous physical presence of the trader and the consumer in a place which is not the business premises of the trader; (b) a contract for which an offer was made by the consumer in the simultaneous physical presence of the trader and the consumer in a place which is not the business premises of the trader; (c) a contract concluded on the business premises of the trader or through any means of distance communication immediately after the consumer was personally and individually addressed in a place which is not the business premises of the trader in the simultaneous physical presence of the trader and the consumer; (d) a contact concluded during an excursion organised by the trader with the aim or effect of promoting and selling goods or services to the consumer (Regulation 2(1)).
512. A distance contract is 'a contract concluded between a trader and a consumer under an organised distance sales or service-provision scheme without the simultaneous physical presence of the trader and the consumer, and with the exclusive use of one or more means of distance communication up to and including the time at which the contract is concluded' (Regulation 2(1)).
513. Regulations 9 and 12.
514. ComReg Information Notice Ref 16/83, available at https://www.comreg.ie/virgin-media-pay-comreg-e255000-penalties-failure-provide-customer-contracts/.

239. Similarly the European Communities (Distance Marketing of Consumer Financial Services) Regulations 2004[515] set out the requirement to provide certain information to the consumer who enters into a distance financial contract, both pre- and post-contract formation. Failure to comply with these requirements may mean that the distance contract is not enforceable against the consumer.[516] The Consumer Credit Act also provides that hire-purchase agreements and consumer hire agreements must be evidenced in writing or will be unenforceable.[517]

II. Evidential Requirement: Proof

A. General

240. In general the terms of a contract can be either written, oral or a mixture of both. Unless it is subject to a statutory requirement of written evidence, as discussed above, an exclusively oral contract is as enforceable as one which has some written evidence as to existence. However, there may be a practical difficulty of trying to persuade the court that such a contract has been made, or its exact terms.[518] Proving any term of a contract therefore is an evidentiary question, and it is open to both sides to call evidence which supports their contention as to either the existence and/or the terms of a contract.[519] The task of fact adjudication in civil cases was once the responsibility of the jury, but the jury has now been abolished in most civil cases[520] and the task of determining what facts are to be taken as proved now rests with the judiciary.

B. Parol Evidence Rule

241. According to the parol evidence rule, oral evidence cannot be admitted to 'contradict, vary, add to or subtract from the terms of a written contract or the terms in which the parties have deliberately agreed to record any part of their contract'.[521] However, the harshness of such a rule has led to multiple exceptions, to the extent that some have claimed that the rule is more honoured in the breach. The following exceptions to the rule are well recognised:

---

515. As amended by the European Communities (Distance Marketing of Consumer Financial Services)(Amendment) Regulations 2005.
516. European Communities (Distance Marketing of Consumer Financial Services) Regulations 2004 Regulation 6(6)(a) (inserted by Regulation 2(b) of the 2005 Regulations).
517. *See Henry Forde & Son Finance Ltd v John forde & General Accident Fire and Life Assurance Co*, Unreported, High Court, 13 June 1986.
518. *See*, for example, *O'Keefe v Ryanair* [2003] 1 ILRM 14; *Clayton (U2) v Cashman* [2006] IEHC 360; *Keena v Coughlan* [2019] IEHC 12.
519. *See* the useful summary regarding the admission and use of documents as evidence in *Leopardstown Club v Templeman Developments* [2010] IEHC 152.
520. Juries are now only used for defamation cases in civil actions.
521. *Bank of Australasia v Palmer* [1897] AC 540; *Jacobs v Batavia & General Plantations Trust* [1924] 1 Ch. 287. The parol evidence rule was applied by the Supreme Court in *Macklin & McDonald v Greacen & Co* [1983] IR 61.

(1) Oral evidence may be admitted into court to show that the written contract does not contain the complete agreement, for example, where the parties have omitted a part of the contract when it was being reduced to writing. For example, in *Clayton Love v B&I Transport*[522] it was held that parol evidence of a telephone call between the parties could be added to the written contract, so that the contract was partly written and partly oral.

(2) Parol evidence may be admitted to explain the circumstances surrounding an agreement. Thus in *Moroney v Revenue Commissioners*[523] the Supreme Court admitted evidence to show that a transaction which appeared in the written agreement to be a sale, was in fact a gift. In *Cuffe v CIÉ and An Post*[524] parol evidence was admitted to show the intended purpose behind a risk allocation clause.

(3) Oral evidence may be admitted to show that no contract had come into existence.[525]

(4) If the written document contains a mistake it is possible to introduce parol evidence, and to seek a remedy through the equitable doctrine of rectification. This is an order from the court ordering that the document be altered so as to reflect the true intention of the parties.[526] The Supreme Court in *Irish Life Assurance v Dublin Land Securities*[527] stated that for rectification to occur there must be:

> convincing proof, reflected in some outward expression of accord, that the contract in writing did not represent the common continuing intention of the parties on which the court can act.

(5) If a contract is silent as to the consideration parol evidence is admissible to prove the price payable.[528] Parol evidence may also be admissable to show that the consideration as stated in a memorandum is inaccurate.[529]

(6) Evidence of custom and practice is usually admitted to interpret the written element of the contract.[530]

242. While the existence of so many exceptions to the rule might seem to suggest that it should be abandoned, Clark has commented that it still serves a purpose

522. (1970) 104 ILTR 157.
523. [1972] IR 372.
524. Unreported, Supreme Court, 22 October 1996.
525. *Pym v Campbell* (1856) 6 E & B 370 (evidence admitted to show that the contract was the subject of a condition precedent).
526. *Monaghan County Council v Vaughan* [1948] IR 306.
527. [1989] IR 253.
528. *Jeffcott v North British Oil Co* (1873) IR 8 CL 17.
529. *Black v Grealy*, Unreported, High Court, 10 November 1977.
530. *Wilson Strain v Pinkerton* (1876) 3 ILTR 86.

in setting out an important presumption: 'a document that looks like a contract will be presumed to be the entire contract unless evidence to the contrary is forthcoming'.[531]

C. Public Notaries

243. In the Irish legal system, Commissioners for Oaths administer oaths and take affidavits (statements in writing) for the purpose of any court or private matter, and judicial notice must be taken of the seal or signature of a Commissioner for Oaths.[532] The purpose of the Commissioner of Oaths is to attest that the individual has signed the relevant document and not the accuracy or truthfulness of the document. From a conveyancing point of view, the execution of any necessary statutory declarations is always witnessed by a Commissioner for Oaths.[533] However, given the lack of formalities involved in making a contract, the use of a Commissioner for Oaths in contractual arrangements is minimal. A fee is charged by the Commissioner for their service. Commissioners for Oaths are appointed by the Chief Justice.[534] Every solicitor holding a current practising certificate is entitled to administer oaths and to use the title 'Commissioner for Oaths', although a non-solicitor can apply to be a Commissioner for Oaths in certain circumstances.

244. A notary public is a public officer who serves the public in non-contentious matters usually concerned with foreign or international business. Notaries certify the execution in their presence of a deed, a contract or other writing. Notaries are appointed by the Chief Justice,[535] and applicants need to show that they have obtained a certificate of competence from the Faculty of Notaries Public in Ireland.[536] As a general rule notaries must be solicitors.[537] When, exceptionally, a person who is not a solicitor applies to be a notary public, an undertaking must be given not to engage in conveyancing or in legal work properly performed by a solicitor.[538]

---

531. Clark, *Contract Law in Ireland* p. 196.
532. *Commissioner for Oaths Act* 1889, s. 3(2).
533. *Statutory Declarations Act* 1938, s. 1(1).
534. Courts (Supplemental Provisions) Act 1961, s 10(b).
535. Courts (Supplemental Provisions) Act 1961, s 10(b). *See*, for example, *In the matter of Karl O'Connor, seeking to be appointed a Notary Public* [2017] IESC 2.
536. Order 127 of the Rules of the Superior Courts.
537. In *Re Alfred McKeon* [1965] Ir Jur Rep 24; *In the Matter of Timothy McCarthy seeking to be appointed a Notary Public for the City and County of Cork* [1990] ILRM 84.
538. *See* Information Note Re: Application to be appointed as a Notary Public, available on the courts' website at https://beta.courts.ie/view/document/6f9428de-dbf8-402b-a32c-f4b3d330d83b/Notary%20Public%20Information%20Note.pdf/pdf.

III. Burden and Standard of Proof

245. The burden of proof is on the plaintiff to prove their cause of action,[539] and the standard of proof in all civil matters[540] is the balance of probabilities.[541] A party seeking to prove any point must do so on the basis that, on the balance of probabilities, it was more likely to have occurred than not. The court's job is 'to determine as best it can in the face of honestly given yet conflicting evidence on the balance of probabilities what happened or did not happen'.[542] If the party succeeds in reaching this burden, then the other party may show that some defence should apply, again on the balance of probabilities.

246. In *Clayton v Cashman*,[543] the court stated that a 'very important aspect of the case in assessing the balance of probabilities is the overall credibility of witnesses'. The court cited with approval the test set out by Lord Bingham:

> The main tests needed to determine whether a witness is lying or not are, I think, the following, although their relative importance will vary widely from case to case:
>
> (1) the consistency of the witness's evidence with what is agreed, or clearly shown by other evidence, to have occurred;
> (2) the internal consistency of the witness's evidence;
> (3) consistency with what the witness has said or deposed on other occasions;
> (4) the credit of the witness in relation to matters not germane to the litigation;
> (5) the demeanour of the witness.[544]

247. To assist with this, the judge 'has the benefit of observing the witness in the witness box in addition to hearing the words spoken and reading the relevant documentary evidence and other papers in the case'. This case concerned whether certain items of U2 memorabilia had been gifted to the defendant, who had acted as a stylist for the band; the court held on the balance of probabilities that they had not been so gifted.

248. However, the standard of proof in civil cases is a flexible one, and where more serious allegations are made, such as in cases of fraud,[545] concealment or departure from a written document where a claim of rectification is sought, 'cogent evidence may have to be adduced to satisfy the requirement of proof on the balance

539. Although *see Clayton (U2) v Cashman* [2006] IEHC 360, where the onus was on the defendant to show that the items had been gifted to her.
540. An exception is in cases of contempt of court: *Competition Authority v Licensed Vintners Association*.
541. *See* generally Declan McGrath, *Evidence* (2nd ed.) pp. 69–73.
542. *Clayton (U2) v Cashman* [2006] IEHC 360.
543. [2006] IEHC 360. *See also* the discussion on credibility of witnesses in *Keegan Quarries Ltd v Mc Guinness* [2011] IEHC 453.
544. Lord Bingham 'The Judge as Juror' in *The Business of Judging* (OUP, 2000) p. 6.
545. *Keegan Quarries Ltd v Mc Guinness* [2011] IEHC 453. The standard is still balance of probabilities even in cases of fraud: *Banco Ambrosiano SPA v Ansbacher & Co Ltd* [1987] ILRM 669.

of probabilities'.[546] The court 'will take into account the gravity of the allegation in considering what evidence is sufficient to discharge the burden of proof'.[547]

Obligation of means versus Obligation of result

249. Irish law does not use phrases such as 'obligation of means' and 'obligation of result'. However, the equivalent distinction can be seen based on the interpretation of contractual obligation. Thus, for example, while the obligation to deliver goods in compliance with the contract is based on strict liability,[548] where performance of obligations is either completed or not, and it matters not whether best efforts were made to perform, a contract to provide a service includes an implied term that the service provider will use reasonable skill and care,[549] without necessarily guaranteeing a particular result. For example, it might be agreed to 'use all reasonable endeavours' to provide services such as maintenance and repair of buildings and fixtures in common areas of a business estate 'in accordance with the principles of good estate management'.[550] A body of case law has built up in the UK[551] surrounding the use of phrases used in contracts such as an obligation to use 'reasonable endeavours' or 'best endeavours' in contract performance, an obligation to use 'reasonable endeavours' being less onerous than an obligation to use 'best' endeavours.[552] In *Drocarne Ltd v Seamus Murphy Properties and Developments Ltd*[553] Finlay Geoghegan J accepted the submission that 'a "reasonable endeavours" obligation must be at least one step down from a "Best Endeavours" obligation', at least where a contract contained both types of obligation. However the phrases are inherently uncertain and can cause difficulty, particularly when variations such as 'all reasonable endeavours' are used, and it can be preferable to set out details of what is expected to meet contractual obligations, rather than couch the obligation in vague terms.

250. A common example of when these phrases might be found is when one contracting party is expected to apply for planning permission – the result of such an application cannot be guaranteed, but under the contract they may be expected to

546. *Leopardstown Club v Templeman Developments* [2010] IEHC 152, para. 7.68.
547. *Keegan Quarries Ltd v Mc Guinness* [2011] IEHC 453, para. 82.
548. *Randall v Newsom* (1876) 45 LJQB 364.
549. Sale of Goods and Supply of Services Act 1980, s. 39.
550. *See Grehan and Glenkerrin Homes v Maynooth Business Campus Owner's Management Company* [2019] IEHC 829.
551. *See*, for example, *IBM United Kingdom Limited v Rockware Glass Ltd* [1980] FSR 335; *Phillips Petroleum Company (UK) Ltd v Enron Europe Ltd* (1997) CLC 32; *Jolley v Carmel Limited* [2000] 2 EGLR 154; *Yewbelle Ltd v London Green Developments Ltd* [2007] EWCA Civ 475; *Rhodia International Holdings Ltd v Huntsman International LLC* [2007] EWHC 292 (Comm); *Jet2.com Ltd v Blackpool Airport Ltd* [2012] EWCA Civ 417; *Astor Management AG v Atalaya Mining Plc* [2017] EWHC 425 (Comm); *Gaia Ventures Ltd v Abbeygate Helical (Leisure Plaza) Ltd* [2019] EWCA Civ 823.
552. *See* Gearóid Carey, 'How Much Should One Endeavour?' (2010) 17(9) Commercial Law Practitioner 175–177; Ben Holland, 'Doing Your Best: Making the Most of the Muddle of the 'Reasonable Endeavours' Undertaking' (2007) 18(1) International Company and Commercial Law Review 349.
553. [2008] IEHC 99.

make reasonable or best efforts when applying. For example in *Lynch v Duffy*[554] the purchasers of land were under an obligation to apply for planning permission as soon as possible after the contract was entered into, and required to make 'all reasonable endeavours' to ensure that the application was successful and permission obtained. The contract provided that if planning permission were not obtained by a particular date, either party could terminate the contract by notice in writing. However, there were significant delays in applying for permission, with an application being rejected because the required application fee was not properly paid, despite multiple reminders from the planning authority. It was held that the defendants had not used all reasonable endeavours to obtain planning permission, as required by the contract. The right to terminate had to be read alongside the requirement that the defendant would use all reasonable endeavours to obtain planning permission; because they had failed to do so, the defendants had lost the right of termination under the contract.

§3. Liability and Negotiations

I. Pre-contractual Liability

251. Pre-contractual liability arises where the parties have had dealings with each other which have not resulted in a completed contract but where one party has incurred expense or suffered a detriment.[555] In general, the remedies available in Irish law in this situation are very limited. It might be possible to bring an action in tort, e.g., for a negligent misrepresentation,[556] or for fraudulent misrepresentation under the tort of deceit, even where no final contract has been entered into. In *Richardson v Silvester,*[557] for example, the plaintiff was entitled to recover expenses wasted as a result of carrying out an inspection of property on the basis of a false statement that it was available to let.

252. Restitution may be available where one party has been unjustly enriched as a result of actions of another and involves the removal of the enrichment.[558] *Quantum meruit* enables a party, in limited circumstances, who has incurred expenditure on the basis of activities that do not form a complete contract to recover the value of such expenditure.[559] In *Folens v Minister for Education*[560] the plaintiff entered into negotiations with the Department of Education to write an education book for

554. [2009] IEHC 59.
555. *See* Dietrich, 'Classifying Pre-Contractual Liability: A Comparative Analysis' (2001) 21(2) Legal Studies 153; Raymond Friel, 'Negotiating Liabilities Without Benefit: the Pre-Contractual Liability Trap' (2000) 7(8) Commercial Law Practitioner 188.
556. *Wildgust v Bank of Ireland* [2006] 1 IR 1; *Ryan v FÁS* [2015] IEHC 777.
557. (1873) LR 9 QB 34.
558. *See* Justin Mannolini, 'Restitution where an Anticipated Contract Fails to Materialise' (1996) 59 (1) Modern law Review 111; Shelley Horan 'Agreements to Agree: Do Restitutionary Concepts Provide a Remedy?' (2009) 16(5) Commercial Law Practitioner 95–102.
559. *Planché v Colburn* (1831) 8 Bing 14; 131 ER 305; *British Steel Corporation v Cleveland Bridge & Engineering Co.* [1984] 1 All ER 504.
560. [1984] ILRM 265.

children, and undertook some preparatory work with the approval of the Department. The Department later decided not to proceed with the contract and the plaintiff succeeded in a claim in quasi-contract for work done. To succeed in this situation, the preparatory work must: (a) have been requested by the defendant and (b) been undertaken by the plaintiff in the expectation of payment for expenses incurred. In *Fanning v Wicklow County Council*[561] building work was completed in the mistaken belief that a contract had been concluded between the parties, and the builder was allowed recover *quantum meruit* for the value of the benefit bestowed upon the defendant.

253. Finally, promissory estoppel enables an individual who has relied on the promise of another, to his detriment, to claim relief where appropriate.[562] However, promissory estoppel is limited as it cannot be used as a cause of action; although proprietary estoppel is not so limited.

II. Breakdown of Negotiations

254. In general, no liability attaches for the breakdown of negotiations prior to the creation of a legally enforceable contract. There is no general duty to act in good faith in Irish contract law,[563] and the Irish courts have adopted the statement from the English case of *Walford v Miles* that a 'duty to negotiate in good faith is as unworkable in practice as it is inherently inconsistent with the position of a negotiating party'.[564] Thus any 'agreement to agree' or 'agreement to negotiate' is unenforceable.[565] It is also likely that any express agreement to use best endeavours to negotiate would be unenforceable.[566] In contrast, a lock-out agreement, whereby a party agrees *not* to negotiate with another party, may be enforceable, provided it is limited in time.[567] In addition, in *Ryan v FÁS*[568] the court held that while an agreement to agree is unenforceable, an action might lie in tort for a negligent misrepresentation where an 'unconditional commitment' to enter in a contract is made which is relied upon by the plaintiff but no contract then ensues. Here there was a clear, unambiguous statement that if the plaintiff bought and refurbished a premise, the defendants would lease it from him. The court emphasised that was 'not an ongoing negotiation but rather a commitment to rent with the term of the lease and the maximum rent agreed and other details to be ironed out'.[569]

561. Unreported, High Court, 30 April 1984.
562. *Central London Properties Trust v High Trees House* [1946] KB 130.
563. *See Flynn v Breccia* [2017] IECA 74.
564. *Walford v Miles* [1992] 2 AC 128, 138. Adopted in *Triatic Ltd v Cork County Council* [2007] 3 IR 57 *Esso Ireland Ltd v Nine One One Retail Ltd* [2013] IEHC 514.
565. *Cadbury Ireland Ltd v Kerry Co-operative Creameries Ltd* [1982] ILRM 77.
566. *See Little v Courage Ltd* (1995) 70 Property &Conveyancing Reports 469 (Eng.).
567. *Triatic Ltd v Cork County Council* [2007] 3 IR 57. *See* Blanaid Clarke 'The Enforceability of Agreements to Negotiate and Lock-Out Agreements' (2000) 5 Bar Review 323.
568. [2015] IEHC 777.
569. [2015] IEHC 777, para. 70.

Chapter 2. Conditions of Substantive Validity

§1. Capacity of the Parties

255. The contractual capacity of certain groups of people is restricted. The rules on capacity reflect different policy considerations depending on the reason for the restriction.

I. Minors

256. The legal framework regulating the capacity of minors – i.e., those under the age of 18[570] – to enter into contracts is a complex mix of common law and statutory rules. These rules aim to protect minors who may enter into ill-advised contracts owing to their inexperience and immaturity, or who may be taken advantage of by others. However, the law is generally perceived as outdated, and fails to keep in line with modern commercial practices and the phenomenon of young celebrities such as sport stars, singers or those on social media outlets. The Irish Law Reform Commission has recommended reform of the law on the contractual capacity of minors,[571] based mainly on restitutionary principles and including the introduction of a validation procedure whereby the court could approve contracts entered into by minors. However, these reforms have not been acted upon to date.

257. Minors are bound by contracts for 'necessary goods'. Section 2 of the Sale of Goods Act states that where necessaries are sold to an infant or minor, they must 'pay a reasonable price therefor', and that necessary goods are 'goods suitable to the condition in life of such infant or minor or other person, and to his actual requirements at the time of the sale and delivery'. The question of what constitutes 'necessary goods' usually arises in the context where goods are sold on credit and the seller is trying to sue for the price of the goods, with the minor using the defence that they did not have the capacity to enter into the contract.[572] However it should be noted that the minor only has to pay a 'reasonable price' for the goods, not necessarily the contract price. By analogy, contracts for a 'necessary service' may also be enforceable – such as a contract for funeral services[573] or legal advice.[574]

258. 'Contracts of service', including contracts of apprenticeship, education or employment, can be entered into by a minor, but they can repudiate any such contract if, viewed as a whole, it is not beneficial to them. The courts will take into account factors such as whether the minor is receiving any training, the financial

570. Minors are defined as those under the age of 18, under the Age of Majority Act 1985.
571. LRC 15-1985.
572. *Skrine v Gordon* (1875) IR 9 CL 479 – hunter horse sold to a young English gentleman during a ball was not a necessary but a luxury. *O Neil v Read* (1845) 7 Ir L Rep 434 – purchase of horse by a minor who claimed his health was delicate, and he required the horse for exercise was a necessary.
573. *Chapple v Cooper* (1844) 13 M&W 252.
574. *Helps v Clayton* (1864) 17 CB (ns) 553.

benefit for the minor, and whether the terms of the contract are disadvantageous to the minor. Contracts where there is no training or educational element, such as management or agency agreements, will be strictly scrutinised – see for example the case concerning footballer Wayne Rooney, whose agency agreement entered into when he was 15 was held to be voidable.[575] In contrast, in a recent Irish High Court case the actor Devon Murray, who was in the Harry Potter movie franchise, was liable to pay unpaid agency fees for work done while Murray was a minor, and, in his own words, 'a completely naïve child'.[576] These contracts are also often regulated either by legislation or by the rules of organisations. In the Wayne Rooney case, for example, the FA rules stated that contracts could not be entered into by minors as young as Rooney.

259. Certain older cases on whether contracts would be binding on a minor could today be dealt with using consumer protection rules. For example, in *Keays v Great Southern Railway*[577] a 12-year-old school girl was injured in a railway accident, but when she sued the defendant sought to rely on a clause of her contract (a season ticket for school transport) which excluded liability. It was held that while this was a valid contract with the child, 'capable of being acted upon while in operation, it is the law that the child is entitled to repudiate it and to have determined by the Court whether a contract of this kind is for her benefit or not'.[578] Hence she could successfully bring a claim in tort for her injuries. Today, this case could alternatively be dealt with under the Unfair Contract Term Regulations,[579] meaning that the clause would most likely be invalid.

260. Where a minor enters into a contract involving a series of recurring obligations, this contract is voidable, i.e., the infant was bound unless they repudiate the contract within a reasonable time after attaining majority.[580] The type of contract included in this category includes: insurance contracts;[581] contracts to subscribe for the purchase of shares;[582] contracts to enter a partnership;[583] family settlements;[584] and the lease or purchase of land with continuing obligations attached to it.

261. Finally, certain contracts are deemed void by the Infants Relief Act 1874. This is a somewhat bizarre piece of legislation, and it has been commented that it is unclear why it was passed or what it achieves.[585] Section 1 provides that 'all contracts … entered into infants for the repayment of money lent or to be lent, or for goods supplied or to be supplied (other than contracts for necessaries), and all

575. *Proform Sports Management Ltd v Proactive Sports Management ltd* [2006] All ER (D) 38.
576. 'Irish Harry Potter actor ordered to pay agent €260,000', Irish Times April 8 2016.
577. [1941] IR 534.
578. [1941] IR 534, 537 per Hanna J.
579. European Communities (Unfair Terms in Consumer Contracts) Regulations, 1995 as amended. *See* paras 42 et seq. below.
580. Clark, *Contract Law in Ireland*, p. 608.
581. *Stapleton v Prudential* (1929) 62 ILTR 56.
582. *Midland Railway v Quinn* (1851) 1 ICLR 383.
583. *Griffiths v Delaney* (1938) 4 Ir Jur Rep 1.
584. *Paget v Paget* (1882) 11 LR (Ir) 26.
585. Clark, *Contract Law in Ireland*, p. 610.

accounts stated with infants shall be absolutely void'. However, this does not apply to contracts valid under statute or valid at common law or in equity.

II. Mental Incapacity and Assisted Decision-Making

262. Ireland has recently moved away from an approach which denied or severely restricted the capacity of those with mental illness or intellectual disability[586] to a rights based approach which focuses on providing safeguards and support for decision-making. The Assisted Decision-Making (Capacity) Act 2015 takes a functional approach to capacity, which acknowledges that an individual's ability to understand the nature and consequences of a decision can vary – the fact that a person lacks capacity in respect of a decision on a particular matter at a particular time does not prevent him or her from being regarded as having capacity to make decisions on the same matter at another time, or on other matters.[587] Section 8 of the Act sets out guiding principles as follows:

- A person is presumed to have capacity unless the contrary is shown.
- A person shall not be considered as unable to make a decision in respect of the matter concerned unless all practicable steps have been taken, without success, to help him or her to do so.
- A person shall not be considered as unable to make a decision in respect of the matter concerned merely by reason of making or being likely to make, an unwise decision.
- There shall be no intervention unless it is necessary to do so having regard to the individual circumstances of the relevant person.
- Any intervention shall be done in a manner which minimises restrictions of that person's rights and freedom of action; have due regard to the need to respect the right of the relevant person to dignity, bodily integrity, privacy, autonomy and control over his or her financial affairs and property; be proportionate to the significance and urgency of the matter the subject of the intervention; and be as limited in duration in so far as is practicable.
- Any intervention must permit the person to participate in the decision-making, and take into account the preferences, beliefs and wishes of the person.
- The intervener must act at all times in good faith and for the benefit of the person.

263. The Act allows individuals over 18 who feel that their capacity might be in question to appoint a 'decision-making assistant', using a 'decision-making agreement',[588] or a 'co-decision maker' under a 'co-decision-making agreement'.[589] The roles of these assistants and co-decision makers are heavily regulated by the Act,

586. *See*, for example, The Lunacy Regulation (Ireland) Act 1871 and the Marriage of Lunatics Act 1811.
587. Section 3(5) and (6).
588. Section 10.
589. Section 17. Such person will be a relative or friend who has had such personal contact with the appointer over such period of time that a relationship of trust exists between them.

including restrictions on who can be appointed, complaints mechanisms, and, in the case of co-decision makers, registration requirements and review of agreements.[590] There is a residual role for the court in appointing co-decision makers or making court orders. However, not all provisions of the Act has not been commenced or implemented.[591]

264. Despite the modern reformulation of the rules on capacity, section 137(1) of the Act essentially restates the rule in section 2 of the Sale of Goods Act 1893:

> A person who lacks capacity to enter into a contract for the sale of goods or services shall pay the supplier a reasonable sum for goods or services supplied at his or her request only if the goods or services are suitable to the person's condition in life and actual requirements, at the time when the goods or services, as the case may be, are so supplied.

265. This blanket statement seems out of keeping with the ethos of the rest of the Act and was likely retained for commercial convenience. It also perhaps reflects the tendency to treat the decision to enter into contracts for goods and services differently to other decisions, for example relating to healthcare.

266. The courts use techniques other than rules on capacity to protect individuals who may be in a vulnerable position due to their mental health, old age or intellectual disability. For example in *Bourke v O'Donnell*[592] a 77-year-old widow living in Portumna Retirement Village, who was ill and frequently in a confused state, was induced to make a gift of a large sum of money to the defendants. The court described the transaction as 'wholly improvident' and set it aside on the basis of undue influence.[593] An action was also brought against the bank that facilitated the transfer in the case. The court noted that, in the absence of knowledge as to any incapacity, the bank was obliged to comply with the plaintiff's instructions:

> The requirement for knowledge of the alleged mental incapacity on the part of the bank is crucial. Clearly, the bank cannot treat every elderly customer as being unable to give instructions in relation to their accounts merely because of their age. Further, although the bank had no knowledge of the fact that the plaintiff had been ill and was now living in fulltime residential care, even if it had, that fact alone would not have been sufficient for the bank to assume that she lacked mental capacity as opposed to being physically infirm.[594]

267. The court found in this case that 'on the balance of probabilities, the plaintiff, at the time of this transaction, was so mentally disordered as to have lost her

590. *See* Parts 3 and 4 of the Act.
591. *See* the detailed list at http://www.irishstatutebook.ie/eli/isbc/2015_64.html.
592. [2010] IEHC 348.
593. [2010] IEHC 348, para. 8.4.
594. [2010] IEHC 348, para. 8.5.

contractual capacity'.[595] Although the bank had no direct notice of this incapacity, it was held that the circumstances of the transaction were such that the bank should have had doubts as to the plaintiff's capacity and made further enquiries. The bank had breached a duty to enquire as to their customer's capacity where substantial grounds to doubt existed, and were held jointly and severally liable for the sum transferred.

III. Prisoners

268. Under the Forfeiture Act 1870, a convict was incapable of making a contract. This Act was repealed by the Criminal Law Act 1997.[596] Thus, in theory a prisoner has a right to enter into a contract; however this right is only exercisable in so far as the prison authorities and the prison rules permit an inmate to conduct such transactions from his cell. The current prohibition on mobile (cell) phones makes such transaction difficult, although it has recently been recommended that this prohibition be relaxed.[597]

IV. Intoxicated Persons

269. A contract entered into while intoxicated may be voidable if the sober party knew that the other party was drunk, although under section 2 of the Sale of Goods Act 1893 the drunk person is bound to pay a reasonable price for any necessaries supplied. The contract might be enforceable if it is affirmed once sober.

270. A court might also find that a contract entered into with someone who is drunk, or an alcoholic, is unconscionable, and it may be set aside on that basis.[598]

V. Corporations

271. Under the Companies Act 2014, the dominant corporate form in Ireland is the company limited by shares, and under section 38 of the Act it has 'full and unlimited capacity to carry on and undertake any business or activity, do any act or enter into any transaction'. The Act also creates a new form of company called the 'designated activity company'. Section 972 states that such a company 'shall have the capacity to do any act or thing stated in the objects set out in its memorandum'.

---

595. [2010] IEHC 348, para. 8.8.
596. Schedule 3.
597. 'Phones for life-sentence prisoners likely to cause surprise' *The Irish Times* 7 June 2018.
598. *See*, for example, *McGonigle v Black* 14 November 1988, High Court.

Section 973 of the Act provides that the memorandum of association of a designated activity company does not limit the contractual capacity of the company but goes on to provide that a member of the company may restrain the commission of an *ultra vires* act by injunction.[599]

§2. Defects of Consent

I. Mistake

272. Cases of mistake which vitiates consent tend to fall into three categories: (a) Common Mistake, where the mistake is shared by both parties; (b) mutual mistake, where the parties are at cross purposes; (c) unilateral mistake, where one party is mistaken but the other party is aware of the true situation. It should be noted that the terminology is not always used, or even used consistently.[600] In addition, a situation can arise where the written document fails to reflect the agreement reached; in this situation the remedy of rectification can be sought to correct the mistake.[601] This sort of mistake does not generally reflect a defect in *consent* so is not dealt with here.[602]

A. Common Mistake

273. Common mistake arises where the parties are in agreement as to the essential terms of the agreement, but share a common mistake. A specific example of common mistake can be seen in *Couturier v Hastie*[603] where both parties to a contract for the sale of corn were under the belief that the corn existed, when in fact it had perished. The result of this case is reflected in section 6 of the Sale of Goods Act 1893, which provides that a contract for the sale of specific goods is void where the goods, without the knowledge of the seller, have perished at the time the contract was made. The concept of 'perished' here includes situations where although technically the goods exist, they have been stolen,[604] or they have been damaged to the extent that are no longer fit for human consumption.[605] This principle also applies outside the context of sales, where the mistake relates to the existence of the

599. *See* generally McGrath, *Annual Review of Irish Law* 2014, 1(1), 82–96.
600. *See O'Neill v Ryan* [1991] ILRM 672.
601. *See*, for example, *Nolan v Graves and Hamilton* [1946] IR 377*; Irish Life Assurance Co Ltd v Dublin Land Securities Ltd* [1989] IR 253; *Boliden Tara Mines Ltd v Cosgrove* [2007] IEHC 60, [2010] IESC 737; *Moorview Developments Ltd v First Active Plc* [2010] IEHC 275; *Byrne v Killoran (No.2)* [2014] IEHC 328; *Tighe v Carey* [2017] IEHC 395.
602. Although in some cases where an order of rectification is refused, the contract might be set aside on the basis of mistake: *Gun v McCarthy* (1884) 13 LR (Ir) 304.
603. (1856) 6 HLC 673.
604. *Barrow Lane & Ballard v Phillip Phillips & Co Ltd* [1929] 1 KB 574.
605. *Rendel v Turnball & Co* (1908) 27 NZLR 1067; *Western Potatoes Co-op Ltd v Durnan* [1985] ILRM 5 (Circuit Court), *see* Clark 'Of Potatoes and Pariahs' (1984) 19(1) Irish Jurist 101.

subject matter of the contract or to the existence of a person essential to the contract.[606] Nonetheless it is not a forgone conclusion that the contract will be declared void, as it is possible that one party will have impliedly or expressly warranted that the subject matter of the contract existed, or that the risk of the mistake occurring had fallen on one party or the other.[607] For example, in *Tighe v Carey*[608] the parties entered into a contract for the sale of land for €230, unaware that the seller did not in fact own a substantial part of the lands that he had purported to sell to the plaintiff. The lands acquired by the plaintiff were 27.7% less than what had been agreed to be sold. The court here found rejected an argument based on mistake, and although the reasoning is unclear,[609] this seems to be based on the fact that the contract itself dealt with a mistake of this kind, with the seller having warranted to sell a particular plot of land that he was now unable to sell in full. The court held that this was instead a breach of contract and awarded damages to the buyer.

274. The common law courts have taken a strict approach to providing relief for a common mistake, restricting it to situations where it related to the existence of subject matter essential to the contract. Thus, a common mistake relating to the surrounding circumstances of the transaction, or the quality or value of the consideration, would not render the contract void.[610] Thus, for example, purchasing a painting in the belief that it is by a famous artist, when in fact it is a modern copy, would not render the contract void, although on a given set of facts it might form the basis of an action for breach of warranty or misrepresentation.[611] The case of *Fitzsimons v O'Hanlon*[612] provides a good example of this strict approach. The parties in this case were in dispute over the division of an estate and entered into an agreement that one party would get a lump sum and the other party would get 'the rest'. It later turned out that the deceased had an additional amount in a bank account, meaning that the second party obtained a greater sum than the parties had originally envisaged. The settlement was upheld despite this mistake – it was foreseeable that additional amounts would be found and the error related to the quality of the consideration and the surrounding circumstances, not to an essential element of the subject matter of the contract. The court will uphold apparent contracts and will not rescue a party from what was essentially a bad bargain. It is only if the shared mistake produces 'a radically different agreement from that which the parties believed to exist' that a remedy might be available.[613]

606. Such as where a life insurance policy is taken out in the mistaken belief that the insured person is still alive: *Strickland v Turner* (1852) Exch. 208.
607. *See*, for example, *Mallett and Son (Antiques) v Rogers* [2005] IEHC 131; *Intrum Justicia BV v Legal and Trade Financial Services* [2005] IEHC 190; *Amalgamated Investments v Walker* [1976] 3 All ER 509 (Eng.); *McRae v Commonwealth Disposals Commission* (1951) 84 CLR 377 (Aus.).
608. [2017] IEHC 395.
609. The court stated that this was not 'common mistake' but rather a 'unilateral mistake' by the seller, but with respect, both parties were under the impression that this land was owned by the seller, and it was thus a common mistake.
610. *Bell v Lever Brothers* [1932] AC 161.
611. *See Harlingdon Ltd v Hull Fine Art Ltd* [1990] 1 Al ER 737; *Gill v McDowell* [1903] 2 IR 463.
612. [1999] 2 ILRM 551.
613. *McCawley v Sweedon Oil Ltd* [2018] IEHC 17, para. 38.

275. Despite the strict common law approach, it might be possible in equity to set aside a contract on such terms as the courts sees fit, 'if the parties were under a common misapprehension either as to facts or as to their relative and respective rights, provided that the misapprehension was fundamental and that the party seeking to set it aside was not himself at fault'.[614] This equitable jurisdiction is more flexible than the common law approach and was approved in Ireland in *O'Neill v Ryan.*[615] The English courts have since denied the existence of an equitable jurisdiction,[616] on the basis that it was not possible for equity to circumvent the common law position set out by the House of Lords in *Bell v Lever Brothers*, but the Irish courts have not been constrained by precedent in the same manner and remain free to set aside contracts on this basis. Moreover, leading Irish commentators have suggested that this equitable jurisdiction is 'more flexible and pragmatic' and should remain.[617] However, it is important to remember that the overriding principle to be applied is to enforce apparent agreements, and mistake will remain difficult to plea regardless of whether the common law or equitable test is used.[618]

B. Mutual Mistake

276. Mutual mistake occurs when the contracting parties have differing views as to the terms of the agreements; where one party believes the contract contains X but the other believes it contains Y. Such a situation might indicate that there is no *consensus ad idem*, and thus no contract. In *Mespil v Capaldi*[619] the Supreme Court upheld the distinction between mistake as to the effect of a bargain and mistake as to the true nature of the agreement. In the latter situation a remedy would be available:

> It is the essence of an enforceable simple contract that there be a consensus ad idem, express in an offer and acceptance. Such a consensus cannot be said to exist unless there is a correspondence between the offer and the acceptance. If the offer made is accepted by the other person in a fundamentally different sense from that in which it was tendered by the offeror, and the circumstances are objectively such as to justify such an acceptance, there cannot be said to be the meeting of the minds which is essential for an enforceable contract. In such circumstances the alleged contract is a nullity.[620]

614. *Solle v Butcher* [1950] 1 KB 671, 693 per Lord Denning.
615. [1991] ILRM 672.
616. *Great Peace Shipping Ltd v Tsavliris (International) Ltd* [2002] 4 All ER 689.
617. Clark, *Contract Law in Ireland* (8th ed., 2016) pp. 361–362.
618. *See*, for example, *Fitzsimons v O'Hanlon* [1999] 2 ILRM 551 and *Intrum Justicia BV v Legal and Trade Financial Services* [2005] IEHC 190, in which both the common law and equitable grounds for relief were denied. Other cases in which a claim based on mistake failed included *McCawley v Sweedon Oil Ltd* [2018] IEHC 17.
619. [1986] ILRM 373.
620. [1986] ILRM 373, 376 per Henchy J.

277. In this case there was 'latent ambiguity and mutual misunderstanding' of a settlement dispute, meaning that the contract was void for mistake. In contrast in *O'Neill v Ryan (No.3)*,[621] where the parties had a different understanding of the scope of a settlement agreement, the court found in favour of the plaintiff's interpretation of the agreement, based on the letter of settlement, and found there was no such latent ambiguity and it was possible to find a valid agreement. In cases such as this 'the parties may have differed in their understanding of the transaction but they freely entered into an unambiguous written agreement'.[622] This strict approach can be seen in *Stapleton v Prudential Assurance*,[623] in which the plaintiff mistakenly believed that a lump sum would be paid on a life insurance contract at the end of the contract term, rather than on her death. Her mistake regarding the meaning of the contract was not sufficient to rescind the contract and allow her to the return of premiums paid.

278. Cases such as this emphasise that the courts will have regard to the objective intentions of the parties, rather than their subjective beliefs regarding the terms of the contract:

> If the intention of one party, objectively ascertained, indicates assent to a particular term, that term will be included in the bargain. The courts will not permit the reasonable expectations of one party to be defeated if they exist because of the conduct of the other party.[624]

279. A good example of this is in *Clayton Love v B & I Transport*,[625] where the parties had different views on the temperature at which frozen scampi would be transported. It was held that because of the way the Transport company had conducted themselves during negotiations they were bound to load the cargo at sub-atmospheric temperatures and were therefore liable for not doing so. Similarly in *Lucy v Laurel Construction*[626] a purchaser of a house relied on a site plan which indicated that the plot would be 170 feet long. This was in fact a mistake, but it was the only objective manifestation of the builders' intentions, and they were unable to rely on their subjective, undeclared intention to only sell a plot which was 120 feet long. Similar reasoning was applied in *Ferguson v Merchant Banking Ltd.*,[627] and *McGrath v Stewart*[628] – as the property to be sold was clearly defined in the contractual documentation there was a consensus *ad idem*.

621. [1992] 1 IR 166.
622. *McGrath v Stewart* [2008] IEHC 348 per Murphy J.
623. (1928) 62 ILTR 56.
624. Clark, *Contract Law in Ireland* (8th ed., 2016) p. 364. *See Smith v Hughes* (1871) LR 2 QB 597.
625. (1970) 104 ILTR 157. *See also O'Neill v Ryan* [1991] ILRM 672 (objective agreement as to the terms of the contract).
626. Unreported, High Court, 18 December 1970.
627. [1993] 1 ILRM 136.
628. [2008] IEHC 348.

C. Unilateral Mistake

280. A contract may be void where one party is aware that the other contracting party is entering into the contract under a mistaken assumption, but seeks to take advantage of this mistake. The most common example of this is where someone jumps to purchase an item at a greatly reduced and obviously incorrect advertised price, such as an offer to sell a printer for $66 instead of $3,854.[629] Even if there is an 'offer' and 'acceptance',[630] the element of sharp practice in 'snapping up' the obviously mistaken price means that any apparent agreement is void. However, if the mistake in the offer would not have been obvious to a reasonable addressee, or if the other party was not aware of the mistake and did not contribute to it, then the contract may be upheld.[631]

281. In *Gun v McCarthy*[632] for example an offer stated that property would be let for £33.10s, when the correct figure was £55.10s. It was clear that the offeree, in accepting, knew that this figure was so low that it must have been a mistake, and the contract was rescinded. A recent example of sharp practice can be seen in *Slattery v Friends First Life Assurance Company*[633] where in the course of negotiations one side deliberately failed to highlight, or 'redline', a change that they had been made to the wording of a guarantee, and the contract was signed by the other side, Friends First, with that amendment going unnoticed by their solicitors. It was found that the party who made the change knew that Friends First would not have agreed to the amendment if they had seen it. They knew that Friends First were mistaken, and 'wilfully closed their eyes to that knowledge', in fact saying 'let's get it signed ASAP!' It was held that this constituted sharp practice, and on the facts an order for rectification of the contract was the appropriate remedy.

D. Mistake of Law

282. If one or both parties enter into an agreement on the basis of a misunderstanding of the law, they may try to argue that it should be void as a result of this mistake; however traditionally the courts would not allow such a claim.[634] Equity could intervene by drawing a distinction between a mistake as to general law (which would not be operative) and private law, including Private Acts of Parliament (which could result in the contract being set aside).[635] The House of Lords abolished the distinction between mistake of fact and mistake of law in the 1990s,[636] and although there has been no similar Irish case it is likely that a similar approach would be taken. It may also be possible to obtain restitution of moneys paid under

629. As occurred in *Chwee Kin Keong v Digilandmall.com* [2005] SGCA 2.
630. In general advertisements are not offers but invitations to treat.
631. *O'Neill v Ryan* [1991] ILRM 672.
632. (1884) 13 LR (Ir) 304.
633. [2013] IEHC 136, [2015] IECA 149.
634. *See*, for example, *O'Loghlen v O'Callaghan* (1874) IR 8 CL 116.
635. *See Cooper v Phibbs* (1865) 17 Ir Ch R 73; (1867) LR 2 HL 149.
636. *Kleinwort Benson Ltd v Lincoln City Council* [1998] 3 WLR 1095.

a mistake of law where there is 'something more in addition to a mistake of law, if there is something in the defendant's conduct which shows that, of the two of them, he is the one primarily responsible for the mistake'.[637]

II. Misrepresentation

283. A misrepresentation is a false representation of fact which induces one party to enter into the contract. The remedy available for a misrepresentation can vary according to the type of misrepresentation made, but in general the plaintiff will be seeking rescission of the contract and/or damages. Whether these remedies will be available depends on the classification of the representation, i.e., whether it is fraudulent, negligent or innocent. In addition, the remedies have been modified in case of contracts for the sale or hire of goods and supply of services by the Sale of Goods and Supply of Services Act 1980. The action for misrepresentation is a meld of contract and tort law – while any claim for damages is tortious in nature, for example for a negligent misstatement or through the tort of deceit, the misrepresentation may also form the basis of a contractual remedy, in particular rescission.

A. *Classifying Pre-contractual Statements*

284. A statement which is made prior to the conclusion of negotiations may be a term of the contract, or a representation, or a statement with no legal consequences, which is often referred to as a 'sales puff'. If it is a contract term, and that term is breached, the normal remedies for breach of contract are available. If the statement is a representation, and it turns out that that representation is false, then the person who was induced to enter into the contract as a result can bring an action for misrepresentation. If the statement is a mere sales puff, it has no legal consequences and no action can be brought as a result. It is thus important to categorise pre-contractual statements, as different legal consequences can result.

285. It is difficult to set down precise guidelines for determining whether a statement is a term or a non-contractual representation. The court may have regard to such matters as when the statement was made,[638] whether the party making the statement was in a better position to ascertain the truth of the statement,[639] and whether it was omitted from a document which purports to contain the terms agreed by the parties.[640] In *Nolan v Allied Irish Banks PLC*[641] it was stated that 'none of

637. *Kiriri Cooton Co v Dewani* [1960] AC 192, approved in *Dolan v Nelligan* [1967] IR 247 and *Rogers v Louth County Council* [1981] ILRM 143. The case of *Lord Mayor of Dublin v The Provost of Trinity College Dublin* [1986] ILRM 283 arguably even goes further in this regard, stating that money is recoverable based solely on the mistake.
638. *Schawel v Reade* [1919] 2 IR 64, 81 (HL).
639. *Cody v Connolly* (1940) Ir Jur Rep 49.
640. *Gill v McDowell* [1903] 2 IR 463.
641. [2016] IEHC 313, para. 27.

these criteria is conclusive and the true test would seem to be whether there is: "evidence of an intention of one or both parties that there should be contractual liability in respect of the accuracy of the statement"'.

286. However, it is possible for a statement to be both a term of the contract *and* a misrepresentation. In this situation, both an action for breach of contract and an action for misrepresentation may be available,[642] and the plaintiff may elect which remedy they prefer. In general, if the agreement entered into was a bad one for the plaintiff, then misrepresentation will be the preferred cause of action as the remedy of rescission may be available; whereas if it was a good deal then an action for breach of contract may be preferable as it may result in a higher level of damages. For breach of a contractual warranty, the level of damages is based on what the plaintiff would have earned had the contract been performed as promised, whereas for a misrepresentation damages are awarded on a tortious basis, putting the plaintiff in the position they would have been in had the tort not occurred, i.e., if they had not entered the contract. The difference in remedy can be seen in the case of *Carey v Independent Newspapers*,[643] where the plaintiff, a journalist, had accepted a contract of employment on the basis of a statement that she could work from home in the mornings owing to childcare needs. The plaintiff was subsequently asked to work the early shift in the office, and was dismissed when she could not do so. It was held that the statement made was both a term of the contract (a warranty) *and* a misrepresentation, and while the defendant could not recover damages under both headings, she could take advantage of the remedy most advantageous to her. Damages for breach of warranty were assessed at €52,266, being two years net loss of earnings from her job with the defendant. Damages for negligent misrepresentation were assessed at €33,276, being two years' loss of earnings had she remained in her previous job. The plaintiff was therefore awarded the higher level of damages for breach of warranty.

287. Perhaps of more importance is the ability to distinguish between statements which have legal relevance (be they a term or a representation) and those which have no legal effect. Recent case law suggests that even statements which are in sales brochures might be viewed as having legal effect; the mere fact of being contained in publicity material does not mean such statements are a 'sales puff'. In *Spencer v Irish Bank Resolution Corporation Limited*[644] brochures which had been sent out to encourage people to invest money in a development contained various misrepresentations, and it was held that it would be 'manifestly unfair and at odds with the principles of good faith upon which the entire law of contract is founded' to allow a claim that such statements were not to be taken seriously or to have no

642. *See* s. 44 of the Sale of Goods and Supply of Services Act 1980.
643. [2004] 15 ELR 45.
644. [2016] IECA 346. *See also McCaughey v Irish Bank Resolution Corporation* [2013] IESC 17.

legal effect.[645] Nor in this case was it possible to argue that the mere fact that further formal documentation would be issued would negate the impact of this initial brochure, when it was clear that the plaintiff had relied on the brochure in deciding to enter into the contract.[646]

B. The Elements of a Misrepresentation

288. To bring an action for misrepresentation, certain elements must be present. First, there must be a representation – mere silence will not constitute a representation, and there is no general duty to disclose information prior to entering into the contract. It must be an unambiguous representation of fact, rather than a representation of law, opinion or intention, and it must be addressed to the party mislead. The representation must have been relied upon, and it must have been a material reason the plaintiff entered into the contract.

Silence as Representation

289. As a general rule, mere silence on a relevant matter will not be construed as a misrepresentation, and there is no general requirement to disclose information prior to entering into a contract. However, there are a number of significant exceptions to this rule.

(i) There can be a representation by conduct, where even though nothing is expressly stated there is 'a nod or a wink, or a shake of the head, or a smile from the purchaser intended to induce the vendor to believe the existence of a non-existing fact'.[647] In these cases, context is often important. For example, in *Gill v M'Dowell*[648] an animal was sold in a market where cows or bulls were sold. It was held that bringing an animal to the market was a tacit representation that it was either a bull or a cow, and failure to disclose that it was in fact a hermaphrodite was a misrepresentation.
(ii) Silence may constitute an actionable misrepresentation where it distorts a positive representation which has been made. In *Doolan v Murray* Keane J. adopted the following as a correct statement of the law in Ireland:

> Silence upon some of the relevant factors may obviously distort a positive assertion. A party to a contract may be legally justified in remaining silent about some material fact, but if he ventures to make a representation upon the matter it must be a full and frank statement, and not such a partial and fragmentary account that what is withheld makes that which is said absolutely false. A half truth may be in fact false because of what it leaves unsaid and

645. [2016] IECA 346, paras 129–130.
646. *Ibid.*
647. *Walters v Morgan* (1861) 3 D F & J 718.
648. [1903] 2 IR 463.

> although what a man actually says may be true in every detail, he is guilty of misrepresentation unless he tells the whole truth.[649]

An example of such a half truth can be seen in *Spencer v Irish Bank Resolution Corporation Limited*[650] where it was stated in a sales brochure that planning permission existed for 80,000 feet of new retail space on a particular plot of land. While this was statement was true, it failed to mention that the consent of a third party was necessary, that that third party had not been told of the plans, and that there would be no access to the land for five years, and there was thus a misrepresentation.
statement may be true when made, but no longer true at the time of contracting because of a change of circumstances. Failure to correct the initial statement in these circumstances may constitute a misrepresentation.[651]
There might be a duty to disclose information if the contract itself imposes a duty to disclose information.[652]
A duty to disclose all material facts can arise in certain types of contracts, where there is a relationship of a confidential or fiduciary nature between the parties.[653] The distinction between the duty of pre-contractual disclosure in contractual relationships and fiduciary relationships was described as follows by the Irish High Court:

> While all who enter into contracts are obliged to discharge them honestly and in good faith, it cannot be supposed, for example, that a retailer is under a positive obligation to disclose to a customer that he or she is aware that exactly the same goods can be purchased for a lower price from a nearby outlet. That would, however, be the position in law if, for example, a retailer were held to be a fiduciary.[654]

290. The classic example of a contract *uberrimae fidei* is a contract of insurance, where a failure to disclose all material facts may invalidate the insurance policy.[655]

Unambiguous Representation of Fact

---

649. Unreported, High Court, 21 December 1993, per Keane J p. 42, approving a statement from Cheshire, Fifoot and Furmston's 'Law of Contract' (12th ed.) at p. 273. *See also Leopardstown Club Ltd v Templeville Developments Ltd* [2015] IECA 164, para. 18: '[S]ilence may constitute an actionable misrepresentation where it distorts a positive representation.'
650. [2016] IECA 346.
651. *With v O'Flanagan* [1936] Ch. 575.
652. *Geryani v O'Callaghan* (Unreported High Court Jan 25, 1995).
653. *Conlon v Sims* [2007] 2 All ER 802 (Eng.) (partnership).
654. *Irish Life and Permanent Plc v Financial Services Ombudsman & Ors* [2012] IEHC 367 Hogan J.
655. *See Chariot Inns ltd v Assicurazioni Generali SPS & Coyle Hamilton* [1981] ILRM 173; *Keenan v Shield Insurance Company Ltd* [1987] IR 113; *Keating v New Ireland Assurance Company plc* [1990] ILRM 110; *Kelleher v Irish Life Assurance* [1993] ILRM 643; *Manor Park Homebuilders Ltd v AIG Europe (Ireland) Ltd* [2008] IEHC 174.

291. There must be an unambiguous representation of fact. In *O'Donnell v Truck and Machinery Sales*[656] a statement that a mechanical shovel was 'comparable' to the market leader, when in fact it was different in a number of respects, was held to be too vague and uncertain to constitute an actionable representation.

292. A statement of opinion will not generally be regarded as a misrepresentation unless the person making it *knows* that is false, or has more knowledge, skill and experience than the other, such that it is reasonable for the other party to rely on the statement made. In the latter situation, a 'statement of opinion by the one who knows the facts best involves very often a statement of a material fact, for he impliedly states that he knows facts which justify his opinion'.[657] By contrast, where the parties have a similar level of knowledge and expertise, it is unlikely that an opinion will constitute a misrepresentation.[658]

293. A statement of intention will not generally be regarded as a misrepresentation unless it was not honestly held at the time.[659]

Representation addressed to the party mislead

294. The representation must be made by the contracting party, or, as in *Smelter Corporation v O'Driscoll*, their agent.[660]

295. The question of to whom the representation must have been made can be more complex. McKendrick has stated that the statement of fact must be 'addressed to the party misled'[661] and in *Stafford v Keane Mahony Smith*[662] a claim against an estate agent who represented that certain property would be a good investment failed because the representation was made not to the plaintiff but to his brother. In some cases the question depends on whether the defendant could be said to owe a duty of care to the plaintiff, and this often involves a consideration of multiple policy issues reaching beyond contract into the realm of tort.[663] However, it would be wise to take note of how far this duty of care can extend – in *Doran v Delaney*[664] the Supreme Court held that in certain circumstances the solicitor for the vendor of property owes a duty of care to the purchaser of property to exercise care in answering questions.

Reliance on the representation

656. [1998] 4 IR 191.
657. *Smith v Land & House Property* (1885) 28 Ch D 778.
658. *Smith v Lynn* (1954) 85 ILTR 57.
659. *Edgington v Fitzmaurice* (1885) 29 Ch Div 459 (intention not honestly held); *The Sunflower* [2000] 2 All ER (Comm) 160 (intention honestly held); *Ryan v FÁS* [2015] IEHC 777 (argument that statement was one of future intention rejected by court).
660. [1977] IR 305.
661. McKendrick, *Contract Law: Text, Cases & Materials* (3rd ed., OUP, 2008), p. 587.
662. [1980] ILRM 53.
663. *See*, for example, cases on negligent misstatement such as *Smith v Eric Bush* [1989] 2 All ER 514 (HL); *Caparo Industries v Dickman* [1990] 1 All ER 568.
664. [1998] 2 IR 161.

296. The representation made must have been relied upon by the plaintiff, and there 'must also be an intention that the other party rely upon the representation of fact'.[665] There can be no misrepresentation if the plaintiff was unaware of the statement,[666] or if the plaintiff did not allow the statement to affect his judgement.[667]

297. There is no misrepresentation if the plaintiff was *actually aware* of the truth, as in this situation they cannot be said to have relied on the representation. For example in *Intrum Justicia BV v Legal and Trade Financial Services*[668] the purchaser of a company was not able to rely on the false statement that there were 'no skeletons in the cupboard' as they had carried out their own due diligence process and relied on this rather than on the misstatement when deciding to enter the contract. Importantly, however, knowledge of the true position must be actual, not merely constructive. It is not sufficient for the defendant to claim that the plaintiff could have ascertained the truth if they had done their own research or that they should have carried out a due diligence check:

> It does not lie with a vendor, who has by his misrepresentation induced the purchaser to enter into a contract to purchase, to have his misrepresentation excused or overlooked and to have the purchaser deprived of a right to rescind because he did not ignore the misrepresentation and pursue matters further so as to establish the truth of what was misrepresented. That would be unconscionable and unfair.[669]

298. The question of whether the representee was actually aware of the truth was recently raised in the case of *Leopardstown Club Ltd v Templeville Developments Ltd.*[670] The plaintiffs leased land to the defendants to run a leisure and sports centre, including plans for a number of tennis courts. The parties' relationship was fraught, and litigation commenced, but they eventually entered into a mediated settlement agreement. However, the defendants claimed they had entered this agreement because of a misrepresentation regarding the presence of two electric cables running under the land. They argued that maps given to them had shown only one cable, but not the second cable. In the High Court, Charleton J found as a matter of fact that they had been aware of the second cable, and thus could not rely on the misrepresentation by the plaintiffs. This was overturned by the Court of Appeal, which in turn was overturned by the Supreme Court on the basis the Court of Appeal did not have the power to overturn a finding of fact by the trial judge. It is important to note that the Supreme Court did not overrule *Gahan v Boland*,[671] or state that there was a duty on the defendant to notice the second cable (e.g., by noting the

665. *Leopardstown Club Ltd v Templeville Developments Ltd* [2015] IECA 164, para. 18.
666. *See O'Leary v Volkswagon Group* [2020] IECA 18.
667. *See* the example of *McCaughey v Irish Bank Resolution Corporation* [2013] IESC 17, discussed below.
668. [2003] IEHC 190. *See also Smith v Lynn* (1954) 85 ILTR 57.
669. *Gahan v Boland and Boland*, Unreported, Supreme Court, 20 January 1984.
670. [2017] IESC 50; Appeal from [2015] IECA 164.
671. Denham C.J. noted that the issue of constructive notice 'does not arise on the facts of this case', para. 99.

presence of ESB manholes on the land), but rather that on the facts the evidence indicated that the defendant was in fact aware of both cables.

Material reason for entering into the contract

299. The representation does not have to be the only reason the plaintiff entered into the contract, but it must be a material reason for doing so. In *Carey* the court set out the following principles:

(i) Where the significance of the truth to the plaintiff of what turns out to be a misrepresentation may be such that, if the plaintiff appreciated the true position, they would not have entered into the contract at all, it is a legally effective inducement.
(ii) Similarly, where a representation may be material to the decision of the plaintiff to enter into the contract without being decisive: had they known the truth, they might still have concluded the contract but perhaps on different terms, it is a legally effective inducement.
(iii) Where, despite the relevance of the representation, had the plaintiff known the truth, they would still have concluded the contract, it does not give rise to operative inducement.
(iv) Where it cannot be said whether the misrepresentation induced the plaintiff to enter the contract, but it might be said that the misrepresentation might have been material, if not decisive, to the decision, it falls between categories (ii) and (iii).

300. The question of how to assess the plaintiff's motivations was discussed by the Supreme Court in *McCaughey v Irish Bank Resolution Corporation.*[672] This case was concerned with the suppression of a facts from an investment prospectus, but the Court was satisfied that the investor would not have chosen another course of action if those facts had been disclosed. The Supreme Court favoured a predominantly objective approach to this question, with some allowance for individual's personal reasons for wanting to have certain facts before entering into a contract:

> When one is assessing a statement of a person as to what he would have done, or not done, had matters developed differently to the way they actually developed, it is reasonable to consider, as a starting point, whether his claimed reaction would have been reasonable. It would quite wrong, of course, to proceed on the basis that only a reasonable reaction was open to him because the Courts very often see instances where people react to particular developments in ways which are irrational, exaggerated, unduly bellicose or unduly timid, or otherwise improbable. But the learned trial judge's finding here made every allowance for the capacity for odd reactions for subjective reasons … .

672. [2013] IESC 17.

301. This decision means that the representation made (or in this case, the failure to disclose) must actually have been a reason for entering into the contract, and not merely used during a dispute as a technical means of escaping a bargain.

C. *Remedies for Misrepresentation*

302. The primary remedy available for misrepresentation is rescission of the contract. In this context, this means that the parties are restored to the parties to the position they were in before they entered into the contract. The contract is said to be 'voidable' as opposed to void, meaning that it remains a valid contract until steps are taken to avoid it. Rescission is available for a fraudulent misrepresentation,[673] a negligent misrepresentation and an innocent misrepresentation. However, the right to rescind is an equitable one which can be lost in a number of situations:

(a) Where the contract was executed, that is, where a contract for the sale or lease of land was completed by the formal conveyance, or formal assignment of a chattel or transfer of a chose in action, for example, shares in a company.[674] This rule is often referred to as the Rule in *Seddon's* case,[675] and was removed by section 44(b) of the Sale of Goods and Supply of Services Act 1980 in relation to goods and services.
(b) Where there was 'laches' or unreasonable delay in seeking the equitable relief of rescission.[676]
(c) Where the representee is taken to have affirmed the contract or declared their intention to proceed with it, or acts in relation to the subject matter in a way which indicates their intention to regard the contract as binding on them.[677]
(d) Where an innocent third party acquired a good title for valuable consideration in the subject matter of the contract before steps were taken to rescind.[678] A specific application of this general rule can also be found in section 23 of the Sale of Goods Act 1893, which states:

> When the seller of goods has a voidable title to them, but his title has not been avoided at the time of the sale, the buyer acquires a good title to the goods, provided he buys them in good faith and without notice of the seller's defect of title.

In cases where property is sold by a fraudster under false pretences, the distinction between cases of unilateral mistake as to identity (which renders the contract void

---

673. *See*, for example, *Carbin v Somerville* [1933] IR 226.
674. *Lecky v Walter* [1914] IR 378.
675. *Seddon v North Eastern Salt Co.* [1905] 1 Ch 326.
676. *Leaf v International Galleries* [1950] 2 KB 86 (Eng.).
677. *Scholey v Central Railway Co. of Venezuela* (1868) LR 9 Eq 266.
678. *Anderson v Ryan* [1967] IR 34.

ab initio) and misrepresentation of identity (which renders the contract voidable) is important, as in the former situation title cannot be passed to an innocent third party, whereas in the latter it can be.[679]
Where it is not possible to restore the parties substantially to their pre-contractual position. A strict requirement of *restitutio in integrum* existed at common law, but this has been eliminated by the less stringent equitable approach that recission will be granted if the parties can be restored at least substantially to their original positions with, if necessary, adjustments being ordered to bring this about which take account of profits, improvements or deterioration in property.[680]

303. In addition, section 45(2) of the Sale of Goods and Supply of Services Act 1980 states that in the case of a non-fraudulent misrepresentation, the court may award damages in lieu of rescission, if it would be 'equitable to do so, having regard to the nature of the misrepresentation and the loss that would be caused by it if the contract were upheld, as well as to the loss that rescission would cause to the other party'. In contrast to the position in England and Wales under the Misrepresentation Act 1967,[681] section 45(2) *only* applies to contracts for the sale or hire of goods, supply of services, or hire purchase agreements, and not to contracts of land.[682] This severely restricts the scope of the provision, and there does not appear to be any Irish cases applying it. However, case law from England would suggest that the right to damages contained therein only applies where rescission would otherwise be available; it is not a stand-alone right to damages.[683]

Damages

304. Whether damages are available, and the type of damages available, depends on the type of misrepresentation.

305. Damages are available for a fraudulent misrepresentation on the basis of the tortious action of deceit.[684] It is necessary for the plaintiff[685] to prove that the false representation was made knowingly, or without belief in its truth, or not caring whether what was stated was true or false.[686] If fraud can be proven, the plaintiff is entitled to be put in the position they would have been in had the fraud not

679. *See Shogun Finance Ltd v Hudson* [2004] 1 AC 919 (HL).
680. *Lagunas Nitrate Co. v Lagunas Syndicate* [1899] 2 Ch 392. *Connor v Potts* [1897] IR 534; *Keating v Bank of Ireland* [1983] ILRM 295.
681. Section 2(2) contains the equivalent provision to s. 45(2).
682. Section 43 of Sale of Goods and Supply of Services Act 1980. *See*, for example, its application in *William Sindall plc v Cambridgeshire CC* [1994] 1 WLR 1016.
683. *Zanzibar v British Aerospace (Lancaster House) Ltd* [2000] 1 WLR 2333.
684. Because the action is in the tort of deceit, a fraudulent misrepresentation does not have to result in a contract. In *Richardson v Silvester* (1873) LR 9 QB 34, for example, the plaintiff was entitled to recover expenses wasted as a result of carrying out an inspection of property on the basis of a false statement that it was available to let.
685. *Keegan Quarries Ltd v McGuiness* [2011] IEHC 453.
686. *Derry v Peek* (1889) 14 App. Cas. 337 at 374.

been committed. They are entitled to be compensated for all damage directly flowing from the inducement, regardless of whether or not it is foreseeable. In *Northern Bank Finance v. Charlton,*[687] the court explained the measure of damages recoverable for fraudulent misrepresentation:

> While it is said that the measure of damages for breach of contract is the amount of money necessary to put the damnified person in the position in which he would have been if the contract had not been broken, the claimant in tort is entitled, by an award of damages, to be notionally restored to the position in which he would have been if the tort had not been committed. As far as the tort of fraud or deceit is concerned, it is well settled that the measure of damages is based on the actual damage directly flowing from the fraudulent inducement, and that the award may include, in an appropriate case (of which this may not be an example), consequential damages representing what was reasonably and necessarily expended as a result of acting on the inducement.

306. For example in *Fenton v Schofield*[688] the seller of land fraudulently represented that over the last four years a river running over the land had yielded 300 salmon a year and that he had spent £15,000 renovating the property. When the purchaser sued in the tort of deceit, damages were recoverable based on the difference between what the land was worth and what it was represented to be worth. In the more recent case of *Keegan Quarries Ltd v McGuiness*[689] the plaintiffs who purchased land as a result of a fraudulent misrepresentation were entitled to damages representing the difference between the value of the land had the misrepresentation been true, i.e., the purchase price of the land (€7 million) and its actual value (€1.5 million).[690] However other damages claimed which did not have a sufficient causal connection to the misrepresentation were not allowed.

307. Historically, all non-fraudulent misrepresentations were classified as innocent, and no damages were available, although rescission was available in equity and an indemnity might be payable in respect of the expenses necessarily incurred in entering the contract. It is still the case that an innocent misrepresentation does not result in damages, although as noted above under section 45(2) of the 1980 Act damages might be awarded *in lieu of* rescission where there is an innocent misrepresentation. However, since the seminal decision in *Hedley Byrne v Heller*[691] there is now a third category of misrepresentation, namely a 'negligent' misrepresentation. In *Hedley Byrne* it was stated that this duty of care could arise even absent a contractual relationship, provided a special relationship existed, and this can be seen

687. [1979] IR 149, 199. *See also Keegan Quarries Ltd v McGuiness* [2011] IEHC 453 where the Irish High Court approved principles in *Smith New Court Services Ltd v Scrimgeour Vickers Assets Management Ltd* [1996] 3 WLR 1051.
688. (1966) 100 ILTR 69.
689. [2011] IEHC 453.
690. They could also recover stamp duty, loan interest paid and legal costs attributable to the additional purchase price of EUR 5.5 million but not the entire amount.
691. [1964] AC 465.

in Irish jurisprudence.[692] It was applied to pre-contractual negligent statements in *Esso Petroleum v Mardon*[693] by the English Court of Appeal and the principle has been approved in Irish law.[694] To bring an action for negligent misstatement under the *Hedley Byrne* principles, one must still prove negligence; moreover damages are more limited to those available for a fraudulent misrepresentation in that they must be foreseeable. An alternative cause of action has been provided by section 45(1) of the Sale of Goods and Supply of Services Act 1980, which states:

> Where a person has entered into a contract after a misrepresentation has been made to him by another party thereto and as a result thereof he has suffered loss, then, if the person making the misrepresentation would be liable to damages in respect thereof had the misrepresentation been made fraudulently, that person shall be so liable notwithstanding that the misrepresentation was not made fraudulently, unless he proves that he had reasonable ground to believe and did believe up to the time the contract was made that the facts represented were true.

308. This rather complicated provision is based on section 2(1) of the Misrepresentation Act 1967, although as noted above the Irish legislation is more limited in scope than that in England and Wales, as it does not apply to contracts for the sale of land. In England and Wales, section 2(1) has been interpreted as meaning that it is possible to claim the same level of damages as that available for a fraudulent misrepresentation, without having to prove the existence of fraud.[695] The onus is on the *defendant* to prove that the misrepresentation was innocent – that they had reasonable grounds to believe and did believe that the representation made was true – in which case they will not be so liable.[696] Thus, the party relying on this section who has been the victim of a negligent misstatement can claim the higher level of damages available for a fraudulent misrepresentation, without having to prove fraud or even negligence. In practical terms this means that section 2(1) is often the most effective course of action for a plaintiff seeking damages for a misrepresentation, but it has been criticised as treating 'the foolish but honest man as if he were dishonest'.[697] There are no Irish cases applying this section, most likely because of its narrow scope, and it remains to be seen if the Irish courts would follow the 'fiction of fraud' approach taken by the English courts.

Misrepresentation and specific performance

309. Specific performance of a contract is an equitable remedy, and misrepresentation may result in the court refusing to order specific performance. In *Smelter*

692. *Doolan v Murray*, Unreported, High Court, 21 December 1993; *Doran v Delaney* [1998] 2 IR 161.
693. [1976] QB 801.
694. *Securities Trust Ltd. v Hugh Moore and Alexander* [1964] IR 417; *Darlington Properties v Meath County Council* [2011] IEHC 70.
695. *Royscott Trust Ltd v Rogerson* [1991] 2 QB 297.
696. *See Howard Marine v Ogden* [1978] QB 574.
697. Hooley 'Damages and the Misrepresentation Act 1967' (1991) 107 Law Quarterly Review 547.

Corporation v O'Driscoll[698] a corporation sought an order of specific performance in relation to a contract for the sale of land. The plaintiff's agent had told the defendant during negotiations that if she did not agree to sell the local authority would compulsorily acquire the lands. It was held that this statement had been made bona fide but was nonetheless untrue, meaning that it would be unjust to grant an order of specific performance.

310. Misrepresentation may also result in an abatement of price as a counterclaim to specific performance,[699] or even where the representee wishes to continue with the contract but to pay a smaller price. In *Moran v Orchanda*[700] the plaintiff had agreed to purchase licence premises from the defendant, but during negotiations the defendant's accounts overestimated the turnover figures for the last two years of operation. The plaintiff successfully claimed a decree of specific performance with regard to the contract of sale and an abatement of the purchase price to reflect the true figures.

D. *Excluding Liability for Misrepresentation*

311. It is possible to exclude liability for misrepresentations. This can be done by an 'entire agreement clause', which states that the agreement is limited to the terms written in the contract, or simply by a disclaimer in which no liability is said to be incurred for statements made prior to entering into the contract.

312. A recent example of this can be seen in the Irish Supreme Court case of *Walsh v Jones Lang Lasalle Ltd*,[701] which concerned the following disclaimer in a sales brochure:

> Whilst every care has been taken in the preparation of these particulars, and they are believed to be correct, they are not warranted and intending purchasers/lessees should satisfy themselves as to the correctness of the information given.

313. Owing to a misrepresentation as to the size of the property in the brochure, a claim of negligent misstatement was brought, but it was held that this disclaimer negated the existence of any duty of care:

> [T]he core issue in determining whether a duty of care exists is whether the existence of the disclaimer by reference to its terms has the effect that there is no assumption of responsibility for the task of furnishing correct information

698. [1977] IR 305.
699. *Connor v Potts* [1897] IR 534; *O'Brien v Kearney*, Unreported, High Court, 3 March 1995.
700. Unreported, High Court, 25 May 2000.
701. [2017] IESC 38.

on the part of the estate agent giving the information to the recipient. If it has that effect, a duty of care is not owed to the recipient.[702]

314. However, there are limitations on the ability of parties to exclude liability for a misrepresentation. First, it is not possible to exclude liability for a fraudulent statement made.[703] Second, in the case of a contract for the sale of goods and supply of services, any such term restricting liability for a misrepresentation must be 'fair and reasonable'.[704] Similarly, in consumer contracts a term which excludes liability for misrepresentations may be considered to be an unfair term, and thus unenforceable against the consumer. For example in *Re Application by the Director of Consumer Affairs*[705] Kearns J in the High Court declared fifteen sample terms in consumer construction contracts in breach of the 1995 Unfair Contract Terms Regulations, including an 'entire agreement' clause which attempted to limit the possibility of any preliminary representation made by the builder or his agents to the consumer from being taken into account.

315. In addition, in some recent cases the courts have expressed disquiet with the possibility of liability for a misrepresentation being excluded without that exclusion having being brought to the attention of the other side. In *McCaughey* the Supreme Court noted the disparity between the reassurances that were given orally to the parties, and the formal disclaimers found in the contract itself:

> It may be, having regard to the scope of the clauses, and to their variance with the nature of the previous relationship between the parties, that such a person's attention should be drawn in absolutely express terms to their enormous scope and to the total exclusion of liability which they attempt.[706]

316. Similarly in *Spencer v Irish Bank Resolution Corporation Limited*[707] an attempt to correct errors in representations previously made was held to be inadequate, as it was 'at best a partial correction' which 'could not be regarded as being sufficient to have removed the impression on investors regarding the potential rate of return which the loose-lead brochures had served to create'. In addition, disclaimers were held not to be effective in this case.

III. Improper Pressure

317. The courts will provide a remedy where improper pressure is placed on a contracting party and can set aside contracts and transfers of property or money where there is evidence of duress or undue influence.

702. *Ibid.*, per Laffoy J.
703. *Pearson v Dublin Corporation* [1907] AC 351.
704. Section 46 of Sale of Goods and supply of services Act 1980.
705. Unreported, High Court, 5 December 2001.
706. *McCaughey v Irish Bank Resolution Corporation* [2013] IESC 17, para. 76.
707. [2016] IECA 346.

A. Duress

318. A party to a contract may claim they were forced into a contract, or forced into modifying a term contained in a contract, under duress. Duress will generally render a contract voidable,[708] and can also be used as a defence to an action of specific performance.[709]

319. Older cases of duress included cases of contracts being entered into after an abduction[710] or the example of a young man who was threatened with imprisonment and dishonour unless he married a young girl he was alleged to have made pregnant.[711] A more recent example can be found in the leading Irish case of *Smelter Corporation v O'Driscoll*[712] in which an agent of Smelter Corporation told the owner of land that if she did not agree to sell the land, that the local authority would compulsorily acquire it. The agent believed this statement to be true, but it was in fact false. It was held in the Supreme Court that the defendant had been under a 'fundamental misapprehension' as to the true position, and it would be unjust to grant specific performance of the sale.

320. Economic duress is when one party exerts illegitimate economic or commercial pressure on another party which causes them to agree to a contract or to certain contract terms:

> The threat of violence is no longer necessary to establish that a contract was entered into under duress. Nor is it necessary that consent to bargain is negatived; rather that consent must have been so wrongfully obtained that it can properly be described as an illegitimate and significant cause of the party ostensibly contracting giving assent.[713]

321. The issue for the courts is to determine whether any pressure exerted in these situations is simply the use of normal bargaining power, to be expected in commercial relationships, or whether it is an illegitimate form of pressure rendering the contract voidable. It may be the case that a party is unhappy with the bargain they have struck, or that they felt they were under a certain amount of pressure to agree to something, but this is enough to warrant a finding that the contract can be set aside for duress. This was discussed recently by Charleton J in *ACC Bank Plc v Dillon*:

---

708. *ACC Bank Plc v Dillon* [2012] IEHC 474, para. 5.0. *See North Ocean Shipping v Hyundai Construction* [1979] QB 705 (contract affirmed so could not be set aside).
709. *Smelter Corporation v O'Driscoll* [1977] IR 305.
710. *Lessee of Blackwood v Gregg* (1831) Hayes 277.
711. *Griffith v Griffith* [1944] IR 35. The contract was held to be void. It seems he was not in fact the father, and if he had been that the marriage would have been valid; however this aspect was rejected in *MK (McC) v McC* [1982] ILRM 277. The current law on duress in marriage can be seen in *OB v R and OB* [2000] 1 ILRM 306.
712. [1977] IR 305.
713. [2012] IEHC 474, para. 5.2.

> In bargaining with each other, the parties to any prospective contract are never entirely free. Either they will be driven by what they want to achieve, which is the purpose of their desire to enter into mutually acceptable commercial relations, or they may be motivated by needs. The purpose driving any party into a bargain may in some instances be so pressing that revealing why they wish to benefit from that which the other side may supply would skew the bargain markedly against any expectation for mutual advantage. Negotiation is therefore a process of careful interaction in order to achieve a consensus. A consensus is nonetheless achieved notwithstanding that one party may be sore at what it has had to give and the other jubilant at what has been achieved. … The doctrine of duress is not part of the law in order to interfere in the context of an imbalance in bargaining powers where that want in balance is merely the result of a difference in commercial bargaining power in negotiations conducted at arms length … [714]

322. In this case the plaintiff bank claimed that the defendants, directors of a construction company, were liable to pay €5.38 million on foot of guarantees made in respect of the company's debts. The loans taken out by the company were not initially supported by personal guarantees, but by mid-2008 the term of the loans had expired and before extending the loans the bank had insisted on personal guarantees being given. The defendants claimed that these guarantees had been entered into under duress, as the bank had said that if guarantee were not provided it would appoint a receiver to the company, potentially resulting in the loss of lucrative contracts and loss of jobs. In assessing whether a particular threat would constitute duress, the court said it would take into account factors such as 'the availability of an alternative course of action, a protest at the term agreed or bargain extracted, the availability of time and space to think and recourse to independent advice'.[715] In this case, the court pointed out that this was simply a difficult situation for both parties, but that the bank had stronger bargaining power and it was lawful for them to appoint, or threaten to appoint, a receiver over the company. The 'circumstances of negotiation were "certainly fraught"' but that did not mean there was illegitimate pressure applied.[716] In addition, the defendants had received financial advice and they had time before making a final decision. This was all said to be 'within the level of appreciation that must be allowed in commercial bargaining', and thus did not constitute duress. In *John K Rogers t/a John Rogers Engineering v Iaralco Ltd*[717] the contracting parties were involved in a dispute over payment for work done, with the plaintiff claiming a payment of £45,000 but eventually accepting a payment of £30,000. The plaintiff then sought to recover the remaining £15,000, on the basis that he had only accepted the lesser payment as a result of economic duress. He stated that the defendant was aware that the plaintiff was under pressure to pay wages to employees, and that the plaintiff had undergone surgery during Christmas, and used this to his advantage. The court refused to find that this

714. [2012] IEHC 474, paras 5.0–5.1.
715. [2012] IEHC 474, para. 5.3.
716. [2012] IEHC 474, para. 5.5.
717. [2007] IEHC 130.

amounted to economic duress, stating that the pressure to pay wages is 'universal' in 'commercial life', and not an illegitimate form of pressure to use in negotiations. The court further found that the settlement reached was a reasonable one, and the defendant had compromised significantly on its own assessment of the sum due. A similar conclusion was reached in the Supreme Court in *Archer and others v O'Connor*,[718] in which it was said that while the appellant had been 'under pressure' that this did not equate to duress 'in the legal sense'.[719]

323. Often these cases arise where parties have already entered into an agreement, but one party seeks more pay or modification of terms, and threatens to breach the existing contract or withhold performance. If the other party has no alterative they may accept these terms but later claim they were obtained by duress. The case of *Williams v Roffey Brothers & Nicholls*[720] confirmed a central role for duress in establishing the enforceability of these promises – as discussed above, in this case the court relaxed the need for consideration in this situation, but explicitly stated that contractual modifications must not have been made under duress.[721] An issue that arises in these cases is whether a threat to breach contract (e.g., by not paying sums due) is an illegitimate or legitimate threat:[722]

> In determining whether there has been illegitimate pressure, the court takes into account a range of factors. These include whether there has been an actual or threatened breach of contract; whether the person allegedly exerting the pressure has acted in good or bad faith; whether the victim had any realistic practical alternative but to submit to the pressure; whether the victim protested at the time; and whether he affirmed and sought to rely on the contract. These are all relevant factors. Illegitimate pressure must be distinguished from the rough and tumble of the pressures of normal commercial bargaining.[723]

324. There are few examples of this defence succeeding in Ireland; however, one example of economic duress should be noted, in relation to the dispute between Whelans Frozen Foods and its only customer, the retailer Dunnes Stores. Dunnes Stores withheld payment as part of an attempt to unilaterally change the terms on which Whelans supplied it with goods, causing serious cash flow problems for Whelans. Although an interlocutory injunction was initially granted against Dunnes

718. [2019] IESC 52.
719. [2019] IESC 52, para. 14.
720. [1990] 1 All ER 512.
721. *See*, for example, *Carillion Construction Ltd v Felix UK Ltd* [2001] Build LR 1; *DSND Subsea v Petroleum Geo Services ASA* [2000] Build LR 530; *North Ocean Shipping v Hyundai Construction* [1979] QB 705; *Atlas Express Ltd v Kafco (Importers and Distributors) Ltd* [1989] 1 All ER 641; *CTN and Carry v Gallaher* [1995] 4 All ER 714.
722. Bigwood 'Economic Duress by (Threatened) Breach of Contract' (2001) 117 Law Quarterly Review 376.
723. *DSND Subsea Ltd v Petroleum Geo-Services ASA* [2000] Build LR 530, Dyson J.

Stores,[724] the case never made it to a full hearing and was supposedly settled.[725] Ultimately, however, the dispute resulted in the end of the relationship[726] and the closure of Whelans Frozen Foods.[727]

325. The other context in which claims of economic duress may be made concern threats made by trade unions in industrial disputes, such as in *Universe Tankships of Monrovia v International Transport Workers Federation*[728] or *The Evia Luck.*[729]

326. In Ireland, there is also legislation protecting consumers from being harassed or coerced into entering a contract or paying money. The Consumer Protection Act 2007[730] prohibits traders from using aggressive commercial practices when dealing with consumers.[731] A commercial practice is deemed to be aggressive:

> if by harassment, coercion or undue influence it would be likely to—
>
> (a) cause significant impairment of the average consumer's freedom of choice or conduct in relation to the product concerned, and
> (b) cause the average consumer to make a transactional decision that the average consumer would not otherwise make.[732]

327. In this context, 'undue influence' means 'exploiting a position of power in relation to the consumer so as to apply pressure, even without using or threatening to use physical force, in a way which significantly limits the consumer's ability to make an informed decision'.[733] Although the court will look at the entire context of the practice,[734] factors that can be taken into account include the use of threatening or abusive language or behaviour by the trader, the exploitation of a consumer's misfortune or circumstance when the trader is aware that the consumer's judgment is impaired, and the use of threats by the trader to do something unlawful, or to take action against the consumer when the trader has no legal basis for taking such action.[735]

328. In addition, section 11 of the Non-Fatal Offences Against the Person Act 1997 provides that a person who makes any demand for payment of a debt shall be

---

724. *Whelan Frozen Foods v Dunnes Stores* [2006] IEHC 171.
725. 'Whelan's and Dunnes Stores resolve High Court dispute' *The Irish Times*, 19 July 2006.
726. 'Dunnes supplier dispute spells end to 25-year trading tie' *The Irish Times*, 26 May 2006.
727. 'Closed food firm files accounts' *The Irish Times*, 6 December 2007.
728. [1982] 2 All ER 67.
729. [1992] 2 AC 152.
730. This Act implemented Directive 2005/29/EC of the European Parliament and of the Council of 11 May 2005 concerning unfair business-to-consumer commercial practices in the internal market.
731. Section 52.
732. Section 53(1).
733. Section 53(4).
734. Section 53(2).
735. Section 53(3).

guilty of an offence if 'the demands by reason of their frequency are calculated to subject the debtor or a member of the family of the debtor to alarm, distress or humiliation', or the person falsely represents that criminal proceedings lie for non-payment of the debt.

B. Undue Influence

329. The courts will not set aside gifts or transactions 'on the ground of folly, imprudence or want of foresight on the part of donors' but the equitable doctrine of undue influence may 'save them from being victimised by other people'.[736] Court interferes not because of any wrongful act, but on grounds of public policy, i.e., the 'dominant' party must be assiduous not to be take advantage.[737]

330. Some forms of relationship are such that there is a presumption of undue influence, meaning that the burden shifts to the 'stronger' party in the relationship to prove that the transaction was freely entered into. There is thus no need for the party looking to set aside the transaction to prove undue influence. These cases of presumed undue influence can be further categorised, into:

(i) those relationships where a presumption of undue influence is automatically raised (e.g., doctor/patient, solicitor/client,[738] parent/child[739]); and
(ii) those where although there is no automatic presumption based on the type of relationship, on the facts the relationship is itself one of trust and confidence.

331. In the latter category, the party looking to set aside the contract has to show that there is a relationship of trust and confidence, and then the burden of proof shifts to the other party to show that it was fair and freely entered into. The classic example of this type of situation is between spouses or those in an intimate relationship, although it can apply to other relationships, e.g., as between neighbours. However, it is not an automatic conclusion that a relationship of trust and confidence will be found. In *Irish Bank Resolution Corporation Ltd v Quinn & Another*[740] a married couple had jointly borrowed a large sum of money, but when the bank sought payment of the sum owed, Mrs Quinn sought to rely *inter alia* on undue influence. The court confirmed the position that there is no presumption of undue influence as between husband and wife.[741] Kelly J then found that there was no suggestion that Mrs Quinn was suffering from 'any intellectual disability, mental

736. *Allcard v Skinner* (1887) 36 Ch D 145, 182–183 per Lindley LJ.
737. *See Carroll v Carroll* [2000] 1 ILRM 210, 225.
738. But not a bank/client relationship: *Bank of Nova Scotia v Hogan* [1996] 3 IR 239.
739. *Croker v Croker* (1870) 4 ILTR 181; *McMackin v Hibernian Bank* [1905] 1 IR 296. There is no automatic presumption of undue influence of a child over the parent, although on the facts there might be a relationship of trust and confidence, and thus the presumption might be raised.
740. [2011] IEHC 470 (High Court, Kelly J, 16 December 2011).
741. *See also Bank of Nova Scotia v Hogan* [1996] 3 IR 239.

illness, feebleness of mind or cognitive impairment'; nor was there evidence of any threats of bullying or such behaviour towards her by Mr Quinn.[742] The presumption was thus not raised.

332. Finally, if there is no presumption of undue influence, the person claiming undue influence will need to show that undue influence was actually exerted. This is more difficult to prove, as the burden of proof is reversed – in the *Quinn* case, mentioned above, there was 'not the slightest evidence to suggest any allegation of actual undue influence could be sustained'.[743] This can be contrasted with *O'Flanagan v Ray-Ger Ltd*[744] in which the court set aside a transfer of property agreement between two shareholders of company on the basis that actual undue influence had been exerted.

333. Of course, in many cases of presumed undue influence there might also be a finding of actual due influence on the facts. In *McGonigle v Black*[745] an elderly farmer transferred land to his neighbour. It was found that the farmer was particularly vulnerable, and that the neighbour was the dominant party in the relationship who had persuaded the farmer to leave his old solicitor. The transaction was set aside, with the court describing it as:

> a grossly improvident transaction which was brought about by undue influence persistently exercised by the defendant over Mr McGonigle who, because of a combination of bereavement, inability to cope, loneliness, alcoholism and ill-health, was vulnerable to manipulation and was so manipulated by the defendant to the vendor's obvious disadvantage.

334. The presumption that is raised in these cases can be rebutted by showing that the transaction was freely and fairly assented to. An important factor in rebutting the presumption of undue influence is whether independent legal advice was given to the weaker party. The leading case on what is required is the Irish Supreme Court decision in *Carroll v Carroll*.[746] In this case, a man transferred a pub with residential accommodation to his son, subject only to the right of the donor to reside in the premises for the remainder of his lifetime, with no power of revocation or any provision for maintenance and support. After his death, the transfer was disputed by other members of the family, who argued that there had been undue influence exerted on the donor. The Supreme Court held that the relationship gave rise to a presumption of undue influence, and the onus was on the recipient of the property to show that the transfer resulted from the exercise of free will. Two main factors would be taken into account when deciding whether the presumption had been rebutted:

742. [2011] IEHC 470, para. 43.
743. *Ibid.*
744. Unreported, 28 April 1983.
745. Unreported, High Court, 14 November 1988. *See also Gregg v Kidd* [1956] IR 183.
746. [2000] 1 ILRM 210 (SC).

(1) Was independent legal advice given?
(2) Was decision to make the gift or transfer a spontaneous and independent act, or did the donor act of their own free will?[747]

335. In this case the solicitor advising the donor was predominantly the solicitor for the recipient, and did not properly advise the donor on the transaction. The transfer put the donor at a serious disadvantage and was found to be improvident. The court concluded that the presumption of undue influence was not rebutted, and the transaction was set aside.

Undue influence from a third party

336. A difficulty arises when the improper pressure to enter a transaction has come from a source other than the other contracting party. A typical example is the situation where a wife signs a bank guarantee form or deed of mortgage because of the undue influence of her husband. If the bank seeks to enforce the guarantee, or seeks possession of the house, they may be faced with the argument that the wife only entered into the agreement because of the undue influence of the husband. This situation is sometimes referred to as an 'emotionally transmitted debt'.[748] The question that arises in this situation is to what extent should the bank be held responsible for the actions of the third party?

337. A series of cases from the UK have been influential in Ireland. In *Barclays Bank v O'Brien*[749] the House of Lords held that a bank which should have been aware of the possibility of undue influence, but failed to take reasonable steps to ensure that the wife's consent was properly obtained, would have constructive notice of the wife's right to have the transaction set aside, and would thus be unable to rely on the agreement. In *Ulster Bank v Roche* Clarke J neatly broke this basic principle down into a two-stage test:

> Constructive knowledge can often usefully be broken down into two separate questions. The first is as to what factors place a party on inquiry. The second is as to the nature of the inquiry or action that may then be required. If, in circumstances where a party is put on inquiry, that party does not carry out the inquiries necessary or take whatever other form of action may be mandated, then the party will be fixed with knowledge of matters which it would have discovered had it made the appropriate inquiries or, at least, may be faced with the situation where the court views the case on the basis that appropriate steps were not taken.[750]

747. [2000] 1 ILRM 210, 223.
748. *See AIB v Rostaff Property Developments Ltd* [2017] IEHC 533.
749. [1994] 1 AC180.
750. [2012] IEHC 166, para. 5.7.

338. In 2001 in *Etridge*[751] the House of Lords produced further clarification on the scope of the test in *O'Brien*, including detailed guidelines on when the bank would be put on inquiry as to the possibility of undue influence, the duties of the bank when put on inquiry and the duties of solicitors who were called on to provide independent legal advice to the weaker party.

339. In relation to when the bank is put on inquiry, Lord Nicholls stated that banks would not only be on inquiry in cases where the debtor and guarantor have a sexual relationship or a relationship where the law presumes the existence of trust and confidence. This would be an arbitrary boundary and undue influence could be exercised in an 'infinitely various' range of relationships.[752] Moreover, there were practical difficulties for banks in attempting to ascertain the kind of relationship that exists between the customer and guarantor. This led Lord Nicholls to the conclusion that 'the only practical way forward is to regard banks as 'put on inquiry in every case where the relationship between the surety and the debtor is non-commercial'.[753]

340. When the bank was put on inquiry, the bank was then expected to 'bring home' to the wife the risk she was running, either by having a private meeting or by requiring her to take independent advice from a solicitor. In the latter case, the bank was expected to contact the wife directly, check the name of the solicitor she wished to act for her, provide information on the husband's financial situation to the solicitor,[754] and receive written confirmation from the solicitor that the advice had been given. The solicitor was expected to advise the wife in a face-to-face meeting in the absence of the husband, and explain the documentation, its practical consequences and inherent risks, based on the financial information provided by the lender. The solicitor was then to check if the wife wished to continue and obtain her consent to the solicitor giving the confirmation required by the lender. Other than in exceptional circumstances, the bank would able to rely on this confirmation from the solicitor and the responsibility for the consent being properly given would thus shift from the bank to the solicitor. The House of Lords stressed that the function of the solicitor was not a mere formality.

341. These developments in the UK lead us to the question of how this issue was to be resolved in Ireland. The principle in *O'Brien* was adopted (mostly) with approval in *Bank of Nova Scotia v Hogan*[755] although on the facts there was no evidence of undue influence. It was also approved by Geoghegan J in *Bank of Ireland v Smyth*,[756] a case concerning the Family Home Protection Act 1976.

---

751. *Royal Bank of Scotland plc v Etridge (No 2)* [2002] 2 AC 773.
752. [2002] 2 AC 773, 795, 814.
753. [2002] 2 AC 773, 814.
754. This would be given with the husband's consent, and if the consent was not forthcoming the transaction should not proceed.
755. [1996] 3 IR 239.
756. [1995] 2 IR 259.

342. The case of *Ulster Bank Ltd v Fitzgerald*[757] was decided only a few weeks after *Etridge. Etridge* was not referred to in *Fitzgerald,* and the case stands in harsh contrast to the protective stance of the UK courts. Mrs Fitzgerald, who was in an abusive relationship with her husband, signed a bank guarantee form in favour of her husband's business in the hope that it would improve the relationship between them and save their marriage. O'Donovan J was prepared to accept that 'inordinate pressure' was placed on Mrs Fitzgerald to sign the guarantees and that 'she believed that she had little option but to sign them'. However, the court focused not on whether there was undue influence, but rather on the knowledge of the bank. The bank was unaware of the undue influence exercised by Mr Fitzgerald, and as the relationship of husband and wife does not give rise to a presumption of undue influence, the court was 'not persuaded' that the bank had constructive notice of the undue influence. In other words, the bank was not put on inquiry merely because a wife guaranteed a loan to her husband's business. The bank was thus not under any obligation to advise Mrs Fitzgerald to obtain independent legal advice, and the fact that they did so was 'above and beyond the call of duty'. The court was also of the view that she had a financial stake in her husband's business, as her family was reliant on it for income.

343. Although there were additional factual circumstances which could make it arguable that this case was exceptional,[758] *Fitzgerald* appeared to set a very low threshold of responsibility for banks and to potentially insufficiently protect parties who signed guarantees under undue influence. Limiting the defence of undue influence to a situation where the bank is aware of any undue influence reduces the incentive on the bank to seek any further information, and is inadequate to protect possible victims of undue influence. Moreover, as wives do generally have a financial interest in their husband's business in the sense mentioned by Donovan J, i.e., they may be reliant on the income, this does not necessarily equate to having financial control over the business, and in and of itself should not be enough to prevent the plea of undue influence, particularly as economic dependency can contribute to the inequality of the parties in an abusive relationship.

344. After the *Fitzgerald* case there was considerable uncertainty as to the scope of undue influence in a three-party situation involving a bank, in particular uncertainty as to the extent to which the House of Lords' decision in *Etridge* would form part of Irish law.[759] Some clarification was provided in *Ulster Bank Ireland Ltd v Roche and Buttimer.*[760] Ms Buttimer was the partner of Mr Roche, and evidence showed that she was in a dependent and abusive relationship. Both Ms Buttimer and Mr Roche signed guarantee documents guaranteeing the liabilities of Mr Roche's Business, Roche Motors, up to a maximum of €50,000. When the guarantee was called in by Ulster Bank, Ms Buttimer argued *inter alia* that she had only signed the

757. [2001] IEHC 159.
758. For example, the bank manager explained the guarantee to the wife in a one-to-one interview and the family home was not at risk.
759. Although *see Tynan v County Registrar for Kilkenny & Anor* [2011] IEHC 250 in which Laffoy J endorsed certain aspects of the approach of the House of Lords in *Etridge*, *see below*.
760. [2012] IEHC 166 (High Court, Clarke J, 29 March 2012).

guarantee because she subject to undue influence from Mr Roche. The court in this case was faced with a decision between following the approach in *Fitzgerald* – in which case Ms Buttimer's defence would have failed – and following the more protective approach in *Etridge* – in which case Ms Buttimer had a greater chance of success. In the High Court, Clarke J agreed with academic criticism of *Fitzgerald*, stating:

> A regime which places no obligation on a bank to take any steps to ascertain whether, in the presence of circumstances suggesting a non-commercial aspect to a guarantee, the party offering the guarantee may not be fully and freely entering into same, gives insufficient protection to potentially vulnerable sureties.[761]

345. As the court in *Fitzgerald* had not been referred to the views expressed in *Etridge* Clarke J was of the view that it was appropriate to consider whether the UK jurisprudence is persuasive.[762] With respect to the circumstances in which the bank would be put on inquiry, Clarke J accepted *Etridge* to the extent necessary to resolve the facts before him:

> While not necessarily accepting that the precise parameters, identified in *Etridge*, are those which give rise to an obligation on the bank to inquire, and thus represent the law in this jurisdiction, I am satisfied that the general principle, which underlies *Etridge*, is to the effect that a bank is placed on inquiry where it is aware of facts which suggest, or ought to suggest, that there may be a non-commercial element to a guarantee.[763]

346. Clarke J held that bank in this case was on inquiry as the facts should have suggested there was a non-commercial element to the guarantee.

347. As regards to the steps which should be taken by a bank when it is put on inquiry, Clarke J found that the bank was 'obliged to take at least some measures to seek to ensure that the proposed surety is openly and freely agreeing to provide the requested security'.[764] As Ulster Bank in this case had taken no steps whatsoever, thus meaning it could not rely on the guarantee, Clarke J found it unnecessary to discuss the precise steps a bank should take, or to discuss which aspects of the *Etridge* guidance to banks would apply in Ireland.

348. However, some guidance on this can be found in the earlier case of *Tynan v County Registrar for Kilkenny & Anor*[765] in which Laffoy J endorsed certain

761. *Ibid.*, para. 5.14.
762. *Ibid.*, para. 5.9.
763. *Ibid.*, para. 5.14.
764. [2012] IEHC 166, para. 5.16.
765. [2011] IEHC 250.

aspects of the approach of the House of Lords in *Etridge* concerning the ability of the bank to rely on confirmation from a solicitor that the surety understands and consents to the transaction:

> A bank, proposing to take a security from a surety wife for whom a solicitor is acting, requires, first, confirmation that the solicitor's instructions do extend to advising her about the nature and effect of the transaction. Subject to that confirmation, however, the bank is, in my opinion, entitled reasonably to believe that the solicitor will have advised her on the matters to which I have referred and, accordingly, that she has had an adequate explanation and has an adequate understanding of the transaction.[766]

349. Laffoy J did not examine in this case whether the solicitor would need to be independent from the party exerting the undue influence. In *Etridge* a practical stance was taken whereby the same solicitor could act for husband and wife, provided that in advising the wife the solicitor acts for the wife alone, is concerned with only her interests and is clear that there is no potential for conflict of interest. However this potentially conflicts with the decision in *Carroll v Carroll*[767] where the Supreme Court held that a solicitor who acts for both parties cannot be independent, although on the facts of that case it was evident that the solicitor in question was acting on behalf of the more dominant party and failed to offer any real independent advice to the vulnerable party. Nonetheless, it has thus been suggested that 'a bank wishing to ensure its security should require verification of legal advice from a legal advisor independent of the principal debtor until the Irish courts have dealt with the issue'.[768]

350. In recent years, and in the aftermath of the recession, a plea of undue influence has been a relatively common feature in cases in which banks seek summary judgment to enforce guarantees and the defendant seeks to resist summary judgment. However, the courts have shown resistance to the plea in the absence of any evidence of undue influence. For example, in *Bank of Ireland v Curran*[769] the defendant claimed that she guaranteed the liabilities of a company (in which she was a director and secretary) as a result of the undue influence of her son. To resist summary judgment, the defendant merely had to show 'that she might credibly argue in the course of a plenary hearing that she had executed the guarantee as a result of the undue influence'.[770] This 'required her to set out on affidavit the type of facts, details and circumstances upon which she would rely at the trial to establish that her will was overborne by her son, Michael Curran, when she executed the guarantee' and a 'bald assertion as to the existence of circumstances which might afford a defence'

766. [2011] IEHC 250, para. 4.6, quoting Lord Scott in *Etridge* [2002] 2 AC 773, para. 171. *See also* [2011] IEHC 250, paras 4.3–4.5.
767. [2000] 1 ILRM 210 (SC).
768. Corcoran, 'Undue Influence and Vulnerable Sureties: A Step Towards Greater Protection' (2012) 6 Commercial Law Practitioner 120, 125.
769. [2016] IECA 399. *See also Bank of Scotland plc v Hickey* [2014] IEHC 202; *Irish Bank Resolution Corporation v Quinn* [2011] IEHC 470; *Bank of Ireland v Mellon* [2017] IEHC 501.
770. [2016] IECA 399, para. 32.

would be insufficient.[771] It was held that here there was insufficient evidence of undue influence to meet even the relatively low threshold[772] required to resist summary judgment. Again, in *Ulster Bank (Ireland) Ltd v DeKretser and Fox*[773] there was a lack of evidence to raise a presumption of undue influence. The defendant was an experienced businesswoman who had previously given guarantees to the bank, was a director of the company that the guarantee was in relation to, and received a monthly payment from that company. It was thus 'entirely unreal to suggest that they did not know what they were doing'[774] and the claim of undue influence was held to be a 'mere assertion' which would not be enough to resist an application for summary judgment.[775] In *ACC Loan Management Ltd v John and Maurice Connolly*[776] the guarantor went even further, and sought to resist summary judgment by relying purely on the fact that the principal debtor was his son, and that thus there was an automatic presumption of undue influence. It was argued that the creditor bank was on notice of this presumption, and should have taken steps to ensure the guarantor understood the nature of the guarantee, even though there was no actual claim of any undue influence by the son on the facts. The court rejected this argument, stating that there was no 'independent or distinct defence for a guarantor, albeit related to the principal debtor, seeking to vitiate a guarantee executed in favour of a bank by reason of a breach of an alleged duty owed by the bank to him to ensure that he has obtained independent legal advice or has taken some further steps to ensure that he fully understood the nature of the guarantee being given.'[777] Thus the principles in *Etridge* and *Roche* would apply only if the guarantor first raises an arguable defence relating to wrongdoing on the part of the principal debtor. Although this seems to negate the 'presumption' of undue influence, whereby the burden of proof is on the person seeking to enforce the agreement to show the agreement was freely entered into, it must be remembered that this is a three-party situation, and the creditor is not normally the party accused of undue influence. It might also seem to be contrary to the principle in *Etridge* and *Roche,* that the bank is on enquiry whenever the guarantor is in a non-commercial relationship with the debtor. However, that principle is really that the bank has constructive notice of the undue influence where there is a non-commercial relationship; if there is in fact no undue influence, then there is nothing for them to have constructive notice of. A bank that fails to take steps to ensure that consent has been freely given takes the risk that it might not have been; it does not automatically mean that they cannot enforce the debt or guarantee even in the absence of undue influence. Furthermore, it is not implausible that this approach was taken to avoid spurious claims of undue influence being made when there is not even an arguable case that there was any undue influence on the facts.

---

771. [2016] IECA 399, paras 31–32.
772. *See AIB v Rostaff Property Developments Ltd* [2017] IEHC 533 where Barrett J. noted: 'It must be very clear that there is no case, no issue to be tried (or only issues that are simple and easily determinable). There must be no arguable defence.' Summary judgment was refused in this case.
773. [2016] IECA 371. There was a dissent by Hogan J.
774. [2016] IECA 371, para. 12 (citing the High Court decision).
775. *Ibid.*, para. 31 (citing the High Court decision).
776. [2017] IECA 119.
777. [2017] IECA 119, para. 29. It should be noted that there was a dissent by Hogan J.

351. Of course, if there is sufficient evidence then a claim based on undue influence may go forward. In *ACC Bank v Walsh*[778] the plaintiff bank sought summary judgment against the defendants, a now-separated couple, for a debt of €938,957. It was held in the High Court that the defendant, Mrs Walsh, had no arguable case of undue influence, but this was overturned on appeal. The bank seemed to have been aware that Mrs Walsh had no direct involvement in the business and that she derived no benefit from the loan, and the bank had not denied that it had never met with or spoken to Mrs Walsh. The Court of Appeal also noted that the couple had represented themselves in the High Court, and that Mr Walsh did most of the talking, and made submissions on their joint behalf, and that she was prevented therefore from making her case properly there. There was thus an arguable case of undue influence, which could go to a full hearing. One difficulty in this case was that Mrs Walsh was a joint borrower, while in *Etridge* and *Roche* the Court was concerned with the enforceability of a guarantee given under the undue influence of the primary borrower.[779] However, the Court held that on the facts of this case the distinction might not be relevant:

> [I]n my view there is arguably some equivalence between a spouse who is unduly influenced to join in a loan application being made by her husband and from which she is to derive no benefit, and one who is unduly influenced to provide a guarantee for her husband's primary loan and from which she is to derive no benefit. In each instance, the spouse is exposing herself to liability for the amount owing to the bank in the event of default.[780]

The Family Home Protection Act

352. In Ireland, further protection is provided to spouses by the Family Home Protection Act, section 3(1) of which states 'Where a spouse, without the prior consent in writing of the other spouse, purports to convey any interest in the family home to any person except the other spouse, then … the purported conveyance shall be void.' This applies regardless of whether the spouse actually owns the home – what matters is that it is the 'family home', rather than ownership. In *Bank of Ireland v Smyth*[781] it was held that consent for the purposes of section 3 is fully informed consent, so where the full repercussions of a conveyance are not explained to a spouse the transaction would be void. However, in 2012 in *Irish Nationwide Building Society v Raftery & Another*[782] an argument that a mortgage was void under section 3 of the Family Home Protection Act 1976 failed because *both* parties had entered into the mortgage agreement. Hedigan J followed the Supreme Court

778. [2017] IECA 166.
779. *See GE Capital Woodchester Home Loans Ltd v Reade* [2012] IEHC 363 where it was suggested that the *Roche* test might not be relevant where there is a joint borrower.
780. [2017] IECA 166.
781. [1995] 2 IR 259.
782. [2012] IEHC 352 (High Court, Hedigan J, 9 August 2012).

decision in *Nestor v Murphy*[783] where it was held that section 3(1) of the Family Home Protection Act 1976 did not apply to a conveyance or a contract of sale which had been executed by both sides by mutual consent, as '[i]n such event no protection is needed for one spouse against an unfair and unnotified alienation by the other of an interest in the family home'.[784] The defendants in *Raftery* also argued that the transaction had been entered into without independent legal advice, but as both defendants were party to all the transactions, and as Mrs Raftery 'in all probability understood very well what she was doing and what she was signing' this argument was also rejected.[785]

Non Est Factum

353. A plea of *non est factum* is often raised in conjunction with a plea of undue influence. *Non est factum* means 'it is not my deed', and amounts to the defendant claiming that they were under a fundamental misapprehension as to the nature of a document they were signing.

354. For a defendant to successfully plead *non est factum* it must be shown:

(a) That there was a radical or fundamental difference between what he signed and what he thought he was signing;
(b) That the mistake was as to the general character of the document as opposed to the legal effect;
and
(c) That there was a lack of negligence i.e. that he took all reasonable precautions in the circumstances to find out what the document was.[786]

355. In many cases where *non est factum* is pleaded it will not succeed, usually because the courts will be of the view that the defendant should have taken better care in signing a commercial document. In the *Quinn* case,[787] discussed above, Mrs Quinn argued that she signed loan documents as a matter of course without giving it any second thought, and therefore did not know what she was signing. Unsurprisingly, this plea did not succeed, as 'the most cursory of glances at the documents which bear her signature would alert any but the illiterate to the fact that this was some form of borrowing transaction'. The court stated 'What could more negligent than willy-nilly signing formal legal documents without giving any thought as to their effect?'[788] Similarly in *Bank of Ireland v Curran*[789] a defence of *non est factum* was rejected on the basis that if Mrs Curran had read the document she would

783. [1979] IR 326.
784. [1979] IR 326, 328 per Henchy J.
785. [2012] IEHC 352, para. 9.
786 *Tedcastle McCormack and Company Limited v McCrystal* (15 March 1999) Morris J. cited by Kelly J. in *IBRC v Quinn* [2011] IEHC 470 and Noonan J in *Allied Irish Banks Plc v Yates* [2016] IEHC 60.
787. [2011] IEHC 470.
788. [2011] IEHC 470, paras 34–35.
789. [2016] IECA 399.

have had no difficulty understanding that she was signing a guarantee for €1m, and providing security to the bank separate from any earlier security provided.[790] The court referred to the decision of Clarke J in *Ulster Bank Ireland Ltd v. Roche and Buttimer*[791] when he stated:

> A person who signs a document which may well have significant legal effect and does so, either without reading the document or without applying themselves to the content of the document, 'must accept the consequences of having signed a commercially binding agreement in those circumstances' and will, prima facie, be bound by what they have signed.[792]

356. In addition, the misunderstanding must be to the general character of the document, rather than a misapprehension as to its legal effect. For example, in *Bank of Ireland v McManamy*[793] members of a co-operative creamery had been approached by the creamery manager who asked them to sign forms as receipts for manure and milk supplied. In fact the forms were bank guarantee forms, but when the bank sought to enforce them the members were able to rely on the defence of *non est factum.* In contrast, in *Allied Irish Banks Plc v Yates*[794] the defendant attempted to argue that she had signed the guarantee 'for administrative purposes only', but did not 'identify what she thought she was signing if it was not a guarantee'.[795] The court held that if she acted under any misapprehension, it was as to the legal effect of the document that she signed, which was not sufficient to raise the defence. Nor, even if she had been under a misapprehension as to what she was signing, had she taken reasonable precautions to find out what the document was.[796]

357. A recent (and rare) example where the defence of *non est factum* succeeded was the decision of Charleton J in *Friends First Finance v Lavelle.*[797] In this case, a financial institution argued that Charlotte Lavelle had borrowed approximately €1.75 million, but she argued that she in fact never borrowed the money, but had signed the relevant documents in the belief that she was signing documents to settle money into a family trust. The financial institution never met her face-to-face, did not know the circumstances under which she signed the documents, did not witness the documents on their premises or through their own personnel and did not know if she had received any of the letters in relation to the borrowing in her name. It was held that the defence of *non est factum* was clearly made out, with the court

790. *Ibid.*, para. 44.
791. [2012] IEHC 166.
792. [2016] IECA 399, para. 45.
793. [1916] 2 IR 161.
794. [2016] IEHC 60.
795. *Ibid.*, para. 33.
796. *Ibid.*
797. [2013] IEHC 201.

adding that it was 'repellent that a financial institution could hold someone to a bargain in the borrowing of a huge amount of money when there was never any meeting of mind, never mind any meeting in person, whereby that individual could truly be called a borrower as a matter of contract'.[798]

C. Gross Disparity

358. In general, the court will not intervene to rescue a party from a bad bargain. The consideration that is provided by each party does not have to be equivalent and the court 'will not enter minutely into it, and see that it is full and ample'.[799] However, equity may intervene where there is such a gross disparity that the contract can be said to be 'unconscionable' or 'improvident'. In the High Court decision in *Carroll v Carroll*[800] Shanley J set out the elements which must be established before equity would intervene on the grounds of unconscionable bargain:

> Firstly, that one party was at a serious disadvantage to another by reason of poverty, ignorance, or otherwise, so that circumstances existed of which unfair advantage could be taken; secondly, that the transaction was at an undervalue and thirdly, that there was a lack of independent legal advice.[801]

359. The doctrine is not only limited to transactions for value but also applies to gifts.[802] In *MC (A Ward) v FC*[803] the court set aside a transaction whereby an elderly widow with dementia transferred over €900,000 to her nephew, and in *Bourke v O'Donnell*[804] a transfer of a large sum of money by a vulnerable elderly woman in a nursing home to (apparent) friends who brought her to the bank was set aside as improvident.[805]

360. These cases tend to arise in the context of the disposition of land by vulnerable individuals to a third party, and it is clear that the Irish courts are 'especially protective of elderly persons who sell or dispose of farmland outside of their family'.[806] Thus in *Grealish v Murphy*[807] an elderly and illiterate farmer transferred land at substantial undervalue in favour of a younger man, and the transaction was set aside. Similarly in *Lyndon v Coyne*[808] a transfer of land by an elderly, ill man to

---

798. *Ibid.*, para. 23.
799. *Grogan v Cooke* (1812) 2 B&B 230, 234 per Manners LC.
800. [1998] 2 ILRM 218.
801. *Ibid.*, para. 22 citing *Hanbury & Martins Modern Equity* Fourth Edition (1991) at page 821. The High Court decision was affirmed by the Supreme Court.
802. *Prendergast v Joyce* [2009] 3 IR 519.
803. [2013] IEHC 272, upheld by the Supreme Court at [2013] IESC 36.
804. [2010] IEHC 348.
805. The case was in fact decided on undue influence, but the transaction was described as improvident.
806. McDermott, p. 968.
807. [1946] IR 35. *See* R. Clark, 'An Everyday Story of Country Folk (Not!) *Grealish v Murphy*' in O'Dell, *Leading Cases of the Twentieth Century* (2000) p. 144.
808. (1946) 12 Ir Jur Rep 64.

his nephew was set aside as being improvident, and in *Keating v Keating*[809] a sale of land by an elderly and sick farmer to a much younger relative was set aside.

361. An argument that there has been an unconscionable bargain often arises in connection with an argument that there has been undue influence, although they are separate doctrines. As with undue influence, during the recession some defendants seeking to avoid liability under guarantees or loans would plead that there had been an unconscionable bargain, but the argument usually failed.[810] If there is a plausible argument that there has been an unconscionable bargain, it is possible nonetheless for the transaction to stand if it can be shown that the transaction was entered into freely and independently, and with the benefit of independent legal advice. For example in *Smyth v Smyth*[811] a sale of land to a trustee by the beneficiary of the trust was upheld where the beneficiary had introduced the idea of the sale and the transaction had taken an 'inordinate' amount of time to complete.[812]

§3. Other Conditions of Validity

I. Existing and Licit Cause

362. Irish contract law does not make use of the concept of an 'existing' or 'licit' cause, or the concept of a 'determined or determinable, possible and licit object'.[813]

II. Initial Impossibility

363. There is not much case law on the situation where there is initial impossibility, such as a contract to jump over the moon. Unlike the civil law, the common law does not consider a promise to do the impossible void. Such a promise is viewed 'not as a promise to perform but as a promise to bear the risk of the promised event not coming to pass'.[814] However, in the interpretation of contracts there is a presumption that a contract does not require performance of the impossible.[815] In *Lynch v Duffy*[816] a contract for the sale of land was essentially agreed in late 2006 and January 2007 and formally executed on 4 April 2007. The contract stipulated

809. [2009] IEHC 405.
810. *See*, for example, *Bank of Ireland v Curran* [2016] IECA 399; *Secured Property Loans v Floyd* [2011] 2 IR 652. *See also O'Reilly v O'Connor* [2005] IEHC 255.
811. 22 November 1978, High Court, Costello J.
812. *See also Kelly v Morrisroe* (1919) 53 ILTR 145.
813. There is even little written on it from this perspective, but for an excellent discussion, *see* Earnest Lorenzen 'Causa and Consideration in the Law of Contracts' (1919) 28(7) The Yale Law Journal 621–646.
814. Swadling 'The Judicial Construction of Force Majeure Clauses' in McKendrick (ed.) *Force Majeure and Frustration of Contract* (2nd ed., 1995) p. 3.
815. *The Epaphus* [1987] 2 Lloyd's Rep 213.
816. [2009] IEHC 59.

that the planning permission be sought before 26 February 2007. As this date preceded the date on which the contract was executed, Murphy J. ruled that compliance with this term was impossible and ordered that the February deadline be deleted from the contract. Instead, planning permission was to be obtained 'as soon as possible' after the formal execution of the contract in April 2007.

364. Most cases of initial impossibility are dealt with under the doctrine of mistake –essentially where both parties enter into a contract under a mistaken belief that the contract is possible, when in fact it is not. The courts might find in such a situation that the contract is void *ab initio*, or as mentioned above it might be found that one party warranted or took the risk that the contract would be possible. There is a statutory provision dealing with initial impossibility in contracts of sale – section 6 of the Sale of Goods Act 1893 provides that if both parties enter into a contract for the sale of specific goods, but in fact unknown to both parties the goods have already perished, then the contract is void *ab initio*. This follows the common law principle set out in *Couturier v Hastie*.[817]

III. Illegality and Public Policy

365. A contract which contravenes the provisions of the Constitution or a statute or some rule of common law is often described as *illegal*. When a statutory provision is breached it is referred to as 'statutory illegality', whereas the phrase 'common law illegality' is used to describe a situation where there is breach of a common law rule. Traditionally, the courts would refuse to intervene or be involved with an illegal contract, meaning that the contract was unenforceable and any losses would simply lie where they fell. This had potential to cause harsh results. However, a more modern approach can be seen in Ireland, which focuses on the policy objectives behind the statute or common law rule that is purported to have been breached when deciding if the illegality necessarily means that an underlying contract is unenforceable.

A. *Statutory Illegality*

366. A contract may be illegal because it breaches a statutory provision, or because it is intended to be performed in a manner which breaches a statutory provision. However, a contract may be *enforceable* even if it is considered to be illegal. The difficulty here is although some statutes clearly set out the impact of the illegality on the enforceability of any underlying contract,[818] others do not, and it was left to the courts to determine on a case-by-case basis whether the contract would be enforceable. The traditional approach to statutory illegality reflected the principle of *ex turpi causa non oritur actio*, i.e., a party cannot ask a court to enforce

817. (1852) 8 Exch. 40.
818. For example, s. 4(1) of the Competition Act 2002 provides that all agreements between undertakings that have as their object or effect anti-competitive practices are 'prohibited and void'.

a transaction which is tainted with illegality. This strict approach meant that losses would simply lie where they fell.[819] Even where the contract itself is not illegal, but a statutory instrument exists which would have the effect of making *performance* of the contract illegal, the court would not enforce the contract because to do so would compel the defendant to perform an illegal act.[820] Particular difficulties were caused where the contract appeared on the face of it to be normal and enforceable, but which was entered into without a particular required licence.[821]

367. Any discussion of the modern approach to statutory illegality must focus on the recent Supreme Court decision in *Quinn v IBRC.*[822] In this case, the Supreme Court set out 'the appropriate modern approach to be applied regarding the question of whether, and if so in what circumstances, a court in this jurisdiction should enforce a contract notwithstanding the fact that the relevant contract may, in some way, have a connection with illegality'.[823] In approaching this issue, the Supreme Court recognised the expansion of regulation by statute since the early cases on illegal contracts were developed, and noted that 'the range of breaches which can arise stem across a spectrum from the minor and technical to the substantive and extremely grave'.[824]

368. In *Quinn* it was alleged that a series of lending transactions entered into by Seán Quinn and Anglo-Irish Bank amounted to illegal contracts. The contracts were loans given by Anglo-Irish Bank in order to facilitate the purchase of shares in the Bank itself, and it was argued that as a result they were in breach of the Market Abuse (Directive 2003/6/EC) Regulations 2005 (which prohibits market manipulation) and/or section 60 of the Companies Act 1963 (which forbids a company from purchasing its own shares, or from offering financial assistance in that regard). The issue that arose in the Supreme Court was whether this meant that guarantees and securities given by other members of the Quinn family in connection with the allegedly illegal loans were invalid.[825] In the Supreme Court it was held that the underlying loan contracts were enforceable, despite their illegality, and the guarantees and securities given in respect of them were also enforceable. In reaching this conclusion, the Court rejected taking a case-by-case approach depending on the individual contract in question and the severity of breach. Instead, the courts should assess the policy of the individual *statute* in question:

---

819. *See*, for example, *McIlvenna v Ferris* [1955] IR 318; *O'Shaughnessy v Lyons* (1957) Ir Jur Rep. 90.
820. *Naamloze Vennootschap De Faam v Dorset Manufacturing Co. Ltd.* [1949] IR 203 and *see Fibretex (Société Personnes Responsabilité Limité) v Beleir Ltd.* 89 ILTR 141.
821. Leading examples of licence cases are *St. John Shipping Corporation v Joseph Rank* [1957] 1 QB 267; *Archbolds (Freightage) Ltd. v S. Spanglett Ltd* [1961] 1 QB 374. Irish cases include *Marrinan v O'Haran*, Unreported, High Court, 17 June 1971; *Hortensius Ltd and Durack v Bishop* [1989] ILRM 294; *O'Shaughnessy v Lyons* (1957) Ir Jur Rep 90; *Gray v Cathcart* (1899) 33 ILTR 35.
822. [2015] IESC 29.
823. *Ibid.*, para. 8.1.
824. *Ibid.*, para. 6.2.
825. *Ibid.*, paras 1.5–1.6.

> [A] a court is required to assess whether the requirements of public policy, in respect of a particular statutory provision rendering … a particular type of activity illegal, require that contracts sufficiently connected with that particular type of illegality are to be regarded as unenforceable. Such an approach requires each statutory regime (or part of a statutory regime) to be independently assessed to determine whether policy requires particular types of contracts to be treated as unenforceable. However, such an approach does not mandate the court to take a different view as to whether one particular contract or another may be regarded as unenforceable by virtue of being in breach of the same statutory provision by reference to, for example, the severity of the breach concerned or the adverse consequences for the parties. The proper approach, in my judgement, is statute specific but is not case specific.[826]

369. If the relevant legislation 'expressly states that contracts of a particular class or type are to be treated as void or unenforceable'[827] – or, indeed, enforceable – then this is the end of the matter. However, if the legislation is silent on this issue:

> the court must consider whether the requirements of public policy (which suggest that a court refrain from enforcing a contract tainted by illegality) and the policy of the legislation concerned, gleaned from its terms, are such as require that, in addition to whatever express consequences are provided for in the relevant legislation, an additional sanction or consequence in the form of treating relevant contracts as being void or unenforceable must be imposed.[828]

370. The Court then set out a non-exhaustive list of factors to be taken into account when considering this issue. These include:

- Whether the contract in question is designed to carry out the very act which the relevant legislation is designed to prevent.[829]
- Whether the wording of the statute itself might be taken to strongly imply that the remedies or consequences specified in the statute are sufficient to meet the statutory end.[830]
- Whether the policy of the legislation is designed to apply equally or substantially to both parties to a relevant contract, or whether that policy is exclusively or principally directed towards one party. Therefore, legislation which is designed to impose burdens on one category of persons for the purposes of protecting another category may be considered differently from legislation which is designed to place a burden of compliance with an appropriate regulatory regime on both participants.[831]

---

826. *Ibid.*, para. 8.3.
827. *Ibid.*, para. 8.9.
828. *Ibid.*, para. 8.9.
829. *Ibid.*, para. 8.32.
830. *Ibid.*, para. 8.34.
831. *Ibid.*, para. 8.37.

- Whether the imposition of voidness or unenforceability may be counterproductive to the statutory aim as found in the statute itself.[832]

371. It was also said to be 'at least arguable' that a court may be required to have regard to:

- Whether, having regard to the purpose of the statute, the range of adverse consequences for which express provision is made might be considered, in the absence of treating relevant contracts as unenforceable, to be adequate to secure those purposes.[833]
- Whether the imposition of voidness or unenforceability may be disproportionate to the seriousness of the unlawful conduct in question in the context of the relevant statutory regime in general.[834]

372. The Court was clear that this question was to be decided on a statute-by-statute basis, and not a case-by-case basis:

> [O]nce it is determined that policy requires that contracts which are deemed unlawful by reference to a particular statutory provision are to be regarded as unenforceable, no assessment of the merits of the individual case arises. The consequences lie where they fall.[835]

373. In addition, the mere fact that a statute might require a relevant contract to be unenforceable does not necessarily mean that 'every supporting or collateral measure, such as a guarantee or the giving of security by a party other than a party to the original contract, is to be treated in exactly the same way as the underlying contract itself, particularly in circumstances where those involved in the connected transaction are unaware of, and are innocent in relation to, the relevant illegality'.[836] It may be the case that while public policy requires the primary contract to be rendered unenforceable, it does not require associated contracts such as contracts of guarantee to be unenforceable.

374. In this case, the contracts were in breach of section 60 of the Companies Act 1963, which makes it illegal for a company to give a loan or financial assistance in connection with a purchase of any shares in the company. However, section 60(14) then stated:

> Any transaction in breach of this section shall be voidable at the instance of the company against any person (whether a party to the transaction or not) who had notice of the facts which constitute such breach.

832. *Ibid.*, para. 8.39.
833. *Ibid.*, para. 8.44.
834. *Ibid.*, para. 8.47.
835. *Ibid.*, para. 8.5.
836. *Ibid.*, para. 8.48.

375. It was held in the Supreme Court that there was a 'clear statutory policy' that a company could still elect to treat the loan contract as enforceable and get its money back.[837] The repercussions for the illegal activity in this case were to be a separate criminal penalty, and not 'the potential injustice of allowing the consequences of that unlawful contract to lie where they fell (meaning, in many cases, that the company whose officers had abused its position will be even worse off to the detriment of its shareholders)'.[838] Hence the lending contracts were enforceable even if it could be established that Anglo had acted in breach of section 60 in making the loans concerned.[839]

376. There was also an alleged breach of the Market Abuse Regulations, which prohibit *inter alia* market manipulation, and set out various criminal and administrative penalties, as well as the possibility of civil liability. As the Regulations are silent as to the effect of the prohibition on any underlying contracts, the Court turned to the factors it had set out earlier in the case. Although all the factors were discussed, the Court focused on the policy objective of the Regulations (and the Directive on which they are based), namely the protection of the interests of investors who might be misled by a share price which is being artificially maintained by illegal transactions. Holding the underlying contracts unenforceable would 'deprive those shareholders … of the benefit of contracts entered into by the company as part of a market abuse scheme' and would be 'likely to only increase the damage done to the very persons whom the legislation is intended to protect'.[840] The contracts were thus enforceable despite the illegality under the Regulations.

377. The underlying loan agreements were thus enforceable, notwithstanding their illegality. The Court further held that the Quinn family had never made a case that the guarantees would be unenforceable in the event that the loan agreements were enforceable and had solely based their case on the premise that the loan agreements were unenforceable.

B. Contracts and Contract Terms Void by Statute

378. Some contracts, or contract terms, may be deemed to be 'void' even though they are not necessarily 'illegal' as such.[841] For example, section 36 of the Gaming and Lotteries Act 1956 states that 'every contract by way of gaming or wagering is void'. This means that while the transaction is not illegal – clearly licensed bookmakers and betting shops exist in Ireland[842] – 'no rights can accrue to either party'.[843] This means that the winner of the bet cannot enforce the bet on the other

837. *Ibid.*, para. 10.7.
838. *Ibid.*, para. 10.7.
839. *Ibid.*, para. 10.9.
840. *Ibid.*, para. 11.19.
841. *See* Clark pp. 547–549.
842. *See* the Betting (Amendment) Act 2015.
843. Clark p. 527.

party and make them pay the money owed.[844] In addition, in *Sporting Index Ltd v O'Shea*[845] the High Court refused to enforce a judgment obtained in London against a party to a gambling contract entered into in the UK, on the basis that 'the rule reflects public policy on the control of gambling' and would not be enforced by the Irish courts.

379. Other contracts may not be 'void' but rather voidable at the instance of the person the statutory provision is trying to protect. For example section 74(3) of the Land and Conveyancing Law Reform Act 2009 provides that any conveyance of property made with the intention of defrauding a creditor or any other person is voidable by any person thereby prejudiced.[846]

380. In other instances, an individual term is held to be void, while leaving the rest of the contract intact. For example, section 90(1) of the Property Services (Regulation) Act 2011 provides that any term in a sale or letting contract that requires an agent's fees or expenses to be paid by the purchaser or tenant is void, with any monies paid being recoverable, and the European Communities (Unfair Terms in Consumer Contracts) Regulations 1995 provide that unfair terms in consumer contracts are unenforceable against the consumer, while leaving the rest of the contract intact.

C. Contracts Contrary to the Constitution

381. It is possible that a contract might be found to be contrary to the Constitution. In *Dalton v Dalton*[847] the High Court refused to support a separation agreement between husband and wife which included a clause on the agreement of the parties to obtain a dissolution of the marriage abroad, as this was contrary to the provisions of the Constitution which at the time prohibited divorce. In *Ennis v Butterly*[848] a cohabitation agreement was found to be contrary to the constitutional protection of marriage.[849] The Law Reform Commission has however suggested that *Ennis v Butterly* does not render all aspects of cohabitation agreements invalid, and in fact has recommended that cohabitation agreements should be more commonly used.[850] The Civil Partnership and Certain Rights and Obligations of Cohabitants Act 2010 now allows cohabitants to enter into a cohabitants' agreement to provide for financial matters during the relationship or when the relationship ends, whether

---

844. *See*, for example, *Puloas v Heaps* (1938) 72 ILTR 96.
845. [2015] IEHC 407.
846. *See*, for example, *Keegan Quarries Ltd v McGuinness* [2011] IEHC 453.
847. [1982] ILRM 418.
848. [1997] 1 ILRM 28.
849. Article 41.3.1° of the Constitution, *Bunreacht na hÉireann*, provides that the State is to 'guard with special care the institution of Marriage' and to 'protect it against attack'.
850. Report *Rights and Duties of Cohabitants* (LRC 82-2006) Chapter 3. The Commission's Report resulted in the 'cohabitation' section (i.e., Part 15) of the Civil Partnership and Certain Rights and Obligations of Cohabitants Act 2010.

through death or otherwise, subject to certain criteria in the Act. The court can vary or set aside such an agreement if it is enforceability would cause serious injustice.

382. The constitutional protection of the institution of marriage has also rendered uncertain the validity of prenuptial agreements in Ireland, although there is no court decision to expressly back up the view that prenuptial agreements are unenforceable. It is most likely that any such agreement might be taken into account by a court and serve as a guide during divorce proceedings, but are not legally binding.[851] In 2006 the Government Study Group on prenuptial agreements was of the opinion that prenuptial agreements could be enforceable under the current law,[852] at least in the sense that they could be taken into account by a court,[853] but in the absence of any court decision to this effect the Group recommended an amendment to the Family Law (Divorce) Act 1996 to expressly provide for the recognition of prenuptial agreements.[854] In 2019, the Law Society was also of the view that while courts might take agreements into account, they were not strictly legally enforceable and reform was required.[855] To date such amendment has not occurred.

D. Illegal Contracts at Common Law

383. Certain contracts are illegal at common law on grounds of public policy, while (rather confusingly) other contracts, or terms of contracts, are considered to be 'void' at common law. The difference is in effect: an illegal contract is invalidated in its entirety and unenforceable as being against public policy, but the 'void' contract or contract term, despite its name, is only unenforceable as regards the illegal portion, at least if the rest of the contract can be severed from that term.[856] This section examines illegal contracts at common law, while void contracts are discussed in the next section.

851. *See* Lucy-Ann Buckley, 'Why aren't prenuptial agreements legally enforceable in Ireland?', available at https://www.rte.ie/brainstorm/2019/0801/1066438-why-arent-prenuptial-agreements-legally-enforceable-in-ireland/.

852. *See also* 'No legal bar to pre-nuptial agreements – McDowell' *The Irish Times* 19 October 2006. This has been doubted, however, *see* Coulter 'Caution advised over prenuptial deals' *The Irish Times* 26 November 2007.

853. The Family Law (Divorce) Act 1996 provides that when granting a decree of divorce the court should make 'proper' provision for the spouses and any dependent children, having regard 'in particular' to certain factors. While this list of factors which can be taken into account by the court includes any separation agreement entered into by the spouses, there is no specific mention of whether the courts should take into account any prenuptial agreement which was entered into. However, the list of factors to be taken into account by the court is non-exhaustive, so the failure to mention prenuptial agreements does not necessarily mean that they are excluded or unenforceable.

854. *Report of the Study Group on Pre-nuptial Agreements* (April 2007) p. 71.

855. Law Society of Ireland *Divorce in Ireland: The Case for Reform* Recommendation 2.6 (April 2019), available at https://www.lawsociety.ie/globalassets/documents/submissions/divorce-in-ireland-april-2019.pdf.

856. *See Goodinson v Goodinson* [1954] 2 QB 118, 121.

384. Clark points out that the categories of public policy are not closed,[857] but the following broadly types of contracts might be found to be illegal at common law, meaning they will not be enforced:

1. Contracts Relating to a Criminal Offence or a Tort

385. A contract to commit a crime or a tort is illegal and will not be enforced. However, this can be extended to the principle that 'a person is not to benefit from his or her wrong, even if the level of moral guilt is minimal'.[858] For example, someone who has been convicted of murder will not be able to claim on a contract of insurance relating to that crime. In *Gray v Hibernian Insurance Company*[859] an insurance company refused to pay on a fire insurance policy on the basis that the insured person was suspected of arson. However, it was held in the High Court that the settlement was enforceable. The onus of proof was on the party claiming the illegality (i.e., the insurance company), and in circumstances such as these where the insured person had been acquitted of arson the burden of proof would be a higher standard of proof than the balance of probabilities.

386. An agreement not to prosecute in respect of a criminal offence,[860] or to compromise criminal proceedings,[861] is illegal and will not be enforced unless the offence is a minor one which might also be sued upon (or compromised) as a civil matter. It has been suggested that rather than a blanket rule which can have harsh results, such promises should be enforceable unless there is some public interest which takes priority.[862]

2. Maintenance, Champerty and Third-Party Litigation Funding

387. Maintenance has been defined 'as the giving of assistance, by a third party, who has no interest in the litigation, to a party in litigation'.[863] Champerty is 'where the third party, who is giving assistance, will receive a share of the litigation succeeds'.[864] Maintenance or champerty agreements are considered illegal under Irish law, on the basis that 'litigation trafficking' is undesirable. Funding of litigation by a third party can 'stir up' litigation, with the funder potentially interfering with the litigation and decisions being made with the interests of the funders in mind, rather

857. Clark p. 510.
858. Clark p. 493.
859. Unreported, High Court, 27 May 1993.
860. *Brady v Flood* (1841) 6 Cir Cas 309, *Nolan v Shiels* (1926) 60 ILTR 143.
861. *Keir v Leeman* (1846) 9 QB 371.
862. Clark p. 497.
863. *Persona Digital Telephony Ltd v Minister for Public Enterprise* [2017] IESC 27, para. 25.
864. *Ibid.*

than the interests of the parties themselves. It was the *risk* of this interference or abuse that rendered the contract void, rather than whether the abuse was likely to occur in any given case.[865]

388. However, if it can be shown that the funder has an interest in the litigation, for example as a shareholder or creditor,[866] or some other 'legitimate concern including charity'[867] then it may fall under an exception to the rule. In *Thema International Fund plc v HSBC International Trust Services Ireland Ltd*[868] Clarke J observed that:

> [There is] a substantial difference between a party who already has an indirect link to the impecunious party and who has, therefore, already got an indirect interest in the relevant litigation, on the one hand, and a party with no such prior link who simply buys into the litigation on the other hand.[869]

389. However, the funding of litigation by third parties can in appropriate cases facilitate access to justice, and it has been said that individuals must not be 'deprived of their constitutional right of access to the courts to litigate reasonably stateable claims'.[870] In *Greenclean Waste Management Ltd. v. Leahy (No.2)*[871] Hogan J stated that 'the scope of application of the law of champerty must … accommodate itself to modern social realities'[872] such as 'legal aid, representative actions, *pro bono* work, "no foal, no fee" arrangements and the involvement in litigation of community and voluntary groups and trade unions in support of their members'.[873]

390. The direct issue of professional third-party litigation funding in Ireland was discussed by the Supreme Court in *Persona Digital Telephony Ltd v Minister for Public Enterprise*.[874] The issue in this case was whether a litigation funding arrangement, whereby a company with no connection to the litigation was willing to fund litigation in return for a share of the proceeds should the action be successful, was prohibited under the rules on champerty and maintenance. The plaintiffs argued that this arrangement was legitimate as it enabled a claim of public importance to proceed[875] and ensured the constitutional guarantee of access to justice,

865. *SPV Osus Limited v HSBC Institutional Trust Services (Ireland) Limited & Ors.* [2018] IESC 44, para. 19 (O'Donnell J).
866. *Thema International Fund plc v HSBC International Trust Services Ireland Ltd* [2011] IEHC 357, para. 5.10.
867. *Ibid.*, para. 5.6.
868. [2011] IEHC 357.
869. *Ibid.*, para. 5.10.
870. *O'Keeffe v Scales* [1998] 1 ILRM 393.
871. [2014] IEHC 314; overturned on other grounds in the Court of Appeal: [2015] IECA 97.
872. [2014] IEHC 314, para. 11.
873. *Ibid.*
874. [2016] IEHC 187; [2017] IESC 27.
875. The main case concerned claims of alleged bribery and corruption in relation to the award of a mobile phone licence.

while leaving control of the litigation with the plaintiffs and their legal team.[876] In a joint decision delivered by Denham CJ, the Supreme Court held that maintenance and champerty were still illegal in Ireland, constituting both a tort and potentially a criminal offence.[877] As the funder in this case had no connection with the litigation, other than funding it, it was a champertous agreement and would not be allowed.[878]

391. As to the argument that the law should be developed in light of modern policy issues, the Court stated that substantial reform of policy would 'involve complex situations more suited to legislation', after the benefit of a Law Reform Commission Report.[879] This is partly an issue of constitutional separation of powers, but also raises a practical point regarding the undesirability of simply liberalising the law on champerty without also regulating any resulting third-party funding system. Indeed, it is clear from the various supporting judgments from the Court that the problem of access to justice raises many policy concerns, for example, regarding judicial workloads, free legal aid and the basis of payment to lawyers, and that there is no 'pain-free solution to the problem'.[880] Clarke J (as he was then) in particular sounds a clear warning to the legislature that the current situation might be in violation of constitutional rights, and that measures might have to be taken by the legislature to attempt to resolve the problem of access to the courts.[881] Clarke CJ reiterated these concerns in *SPV Osus Limited v HSBC Institutional Trust Services (Ireland) Limited & Ors.*:[882]

> I remain very concerned that there are cases where persons or entities have suffered from wrongdoing but where those persons or entities are unable effectively to vindicate their rights because of the cost of going to court. That is a problem to which solutions require to be found. It does seem to me that this is an issue to which the legislature should give urgent consideration. But it is not open to the courts to fashion a carefully regulated scheme that balances advantages and risks.[883]

876. [2017] IESC 27, para. 14. This claim was disputed by counsel for the defendants, who argued that litigation agreement application coincided with 'a revival of the proceedings, and a change in the legal representation, which indicates an impact on the litigation' (para. 17).
877. Under the Maintenance and Embracery Act 1634, which was retained by the Statute Law Revision Act 2007.
878. [2017] IESC 27, para. 54(i)–(iii).
879. *Ibid.*, para. 54(v). In its *Issues Paper on Contempt of Court and Other Offences and Torts involving the Administration of Justice* (LRC IP 10-2016), the Law Reform Commission stated at para. 6.33 that that it is 'certainly arguable that legislation should be introduced to allow for third party funding of litigation by person or body who does not have a legitimate interest in the proceedings'. However, detailed proposals have not yet been made; nor is it listed as an issue on the Fifth Programme of Reform.
880. [2017] IESC 27, para. 3.7 (Clarke J).
881. *Ibid.*, paras 4.1–4.4 (Clarke J).
882. [2018] IESC 44.
883. *Ibid.*, para. 2.5 (Clarke CJ).

392. *SPV Osus Limited v HSBC Institutional Trust Services (Ireland) Limited & Ors.*[884] concerned the assignment of a cause of action:

> Assignments of a bare cause of action can therefore be seen as almost the obverse of champerty: whereas in champerty support for litigation is provided in return for payment, in assignment payment is made in return for the action itself. As such, assignment is perhaps if anything more offensive to public policy: in its purest form, an assignment of a bare cause of action involves the outright sale of a cause of action which is then pursued by the assignee (who has no interest or connection to the action other than that created by the assignment itself) to the exclusion of the assignor.[885]

393. The Supreme Court followed its decision in *Perona* to hold that the assignment of a bare cause of action where the assignee has no commercial interest in the assignment is void:

> Following *Persona*, if it is offensive to public policy to permit a person to fund a plaintiff's litigation in return for some part of the proceedings, then the same public policy must apply a fortiori where the third party purchases the claim outright, removes the party from his or her proceedings, and converts them into a mere witness at best.[886]

394. In contrast in *Morrissey v Irish Bank Resolution Corporation Ltd & ors*[887] the Court of Appeal held that a loan sale agreement, comprising the assignment of the loans and the associated right to sue in respect of the recovery of the loans, was not champertous as the assignee had a legitimate interest in the enforcement of the loans.

395. Earlier case law on champerty and maintenance was concerned with 'heir location' agreements rather than third-party funding of litigation. For example, in *McElroy v Flynn*[888] a contract which provided that 25% of the shares in an estate would be paid to the plaintiff, a specialist in tracing next of kin, for assistance in recovering the shares, was held to be champertous and void. However, if the contract was merely to provide information it would have been held to be lawful: *see Fraser v Buckle.*[889]

---

884. [2018] IESC 44.
885. *Ibid.*, para. 15 (O'Donnell J).
886. *Ibid.*, para. 83 (O'Donnell J).
887. [2017] IECA 162.
888. [1991] ILRM 294.
889. [1996] 2 ILRM 34.

3. Contracts to Defraud the Revenue

396. Agreements to defraud the revenue have been held illegal in such cases as understating the purchase price in a sale of real property to avoid or reduce stamp duty liability.[890] However, the burden of proving an illegal contract lies with the party alleging the illegality, and it must be shown that there was an illegal intention.[891] This might be a difficult burden to discharge, particularly where a contract is lawful on its face. In the recent case of *Leggett v Crowley*[892] the defendant alleged that a contract for the sale of property was unenforceable because it was intended to defraud the Revenue by providing for an additional cash payment, over and above the contract price, using untaxed income, but on the balance of probabilities the court held that the additional cash payment had not been agreed to, and therefore the defendant could not rely on illegality as a ground of defence.

397. In unfair dismissals cases employees have been denied compensation where the Employment Appeals Tribunal finds that salary returns by the employer to the Revenue Authority have been reduced, with the knowledge of the employee, to reduce the tax payable on the true remuneration.[893] The Unfair Dismissals (Amendment) Act 1993 now provides that a contravention of the Income Tax Acts or Social Welfare Acts should not prevent a claim for unfair dismissal, but in the absence of this protection employees who are aware of attempts to defraud the Revenue might find their contracts tainted with illegality.[894] The difficulty with these cases is, of course, that the employee often has no say in the matter of how they are paid. In *Red Sale Ltd (In Receivership)* Laffoy J adopted the 'requirement of active participation in addition to knowledge of the facts to render a contact of employment unenforceable',[895] but it is unclear what standard will be applied in future cases.

398. In *Hussein v The Labour Court*[896] a chef from Pakistan who was working long hours in a restaurant in Ireland and being paid with 'pocket money' won an action before the Rights Commissioner which held that there had been multiple breaches of employment legislation, including the National Minimum Wage Act. When the employer failed to pay, the Labour Court ordered it to do so. This was then appealed to the High Court, which held that because the chef was working illegally, his employer having failed to renew his work permit, he was not protected by Irish employment law. This was overturned by the Supreme Court, but on the basis that the High Court was not permitted to review the decision of the Labour Court in the manner in which it did. The case dealt with 'an inherently lawful subject matter, namely, the relationship of employer and employee', as opposed to, say something

890. *Starling Securities Ltd. v Woods*, Unreported, High Court, 24 May 1977.
891. *See Whelan v Kavanagh* [2001] IEHC 14; *Kavanagh v Caulfield* [2002] IEHC 67, para. 7.1.
892. [2019] IEHC 182.
893. *Lewis v Squash (Ireland) Ltd.* [1983] ILRM 363; *Hayden v Sean Quinn Properties Ltd*, Unreported, High Court, 6 December 1993.
894. *See* the argument raised in *Red Sail Ltd (In Receivership)* [2007] 2 IR 361.
895. *Ibid.*
896. [2015] IESC 58.

'inherently against the public interest, such as an agreement to rob or to distribute the proceeds of a robbery', so the Court could focus on the judicial review aspects of the case without examining the rules on legality.[897]

4. Contracts Which Serve to Corrupt Public Officials

399. Contracts which encourage corrupt practices among public officials are, unsurprisingly, illegal and unenforceable.[898]

5. Contracts That Encourage Immorality

400. A contract that might promote or encourage immoral behaviour, particularly behaviour which is viewed as sexually immoral, is illegal.[899] Public policy is of course likely to change over time, and contracts that were in the past considered immoral might now be allowed.

6. Contracts Prejudicial to the Security of the State or to Good Relations with Friendly Foreign States

401. Contracts between nationals and an enemy of the State may be contrary to public policy and unenforceable.[900] In addition, a contract might not be enforced if its performance would be illegal according to the law of the place of performance, even if it would be legal in Ireland.[901]

E. *Void Contracts at Common Law*

402. There are three main kinds of contracts which are deemed to be 'void' at common law. This means that rather than finding the entire contract is unenforceable, the court will attempt to sever the undesirable aspect of the contract and enforce the rest.

1. Agreements to Oust the Jurisdiction of the Courts

403. Agreements which deny recourse to the courts are invalid. However, parties can make provision for a private tribunal or arbitrator to have sole competence

897. *Ibid.*, para. 53.
898. *Lord Mayor of Dublin v Hayes* (1876) 10 IRCL 226.
899. *Pearce v Brooks* (1866) LR 1 Exch. 213.
900. *Ross v Shaw* [1917] 2 IR 367.
901. *Stanhope v Hospitals Trust Ltd* (1936) Ir Jur Rep 25; *Whitecross Potatoes v Coyle* [1978] ILRM 31.

on issues of fact, provided that the rights of the parties to seek review on the basis of an error of law is upheld. It is thus possible to include an arbitration clause in a contract, provided that it does not entirely prevent access to the courts.[902] The effectiveness and interpretation of arbitration clauses is discussed in more detail below.

404. In addition, clauses which provide that an individual is contracting out of a statutory right, such as spousal maintenance, may be void as ousting the jurisdiction of the courts in relation to the statutory right.[903]

2. Agreements Which Subvert the Sanctity of Marriage

405. Historically, agreements which subvert the sanctity of marriage have been held to be void at common law.[904] In Ireland, this is heavily influenced by the constitutional protection of marriage, and this is discussed above.

3. Contracts in Restraint of Trade

406. A contract in restraint of trade is one in which one party agrees to restrict their ability to trade with or work with third parties in the future. A restraint of trade clause may also be referred to as a 'non-compete' clause or a 'restrictive covenant'. In the absence of justifying circumstances a restraint of trade clause is contrary to public policy and void. The party who wishes to enforce the clause must show that it is reasonable in the interests of the contracting parties and the public. In *Macken v. O'Reilly*[905] O'Higgins CJ stated:

> All interference with an individual's freedom of action in trading is per se contrary to public policy and, therefore, void. The general prohibition is subject to the exception that certain restraints may be justified. Restraints, restrictions or interferences are permitted if they are, in the circumstances obtaining, fair and reasonable. Whether what is complained of can be justified on this basis involves a careful examination of all the circumstances – the need for restraint, the object sought to be attained, the interests sought to be protected and the general interest of the public. What is done or sought to be done must be established as being reasonable and necessary and on balance to serve the public interest.[906]

902. *Scott v Avery* (1856) 5 HL Cas 811; *Mansfield v Doolin* (1868) 4 IRCL 17; *Gregg & Co v Fraser & Sons* [1906] 2 IR 545.
903. *Hyman v Hyman* [1929] AC 60; *HD v PD*, Unreported, Supreme Court, 8 May 1978.
904. *See* Clark pp. 552–559.
905. [1979] ILRM 79.
906. [1979] ILRM 79, 90.

407. The law on restraint of trade was recently restated by Clark J in *Murgitroyd & Company Ltd v. Purdy*:[907]

> A restraint on a person working or being engaged in one or more lines of business is by definition a restraint of trade. It is well settled that such a term will not be enforced by the courts unless it meets a two fold test:
>
> (a) it is reasonable as between the parties; and
> (b) it is consistent with the interests of the public. […]
>
> The test seems to be, therefore, as to whether in all the circumstances of the case both the nature of the restriction and its extent is reasonable to protect the goodwill of the employer.[908]

408. The court identified 'duration of the prohibition and the geographical scope of same' as 'important matters to be considered having regard to the nature of the work in question and the structure of the business'.[909] In addition, a more restrictive view is taken of clauses in employment contracts than is taken of covenants given on sale of a business.[910] In that case, a restriction on a patent attorney working in competition with his previous employer in Ireland for a period of twelve months was held to be too wide and unenforceable. A prohibition on soliciting or dealing with customers of the previous employer would have been 'reasonable and sufficient to meet any legitimate requirements' of the employer, i.e., to protect their existing customer base, but a more general prohibition on competition, or restrictions on dealing with potential customers, was held to be unenforceable. It was accepted by the court that there *may* be types of business where it is not practical to distinguish between customers and non-customers, but this was not one of them, as the number of customers was small and identifiable.

409. In *Murgitroyd*, the defendants' legitimate interest was in protecting its existing client base, but it is clear that the principles apply to other legitimate interests, such as the protection of confidential information. In the recent case of *Ryanair v Bellew*[911] the High Court held that Ryanair's departing Chief Operations Officer Peter Bellew was free to join the competitor EasyJet, despite a term in his contract with Ryanair restraining him from working 'in any capacity in any business wholly or partly in competition with [Ryanair] for air passenger services in any market' for twelve months.[912] The High Court found that Ryanair had shown it had

907. [2005] IEHC 159.
908. *Ibid.*, paras 15–17.
909. *Ibid.*
910. *Ibid.*, para. 21. *See also Ryanair v Bellew* [2019] IEHC 907, para. 139.
911. [2019] IEHC 907.
912. The clause stated: 'For a period of 12 months after the termination of your employment you shall not, without the prior written consent of the Company, directly or indirectly in any capacity either on your own behalf or in conjunction with or on behalf of any other Person; a. be employed, engaged, concerned or interested in any capacity in any business wholly or partly in competition with the Company for air passenger services in any market; b. solicit or entice or endeavour to

a 'legitimate interest in exacting a covenant from the defendant to protect the valuable sensitive and confidential commercial, operational and financial information that would come to the defendant's knowledge in the course of his employment'.[913] However, this legitimate interest was limited to roles which would risk the disclosure or use of its protectable information, i.e., roles in airlines in competition with Ryanair in the low cost or low fare sector. The clause in this case, properly construed, would prevent the defendant from taking up employment with *any* European airline, including the 'legacy' or 'high cost' sector, and thus went beyond what was justified.[914] Of course, what is interesting here is that Bellew was not *in fact* going to work with a legacy or high-cost sector; he was intending to work with exactly the kind of airline that Ryanair was said to have a legitimate interest in preventing him joining. However, the Court held that 'the enforceability of the restraint is to be judged by reference to what the employee agreed not to do, rather than what he or she proposes to do after the cessation of employment'.[915] The time at which the court assess the reasonableness of the restraint is the date of the contract.[916]

410. A similar approach had been taken in the previous case of *Net Affinity Ltd. v Conaghan*,[917] in which an agreement not to work for any individual or company providing services similar to that of the plaintiff (a hotel marketing and booking agency) was held to be unenforceable as it was not geographically limited and was too wide to protect the legitimate interest of the plaintiff. The clause in question would have prevented the defendant from working for a company based outside Ireland; the fact that the defendant did not in fact propose to do so was irrelevant. *Net Affinity* also shows that in certain cases, orders might be made to protect confidentiality, even in the absence of a valid restraint of trade or non-compete clause.[918] In this case, although the clause was unenforceable, and the defendant could not be prevented from taking up employment with a new company, Avivo, the court ordered that 'Ms. Conaghan should not approach, solicit or deal with any existing customers of Net Affinity' for a period of twelve months. This was to prevent the defendant from breaching her duty of confidentiality as set out in express terms in her contract of employment.

§4. The Consequences of a Defect of Consent or a Lack of Substantive Validity

411. The consequences of issues of consent are dealt with under each of the sections headings above.

---

solicit or entice away from the Company any person who was employed within in (sic.) a senior executive, managerial, or technical capacity by the Company.'

913. [2019] IEHC 907, para. 208.
914. *Ibid.*, paras 209–210.
915. *Ibid.*, para. 156.
916. *Ibid.*, para. 155.
917. [2011] IEHC 160, [2012] 3 IR 6.
918. *See* [2019] IEHC 907, para. 141.

Chapter 3. The Contents of a Contract

§1. The Different Clauses

I. Ascertaining of Express Terms

412. The express terms of a contract may be oral or in writing, and the lack of formal requirements for the formation of a valid contract and the lack of formal requirements to prove a contract (with the exceptions noted above) may make it difficult to establish precisely what terms were agreed upon by the parties. Negotiations may have been conducted by correspondence, by telephone, by conferences between the parties, and may have taken place over a long period. Not all statements made orally or in writing during negotiations may have been intended to form part of the eventual contract, and the court may have to distinguish between the contents or terms of the contract, and statements made which were not part of the contract, although they may have had some influence in its formation. In addition, it may not always be clear whether certain terms have in fact been incorporated into the contract.

A. *Incorporation of Terms*

413. The issue of whether terms have been incorporated in the contract can arise in a number of different, sometimes overlapping, contexts. A contracting party may sign a contractual document without reading the terms, and then later claim that these terms did not form part of the agreement. Not all the terms of a contract may be written in the main contractual document, but may be in other located in other documents, which may be referred to in the main contractual document or elsewhere. A party may deal with another party on such a regular basis that certain terms are incorporated into each contract because of that course of dealing, even if they are not referred to on each occasion. In addition, if the terms which one party claims are incorporated are particularly onerous, such as exclusion clauses, then additional policy considerations and statutory provisions might apply. At the core of these cases is the question of whether the party was given reasonable notice of the term, and what is 'reasonable' may vary depending on the nature of the clause.

(i) Incorporation by Signature

414. Incorporation by signature is generally seen as the best way to incorporate terms into a contract. Where a party signs a contractual document containing the clause, that party will generally be held bound by the clause, whether he has read it or not.[919] The only exceptions arise if there is fraud, misrepresentation or a plea of

919. *Duff v Great Northern Railway Co.* (1878) 4 LR IR 178; *Clubgear v Mitre Sports International Ltd* [2015] IEHC 708.

non est factum. As a preliminary point, however, the signature must be on a document which a reasonable person would expect to contain contractual terms. In *James Elliott Construction Ltd v Irish Asphalt Ltd*[920] the Irish Supreme Court held that a signed delivery note was not a contractual document, in the sense of a document containing binding contractual terms. The purpose of the delivery docket was to record the material and date delivered, not to set out the contractual arrangement between the parties. The Court also stressed that the document that is signed must actually contain the terms and conditions, and a 'bland reference to terms and conditions alone cannot suffice'.[921]

(ii) Incorporation of a set of terms by reference

415. It is possible to incorporate a set of written conditions into a contract by express reference. For example in *Tierney v An Post*[922] the rules in the Postmaster's Manual were incorporated into the contract by reference, and in *Sweeney v Mulcahy*[923] the conditions of the Royal Institute of Architects of Ireland were incorporated into a contract for renovation works on a house. In this case, the defendant had set at the outset that this was the basis on which she was contracting, and the plaintiff never objected to this. A similar result was reached in *Lynch Roofing Systems Ltd v Bennett & Son Ltd*[924] where there was said to be a shared assumption that the standard conditions of the RIAI would apply. However, in *Irish Pharmaceutical Union v Minister for Health and Children*[925] the Supreme Court held that an agreement between pharmacists and the Health Boards in 1996 did not incorporate the terms of a 1971 memorandum entered into between the Minister for Health and the Irish Pharmaceutical Union:

> Although it is possible, in law, to have a term of a contract imported into another contract, provided the intention to do so is clearly found, it seems to me that, having regard to the background and the context in which the arrangements were negotiated … this intention is not borne out by a proper or reasonable interpretation of any of the terms in either of the agreements reached in 1996.

(iii) Incorporation by reasonable notice

416. Where a set of terms is contained in an unsigned document, or displayed on a sign, the rule is that the court must be satisfied that reasonable notice of the clause was given at or before the time the contract was concluded.[926] Again in this

920. [2014] IESC 74. *See also Noreside Construction ltd v Irish Asphalt Ltd* [2014] IESC 68.
921. [2014] IESC 74, para. 117.
922. High Court, 7 July 1998.
923. [1993] ILRM 289. *See also Kastrup Trae-Aluvinduet A/S v Aluwood Concepts Ltd* [2009] IEHC 577; *Mount Juliet Properties Ltd v Melcarne Developments Ltd & others* [2013] IEHC 286.
924. [1999] 2 IR 450.
925. [2010] IESC 23.
926. *Early v Great Southern Railways Co.* [1940] IR 409.

case, it is not necessary that the party affected should actually have read and understood the clause; it is sufficient if they had reasonable notice of it. In some of the earlier 'railway ticket cases' the courts applied a rather lenient test of what was reasonable notice, for example, holding it to be reasonable notice where a ticket given to a passenger referred to 'conditions and regulations in the company's timetables, books, bills and notices', even though no document containing those conditions was available for inspection by intending passengers at the station where the ticket was issued.[927] Although the cases have not been entirely consistent,[928] McDermott has summarised four principles which can be drawn from the case law:[929]

(1) If you know that the ticket contains conditions, you are bound by them whether you read them or not.
(2) If you did not see or know that the ticket contained any writing, you are not bound by the conditions.
(3) If you knew that there was writing on the ticket and knew or believed that the writing contained conditions, then you are bound by the conditions.
(4) If you knew that there was writing on the ticket but did not know or believe that the writing contained conditions, you will be bound if you were given reasonable notice that the writing contained conditions.[930]

417. The same test of reasonable notice applies where a document such as a ticket is not given but a notice of the terms of the contract, including the exemption clause, is displayed on a notice or notices at the place of contracting.[931] The fact that the affected party may not actually have seen or read the notice is immaterial, provided it was displayed in a reasonably conspicuous manner.

418. Notice of conditions must be given *before* the contract is concluded or it will be ineffective.[932] The leading English authority on this point is *Thornton v Shoe Lane Parking*[933] in which an individual who had parked their car in a car park was not bound by terms contained on a notice located inside the car park, which could only be read *after* having entered into the contract. Although there are Irish 'car park' cases in which it was held that reasonable notice had been given in similar circumstances, these appear to be based on a different interpretation of when the contract was concluded and based on the (unrealistic) premise that the individual could leave the carpark without paying when they became aware of the terms.[934] In

927. *Ibid.*
928. Contrast the result in *Ryan v Great Southern and Western Railway Co* (1898) 12 ILTR 108 (reasonable notice not given).
929. In particular *Parker v South Easter Railway Co* (1877) 2 CPD 416; *Shea v Great Southern Railways Co.* (1944) Ir Jur Rep. 26; *Carroll v An Post* [1996] 1 IR 443.
930. McDermott and McDermott, pp. 458–459.
931. *Shea v Great Southern Railways Co.* (1944) Ir Jur Rep 26; *Henigan v Ballybunion Picture House Ltd.* (1944) Ir Jur Rep 62.
932. *Sproule v Triumph Cycle Co.* [1927] NI 83; *Olley v Marlborough Court Hotel* [1949] 1 KB 532.
933. [1971] 2 QB 163.
934. *O'Beirne v Aer Rianta* (20 May 1987) High Court *ex tempore* Barrington J. *See also Brady v Aer Rianta* (1974), cited in *O'Beirne v Aer Rianta* and McDermott and McDermott p. 465.

addition, the results in these cases have been criticised,[935] and it is unlikely that a similar conclusion would be reached today, particularly in light of the European Communities (Unfair Terms in Consumer Contracts (Regulations) 1995.[936]

(iv) Incorporation of onerous terms

419. When the term which is claimed as part of the contract is a particularly onerous one, then it must be drawn to the other party's attention. This is sometimes known as the 'red hand rule', in reference to Lord Denning's comment that such a term 'would need to be printed in red ink with a red hand point to it – or something equally startling'.[937] In *Carroll v An Post*[938] Costello P adopted this approach in Ireland, stating that 'if the condition relied on by the party tendering the document is particularly onerous or unusual that party must show that it has been fairly and reasonably brought to the other party's attention'.[939] In this case the clause in question – a clause excluding liability for any acts or omissions of National Lottery agents – was held to not be particularly onerous or unusual, and reasonable notice was given of them. Similarly in *Western Meats Ltd. v National Ice and Cold Storage Co. Ltd* it was held that where a specialist service is being offered by a business enterprise, and a standard condition of the contract excludes responsibility, a greater effort may be required to bring notice of such an exemption to the attention of the affected party to incorporate it into the contract.[940] In *Elliott Construction ltd v Irish Asphalt Ltd*[941] the Supreme Court held that a limitation clause in a contract was onerous in nature, and that it had not been brought to the attention of the other contracting party; hence it was not incorporated. In the related case of *Noreside Construction v Irish Asphalt Ltd* the Supreme Court stated:

> It is for the party relying on an exemption clause to give reasonable notice of its terms and conditions and not for the party to be bound to be put on enquiry as to whether or not there may be terms and conditions containing an onerous exemption clause.[942]

420. In *James Elliott* the Supreme Court also noted the importance of the corporate structure, and stated that notification of the term must be 'at a level within the corporation which might reasonably be expected to be effective in terms of bringing the clause to the attention of the appropriate decision making level within

935. McDermott and McDermott pp. 464–465.
936. Although these regulations relate to the enforceability of incorporated terms, rather than incorporation per se.
937. *Thornton v Shoe Lane Parking* [1971] 2 QB 163, 170. *See also Interfoto Picture Library Ltd v Stiletto Visual Programmes Ltd* [1989] QB 433.
938. [1989] IR 443.
939. *Ibid.*, 462. It should be noted that this was based on s. 40 of the Sale of Goods and Supply of Services Act 1980 which provides that reasonable notice must be given of any clause which attempts to exclude liability under s. 30 of the Act, in relation to the provision of services.
940. *Western Meats Ltd. v National Ice and Cold Storage Co. Ltd.* [1982] ILRM 99.
941. [2014] IESC 74.
942. [2014] IESC 68.

that corporation'.[943] Thus, giving notice to the foreman of a site, who would not make management level decisions, would not be equivalent to giving notice to the corporation entering into the contract.

(v) Incorporation by a course of dealing

421. If parties deal with each other on a regular basis it may be possible to incorporate a term by course of dealing. In such a case, it may be held that there is reasonable notice of the terms on which contracting occurs, even if the terms are not explicitly referenced each time a contract is entered into.[944] In *Miley v R. & J. McKechnie*[945] the plaintiff was a regular customer with a dry cleaners, and each time would receive a receipt which stated that all orders were 'accepted without guarantee'. Although technically notice of this term was given after the contract was made, it was nonetheless incorporated by a course of dealing, as the plaintiff had been given the same receipt on a frequent basis in the past and was thus held to have notice of the term. This is a relatively old case in which the plaintiff was a consumer, and it is unlikely that a sufficient 'course of dealing' would be found on similar facts today.[946] The more likely scenario is in the commercial context, where there is a course of dealing between commercial undertakings and thus the parties are on notice of certain terms. In *Clare Taverns v Gill*[947] an exclusive jurisdiction clause contained on the back of an invoice was incorporated into a contract by means of a statement on the face of the invoice stating 'All Transactions are subject to standard conditions of sale overleaf'. McGuinness J stated:

> In the submissions made before this Court it was not seriously suggested that the practice of printing general conditions of sale on the reverse side of invoices and similar documents, with a reference on the face of the document to the said conditions, was not a common commercial practice in the type of international trade with which we are concerned here. Indeed, from the point of view of practical experience every ordinary consumer, and still more anyone engaged in trade or commerce, must be familiar with this type of document.[948]

422. This statement was subsequently approved by the Supreme Court.[949] Accepted commercial practice and an established course of dealings might also explain the otherwise strange result in *Leo Laboratories v Crompton BV*,[950] where the defendant stated that the order had been accepted 'subject to our general terms

943. [2014] IESC 74, approving [2011] IEHC 269, para. 252.
944. *See Sugar Distributors Ltd v Monaghan Cash and Carry Ltd* [1982] ILRM 99.
945. (1949) 84 ILTR 89.
946. And even if it were found, such a clause would most likely be unfair under the European Communities (Unfair Terms in Consumer Contracts) Regulations 1995 and thus invalid.
947. [2000] 1 IR 286. This case concerned the Brussels Convention.
948. [2000] 1 IR 286, para. 24. *See also Sugar Distributors Ltd v Monaghan Cash and Carry Ltd* [1982] ILRM 99.
949. *McCabe Builders (Dublin) Ltd v Sagamu Developments Ltd* [2011] 3 IR 480.
950. [2005] 2 IR 225.

and conditions of sale and delivery as stated on the back hereof'. Even though the terms were not in fact on the back of the document, the plaintiff was held to be on notice of them, and they were incorporated into the contract.

B. *Terms and Mere Representations*

423. The courts may have to decide whether a particular statement made during negotiations is a term (sometimes referred to as a 'warranty' in a general sense), giving rise to contractual liability, or a mere representation, which induced the making of a contract but which was not intended to form part of the concluded contract. If the statement is a term, the remedies that are available for breach of this term will depend on whether the term is classified a 'warranty' (in the technical sense),[951] 'condition' or 'innominate term'. If a statement is classified as a mere representation, then if it is false it may give rise to an action in misrepresentation. Alternatively, the statement might be a sales 'puff', or a statement with no legal consequences, in circumstances where no reasonable person could believe it was intended to be relied upon. It is also possible for a statement made to be classified as a representation *and* a warranty, with the plaintiff free to choose the most suitable remedy.[952] The preferable situation will usually be to show that it is a warranty, as the remedies for misrepresentation may be limited.[953]

424. The onus of proof is on the party claiming that a particular statement is a warranty.[954] In deciding whether a particular statement is a term or a mere representation, the court will take into account certain considerations:[955]

(i) The time the statement was made

In contracts for the sale of goods, statements made about the goods at, or just about, the time the contract was concluded will generally be regarded as terms of the contract.[956]

(ii) If the contract is later reduced to writing, whether the statement was included in a written contract

If the contract is reduced to writing and a statement made in the previous negotiations is not included in the document it may suggest that it was intended to be a mere representation. However, it must be remembered that the courts have found that oral statements might be coupled with written terms to form the complete contract.

(iii) The special knowledge or skill of the representor

---

951. Warranty here refers to the technical meaning of a warranty, as a contractual term giving rise to a remedy in damages for breach.
952. *Carey v Independent Newspapers Ltd* [2003] IEHC 67.
953. *See* the discussion above at para. 286.
954. *Fitzpatrick v Harty and Ballsbridge International Bloodstock Sales Ltd* High Court, 25 February 1983.
955. *See* McDermott and McDermott p. 352.
956. But in *Schawel v Reade* [1913] 21 R 81 (H.L.) the House of Lords accepted a statement made three weeks before the negotiations concluded as a term of the contract.

In *Bank of Ireland v Smith*[957] it was stated that there is a 'welcome tendency to treat a representation made in connection with a sale as being a warranty, unless the person who made it can show that he was innocent of fault with it'. The court is more likely than not to regard a statement made by a party to the contract who has expert or special knowledge of the subject matter as intended to be a term of the contract, whereas a statement by someone who is not an expert (or who is essentially a consumer) will be viewed as a representation. In *Oscar Chess v Williams*[958] an individual exchanged his car with a car dealer in return for a new car, with both parties relying on the registration book in their belief that this was a 1948 model. When it transpired that the car was in fact a 1939 model, the buyer attempted to argue that there had been a warranty that the car was a 1948 mode, and claimed damages for breach of that warranty. It was held however that this was merely a representation. In contrast, in *Dick Bentley Productions v Harold Smith*[959] a statement by a car dealer regarding the car's mileage was held to be a warranty, as the dealer was in a better position that the buyer to verify the truth of the statement. Although these are English cases, they are generally accepted in Ireland.

(iv) The importance of the statement

In *Carey v Independent Newspapers*[960] the plaintiff, a journalist, had accepted a contract of employment on the basis of a statement that she could work from home in the mornings owing to childcare needs. The plaintiff was subsequently asked to work the early shift in the office and was dismissed when she could not do so. It was held that the statement made was both a term of the contract (and a misrepresentation), with the court stating that the importance of the representation to the entry into the contract by the parties was a significant factor in finding that there was a warranty. In *Rothwell*[961] the buyer of a car specifically sought a car with a fuel consumption of fifty miles per gallon. A reassurance to this effect by the seller seems to have been treated as a warranty, with damages being awarded when the car's fuel consumption failed to meet this standard.

(v) An indication that the statement can be relied upon and need not be verified

In *Schawel v Reade*[962] the seller of a horse stated during an inspection of the horse 'You need not look for anything; the horse is perfectly sound. If there was anything the matter with the horse I would tell you.' This was held to be a warranty.

(vi) The description used by the parties

957. [1966] IR 646. *See also Murphy v Hennessy* (1897) 31 ILT 404.
958. [1957] 1 WLR 370.
959. [1965] 1 WLR 623.
960. [2004] 3 IR 52. *See also King v Aer Lingus* [2002] 3 IR 481; *McGrath v Trintech Technologies Ltd* [2005] 4 IR 382; *AIB Mortgage Bank v Hayes* [2016] IEHC 280.
961. *Rothwell v Arrowdale Ltd t/a Sheehy Motors* [2007] IEHC 395.
962. [1913] 2 IR 64.

Whether or not the parties use words like 'warrant' or 'warranty' are not determinative of whether the statement is a warranty[963] although it may be indicative.[964]

II. Implied Terms

425. Terms may be implied into a contract by the court, by legislation or by the Constitution.

A. *Terms Implied by the Court*

426. The courts have been traditionally slow to interfere with the bargain the parties themselves have made by implying further terms into a contract. In *Tradax Ireland v Irish Grain Board*[965] McCarthy J stated:

> It is not the function of a court to write a contract for parties who have met upon commercially equal terms; if such parties want to enter into unreasonable, unfair or even disastrous contracts, that is their business, not the business of the courts.[966]

427. In the same case, O'Higgins J stated that:

> [T]his power [to imply terms] must be exercised with care. The courts have no role in acting as contract makers, or as counsellors, to advise or direct what agreement ought to have been made by two people, whether businessmen or not, who choose to enter into contractual relations with each other.[967]

428. Where the courts imply a term, they have justified it on the basis that they were merely implementing the unexpressed intention of the parties themselves. As Maguire CJ put the matter in *Ward v Spivack Ltd.*,[968] where there has been a failure by the parties to express their intention on a matter 'the judge may supply the further terms which will implement [the parties'] presumed intention and in a hallowed phrase give 'business efficacy' to the contract. In doing this he purports at least to do merely what the parties would have done themselves had they thought of the matter'.[969] Thus, the courts are not creating a new term; they are finding a term that was there all along, but merely unexpressed in the contract.

963. *Scales v Scanlan* (1843) 6 ILRCL 432.
964. *Manor Park Homebuilders Ltd v AIG Europe (Ireland) Ltd* [2008] IEHC 174.
965. [1984] IR 1.
966. [1984] IR 1, 26 per McCarthy J.
967. *Tradax (Ireland) Ltd. v Irish Grain Board Ltd.* [1984] IR 1, 14 per Higgins CJ.
968. [1957] IR 40.
969. [1957] IR 40, 61.

429. In *Flynn v Breccia*,[970] the High Court found that that the following principles emerged when considering implied terms:

(1) it must be reasonable and equitable;
(2) it must be necessary to give business efficacy to the contract, so that no term will be implied if the contract is effective without it;
(3) it must be so obvious that 'it goes without saying';
(4) it must be capable of clear expression; and
(5) it must not contradict any express term of the contract … .[971]

430. Three tests have emerged which can help in ascertaining when a term might be implied as a matter of fact: the business efficacy test, the officious bystander test, and terms which are implied as a matter of custom. However, there is not always a clear delineation between the officious bystander test and the business efficacy test – they overlap and are often applied in conjunction with each other. Moreover, although they are listed separately in *Flynn v Breccia*, as (2) and (3) respectively, in the Court of Appeal it was stated that the parties agreed that 'that (2) and (3) may be alternatives (and not necessarily cumulative) accords with the law in this jurisdiction as set out in *Sweeney v Duggan*'.[972]

431. There is a separate line of jurisprudence regarding terms implied as matter of law, based not on the intentions of the parties but rather as a matter of policy based on the nature of the contract itself. Thus certain terms have been implied as a matter of policy into landlord/tenant contracts, particularly in relation to social housing,[973] or in employment contracts.[974] For example in *Berber v Dunnes Stores*[975] there was said to be implied in a contract of employment a mutual obligation that neither the employer nor the employee will conduct themselves in a way likely to damage the relationship of confidence and trust between them. However, we now turn to the tests used by the courts when implying a term as of fact, as opposed to law.

---

970. Haughton J, High Court, 13 August 2015, para. 126.
971. Referring to *BP Refinery (Westernport) Pty. Ltd. v Shire of Hastings* [1977] 180 CLR 266 and cited by the Court of Appeal in *Flynn v Breccia* [2017] IECA 74, para. 77. *See also* the slightly different list in *Meridian Communications v Eircell Ltd* High Court, 5 April 2001, O'Higgins J.
972. [2017] IECA 74, para. 77.
973. *Liverpool City Council v Irwin* [1977] AC 239, which was referred to in *Sweeney v Duggan* [1997] 2 ILRM 216; *Siney v Dublin Corporation* [1980] IR 400; *Burke v Corporation of Dublin* [1991] IR 341.
974. On terms implied into employment contracts, *see McGrath v Trintech Technologies* [2004] IEHC342; *Quigley v Complex Tooling and Moulding* [2009] IESC 526; *Sheehy v Ryan* [2008] IESC 14.
975. [2009] IESC 10.

1. The Officious Bystander Test

432. The officious bystander test is based on the premise that the term was so obvious that there was no need to state it. If a third party (the 'officious bystander') overheard the contractual negotiations and decided to ask the parties whether this term was part of their contract, they would both say that it was:

> *Prima facie* that which in any contract is left to be implied and need not be expressed is something so obvious that it goes without saying; so that if while the parties were making their bargain, an officious bystander were to suggest some express provision for it in the agreement, they would testily suppress him with a common 'oh of course!'[976]

433. This test is only fulfilled where both parties would have answered the bystander's hypothetical question in the affirmative. In *Carna Foods Ltd v Eagle Star Insurance*[977] the defendant was the plaintiff's insurer, but refused to renew the insurance policy and also further gave no reason for this. The plaintiff claimed that there was an implied term that reasons must be given by the insurer in the event of refusal to renew, but the court refused to imply such a term as it was likely that had this arisen as an issue during contract formation that the insurer would have refused such a term.

434. An unusual context for this type of implied term was the case of *M.R. v T.R. (Frozen embryos)*.[978] In this case a married couple underwent in vitro fertilisation treatment and had embryos frozen as a result of that treatment. Subsequently their relationship broke down, and a question arose as to whether there these frozen embryos could still be used. The agreement they had entered into when starting the treatment made no mention of what was to happen if the couple separated, nor was there any express agreement regarding what was to happen to these embryos. The court held that it could not be said to be the presumed intention of the parties that the remaining frozen embryos would be implanted in these circumstances, and thus refused to imply a term that they could be used.

435. In *Horan v O'Reilly*[979] the plaintiff claimed to be entitled to one-fifth of a sum of money won by a lottery syndicate. The lottery syndicate was an informal arrangement, whereby one individual, Mr O'Brien, would collect money weekly from the members of the syndicate to purchase lottery tickets, and any winnings would be shared equally between the members of the syndicate. The difficulty arose because the plaintiff was in arrears when the syndicate won a large sum of money. The court thus had the difficult job of ascertaining the terms of the contractual agreement between the parties, but it was held by the Supreme Court that it had not

976. *Shirlaw v Southern Foundries* [1939] 2 KB 206, cited with approval in *Sweeney v Duggan* [1997] 2 ILRM 211, 216.
977. [1997] 2 ILRM 499.
978. [2006] IEHC 221 (*see also* [2006] IEHC 359 and [2009] IESC 82 on the Constitutional issues).
979. [2008] IESC 65.

been part of the original arrangement between the syndicate that individual members could pay in arrears and nonetheless remain a member of the syndicate. Nor could any such arrangement be implied, as 'it would not be obvious to any innocent bystander that such an obligation was imposed on Mr O'Brien on behalf of the other syndicate members'.[980]

2. The 'Business Efficacy' Test

436. The leading case on the business efficacy test is *The Moorcock,*[981] which has been applied in Ireland on a number of occasions.[982] The court presumes that both parties intended the contract to be workable (that it has 'business efficacy'), and it may imply an unexpressed term into the contract because it is necessary to make it workable. It is important here that the term must be *necessary* and not merely 'fair and reasonable'.[983] In *Sweeney v Duggan,*[984] for example, an employee was injured while operating a drill, but could not claim compensation from his employer as they were in liquidation and had no employer liability insurance. He argued that it was a term of his contract of employment that the managing director of the employer company had a personal duty to procure employer's liability insurance or warn the plaintiff that no such insurance existed. The term could not implied as it was not necessary, and the contract operated without it. In addition, it was not possible to formulate the term with 'reasonable precision'.[985]

437. In *Airscape Ltd v Heaslon Properties Ltd*[986] it was held that the business efficacy test required the implication of a term that the defendant would not unreasonably delay or withhold co-operation for the carrying out of works by the plaintiff. Similarly in *Meridian Communications v Eircell Ltd*[987] the actions of the defendant in failing to supply the plaintiff with transfer books amounted to a breach of an implied term that either party would not deliberately seek to frustrate the operation by the other party. However, the Irish courts do not generally recognise a general implied duty of good faith in contractual performance: *Flynn v Breccia.*[988] Again, the question is what is necessary to make the contract work, rather than what may seem to be reasonable or fair. This is illustrated by *Harrington v Gulland Property Finance Ltd (No. 2)*[989] in which it was argued that there was an implied term in a loan contract that the lender 'could not unilaterally and without cause, call in

980. *Ibid.*, para. 36.
981. (1883) 14 PD 64.
982. *See*, for example, *Ward v Spivack Ltd.* [1957] IR 40; *Grehan v Medical Incorporated* [1986] IR 528.
983. *Dakota Packaging ltd v Wyeth Medica Ireland / AHP Manufacturing BV* [2005] 2 IR 54, 106.
984. [1997] ILRM 211.
985. *Ibid. Dakota Packaging ltd v Wyeth Medica Ireland / AHP Manufacturing BV* [2005] 2 IR 54.
986. [2008] IEHC 82.
987. High Court 5 April 2001 O'Higgins J.
988. [2017] IECA 74, [99] per Finlay Geoghegan J.
989. [2018] IEHC 445.

the loan in a way that was capricious, arbitrary or unreasonable'.[990] Although this possibility had been suggested in a previous case,[991] it was rejected here on the basis that it would be contrary to the express term that demand for the repayment of loan facilities could be made at any time and without stating any reason, and there was no obligation to exercise this unilateral right in good faith. In *Cheldon Property Finance Dac v Hale*[992] an attempt to imply a term into a loan agreement that the loan would not be transferred to a third party similarly failed as it contradicted an express term of the agreement.

438. In long-term commercial relationships, one party may seek to imply a term that the other must give reasonable notice before terminating their arrangement. As a starting point, it is clear that there must first be a contract in which to imply such a term – an ongoing supply arrangement between two parties which falls short of a binding contractual arrangement can be terminated at any point, and there is no need (and indeed, no method) to imply a term regarding the giving of reasonable notice.[993] In *Irish Welding v Philips Electrical (Ireland) Ltd*[994] it was held that a sole agency agreement could be terminated after a reasonable period of time (rather than without any notice), but these cases will depend on the intentions of the parties and the context of the contract formation. Moreover, it must be possible to formulate the notice period and parties' contractual obligations during that period with sufficient precision.[995]

3. Terms Implied by Custom

439. A term may be implied into a contract where it is clear that people in the particular industry in question regard the custom as contractually binding. The principles according to which terms may be implied by custom and usage were restated by Finlay Geoghegan J. in *Noreside Construction Ltd. v Irish Asphalt Ltd.*:[996]

> The principles according to which terms will be implied in a contract by custom are not in dispute. McDermott on '*Contract Law*' … identifies the basic question … as being whether, 'there was in the trade, a uniform … practice, so well defined and recognised that the contracting parties must be assumed to have had it in their minds when they contracted'. McDermott further identifies … the following as a non-exhaustive list of the requirements which must be fulfilled before a custom may be implied:

990. *Ibid.*, para. 100.
991. *ACC Bank Plc. v Kelly* [2011] IEHC 7, para. 7.7, per Clarke J. *See also O'Flynn v Carbon Finance Ltd.* [2014] IEHC 458, paras 151–152 per Irvine J.
992. [2017] IEHC 432.
993. *Dakota Packaging ltd v Wyeth Medica Ireland / AHP Manufacturing BV* [2005] 2 IR 54.
994. Unreported, High Court, 8 October 1976. *See also Ward v Spivack Ltd* [1957] IR 40.
995. *See Dakota Packaging ltd v Wyeth Medica Ireland / AHP Manufacturing BV* [2005] 2 IR 54.
996. [2011] IEHC 364, affirmed on appeal by the Supreme Court [2014] IESC 68.

(i) The custom must have acquired such notoriety that the parties must be taken to have known of it and intended it should form part of the contract.
(ii) The custom must be certain.
(iii) The custom must be reasonable, and the more unreasonable it is the harder it will be to prove that it exists.
(iv) Until the courts take judicial notice of a custom it must be proved by clear and convincing evidence.
(v) The custom must not be inconsistent with the express contract.[997]

440. For example in *O Connaill v The Gaelic Echo*[998] a term was implied into a Dublin journalist's contract of employment that he would receive holiday pay, on the basis of evidence that holiday pay for journalists was the custom in Dublin. However, any such custom must be 'so notorious, well known and acquiesced in that in the absence of agreement in writing it is to be taken as one of the terms of the contract between the parties'.[999] In *Carroll v Dublin Bus*[1000] there was held to be a custom that a bus driver returning to work after illness would be given a light route, where possible.

441. However, in general it is difficult to prove the existence of a custom. In *O'Reilly v Irish Press*[1001] it was stated:

> [A] custom or usage of any kind is a difficult thing to establish. Before a usage such as is contended for here can be held to be established it must be proved by persons whose position in the world [being considered by the Court] entitles them to speak of with certainty and knowledge of its existence. I have to be satisfied that it is so notorious, well known and acquiesced in that in the absence of agreement in writing it is to be taken as one of the terms of the contract between the parties.[1002]

442. In this case there was held to be no custom that chief sub-editors in newspapers were entitled to six months' notice, and hence no term could be implied on this basis. In *P.H. and others v An tAire Dlí Agus Cirt, Comhionannas Agus Cosanta*[1003] the court refused to imply a term that an allowance over and above the contractual rate of pay was to be paid to the plaintiff on the basis of a custom in the Criminal Assets Bureau. It was held that while 'Bureau officers' might have customarily been entitled to such an allowance, the plaintiff was not a 'Bureau officer', but rather an accountant, and there was no such custom regarding accountants. In addition, it was held that any such implied term would contradict the express terms

997. [2011] IEHC 364, para. 46.
998. (1958) 92 ILTR 156.
999. *O'Reilly v Irish Press* (1937) ILTR 194.
1000. [2005] IEHC 278.
1001. (1937) ILTR 194.
1002. This statement has recently been confirmed by Hedigan J. in *McCarthy v Health Service Executive* [2010] IEHC 75.
1003. [2019] IEHC 335.

of the contract. In *Noreside Construction Ltd. v Irish Asphalt Ltd.*[1004] there was no limitation of the liability of the defendant for defective product implied by custom into the contract of supply between the plaintiff and the defendant.

B. Terms Implied by Statute

443. Numerous statutes imply terms into particular kinds of contract, e.g., sale of goods, hire purchase, contracts of tenancy, employment contracts. It is not possible in a work of this nature to deal in detail with all of these statutes, but some of the more important are considered further in the special contracts in Part II.

C. Terms Implied under the Constitution

444. Terms may be implied in a contract in order to give effect to a constitutional right.[1005] In *Meskell v C.I.É.*[1006] the Supreme Court held that the constitutional right of disassociation (the right not to join an association or union)[1007] must be respected by an employer and would trump any common law right to dismiss an employee. In *Glover v BLN*[1008] it was held to be an implied term of a contract of employment that the employee will have a fair hearing before being dismissed,[1009] and principles of constitutional justice dictate that disciplinary proceedings for breach of club or association rules must be fair.[1010]

III. Standard Terms and Exemption Clauses

445. Standard terms, including exemption clauses, are widely used in commercial practice. The Irish Law Reform Commission has recognised that exemption clauses serve a purpose in the allocation of risk between the parties:

> In modern commercial transactions, contracting parties use exemption clauses in order to allocate the risk of certain events. For example, if A hires B to store his goods, a clause in the contract between A and B may exclude B's liability to compensate A for in the event that the goods are damaged in storage. Hence, A takes the risk that he may suffer a loss. This will be reflected in the price of the contract between A and B: A will have to either insure against the risk of

---

1004. [2011] IEHC 364, affirmed on appeal by the Supreme Court [2014] IESC 68.
1005. *See* Clark *Contract Law in Ireland* pp. 226–234 for discussion.
1006. [1973] IR 121.
1007. Article 40.6.1 and 40.6.2, *Bunreacht na hÉireann*.
1008. [1973] IR 388.
1009. Article 40.3, *Bunreacht na hÉireann*. *See also Gunn v Bord an Choláiste Náisiúnta Ealaíne is Deartha* [1990] 2 IR 168 (termination of employment must be in line with principles of natural and constitutional justice).
1010. *Bolger v Osborne* [2000] 1 ILRM 250; *O'Connell v Turf Club* [2015] IESC 57; *McMahon v Irish Road Haulage Association* [2009] IEHC 145.

loss, or self-insure, and thus the price payable to B will be reduced. If A wants to enter into a contract with B under which he has a right of recourse to B if the goods are damaged, i.e. a contract where B takes the risk of damage to the goods, then the price payable to B will increase.[1011]

446. However, certain standard terms can be viewed as onerous or unfair, particularly where they are very one-sided, and one party has not had a genuine opportunity to become acquainted with the term or to negotiate it with the other party. This is more likely to happen in a business-to-consumer (B2C) relationship, and less likely to happen where contracting parties are of equal bargaining strength and have had a genuine opportunity to negotiate important terms such as exclusion clauses. The response to this problem has been multifaceted, and includes strict judicial approaches to the incorporation of onerous standard terms (as discussed above), strict judicial rules on the interpretation of those terms, and finally legislative intervention, particularly in the area of consumer protection.

A. *The Interpretation of Exclusion Clauses*

(i) The contra proferentem rule

447. The most well-known principle when interpreting an exclusion clause is the *contra proferentem* rule, which provides that the *'proferens'* (the person who inserted the exemption clause, and who is usually the person seeking to rely on it) should draft the clause clearly and explicitly. Any ambiguity would be resolved against them in favour of the party adversely affected by the clause.[1012] For example, in cases concerning contracts for the sale of goods, clauses exempting liability for 'breach of warranty' were held not to be sufficient to exclude liability for 'breach of condition' (in particular the implied conditions found in the Sale of Goods Act 1893).[1013] This rule can also apply outside the context of exclusion clauses – for example in *Danske Bank v RQB Ltd*,[1014] McGovern J. stated that guarantees must be strictly construed with ambiguities being resolved in the guarantor's favour.

448. The *contra proferentem* rule was applied by the Irish Supreme Court in *Analog Devices BV v Zurich Insurance.*[1015] In this case the plaintiffs claimed on insurance policies for loss arising from the negligence of an employee who was working on the 'maintenance' of equipment. The insurers sought to rely on exclusion clauses in the policies which excluded, *inter alia*, liability for loss or damage resulting from 'faulty workmanship', and did not mention 'maintenance', despite

1011. Law Reform Commission, *Report on Privity of Contract and Third Party Rights* (LRC 88-2008) para. 2.40.
1012. *See Alexander v Irish National Stud Co. Ltd.*, Unreported, High Court, 10 June 1977.
1013. *Wallis, Son and Wells v Pratt and Haynes* [1910] 2 KB 1003.
1014. *Danske Bank a/s trading as National Irish Bank v RQB Ltd (formerly known as Redquartz Boundary Ltd)* [2010] IEHC 347.
1015. *Analog Devices BV v Zurich Insurance* [2005] IESC 12.

the existence of such clauses in standard exclusions used in the insurance industry and in other policies issued by the first defendant. The Court held that in interpreting the policies, the Court had to give effect to the intentions of the parties, ascertained objectively from the words used in the policies and taking into consideration the surrounding circumstances or factual matrix.[1016] Any ambiguity in the exclusion clauses in the policies had to be construed *contra proferentem*, i.e., against the insurer. It was held that in excluding liability for 'faulty workmanship' in the insurance policies, the defendants had not excluded liability for negligence in the course of carrying out maintenance work.[1017]

449. When parties are of equal bargaining power, and use greater sophistication and care in drafting exemption clauses, the courts find it more difficult to apply the *contra proferentem* rule,[1018] pointing out that it is not always clear who is the *proferens*.[1019] This restriction of the *contra proferentem* principle can be seen recently in the Irish Supreme Court, with O'Donnell J stating it 'may usefully be applied not just to exemption clauses but to a contract in general but normally only as a last resort in the case of ambiguity and not as a general approach'.[1020] In *Law Society of Ireland v MIBI* Clark J in the Supreme Court viewed the *contra proferentem* principle as merely an application of the general rules on contractual interpretation:

> The reasonable and informed person would be likely to assume that an individual who wished to insert a clause into a contract specifically for their own protection or benefit would ensure that the clause was expressed in clear terms. It would follow that, provided that the terms were clear and that there was no ambiguity, the clause should stand and provide whatever protection its terms permitted. However, if the clause were unclear and an ambiguity existed, then the clause should be construed against the profferer for the reasonable and informed observer would be likely to take the view that, if greater protection or benefit had truly been agreed, the profferer would have ensured that it was clearly specified.[1021]

(ii) The interpretation of clauses which restrict liability for negligence

450. In drafting an exemption clause the onus is placed on the *proferens* to cover clearly all the possible grounds of liability he wishes to be exempted from, that is,

1016. Following *I.C.S. Ltd. v West Bromwich B.S.* [1998] 1 WLR 896, discussed below in para. 495. In this case, the surrounding circumstances included the fact that maintenance would have been mentioned in other contracts in the industry.

1017. It was also held that exclusion clauses in both policies relating to contamination and pollution were intended to exclude only environmental damage and not the damage which in fact occurred.

1018. *Tokn Grass Products Ltd. v Sexton & Co.*, Unreported, High Court, 1 October 1983.

1019. *See Transocean Drilling UK Ltd v Providence Resources Plc* [2016] EWCA Civ 372, para. 20 (UK).

1020. *ICDL GCC Foundation FZ-LLC & Another v European Computer Driving Licence Foundation Limited* [2012] IESC 550.

1021. *Law Society of Ireland v MIBI* [2017] IESC 31, para. 10.46 Clark J.

contractual, statutory, or tortious, because any omission or ambiguity in drafting may result in a decision adverse to him. A difficulty can arise when the clause in question does not specifically mention a cause of action – e.g., negligence – but uses wording which could potentially cover this cause of action. In *Regan v RIAC*[1022] for example, an exclusion clause which excluded 'liability arising out of accidents howsoever caused, resulting in damage and/or personal injury to my person and/or property' was held to be wide enough to cover accidents caused by negligence, even though there was no express reference to negligence. In contrast, in *Alexander v Irish National Stud Co. Ltd*[1023] a disclaimer of responsibility 'in the event of an accident occurring' to horses was not effective to exempt the National Stud from liability for an accident to a horse caused by the negligence of its employees of the Stud.

451. Of course, it needs to be remembered that to bring a claim for breach of contract it is not necessary to show 'negligence'.[1024] Hence a clause which excludes liability for 'negligence' will not exclude a claim for breach of contract, and a clause which excludes liability for breach of contract will not exclude a claim for negligence, and the plaintiff remains free to bring any cause of action appropriate to them.[1025]

452. In some cases, a clause might exclude or limit liability provided loss is not caused by 'a wilful act' or 'gross negligence'. For example in *ICDL GCC Foundation FZ-LLC v European Computer Driving Licence Foundation Ltd*[1026] the relevant clause stated:

> The Licensee's exclusive remedy and the total liability of ECDL-F in respect of any cause of action relating to or arising out of this Contract will, to the extent that it is not caused by a wilful act or gross negligence by ECDL-F, not exceed 10 per cent of the total amounts paid to ECDL-F by the Licensee, or €50,000.00, whichever is the lesser amount.

453. In relation to the concept of a 'wilful act' it was held that it suffices that the act is 'done deliberately' and it is 'not necessary that it be committed with the intention to injure or that the person committing it knows that it is unlawful'. Here the

1022. [1990] 1 IR 278.
1023. *Alexander v Irish National Stud Co Ltd.*, Unreported, High Court, 10 June 1977.
1024. *ICDL GCC Foundation FZ-LLC v European Computer Driving Licence Foundation Ltd* [2012] IESC 55.
1025. *See Henderson v Merrett Syndicates Ltd* [1995] 2 AC 145, per Lord Goff: 'I do not find it objectionable that the claimant may be entitled to take advantage of the remedy which is most advantageous to him, subject only to ascertaining whether the tortious duty is so inconsistent with the applicable contract that, in accordance with ordinary principle the parties must be taken to have agreed that the tortious remedy is to be limited or excluded.'
1026. [2012] IESC 55.

parties had purported to terminate the contract, but it transpired that that this termination was a breach of contract. It was held that this act (i.e., purporting to terminate) was 'intentional' and thus a 'wilful act', meaning that the party could not then rely on the limitation clause in the contract.

454. The Supreme Court had difficulty interpreting the rather ambiguous concept of 'gross negligence', as this is not in fact a concept used in Irish tort law. However, it accepted that the phrase was intended to create a distinction between 'ordinary' negligence and 'gross' negligence, and approved the definition of Clark J that it was 'a degree of negligence where whatever duty of care may be involved has not been met by a significant margin'. Thus the limitation clause would be sufficient to limit liability unless the plaintiff could prove negligence (which, again, is not normally required for a claim of breach of contract) *and* that the negligence 'amounted to a significant degree to a breach of that party's duty to the other party under the contract'.[1027]

(iii) The interpretation of clauses which exempt liability for fundamental breach of contract

455. The courts will refuse to give effect to a clause which exempts liability for a fundamental breach of contract. Sometimes this can be done by utilising rules of interpretation, such the 'main purpose' rule which provides that an exemption clause should be construed so as to ensure that it does not defeat the main purpose of the contract.[1028] However, even a clause which clearly intends to exempt liability for fundamental breach may not be relied upon. This is often described as the 'doctrine of fundamental breach of contract' – a phrase which rather confusingly refers to the approach of the courts to clauses excluding liability for fundamental breach of contract, rather than the fundamental breach itself. In *Clayton Love v B. & I. Steampacket Co.* the Irish Supreme Court held that this was a rule of law in Ireland – in other words, it would not be possible to exclude liability for fundamental breach, even if the parties intended to include the exclusion. However, in the UK in *Photo Production Ltd v Securicor Transport Ltd*[1029] the House of Lords stated that it was not a rule of law, but a principle of construction – parties of equal bargaining power who wish to exclude liability for a fundamental breach should be able to do so. Some Irish judges[1030] have since indicated that they approve the reasoning in *Photo Production Ltd. v Securicor Transport Ltd* but a Supreme Court decision would be necessary to adopt this approach.

(iv) Excluding liability for a misrepresentation

1027. The clause could not however be relied upon as the act was considered a 'wilful act'.
1028. *Glynn v Margetson* [1893] AC 351.
1029. [1980] AC 827.
1030. Barrington J in *Western Meats Ltd. v National Ice and Cold Storage Co. Ltd.* [1982] ILRM 99; O'Hanlon J in *Fitzpatrick v Harty Ballsbridge International Bloodstock Sales*, Unreported, High Court, 25 February 1983.

456. The exclusion of liability for a misrepresentation is discussed above.[1031]

B. Statutory Control of Exemption Clauses and Unfair Terms

457. It is well recognised that in certain situations exemption clauses and other standard form terms may be one-sided and unfair to a contracting party (in particular a consumer) who might not have the ability to become acquainted with the term or to negotiate it. In *McCord v ESB* the Irish Supreme Court recognised that consumers often enter into 'contracts of adhesion' where the consumer 'has no standing to ask that a single iota of the draft contract presented to be changed before he signs it. He must lump it or leave it'.[1032] The Court added that an approach which assumes that the consumer has freedom of choice would be 'largely based on legal fictions'.[1033] Although the courts were able to develop doctrines, such as the rules on incorporation of contract or the doctrine of fundamental breach, to protect the weaker party in this situation, legislative intervention was also necessary. The two main pieces of legislation which restrict the use of exemption clauses are the Sale of Goods and Services Act 1980 and the Unfair European Communities (Unfair Terms in Consumer Contracts) Regulations 1995, as amended. The Regulations control unfair terms in consumer contracts generally and are not limited to exclusion clauses; however the 1980 Act applies in certain respects to both consumer and commercial contracts.

(i) The Sale of Goods and Supply of Services Act 1980

458. Section 55 of the Sale of Goods Act 1893, as substituted by section 22 of the Sale of Goods and Services Act 1980, restricts the use of exclusion clauses in contrast for the sale of goods. Section 12 of the Sale of Goods Act 1893, which states that the seller must have the right to sell the goods, can *never* be excluded, *even if* both parties are non-consumers. Any attempt to exclude section 12 is void. If the buyer is a consumer,[1034] then sections 13 (sale by description), 14 (merchantability and fitness for purpose) and 15 (sale by sample) of the Sale of Goods Act cannot be excluded. However, even if the buyer is not a consumer, any attempt to exclude sections 13, 14 or 15 must be 'fair and reasonable'. The onus is on the party relying on the clause to show that it is fair and reasonable.

459. In addition, section 40 of the Sale of Goods and Supply of Services Act 1980 provides that any attempt to exclude or restrict the provisions of section 39

1031. At paras 311 et seq.

1032. *Mc Cord v ESB* [1980] 1 ILRM 153, 161.

1033. *Ibid.* It should be noted that this case concerned contracts entered into with an electricity supplier who at the time had a monopoly on electricity supply in Ireland.

1034. Section 3 of 1980 Act provides that a party is a consumer if he neither makes the contract in the course of a business nor holds himself out as doing so, the other party does make the contract in the course of business, and the goods or services supplied are of a type ordinarily supplied for private use or consumption. *See O'Callaghan v Hamilton Leasing (Ireland) Ltd* [1984] ILRM 146; *Cunningham v Woodchester*, Unreported, 16 November 1984.

(which implies certain terms with regard to services) in a consumer contract must be 'fair and reasonable' and specifically brought to the attention of the consumer.[1035] Donnelly and White comment that there 'seems no principled reason why the rules on the exclusion of liability are more lax in relation to contracts for the supply of services'.[1036]

460. The Schedule to the 1980 Act provides that in determining if a term is fair and reasonable, the following factors should be taken into account:

(a) the strength of the bargaining positions of the parties relative to each other, taking into account (among other things) alternative means by which the customer's requirements could have been met;
(b) whether the customer received an inducement to agree to the term, or in accepting it had an opportunity of entering into a similar contract with other persons, but without having to accept a similar term;
(c) whether the customer knew or ought reasonably to have known of the existence and extent of the term (having regard, among other things, to any custom of the trade and any previous course of dealing between the parties);
(d) where the term excludes or restricts any relevant liability if some condition is not complied with, whether it was reasonable at the time of the contract to expect that compliance with that condition would be practicable;
(e) whether any goods involved were manufactured, processed or adapted to the special order of the customer.

461. For example, in *McCarthy v Joe Walsh Tours*[1037] a package holiday agreement contained a standard arbitration clause which required the consumer to submit any dispute to an Irish Travel Agents arbitrator, with maximum damages of £5,000. It was held that this was an exclusion which was not fair and reasonable as it limited the damages available and had not been specifically drawn to the consumer's attention.[1038]

(ii) The Unfair European Communities (Unfair Terms in Consumer Contracts) Regulations 1995

462. Consumers who enter into contracts containing standard terms which have not been individually negotiated are protected by the European Communities (Unfair Terms in Consumer Contracts) Regulations 1995,[1039] which implements the

1035. *Carroll v An Post National Lottery* [1996] 1 IR 433 (exemption clause printed on payslip brought to attention of the consumer as required by s. 40).
1036. Donnelly and White, *Consumer Law Rights and Regulation* (Round Hall 2014) p. 160.
1037. [1991] ILRM 813.
1038. *See* now s. 31 of the Arbitration Act 2010, which puts the specific result of this case on a statutory basis.
1039. SI No. 27 of 1995, as amended by the European Communities (Unfair Terms in Consumer Contracts) (Amendment) Regulations 2000 (S.I. No. 307 of 2000).

Unfair Contract Terms Directive.[1040] These Regulations provide that unfair terms in a consumer contract are not binding on the consumer.[1041]

(a) Scope

463. In Ireland, the Unfair Contract Terms Directive only applies to terms which have not been individually negotiated.[1042] Regulation 3(4) states that a term is not individually negotiated 'where it has been drafted in advance and the consumer has therefore not been able to influence its substance, particularly in the context of a pre-formulated standard contract'. The burden of showing that a term has been individually negotiated is on the seller/supplier.[1043] However, the fact that a specific term or any aspect of a term has been individually negotiated does not exclude the application of the Regulations to the rest of the contract.[1044] The Consumer Rights Bill 2015 proposed extending the scope of the unfair terms provisions to include contract terms that have been negotiated between the consumer and trader,[1045] but this has not yet been enacted.

(b) When is a term 'unfair'?

464. A contract term is unfair if 'contrary to the requirement of good faith, it causes a significant imbalance in the parties' rights and obligations under the contract to the detriment of the consumer'.[1046]

465. The concept of 'good faith' is relatively new to the Irish common law system. In the Irish High Court decision in *AIB v Counihan*, it was explained as follows:

> In essence, the requirement of good faith mandates fair and open dealing, with the result that contractual terms must be expressed fully, clearly, and legibly by a seller/supplier, with suitable prominence being given to any disadvantageous terms, and all concealed pitfalls and traps avoided, in effect adherence to what might be described as good standards of commercial practice. A significant issue arising in this regard is whether a seller/supplier, dealing fairly and equitably with a consumer, could reasonably assume that the consumer would have agreed to an impugned term in individual contract negotiations. As

1040. 93/13/EEC.
1041. Regulation 6.
1042. Regulation 3(1). Subject to the provisions of Schedule 1, these Regulations apply to any term in a contract concluded between a seller of goods or supplier of services and a consumer which has not been individually negotiated. Some exceptions apply.
1043. Regulation 3(6). *See*, however, *Allied Irish Banks Plc v O'Donohoe* [2018] IEHC 599 in which the Court found that the defendant (consumer) had expressly chosen the interest rate in question and was thus 'individually negotiated'.
1044. Regulation 3(5).
1045. Head 71.
1046. Regulation 3(2).

for fair and equitable dealing, what this requires in effect is that a seller/ supplier should not take advantage of, inter alia, a consumer's necessity, indigence, inexperience, unfamiliarity with the subject-matter of a contract, or like characteristics or traits, and must take a consumer's legitimate interests into account.[1047]

466. Schedule 3 to the Regulations sets out a 'grey list' of terms which are assumed to be unfair; however, this list is indicative and non-exhaustive, and terms which are not on the list may be deemed to be unfair under the general test. For example, terms which have the effect of 'excluding or limiting the legal liability of a seller or supplier in the event of the death of a consumer or personal injury to the latter resulting from an act or omission of that seller or supplier' are presumed to be unfair.[1048]

467. Early cases applying the Regulations included *Re an Application pursuant to Regulation 8(1) of the Unfair Terms in Consumer Contracts 1995*[1049] in which Kearns J declared fifteen sample terms and an interim payment schedule invalid under the Regulations, without giving reasons for that order.[1050] This case arose in the context of the Irish housing boom, when the Law Society of Ireland and the Construction Industry Federation became aware that a number of building agreements were departing from the standard agreement which had been negotiated by the two bodies and recommended to their members, and that potentially unfair terms were being inserted into consumer construction contracts by solicitors acting for builders. In *Malcolm Marshall v Capital Holdings Limited t/a Sunworld*[1051] it was held that a clause providing for arbitration of disputes relating to a package holiday as not an unfair term. Schedule 3, subparagraph 1(q) states that a term may be unfair if it excludes the consumer's right to take legal action 'particularly by requiring the consumer to take disputes exclusively to arbitration not covered by legal provisions' – but here the arbitration in question *was* regulated by legal provisions, and was not unfair.

468. More recently, individuals in mortgage arrears who are faced with a court action for possession of their homes have sought to rely on the Regulations, albeit with limited success. In a number of cases[1052] it has been argued that the terms and conditions concerning the variable interest rate in a mortgage or loan were unfair because they permit the lender to alter the terms of the contract price unilaterally without a valid reason specified in the contract. Although it was held in all these cases that the term in question was not in fact subject to the fairness test (*see*

1047. *AIB v Counihan* [2016] IEHC 752, para. 17.

1048. Schedule 3, subpara. 1(a).

1049. Unreported, High Court, 5 December 2001 (Hearing and Judgment) and 20 December 2001 (order).

1050. For criticism, *see* Kelly, 'The Impact of Europe on Irish Contract Law' in Devenney and Kenny (eds), *The Transformation of European Private Law* (Cambridge University Press, 2013).

1051. [2006] IEHC 271.

1052. *Permanent TSB Plc. v Davis* [2019] IEHC 184; *Allied Irish Banks Plc v O'Donohoe* [2018] IEHC 599.

below), it was also held that even if it was to be assessed for fairness it was in fact fair. Although the 'grey list' of unfair terms includes both 'enabling the seller or supplier to alter the terms of the contract unilaterally without a valid reason which is specified in the contract'[1053] and 'terms which have the object or effect of … allowing a seller of goods or supplier of services to increase their price without … giving the consumer the corresponding right to cancel the contract if the final price is too high in relation to the price agreed when the contract was concluded',[1054] these are expressly subject to exceptions in paragraphs 2(b)[1055] and 2(c)[1056] of the Annex concerning financial services. A fuller explanation of why such terms would not be viewed as unfair is provided in *Grant*, where the court held that such a term was normal and common, 'a well-recognised feature of family home purchase and finance in Ireland' and in fact serves an 'important social purpose'.[1057] It was furthermore pointed out that protections exist against the abuse of variable loan terms[1058] and such a term is 'subject to an implied contractual term that it will not be exercised 'dishonestly', for an improper purpose, capriciously or arbitrarily'.[1059] Similarly, an acceleration clause in the contract was deemed to be fair in light of consumer protections which exist regarding its operation, such as for example the Central Bank's Code of Conduct on Mortgage Arrears (CCMA), which ensures that 'these clauses cannot be invoked unreasonably, arbitrarily or capriciously but only after an extensive process when other reasonable or practicable options have been explored'.[1060] Thus 'any perceived imbalance in the acceleration term under review is appropriately addressed under the terms of the statute and the Code'.[1061] A power of entry given to the banks was also deemed fair on the basis that it could only be exercised with a court order.[1062] A clause allowing the notice party to sell on the security to any person without notice to the applicants was also upheld as fair,[1063]

1053. Schedule 3, para. (j).
1054. Schedule 3, para. (l).
1055. Subparagraph 2(b) states that subpara. (*j*) 'is without hindrance to terms under which a supplier of financial services reserves the right to alter the rate of interest payable by the consumer or due to the latter, or the amount of other charges for financial services without notice where there is a valid reason, provided that the supplier is required to inform the other contracting party or parties thereof at the earliest opportunity and that the latter are free to dissolve the contract immediately.'
1056. Subparagraph 2(c) states that subparas 1(j) and 1(l) do not apply to 'transactions in transferable securities, financial instruments and other products or services where the price is linked to fluctuations in a stock exchange quotation or index or a financial market rate that the seller or supplier does not control'.
1057. *Grant v The County Registrar from the County of Laois and Pepper Finance Corporation (Ireland) Designated Activity Company* [2019] IEHC 185, para. 105.
1058. Such as a complaint to the Financial Services Ombudsman, *see Millar v Financial Services Ombudsman* [2015] IECA 126.
1059. *Grant v The County Registrar from the County of Laois and Pepper Finance Corporation (Ireland) Designated Activity Company* [2019] IEHC 185, para. 111, citing (*Paragon Finance plc v Nash* [2002] 1 WLR 685).
1060. *Ibid.*, para. 117.
1061. *Ibid.*
1062. *Ibid.*, para. 119.
1063. *See also Permanent TSB Plc v Burns* [2020] IEHC 24; *AIB Mortgage Bank v Gerard Cosgrove* [2017] IEHC 803, para. 54. In a series of cases the courts have determined that securitisation is a normal banking practice that has no impact on the end user or consumer and cannot amount to

as 'each party would remain bound to the mortgage loan and deed and the obligations and rights thereunder' and 'any borrowers under a loan contract containing this clause would retain the same statutory protections as heretofore and any remedy sought by the lender to enforce its rights to possession is subject to the same law applicable to the notice party'.[1064] However in *Tanager Dac v Rolf Kane* it was stated that if 'the consequence of transferring the defendant's mortgage from a regulated to an unregulated entity was to deprive the consumer of the benefit of the CCMA,[1065] then one could readily see how it might be suggested that this could infringe the unfair contract terms regulations'.[1066]

469. In other cases the court has emphasised the importance of independent legal advice. For example in *Permanent TSB Plc v Fox*[1067] the borrowers claimed that a provision in the mortgage conditions which stated that the secured debt became repayable if there was a two-month default in making repayments was unfair, but it was held that the term was not unfair as the borrowers had been aware of it and had had independent legal advice before they entered into the agreement.

(c) The court's obligation to assess unfair terms

470. In *AIB v Counihan*[1068] the Irish High Court acknowledged for the first time the European Court of Justice's position in *Aziz* that 'the national court is required to assess of its own motion whether a contractual term falling within the scope of the directive is unfair'.[1069] However, this requirement appears to remain problematic in practice in a common law system which is adversarial rather than inquisitorial in nature.[1070] The approach of the courts is that the court can only undertake this assessment where the court has the 'the legal and factual elements necessary for that task'.[1071] The assessment is not to be conducted 'in a forensic vacuum on

a defence to an action for possession: *Kearney v KBC* [2014] IEHC 260; *Harrold Nua Mortgages* [2015] IEHC 15 and *Danske Bank v Scanlan* [2016] IEHC 118.

1064. *Grant* para. 124.

1065. The Central Bank's Code of Conduct on Mortgage Arrears.

1066. *Tanager Dac v Rolf Kane* [2019] IEHC 801, para. 16.

1067. [2018] IEHC 292. The availability of independent legal advice was also relied upon by the same judge in *AIB Mortgage Bank and Allied Irish Banks plc v Gerard Cosgrove* [2017] IEHC 803, para. 60 and mentioned as relevant by Binchy J in *The Governor and Company of the Bank of Ireland v McMahon & anor* [2018] IEHC 455.

1068. *AIB v Counihan* [2016] IEHC 752.

1069. *Aziz v Caixa d'Estalvis de Caralunya* C-415/11, para. 46. It has been stated that 'the obligation that the Court of Justice perceives to arise as a matter of European Union law would appear logically to apply with as much vigour to a court that is hearing a de novo appeal as to the trial court' (*EBS Limited v Kenehan and Ryan* [2017] IEHC 604, para. 26).

1070. *AIB v Counihan* [2016] IEHC 752, para. 10; *Allied Irish Banks Plc v O'Donohoe* [2018] IEHC 599, para. 21.

1071. *Permanent TSB Plc. v Davis* [2019] IEHC 184, para. 26; *Allied Irish Banks PLC v Counihan and Counihan* [2016] IEHC 752; *EBS Limited v Kenehan and Ryan* [2017] IEHC 604; *Ulster Bank Ireland Limited v Costelloe* [2018] IEHC 289; *Permanent TSB PLC v Fox* [2018] IEHC 292.

the basis of pure hypothesis or conjecture: the court must conduct its review within an established legal and factual reality'.[1072]

471. The first difficulty here arises where the parties have not in fact raised the possible issue of unfair terms at first instance – in such a situation is the court obliged to raise the issue entirely of its own volition? In *Grant* the High Court answered this question as follows:

> It is clear therefore from the established jurisprudence of the CJEU that legislation or rules of court which do not allow the court before which an application for an order for possession has been brought to assess of its own motion, *in limine litis* or at any other stage during the proceedings whether the term of a mortgage contract which falls within the scope of the directive is unfair do not comply with the principle of effectiveness if it makes it impossible or excessively difficult in proceedings initiated, in this instance by the bank, against the consumer to give effect to the protections which Directive 93/13 seeks to provide. This is so *even though the consumer has not raised or lodged an objection during the course of the proceedings for possession where the court has before it, the legal, financial and factual elements necessary* for the assessment of whether the terms of the contract are covered by the provisions of the Directive and if so, whether they are unfair.[1073]

472. In *Grant* it was held that the County Registrar had failed to review whether the terms of the loan agreement or mortgage deed fell within the scope of or were unfair under the Regulations or the Directive.[1074] Thus it did not seem to the Court that 'the requirements of the developing jurisprudence of the CJEU on this issue had been absorbed into the [Registrar's] practice'.[1075] Nonetheless it was held that the Registrar did have jurisdiction to review the terms, and existing procedures allowed for the Register to assess the terms of the mortgage for fairness. The Court set out the procedure to be followed:

> If [the Registrar] considers that one or more of the terms falls within the scope of the directive and regulations and may be unfair, submissions or evidence should be invited from the parties prior to a ruling on the issue. If the County Registrar considers then that there may be a defence available to the defendants on the grounds that the loan contract or mortgage is void and unenforceable because a term may be unfair and that it is necessary to resolve that issue before granting the order the case should be sent forward to the Circuit Court

1072. *Grant v The County Registrar from the County of Laois and Pepper Finance Corporation (Ireland) Designated Activity Company* [2019] IEHC 185, para. 105.
1073. *Ibid.*, para. 76 (emphasis added).
1074. *Ibid.*, para. 80.
1075. *Ibid.*, para. 80.

for further consideration and determination: in that regard the County Registrar has power to direct that further affidavits be filed in relation to that issue.[1076]

473. In *Allied Irish Banks v Donohoe*[1077] the court was of the view that this requirement was to protect weaker parties, and where the parties are both legally represented before the court, and there is an 'equality of arms', that there is less of an imbalance between the parties. Meenan J stated that it was 'unclear as to what this Court is expected to do when carrying out an assessment 'of its own motion' in circumstances where both the supplier and consumer are fully and ably legally represented'.[1078] The court in this case relied on arguments put forward by counsel as regards the disputed term (the variable interest rate), finding that it was enforceable.

474. The second question that arises is the consequences of a failure to assess the contract terms. In *Grant,* the Court stated that the Registrar had failed to 'take a step which was a *necessary pre-requisite* to a lawful order for possession in the circumstances'.[1079] Without an assessment the Court would not make such an order, citing 'the importance … of ensuring that the standalone obligation imposed upon the national judicial authorities is observed'.[1080] However the Court itself went on to assess the terms in question, finding that they were not in fact unfair.

475. A more complicated situation arises if the court does not have the legal and factual elements necessary to conduct the fairness assessment. In *Donohoe* above, in relation to two other terms, it was stated that 'the Court is not required to reach a conclusion as it does not have "available to it legal and factual elements necessary for that task"'.[1081] The clauses were allowed stand, i.e., the obligation itself did not arise on the facts, and it was not ultimately necessary to decide the case as the plaintiffs were not relying on those clauses. However, in *EBS v Kenehan*[1082] it was found that the absence of documentation before the court meant that it was 'unable to perform a task incumbent upon it as a matter of European Union law before the order for possession may stand', and the court thus refused to make an order for possession.[1083] The court in this case clearly felt that court was placed in this position by the plaintiff bank's failure to produce the relevant documentation, and stated that it was 'in EBS's self-interest to place the court in a position where it could discharge its Aziz-Counihan obligations'.[1084]

(d) The 'Core Term' Exemption

1076. *Ibid.*, para. 86.
1077. [2018] IEHC 599, para. 21.
1078. *Ibid.* It should be noted, however, that the second defendant was not represented by counsel in the case.
1079. *Grant v The County Registrar from the County of Laois and Pepper Finance Corporation (Ireland) Designated Activity Company* [2019] IEHC 185, para. 87.
1080. *Ibid.*, para. 92.
1081. [2018] IEHC 599, para. 21.
1082. [2017] IEHC 604.
1083. *Ibid.*, para. 27.
1084. *Ibid.*, para. 28.

476. Regulation 4 provides for the so-called core term exemption, which provides that the unfairness test does not apply to the definition of the main subject matter of the contract or the adequacy of the price or remuneration, although any such term must still be in plain, intelligible language.[1085] In *Permanent TSB PlC v Davis*[1086] the Irish High Court held terms of a mortgage agreement relating to the variable interest rate were standard core terms in such contracts and did not fall within the scope of the unfair test in the Regulations:

> [I]t is clear that the main subject matter of the agreement was that all monies advanced under the loan would be repaid by monthly instalments and at a variable interest rate over a period of thirty-five years. The loan would be secured on the family home: it was so secured. If the borrowers defaulted on their repayments the plaintiff became entitled to seek an order for possession having made the appropriate demand for repayment and make good their security. These terms were in clear and intelligible form and were fully understood by each of the parties to involve the offering of the defendants' family home and principal place of residence as security for the loan and that in default of making the agreed repayments the security might be realised by the lender.[1087]

477. Similar conclusions regarding the rate of interest in loans and mortgages were reached in *AIB Mortgage Bank and Allied Irish Banks plc v. Gerard Cosgrove*[1088] and *Allied Irish Banks Plc v O'Donohoe.*[1089] In the latter case the Court cited a Circuit Court decision in which it was stated that 'the obligation to pay instalments and repay the loan is the defendants' main contractual obligation'.[1090]

478. The UK Supreme Court in *The Office of Fair Trading v Abbey National*[1091] gave a particularly broad interpretation of the core terms exemption, potentially reducing the scope and impact of the Regulations. In light of criticisms of this approach, the wording of the exclusion was changed in the UK Consumer Rights Act 2015 to ensure that ancillary terms (such as charges for unauthorised overdrafts) would be subject to the fairness test.[1092] Although there had been no similar judicial interpretation in Ireland, for the sake of clarity a similar change was proposed in the Irish context, in the proposed scheme for a Consumer Rights Bill

1085. Regulation 5(1).
1086. [2019] IEHC 184.
1087. *Ibid.*, para. 30.
1088. [2017] IEHC 803, para. 60 (the disputed terms of the relevant mortgage deed could be deemed to be unfair because the borrowers had received independent legal advice).
1089. [2018] IEHC 599, applied in *Bank of Ireland Mortgage Bank v Brian Kane* [2019] IEHC 421.
1090. *Bank of Ireland Mortgage Bank v Mahon & Woods* (Circuit Court, Judge Linnane, 9 August 2017).
1091. [2009] UKSC 52.
1092. Section 64 provides that a term of a consumer contract may not be assessed for fairness to the extent that: (a) it specifies the main subject matter of the contract, or (b) the assessment is of the appropriateness of the price payable under the contract by comparison with the goods, digital content or services supplied under it.

2015.[1093] However as noted before, this Bill has been delayed, so the matter remains unclear. The interpretation in *Abbey National* is by no means inevitable in an Irish court, but there remains the risk that it would be followed. More recently in *Grant* the Court indicated that rather than a definitive rule, whether a term is a 'core term' would depend on 'the particular facts and circumstances of the agreement made and an understanding of whether any particular terms … constitute the main subject matter of the contract or the price or remuneration for the service provided.'[1094]

IV. Penalty Clauses and Liquidated Damages Clauses

479. A clause in a contract may provide that certain or ascertainable sums are to be paid to the injured party in respect of a breach of the contract. For example, a construction contract might provide for the payment of a compensatory sum for each day's delay in completing the contract after the agreed date of completion. If this clause is a genuine attempt to pre-estimate the loss that would be incurred by the breach, it is called a liquidated damages clause and is enforceable.[1095] However, if the clause provides for payment of a sum which is unreasonably high in relation to the injury caused by the breach in question, then it may be deemed a penalty clause, which is unenforceable. The distinction was recently explained by the Irish courts as follows:

> Parties entering into a contract are always aware that it may be broken. Since parties are free to contract … it is also within their rights to genuinely pre-estimate what loss would occur in the event of a breach. A damages clause within a contract is to be upheld by the courts as having equal validity to any other term of the contract as thereby the parties are shown to contemplate and agree on their future losses. The difficult question of quantification is therefore removed from any future dispute as to the effect of a breach. What parties are not allowed to do however is to terrorise against a breach of contract through a clause disguised as a damages clause but which considerably overloads the party in breach with a liability to pay that is unrelated to what the contemplation of the parties genuinely would be as to loss.[1096]

480. If the clause in dispute is held to be a penalty clause, the contract itself remains[1097] but the clause is not enforceable. Indeed, the clause is *technically* valid, but 'simply will not be enforced beyond the actual loss suffered by the innocent party'.[1098] This means the injured party may still prove and recover his actual loss

1093. Head 74(2) clarified that any 'payment that is incidental or ancillary to the main subject matter of the contract' may be assessed for fairness.
1094. *Grant v The County Registrar from the County of Laois and Pepper Finance Corporation (Ireland) Designated Activity Company* [2019] IEHC 185, para. 98.
1095. As in *Toomey v Murphy* [1897] 2 IR 601.
1096. *Durkan New Homes Ltd v Minister for Environment* [2014] 2 IR 440, 456.
1097. *Launceston Property Finance v Burke* [2017] IESC 62, para. 48.
1098. *Ibid.*

according to the general principles of contract law damages.[1099] If the clause is held to be a valid liquidated damages clause, the amount agreed upon is recoverable for the relevant breach, even if the actual loss sustained is less than (or more than) the agreed pre-estimate.[1100]

481. A substantial amount of case law has emerged on the distinction between a penalty clause and a liquidated damages clause. The courts will examine the intentions of the parties, but merely labelling the clause as a 'liquidated damages clause' or 'penalty clause' will not necessarily be decisive.[1101] The principles set out by Lord Dunedin in *Dunlop Pneumatic Tyre Co. v New Garage & Motor Co.*[1102] are still applied in Ireland. They are as follows:

(i) *'The sum will be held to be a penalty if the sum stipulated for is extravagant and unconscionable in comparison with the greatest loss that could conceivably be proved to have followed from the breach.'*

This is the most important principle from the *Dunlop* case, and it focuses on whether the sum stipulated for is arbitrary or a genuine pre-estimate of loss.[1103] In *Durkan New Homes v Minister for the Environment*[1104] a contract for a sale of land contained a special condition for damages for late completion on an ascending scale of €20,000–€50,000 per week. It was held that the penalty was arbitrary and the clause was struck out on the basis of the first of Lord Dunedin's principles.

(ii) *'The sum will be a penalty if the breach consists only in not paying a sum of money and the sum stipulated is a sum greater than the sum which ought to have been paid.'*

This means for example that if someone fails to pay €100 due under a contract, an obligation to pay €200 would be struck out as penal. This rule applies where the sum due (or loss suffered on breach) is certain – no question of attempting to pre-estimate the loss arises. Several cases here concern the issue of the rate of interest which is payable in these circumstances.[1105] In *O'Donnell v Truck and Machinery Sales*[1106] for example, it was held in the

---

1099. *Ibid.*, para. 49.
1100. *Clydebank Engineering and Shipbuilding Co. v Castaneda* [1905] AC 6.
1101. *Dunlop Pneumatic Tyre Company Limited v New Garage and Motor Company Limited* [1915] AC 79, 86. *See*, for example, *Toomey v Murphy* [1897] 2 IR 601 (although both phrases were used here).
1102. [1915] AC 79, 87.
1103. *See also* the statement of Parker LJ [1915] AC 79, 97.
1104. [2014] 2 IR 440.
1105. *See* Horahan, 'The Rule against Penalties and the Enforceability of Default and Surcharge Interest Clauses in Loan Agreements' (2018) 25(5) Commercial Law Practitioner 107–114.
1106. [1998] 4 IR 191.

Supreme Court that where a contract provides for the payment of money, compensation for breach involves the payment of the money and interest at commercial rates. Any formula providing for excess interest is penal and unenforceable as in effect it provides for the payment of larger sum in place of a smaller one.[1107]

In *Sheehan v Breccia*[1108] the question that arose was whether surcharge interest at a rate of 4% over the facility interest rate, found in the general conditions of a loan facility, was an unlawful and unenforceable penalty clause. However, in this case the court did not operate on the assumption that this was a case where a certain sum was due (and thus no more than the commercial rate of interest could apply) but rather a based its decision on an assumption that there was a 'claim recognisable in law for damages for loss and damage which [the creditor] might suffer by reason of the failure of Mr. Sheehan to make a payment due under the agreements on a due date which went beyond the sum in question and interest thereon at a commercial rate'.[1109] This meant that more latitude was to be given, as there may genuinely be a difficulty in pre-estimating the damage suffered in the event of breach.[1110] However, despite this, it was held that the 4% surcharge interest was 'not a genuine attempt to agree upon liquidated damages or estimate the loss which Anglo might suffer by reason of a default to which it relates'.[1111] The same result was reached in the related case of *Flynn v Breccia*,[1112] which was heard at the same time.

This is similar to the approach taken by the same judge in *ACC Bank Plc. v Friends First Managed Pension Funds Ltd.*,[1113] in which a default surcharge rate of 6% interest was held to be a penalty designed to dissuade the borrower from breaching the contract, rather than a genuine pre-estimate by ACC of its losses. In this case AAC could not explain why it chose 6% as its surcharge rate, and moreover it applied not only to principal but also any sum in respect of interest, costs or charges.

A further complication arises in relation to acceleration clauses. Acceleration clauses are generally found in contracts requiring payment in instalments, and provide that the failure to pay an instalment means that immediate payment in full of the balance is required. This obligation to pay the entire sum is usually more expensive for the party in breach. These are generally allowable,[1114] but care is required to ensure they are not penal,[1115] and it may be necessary to make discounts to allow for the fact that payment has been made sooner than

1107. [1998] 4 IR 191, 213–217.
1108. [2018] IECA 286.
1109. *Ibid.*, para. 33.
1110. *Ibid.*, para. 37.
1111. *Ibid.*, para. 49.
1112. [2018] IECA 273.
1113. [2012] IEHC 435.
1114. *National Telephone v Griffen* [1906] 2 IR 115.
1115. *UDT Ltd v Patterson* [1975] NI 142; *Trustee Savings Bank Dublin v Maughan*, Unreported, High Court, 8 October 1981.

it was due. In *Irish Telephone Rentals Ltd v Irish Civil Service Building Society Ltd*,[1116] for example, a clause which required the hirer of telephone equipment to pay the entire sum due under the contract upon breach was invalid as a penalty clause, despite the fact that discounts were given to reflect for example the fact that the other party would save on maintenance costs. The court held that the discount was not sufficient and the clause failed to identify or compensate the actual loss suffered.

It is also possible that in cases for the sale of land the courts may approach the issue of interest rates differently, at least in relation to an interest rate applicable to any delays in the purchaser complying with the agreed closing date. The Supreme Court has stated, albeit in an *obiter* statement, that 'the principles relating to penalties would not apply since the payment of interest is being paid in the course of the performance of the contract and before the mutual obligations of the parties had been finally discharged'.[1117] Similarly in *Launceston Property Finance v Burke*[1118] the McKechnie J emphasised in the Supreme Court that the rules on penalties apply when the clause under dispute is 'related to or dependent upon a potential breach of the arrangements'.[1119] Thus in this case the payment of arrangement fees was not to be assessed under the principles in *Dunlop* as they were to be paid in the performance of the contract, and not in anticipation of any default.

(iii) *'There is a presumption that a clause is penal when a single lump sum is payable on the occurrence of one or more or all of several events, the events occasioning varying degree of loss.'*

A clause which provides that a lump sum is payable for a number of different breaches of varying consequences and types of loss will most likely be considered to be a penalty clause. In *Schiesser International (Ireland) v Gallagher*[1120] for example the defendant had to pay a sum to reimburse his employer's training expenses if he quit employment at any point within a three-year period, be that on the first day or the last day of employment. This was struck out as a penalty clause.

(iv) *'If the consequences of the breach are difficult to estimate in financial terms this, far from being an obstacle to the validity of the clause, will point in favour of upholding it, the courts taking the view that it is better for the parties themselves to estimate the damages that will result.'*

Where it is almost impossible to make a precise pre-estimation of damages, it is probable that the pre-estimated damage clause was the true bargain between the parties.

1116. [1991] ILRM 880.
1117. *O'Donnell v Truck and Machinery Sales Ltd* [1998] 4 IR 191, 218 per Barron J. *See also Donegan, O'Connell and Doran v O'Regan* [2018] IEHC 617, paras 36–37.
1118. [2017] IESC 62.
1119. [2017] IESC 62, para. 45.
1120. (1971) 106 ILTR 22.

482. The overarching test applied in Ireland is to be derived from the first principle in *Dunlop Pneumatic Tyre Co. v New Garage & Motor Co.*[1121] and essentially asks whether the clause is a genuine pre-estimate of loss. However, recent cases in the United Kingdom have shown a move away from this traditional test, with an increased focus on the commercial justification for the clause.[1122] In *Cavendish Square Holdings v Makdessi*[1123] and *ParkingEye Limited v Beavis*[1124] the UK Supreme Court stated that the test was 'whether the impugned provision is a secondary obligation which imposes a detriment on the contract-breaker out of all proportion to any legitimate interest of the innocent party in the enforcement of the primary obligation'. Under this test, which favours freedom of contract and the upholding of commercial agreements, a clause is more likely to be a liquidated damages clause, and enforceable.[1125] It does not have to be shown that the clause is a 'genuine pre-estimate of loss', merely that it is not 'out of proportion to any legitimate interest' a contracting party might have in the enforcement of the contract.

483. The question which then arose was whether the Irish courts would or should follow suit. In *ACC Bank Plc. v Friends First Managed Pension Funds Ltd.*[1126] Finlay Geoghegan J seemed to approach the issue of penalty clauses from the question of whether they were commercially justifiable, although the principles in *Dunlop* were still applied. In the aftermath of the *Cavendish* case, lower courts were bound by the rules of precedent to apply the *Dunlop* standard, as it had been approved by the Supreme Court in *O'Donnell v Truck and Machinery Sales.*[1127] It was thus for the appellate courts to decide whether the approach in *Cavendish* should be followed.[1128]

484. In *Launceston Property Finance v Burke*[1129] McKechnie J in the Supreme Court stated that 'the starting point for an assessment of the law relating to penalty clauses remains the principles set out in the speech of Lord Dunedin in *Dunlop Pneumatic Tyre Co. Ltd*' and added that he was 'not immediately convinced that any change to the test is necessary, nor that the route taken by the UK Supreme Court is necessarily a superior one'.[1130] However, these comments were *obiter*, and McKechnie J stressed 'that the live debate must be left over for a more suitable case, if and when that should arise'. [1131]

1121. [1915] AC 79.
1122. *See*, for example, *Lordsvale Finance Plc v Bank of Zambia* [1996] QB 752.
1123. [2016] AC 1172.
1124. *Ibid.*
1125. It is thus questionable whether (and, if so, why) the appellants in *Launceston Property Finance v Burke* [2017] IESC 62 would have sought to apply the test in *Cavendish* rather than the traditional test in *Dunlop* when seeking to have an interest rate declared a penalty (para. 39).
1126. [2012] IEHC 435.
1127. [1998] 4 IR 191.
1128. *See*, for example, the comments of Haughton J in *Sheehan v Breccia* [2016] IEHC 67.
1129. [2017] IESC 62. *See also First Active Plc v Brian Cunningham* [2018] IESC 11 McKechnie J where these points were again made.
1130. [2017[IESC 62, paras 34 and 42.
1131. *Ibid.*, para. 42.

485. Subsequently, Finlay Geoghegan J in the Court of Appeal confirmed that the courts remained bound to apply the *Dunlop* principles, but again there was a suggestion that this might need to be considered by the Supreme Court in a suitable case:

> The High Court and this Court remain bound in accordance with the *Supreme Court judgment in Pat O'Donnell* to apply the *Dunlop* principles in determining whether the surcharge interest clause is or is not a penalty. In so stating I do not wish to be taken as indicating that a reconsideration of those principles in the 21st century by the Supreme Court certainly insofar as they relate to additional default or surcharge interest may not be desirable. However, that remains a matter for the Supreme Court in this jurisdiction.[1132]

486. However, within the confines of the *Dunlop* principles, Finlay Geoghegan J appears to take an approach which favours commercial freedom to contract, and a certain amount of latitude when assessing the parties' attempt to plan for the unknown consequences of breach. In this context, whether the clause is a 'genuine pre-estimate of loss' is only *one* factor to take into account when assessing the clause, and the main question to ask is whether there was a 'genuine agreement'.[1133] She concluded:

> I would respectfully agree that expressing the question to be determined as to whether 'the clause is a genuine attempt by the parties to estimate in advance the loss which will result from the breach' may be a better way of putting the question. This approach permits the courts to uphold a clause which is a genuine attempt by the parties to estimate in advance the loss which will result from the breach but where by reason of the uncertainty of the loss it may be a sum which differs from the actual loss anticipated.[1134]

487. Thus there may be a 'third way', under which the approach in *Dunlop* is retained, but with a refocus on whether there was a genuine agreement rather than whether there was a genuine pre-estimate of loss. It is worth noting that on the facts of this case it was held that the clause in question *was* in fact a penalty clause, but this aside this approach appears to reflect a more flexible attitude to liquidated damages clauses. It remains, however, for the Supreme Court to have the final say on the matter.

1132. *Sheehan v Breccia* [2018] IECA 286, para. 21.
1133. *Ibid.*, para. 40.
1134. *Ibid.*, para. 44.

V. Arbitration Clauses

488. As discussed above, it is not possible to include a clause in a contract which ousts the jurisdiction of the courts in respect of that agreement. Such a clause is contrary to a traditional common law rule of public policy and is reinforced by the Constitution.[1135] It is however quite common and legally acceptable to include an arbitration clause providing for the submission of a dispute arising out of a contract to a nominated third party. The House of Lords in *Scott v Avery*[1136] held that it is lawful to make the award of an arbitrator a condition precedent to the institution of proceedings in the normal courts, but not to have a clause which absolutely prohibits submission of a legal dispute to the courts.

489. Arbitration is a long established and favoured method of settling disputes arising out of business contracts. In Ireland, arbitration agreements are currently regulated by the Arbitration Act 2010,[1137] which replaced the Arbitration Acts 1954–1998. The Act provides that the UNCITRAL Model Law on International Commercial Arbitration (the 'Model Law') has the force of law in the State and applies to arbitration agreements concerning international and non-international (domestic) commercial arbitrations.[1138] The Act does not apply to arbitrations concerning contracts of employment or industrial relations.[1139]

490. Hutchinson has identified the main changes introduced by the Act as follows:

- the adoption of the Model Law in Ireland as the law governing arbitrations taking place in the State;
- the unification of the regimes governing domestic and international arbitrations in Ireland;
- the default requirement that arbitrators' awards state the reasons on which they are based;
- the requirement that questions of arbitrators' jurisdiction be decided in the first place by the arbitrators themselves, including questions relating to the existence and validity of the arbitration agreement;
- the requirement that complaints about impartiality or independence of arbitrators be raised and determined first before the arbitrators themselves;
- the lifting of the prohibition against agreements within which parties agree in advance to bear their own or the other side's costs in any event regardless of the outcome;
- the granting of injunctive and interim powers to arbitrators;
- the narrowing of the grounds upon which an arbitrator's award can be set aside by the courts;

1135. Articles 34.1. and 34.3.10. *Bunreacht na hÉireann.*
1136. (1856) 5 HL Cas 811.
1137. *See* generally Mansfield, *Arbitration Act 2010 and Model Law: A Commentary* (Clarus Press, 2012); Dowling-Hussey and Dunne, *Arbitration Law* (2nd ed., Round Hall, 2014).
1138. Section 6.
1139. Section 30.

- the abolition of the case-stated procedure whereby arbitrators could refer a question of law to the High Court for an answer;
- the removal of the right to appeal court decisions on arbitration-related matters beyond the High Court, and the designation of the 'arbitration judge' tasked with deciding arbitration-related matters in the High Court.[1140]

491. The 2010 Act states that where parties agree that disputes under a contract or agreement or disputes arising out of a contract or agreement shall be submitted to arbitration, this shall include disputes as to the existence or validity of the contract or agreement.[1141] The court does not have jurisdiction to refuse any party seeking a stay pending arbitration unless satisfied that the agreement to arbitrate is 'null and void, inoperative or incapable of being performed'.[1142]

492. The agreement to arbitrate is separate to the main contract; it may be that performance of the main obligations of the contract have ceased, for example, by fundamental breach or frustration, but the contract itself continues to exist for the purpose of deciding claims, and the obligation established by the arbitration clause continues to exist to determine settlement of these issues.[1143]

493. The attitude of Irish courts to arbitration and arbitration awards is that the procedure should be interfered with as little as possible, and the arbitrator's decision should be considered final.[1144] This attitude is reflected in the comment by Murphy J in *Hogan v St. Kevins Co.*, that 'the court should be slow to usurp the functions of the chosen tribunal by intervening, whether by way of setting aside an award, remitting an award or directing a case to be stated'.[1145] Under Article 34 of UNCITRAL, as incorporated by the 2010 Act, an arbitral award may be set aside by the High Court only under certain limited grounds. In *Delargy v Hickey*[1146] Gilligan J stated that the grounds for setting aside an award 'are to be construed narrowly' and *Snoddy v Mavroudis* it was stated that an award 'may not be set aside for some reason not specified in the Model Law as a result of the courts' inherent jurisdiction'.[1147] In *Ryan and Ryan v Kevin O'Leary (Clonmel) Ltd and General*

1140. Brian Hutchinson, 'A Ten-Year Review of the Arbitration Act 2010?' (2019) 26(9) Commercial Law Practitioner 162. *See also* Aengus Ó Corráin 'The Arbitration Act 2010 and *Scott v Avery* Clauses – Safeguarding Professional Indemnity Insurance Premiums' (2015) 22(3) *Commercial Law Practitioner* 73.
1141. Section 8(3).
1142. Article 8, UNCITRAL, as incorporated into the 2010 Act. *See* Brian Hutchinson 'The Existence of the Arbitration Agreement and the Kompetenz-Kompetenz Principle in Irish Law' (2014) Arbitration 73; *Lisheen Mine v Mullock Shipbrokers* [2015] IEHC 50; *G. Burns Ltd v Grange Construction & Roofing Company Ltd* [2013] IEHC 284; *Mount Juliet Properties Ltd v Melcarne Developments* [2013] IEHC 286.
1143. *Heymans v Darwins Ltd.* [1942] AC 356, 366–367.
1144. *Keenan v Shield Insurance Co. Ltd.* [1988] IR 89; *Brostrom Tankers AB v Factorias Vulcano SA* [2004] 2 IR 191.
1145. [1986] IR 80, 88.
1146. [2015] IEHC 436.
1147. *Snoddy v Mavroudis* [2013] IEHC 285, approving a statement in Mansfield, *Arbitration Act 2010 and Model Law: A Commentary* (Clarus Press, 2012) p. 213. *See also Delargy v Hickey* [2015]

Motors[1148] it was stated that 'an application to set aside an award is not an appeal from the decision of the arbitrator and does not afford the court the opportunity of second-guessing the arbitrator's decision on the merits, whether on the facts or on the law'.[1149]

§2. INTERPRETATION

494. The overarching principle for interpreting the contents of a contract is that an objective approach is to be taken:

> Insofar as Irish law is concerned, the contract is to be interpreted objectively in accordance with the meaning of the words the parties have used.[1150]

495. However, beyond this questions arise regarding what can and cannot be taken into account when assessing how the reasonable person would view the contract, or whether every word should be taken literally or given a purposive interpretation, or the approach to be taken when clauses appear to be inconsistent with each other. The starting point for any discussion of contract interpretation is the five principles set out by Lord Hoffman in *Investors' Compensation Scheme Ltd v West Bromwich Building Society*:[1151]

> (1) Interpretation is the ascertainment of the meaning which the document would convey to a reasonable person having all the background knowledge which would reasonably have been available to the parties in the situation in which they were at the time of the contract.
> (2) The background was famously referred to by Lord Wilberforce as the 'matrix of fact', but this phrase is, if anything, an understated description of what the background may include. Subject to the requirement that it should have been reasonably available to the parties and to the exception to be mentioned next, it includes absolutely anything which would have affected the way in which the language of the document would have been understood by a reasonable man.
> (3) The law excludes from the admissible background the previous negotiations of the parties and their declarations of subjective intent. They are admissible only in an action for rectification. […]
> (4) The meaning which a document (or any other utterance) would convey to a reasonable man is not the same thing as the meaning of its words. The meaning of words is a matter of dictionaries and grammars; the meaning

IEHC 436, para. 31; *Hoban v Coughlan* [2017] IEHC 301; *Ryan and Ryan v Kevin O'Leary (Clonmel) Ltd and General Motors* [2018] IEHC 660.

1148. [2018] IEHC 660. *See* Gearóid Carey, 'Set Aside of Arbitral Awards: Limited Grounds Confirmed' (2019) 26(1) Commercial Law Practitioner 3.

1149. [2018] IEHC 660, para. 31.

1150. *Fitzpatrick v the Board of Management of St. Mary's Touraneena National School and Anor.* [2013] IESC 62, para. 39, citing *Analog Devices BV v Zurich Insurance* [2005] IESC 12.

1151. [1998] 1 WLR 896, 912–913.

of the document is what the parties using those words against the relevant background would reasonably have been understood to mean. The background may not merely enable the reasonable man to choose between the possible meanings of words which are ambiguous but even (as occasionally happens in ordinary life) to conclude that the parties must, for whatever reason, have used the wrong words or syntax […]

(5) The 'rule' that words should be given their 'natural and ordinary meaning' reflects the common sense proposition that we do not easily accept that people have made linguistic mistakes, particularly in formal documents. On the other hand, if one would nevertheless conclude from the background that something must have gone wrong with the language, the law does not require judges to attribute to the parties an intention which they plainly could not have had. Lord Diplock made this point more vigorously when he said …: 'if detailed semantic and syntactical analysis of words in a commercial contract is going to lead to a conclusion that flouts business commonsense, it must be made to yield to business commonsense'.

496. The key changes to the law under *ICS* was that background evidence was always admissible when interpreting contract documents, as opposed to only being admissible where there was an ambiguity, and the scope of the background evidence that could be taken into account – the 'factual matrix' – now extended to '*absolutely anything* which would have affected the way in which the language of the document would have been understood by a reasonable man',[1152] provided it was available to the parties.[1153] However, the factual matrix excludes prior negotiations[1154] and subjective declarations of intent,[1155] and the subsequent conduct of the parties.

497. This statement was approved in by the Irish Supreme Court in *Analog Devices BV v Zurich Insurance*,[1156] and discussed more recently by the Supreme Court in *Law Society of Ireland v MIBI*.[1157] In this case the Court emphasised the 'importance of approaching the Agreement in a holistic way rather than having immediate resort to case law'.[1158] The Court viewed contracts as forms of communication susceptible to the same errors and rules of interpretation applicable to other forms of human communication:

1152. Emphasis added.

1153. For discussion, *see* Lord Bingham 'A New Thing under the Sun? The Interpretation of Contracts and the ICS Decision' Edin LR Vol 12, 374–390.

1154. *Prenn v Simmonds* [1971] 1 WLR 1381 and *Chartbrook Limited v Persimmon Homes Limited* [2009] UKHL 38, cited in *Point Village Developments and Anor v Dunnes Stores* [2019] IECA 233, paras 59–60.

1155. *Point Village Developments and Anor v Dunnes Stores* [2019] IECA 233, paras 67, 72, 74, 86; *Danske Bank v Hegarty* [2012] IESC 30, para. 7.7.

1156. *Analog Devices BV v Zurich Insurance* [2005] IESC 12. *See also Fitzpatrick v The Board of Management of St. Mary's Touraneena National School and Anor.* [2013] IESC 62, para. 39.

1157. [2017] IESC 31.

1158. *Law Society v MIBI* [2017] IESC 31, para. 8.

A contract is a form of communication intended to convey the meaning agreed upon by the parties. Words are the vehicle through which that meaning is conveyed but the meaning of a document is much more than the meaning of the words. It is what the parties would reasonably have been understood to mean from a consideration of all the available guides to the meaning of the agreement. Words are an important and very often the only necessary guide to discerning the meaning, but they are only a guide, and as recognised by Lord Hoffman, they can be ambiguous, and sometimes even, as happens in real life, it may be apparent the parties have for whatever reason used the wrong words or syntax. In those circumstances, the words must give way.[1159]

498. O'Donnell J emphasised the importance of having an understanding of the commercial or practical background to the contract:

Agreements are intended to express in a clear and functional manner what the parties have agreed upon in respect of their relationship … . It is not merely therefore a question of analysing the words used, but rather it is the function of the court to try and understand from all the available information, including the words used, what it is that the parties agreed, or what it is a reasonable person would consider they had agreed. In that regard, the Court must consider not just the words used, but also the specific context, the broader context, the background law, any prior agreements, the other terms of this Agreement, other provisions drafted at the same time and forming part of the same transaction, and what might be described as the logic, commercial or otherwise, of the agreement. … The reasonable person who is the guide to the interpretation of the agreement is expected not merely to possess linguistic skills but must also have, or acquire, a sympathetic understanding of the commercial or practical context in which the agreement was meant to operate, and perhaps even an understanding of the many ways in which even written, formal and legal communication falls short of the standard clarity and precision set by the early editions of Fowler's *Modern English Usage.*[1160]

499. The contract must be read as a whole:[1161]

An agreement is an exercise in communication and there is a working, though by no means irrebuttable, presumption of coherence. It is important therefore to test any interpretation of a clause against the understanding of the agreement to be gleaned from what is said, and sometimes not said, elsewhere in the agreement.[1162]

500. Thus, when a dispute arises, rather than focusing immediately on the meaning of the individual clause(s) under dispute, the Court stated that the correct

1159. [2017] IESC 31, para. 9.
1160. *Ibid.*, para. 12.
1161. *O'Leary v Volkswagon Group* [2020] IECA 18, para. 37.
1162. *Law Society v MIBI* [2017] IESC 31, para. 6.

approach is to *first* ascertain the overall purpose and meaning of the *entirety* of the agreement, and then to ascertain what that means for the specific issue at hand. This necessary to 'see the agreement and the background context, as the parties saw them at the time the agreement was made, rather than to approach it through the lens of the dispute which has arisen sometimes much later'.[1163] This was particularly important on the facts of this case, which concerned an agreement entered into by the Motor Insurance Bureau of Ireland. The Motor Insurance Bureau of Ireland pays compensation to individuals injured in road traffic accidents where the party who caused the accident does not have insurance, or is untraceable. The question that arose in this case was whether the agreement covered situations where the party who caused the accident had insurance, but the insurance company has since become insolvent. Rather than simply interpreting individual terms of the contract to see whether they could technically give rise to this interpretation, the Court looked to the entirety of the agreement in order to interpret it, and *began* this process by looking at the commercial, factual and legal context in which the Agreement was entered into.[1164] In particular, the Court examined the level of risk assumed by the parties in the 'traditional' interpretation of the Agreement (i.e., one where the MIBI was only to pay compensation where a driver was uninsured) and the interpretation sought by the Law Society (i.e., one where the MIBI would potentially be liable to pay compensation where the insurance company was insolvent.) The risk in the latter situation was 'not just a significantly different risk, but … one which is potentially ruinous for the remaining insurers',[1165] i.e., the insurance companies who are members of and fund the MIBI. Such an agreement would be 'plainly foolish to the point of threatening the financial viability of the companies', such that it must be asked why this sort of Agreement would be entered into. The commercial background to this Agreement thus made it very unlikely that the MIBI would have agreed to cover insolvent insurers.[1166] The Court then proceeded to look at individual clauses in the contract with this commercial background in mind. While the words used in the agreement were general in nature, and could feasibly include a situation where an insurer became insolvent, it was held that, given the commercial background to the contract, specific language and detailed provisions would need to have been included to infer that MIBI were to be liable in this situation. The Court could not accept that the parties intended to cover this scenario 'yet did not address themselves to the commercial and legal issues involved'.[1167]

501. Clarke J gave a separate concurring judgment, in which he referred to the approach to be taken as a 'text in context' method of interpretation:

> The modern approach has sometimes been described as the 'text in context' method of interpretation. It might be said that the older approach in the common law world placed a very high emphasis indeed on textual analysis without

1163. *Ibid.*, para. 14.
1164. *Ibid.*, para. 22.
1165. *Ibid.*, para. 24.
1166. *Ibid.*, para. 27.
1167. *Ibid.*, para. 66.

> sometimes paying sufficient regard to the context or circumstances in which the document in question came into existence. On the other hand, it is important not to lose sight of the fact that the document whose interpretation is at issue forms the basis on which legal rights and obligations have been established. That is so whether the document in question is a statute, a contract, the rules of an organisation, a patent or, indeed, any other form of document which is designed, whether by agreement or unilaterally, to impose legal rights and obligations on either specific parties or more generally. To fail to have sufficient regard to the text of such a document is to give insufficient weight to the fact that it is in the form of the document in question that legal rights and obligations have been determined. However, an over dependence on purely textual analysis runs the risk of ignoring the fact that almost all text requires some degree of context for its proper interpretation. Phrases or terminology rarely exist in the abstract. Rather the understanding which reasonable and informed persons would give to any text will be informed by the context in which the document concerned has come into existence.
>
> Perhaps it is fair to say that the main underlying principle is that a document governing legal rights and obligations should be interpreted by the courts in the same way that it would be interpreted by a reasonable and informed member of the public who understands the context of the document in question. Such a person would, necessarily, pay a lot of attention to the text but would also interpret that text in its proper context.

502. Clarke J referred to the 'text in context' approach in the context of planning permission in *Lanigan and ors. v Barry and ors*[1168] and again in the context of a settlement agreement in *Jackie Greene Construction Ltd v Irish Nationwide Building Society.*[1169] In this case, Clarke J emphasised that both the text and the context should be given due consideration:

> [I]t is important to give due recognition both to the text of any document creating legal rights and obligations and to the context in which the words used in the measure concerned were chosen. To fail to give adequate weight to the words is to ignore, or downplay, the fact that those were the words that were chosen to define the relevant legal arrangement. To fail to give adequate weight to context is to ignore the fact that all language is inevitably interpreted by reasonable persons in the light of the context in which that language is used.
>
> In addition, it is clear from the authorities referred to that part of the relevant context is the nature of the document governing legal rights and obligations whose construction is at issue. The more formal the document the less one would expect to find errors or looseness of language. Contractual documents entered into after careful negotiations between experienced lawyers on behalf of the parties may be seen to operate in a different context to, for

1168. [2016] IESC 46. 'The "text in context" approach requires the Court to consider the text used in the context of the circumstances in which the document concerned was produced including the nature of the document itself.'

1169. [2019] IESC 2.

example, the informal rules of a small association. In all cases the text is important, but part of the context in which that text needs to be considered is the manner in which that text was arrived at, and the circumstances which led to the text being required and/or agreed.[1170]

503. This was applied by the Court of Appeal in *Point Village Development Ltd. (In Receivership) v Dunnes Stores*.[1171] In this case, the Court took into account that the Agreement in question was a 'commercial contract which was negotiated on an arm's length basis with the benefit of extensive legal and expert advice by two highly experienced counterparties in the context of a commercial transaction and the compromise of subsequent litigation'.[1172] The Court thus rejected the argument that an agreement with an obligation to secure 'tenants' should be interpreted as an obligation to secure 'high quality tenants', as to do so would be 'to obliquely impeach the clauses' clear words and distort its simple, plain language' and 'supplant certainty with uncertainty'.[1173] The approach in this case places considerable emphasis on the text of the agreement, at least in a commercial context where the agreement has been carefully drafted with the benefit of legal advice.

§3. Conditional Contracts

504. A contract may be entered into on the basis that it will not become operative unless some condition is first satisfied or, having become operative, that it will terminate on the occurrence or non-occurrence of some condition:

> If the condition is one to be fulfilled before the agreement comes into force, it is what lawyers have called a condition precedent (or a contingent or causal condition), that is, a condition of the agreements coming into force; and if it is not performed there is no agreement. If the condition is to be performed after the agreement has come into force, it is what lawyers have called a condition subsequent, or a condition inherent (or a promissory condition), that is, a condition of the agreements continuing; and if it is not performed the agreement comes to an end.[1174]

505. However, the distinction between different types of conditional contracts, and the impact of failure to complete a stated condition, is not always easy to adduce. In *O'Connor v Coady*[1175] property was sold subject to the obtaining of planning permission within four months and with the provision that the sale was to be closed within seven days of the granting of the permission. It was held in the Supreme Court that once the date mentioned in the condition had passed without

1170. *Ibid.*, paras 5.4–5.5.
1171. [2019] IECA 233, para. 84.
1172. *Ibid.*, para. 70.
1173. *Ibid.*, para. 106.
1174. *Wickman Machine Tool Sales Limited v L. Schuler AG* [1972] 1 WLR 840 cited in *Point Village Development Ltd. (In Receivership) v Dunnes Stores* [2019] IECA 233, para. 95.
1175. [2005] 1 ILRM 256.

the planning permission being available there was an entitlement to bring the contract to an end. This would not happen automatically, but there would have to be notification by one party to the other. The Court approved of McWilliam J's statement in *O'Mullane v Riordan* which concerned similar facts:

> [I]t has been argued that, as this contract was subject to a condition (i.e., the obtaining of planning permission) there was no contract until the planning permission had been obtained … . I was referred in this context to the case of *Aberfoyle Plantations Limited v. Kajw Bien Cheng* [1960] AC 115. I cannot accept this argument. The fact that a contract is subject to a condition has the effect of making it unenforceable until the condition is fulfilled, but it does not mean that there is no contract at all and the case cited decided that the purchaser was entitled to recover his deposit under a term of the agreement. A conditional contract is one which becomes enforceable provided the condition is fulfilled within the time provided by the contract or if no time is provided within a reasonable time.[1176]

506. Geoghegan J stated:

> Normally, a conditional contract will not mean a contract which only comes into existence upon fulfilment of the condition but rather a contract which can only be enforced upon fulfilment of the condition. That is what this contract was.[1177]

507. Where the fulfilment of the condition is outside the control of either party to the contract, e.g., the grant of a mortgage or the obtaining of planning permission for a particular use of land, nevertheless, the condition may impliedly involve an obligation on a party to take reasonable steps to obtain the mortgage or the permission and failure to do so will be an actionable breach of the contract.[1178]

508. In accordance with the normal rule that a party to a contract may waive any term which is wholly for his benefit, so also a party to a 'conditional' contract may unilaterally waive the condition, if it is exclusively for his benefit, and thus enable the contract to operate without the inhibiting condition.[1179] For example, in *McKenny v Martin*[1180] a contract for the sale of land was made subject to the purchaser obtaining planning permission to build a house on the site. The contract could be rescinded if planning permission was not obtained. Over the next few years the purchaser made numerous unsuccessful attempts to obtain planning permission. The court held that this condition had been inserted exclusively for the benefit of the purchaser, and therefore the purchaser could waive compliance with this condition.

1176. [1978] ILRM 73, 77.
1177. *O'Connor v Coady* [2005] 1 ILRM 256.
1178. *Rooney v Byrne* [1933] IR 609; *Lynch v Duffy* [2009] IEHC 59.
1179. For example, as in *O'Mullane v Riordan*, Unreported, High Court, 20 April 1978. (The purchaser agreed to buy land subject to obtaining planning permission. If planning permission is refused, the purchaser might elect to purchase the land anyway. The condition is wholly for his benefit.)
1180. [2010] IEHC 293.

However, this waiver must be communicated before the other party communicates an intention to avoid the contract.[1181] In *ACC Loan Management Ltd v Sheehan*[1182] thc bank had made a condition of drawdown of a loan the receipt of a letter from the guarantor's solicitor confirming that the guarantor had received independent legal advice prior to execution of the guarantee document. Only a letter from the borrower's solicitor was received. In this case it was said to be arguable that the bank was not entitled to unilaterally waive a condition it had imposed but which arguably was for the benefit of both parties.

1181. *Hand v Greaney* [2004] IEHC 391.
1182. [2016] IECA 343.

Chapter 4. Privity of Contract

§1. The Rule of Privity of Contract

I. The Rule of Privity of Contract

509. The rule of privity contract provides that someone who is not a contracting party cannot have contractual obligations enforced against them. The rule has been applied in Ireland since the 1860s, and can be seen in *Murphy v Bower,*[1183] where a contractor agreed to perform certain work for a railway company. The contractor was to be paid when an engineer certified that the work had been completed, but the engineer subsequently refused to do so. It was held that the contractor could not bring a case against the engineer in contract, as the engineer was not a party to the contract between the contractor and the railway company.

510. The privity rule also means that a third party cannot enforce a contract, even if that contract was intended to benefit them. This rule is well illustrated in Ireland by cases such as *McCoubray v Thompson.*[1184] Here, a contract provided that a farm would be transferred to Thompson if he agreed to pay half the value of the farm to McCoubray, who was not a contracting party. After the land was transferred to Thompson, he refused to pay the amount promised in the contract to McCoubray, but McCoubray could not recover the amount owed to him as he was not party to the contract. Similarly in *Cadbury (Ireland) Ltd v Kerry Co-Operative Creameries Ltd and Dairy Disposal Co Ltd*[1185] a contract was entered into between Kerry Co-Op and Dairy Disposal which included an undertaking from Kerry Co-Op that adequate milk supplies would continue to Cadbury's factory. This was held not be enforceable, as even though it was clearly intended to benefit Cadbury's, Cadbury's were not party to the contract. More recently, the Supreme Court has stated that privity of contract 'can be a valid defence against the binding nature of a collective agreement entered into between an employer and a trade union', as 'the membership of a union, or of an employers' group, may be at one remove from such a contract and not privy to it'.[1186]

511. A third effect of the privity rule is that third parties may not be able to rely on exclusion clauses contained in contracts to which they are not party. The law in Ireland is not entirely clear in this regard – although the English Court of Appeal in *Scruttons Ltd v Midland Silicones Ltd*[1187] set out the limited conditions under which it might be possible for a third party to rely on an exclusion clause which purports

1183. (1868) IR 2 CL 506.
1184. (1868) 2 IRCL 226.
1185. [1982] ILRM 77.
1186. *Martin Reid and James Turner v The Health Service Executive* [2016] IESC 8, para. 17. *See also Goulding Chemicals Ltd v Bolger* [1977] IR 211. However a situation could arise where a union is said to act as an agent for its members, *see Pattison v Institute for Industrial Research and Standards*, Unreported, High Court, 31 May 1979.
1187. [1962] AC 446 (Eng.). *See also New Zealand Shipping Co Ltd v AM Satterthwaite & Co Ltd (The Eurymedon)* [1975] AC 154 (Privy Council).

to benefit them, this does not appear to have been expressly adopted in any Irish case.[1188] Section 34(1)(b) of the Civil Liability Act 1961 provides that a defence arising under a contract is available in respect of a negligence action, but it is unclear whether this refers to a defence in *any* contract, or merely a contract to which the defendant is privy.[1189]

512. A final implication of the privity rule is that contractual remedies aim to compensate parties to the contract rather than third parties. As a general rule it is not possible to recover damages in contract for the loss suffered by a third party,[1190] although there are exceptional situations where this might be possible.[1191]

II. Exceptions to the Rule of Privity of Contract

513. There are several common law exceptions to this rule. One of the most important of these exceptions is agency, which allows a principal to sue and be sued on a contract entered into by their agent on their behalf, and which forms a discrete area of contract law in its own right.[1192]

514. Under the law of trusts a third party can enforce a contract if a completely constituted trust was created in their favour by the contract. In some earlier cases the courts were willing to imply the existence of a trust to give rights to third parties,[1193] but this has been criticised as 'intellectually dishonest'[1194] and a 'cumbrous fiction',[1195] and today courts are reluctant to find that there is a trust unless it is clear that this was the intention of the parties.[1196] This is in part because the finding of the existence of a trust means that the contracting parties are no longer free to rescind or vary their agreement, and can have consequences beyond normal contractual obligations.

515. It is of course possible to sue for negligence in tort where there is no privity of contract.[1197] However, the limitation imposed by privity rule is at least partly

1188. Although the decision in *Hearn and Matchroom Boxing Ltd v Collins*, Unreported, High Court, 3 February 1998, purports to apply the test, it does so in an unusual context and arguably one where normal agency principles could simply have applied.
1189. *See* Quill, 'Sub-contractors, Exclusion Clauses & Privity' (1991) Irish Law Times 211.
1190. *See Woodar Investment v Wimpey Construction* [1980] 1 All ER 571 (Eng.), cited with approval in *Burke v Dublin Corporation* [1991] 1 IR 341.
1191. *See Burke v Dublin Corporation* [1991] 1 IR 341, 353 where Finlay CJ said that consumer cases where one party enters into a contract on behalf of a group may call for 'special treatment' in the relation to the measure of damages.
1192. *See* Part II Chapter 1 below.
1193. *See*, for example, *Drimmie v Davies* (1899) 1 IR 176; *Kenny v Employer's Liability Insurance Corp* [1901] 1 IR 301; *Kelly v Larkin* [1910] 2 IR 550.
1194. Clark, *Contract Law in Ireland* (8th ed., 2016) 632.
1195. Lord Wright (1939) 55 Law Quarterly Review 189, 208.
1196. *See*, for example, *Cadbury (Ireland) Ltd v Kerry Co-op Creameries Ltd* [1982] ILRM 77; *Inspector of Taxes Association v Minister for the Public Service* High Court, 24 March 1983.
1197. The leading English case of *Donoghue v Stevenson* [1932] AC 562 was approved in Ireland in *Kirby v Burke* [1944] IR 207.

responsible for the expansion of the law of negligence to encompass cases of 'pure economic loss', that is, pure financial loss independent of any personal injury or injury to property. Actions for pure economic loss tend to be brought where it is not possible to sue for breach of contract because there is no contractual relationship, and may be viewed as an attempt to circumvent the privity rule.[1198] The expansion of negligence in this manner has been criticised, and the English Court of Appeal[1199] has restricted recovery for pure economic loss to particular cases such as negligent misstatement and professional negligence. In *Glencar Exploration plc v Mayo County Council*[1200] the Irish Supreme Court refused to allow an action for pure economic loss on the facts, and Keane CJ expressly reserved for another occasion the question of whether this type of action should be allowed in Ireland. In *Beatty v The Rent Tribunal*[1201] Geoghegan J stated that the law on this question has not been finally determined in Ireland. In *Hu v Duleek Formwork Ltd & Anor*[1202] the High Court rejected the argument that the insurance company owed a duty of care to a potential claimant against the insured party, in the absence of a contractual relationship between the two.

516. There are several statutory exceptions to this rule. These were developed in an ad hoc fashion as a response to specific situations where the legislature ascertained a need to grant third parties the right to enforce a contract made for their benefit. Section 8 of the Married Women's Status Act 1957 provides that any contract entered into by a person that confers a benefit on their spouse or their children can be enforced by the spouse or children.[1203] However this is limited in that it only applies to a spouse or children (not cohabiting partners or other relatives) and the contract must expressly confer a benefit on that individual.[1204] Section 76(1) of the Road Traffic Act 1961 provides that a person who is claiming against an insured motorist can bring an action against the motorist's insurer where the owner is outside the State or cannot be found, or where 'for any other reason it is just and equitable that the application be granted'.[1205]

517. Section 62 of the Civil Liability Act 1961 states that where an individual who has effected a policy of insurance in respect of liability or a wrong becomes a bankrupt or dies,[1206] moneys payable to the insured under the policy are only applicable in discharging valid claims against the insured, and cannot be used to pay off

1198. *See*, for example, *Junior Books Ltd v Veitchi Co Ltd* [1983] 1 AC 520, which was approved in Ireland in *Ward v McMaster* [1988] IR 337.
1199. *Murphy v Brentwood District Council* [1991] 1 AC 69.
1200. [2002] 1 IR 84.
1201. [2006] 1 ILRM 164, 173.
1202. [2013] IEHC 50.
1203. *See also* s. 7 of the Married Women's Status Act 1957 which provides that a policy of life assurance or endowment which is expressed to be for the benefit of, or by its express terms purports to confer a benefit upon, the spouse or child of the insured, is enforceable by that spouse or child.
1204. *See*, for example, *Burke v Dublin Corporation* [1991] 1 IR 341.
1205. *Sinnott v Quinnsworth* [1984] ILRM 523.
1206. The section also applies to insured companies and partnerships which are wound up or dissolved, so that, for example, insurance money cannot be used by a liquidator in an insolvency situation but must be paid to the injured party.

other debts. Although this section gives an entitlement to an injured party to sue the insurers of a bankrupt party to ensure compliance with the section,[1207] its function is to protect insured debts from insolvency proceedings, and it cannot be used as a more general means of circumventing the privity rule. In *Hu v Duleek Formwork Ltd & Anor*[1208] it was held that there was no privity of contract between an employee and the employer's insurance company, and section 62 could not be used to create a right of action against the insurance company. This decision has been criticised, and the Law Reform Commission has recommended that third-party consumers who may be entitled to benefit under the terms of a contract of insurance should be able to enforce those rights directly against the insurer, on a similar basis to the Road Traffic Act 1961.[1209]

518. Until recently, Irish law adopted the common law rule in *Tulk v Moxhay*[1210] that negative covenants concerning land may be enforced against subsequent owners of the land, even though they were not party to the original covenant.[1211] However, the common law rule was abolished by section 49 of the Land and Conveyancing Law Reform Act 2009, and replaced by a rule which makes any freehold covenants enforceable by and against successors in title. Hence, successors in title to land can gain responsibilities under a contract to which they were not a party.[1212]

519. Ownership of the rights contained in negotiable instruments can be transferred to and enforced by a third party, referred to as the holder in due course. Section 38(2) of the Bills of Exchange Act 1882 provides that the holder in due course may take an action against not only the original debtor on the instrument if he fails to pay, but also against any other previous signatories of the instrument who have had the debt negotiated to them.

520. A number of statutory exceptions to the rule concern consumers. Section 80 of the Consumer Credit Act 1995 provides that where a consumer enters into a hire-purchase agreement, the consumer has a remedy against both the seller and the hire-purchase company in the event of a breach of the agreement or a misrepresentation by either the seller or the hire-purchase company. Section 14 of the Sale of Goods and Supply of Services Act 1980 provides that where goods are sold to a consumer under an arrangement with a 'finance house', the finance house and the seller are jointly answerable to the buyer for breach of the contract of sale and for any misrepresentations made by the seller with respect to the goods. Section 13 of the Sale of Goods and Supply of Services Act 1980 provides that there is an implied condition in a contract for the sale of a motor vehicle that at the time of delivery the

---

1207. *Dunne v PJ White* [1989] 1 ILRM 803.
1208. [2013] IEHC 50. *See also McCarron v Modern Timber Homes Ltd* [2012] IEHC 530; *Murphy v Allianz plc* [2014] IEHC 692.
1209. Law Reform Commission, *Report on Consumer Insurance Contracts* (LRC 113-2005) para. 6.35.
1210. (1848) 2 Ph 774. The covenant could not be enforced against a *bonafide* third-party purchaser who did not have notice of the covenant.
1211. *See*, for example, *Whelan and Whelan v Cork Corporation* [1991] ILRM 19.
1212. *See* McGrath and Howlin, *Lyall's Land Law in Ireland* (4th ed., Round Hall, 2018).

vehicle is free from any defect that would render it a danger to the public, including people travelling in the vehicle. The parties to the contract of sale are the buyer and seller, but third parties who use the vehicle with the consent of the buyer and suffer a loss because of a breach of this condition may maintain an action for damages against the seller.[1213] The Liability for Defective Products Act 1991 gives consumers rights of action in tort where they suffer an injury caused by a defect in a product, even if they did not buy the product themselves. The protections in the Package Holidays and Travel Trade Act 1995 as amended[1214] extend not only to the person who purchases the holiday, but also to third parties who benefit from the contract.

521. In addition, contractual devices are used to circumvent the effect of the privity rule. For example, collateral warranties are used extensively to circumvent the privity rule, particularly in the construction industry, and contractual rights may be assigned to another party.[1215]

III. The Need to Reform the Rule of Privity of Contract in Ireland

522. Unlike many other jurisdictions, in Ireland there is no general exception to the privity rule where the contract is for the benefit of a third party. This position has been criticised by the Law Reform Commission which in 2008 issued a report recommending legislative reform of the privity rule to allow third parties to enforce rights under contracts made for their benefit.[1216] The Law Reform Commission identified several problems with the current state of the privity rule in Ireland. The privity rule applies even if the parties intended to benefit a third party, and thus can 'thwart the intentions of the contracting parties',[1217] a result which appears to be incompatible with the principle of freedom of contract. In the situation where the application of the privity rule means that a third party cannot rely on an exemption clause intended to benefit them, there may also be interference with the risk allocation agreed upon by the parties. The privity rule often does not accord with commercial expectations – many contracting parties may assume that the third party can enforce the promise, for example in a situation where a consumer buys a gift intended for a third party. The Law Reform Commission further pointed out that devices used to circumvent the rule, such as collateral contracts, cause extra expense and inconvenience for contracting parties. The privity rule can result in the anomalous position that the party who has suffered a loss cannot sue for damages, while

1213. *See*, for example, *Glorney v O'Brien*, Unreported, High Court, 14 November 1998.

1214. This Act was recently amended by the European Union (Package Travel And Linked Travel Arrangements) Regulations 2019.

1215. Law Reform Commission, *Report on Privity of Contract and Third Party Rights* (LRC 88-2008) paras 1.26–1.29.

1216. Law Reform Commission, *Report on Privity of Contract and Third Party Rights* (LRC 88-2008). The Report follows the publication in 2006 of a Consultation Paper *Privity of Contract: Third Party Rights* (LRC CP 40-2006). *See* Kelly, 'Privity of Contract – The Benefits of Reform' 2008(1) *Judicial Studies Institute Journal* 145–170.

1217. Report para. 2.04.

the party who can sue has not suffered a loss and can only recover nominal damages. A significant number of exceptions exist both at common law and in statute, but they do not cover every situation which might arise; moreover it is not always clear when the courts will apply the rule or an exception to the rule. It has been suggested, for example, that the rule could be circumvented by means of devices such as constructive trusts or estoppel, but, while this may provide a just result in an individual case, it would cause considerable uncertainty.

523. The Law Reform Commission Report recommended the introduction of detailed legislation which would allow a third party to enforce a term of the contract when the term expressly benefits the third party, provided this was the intention of the contracting parties. Second, it was recommended that a third party should be able to enforce a term of the contract when the contract expressly states that the third party has a right of enforcement, regardless of whether or not the contract benefits the third party. Third, the Commission recommended that a third party should have a right to rely on a term of a contract which excludes or limits the liability of the third party, provided that was the intention of the parties. The Commission's proposed statutory scheme also dealt with issues such as how the third party is to be identified, the ability of the contracting parties to cancel or vary the contract, the defences available to the promisor, the remedies available to the third party and the possibility of overlapping claims. As mentioned above, a second report also recommended reforms to the privity rule in relation to consumer insurance contracts.[1218]

524. Despite the recommendations of the Law Reform Commission, to date no legislation has been passed by the Oireachtas. The Consumer Rights Bill 2015 included provision to protect consumers who receive presents as a gift, in that the protections in the Bill would apply to them as though they had bought the item themselves, but this Bill has been abandoned pending European developments.[1219]

§2. Transfer of Contractual Rights

525. Section 28(6) of the Supreme Court of Judicature (Ireland) Act 1877 provides that an 'absolute assignment' by the assignor of any debt or other legal chose in action can pass the legal right to the debt or chose in action to the assignee. The assignment must be in writing by the assignor and the debtor must be given express notice in writing of the assignment. A statutory assignment does not need valuable consideration (i.e., any form of payment) to be valid. The assignee can then sue the debtor in their own name, without joining the assignor as a party to the action. Specific legislative provisions provide for the formal assignment of contractual rights in particular situations. For example, the Policies of Assurance Act 1867 allows for

1218. Law Reform Commission, *Report on Consumer Insurance Contracts* (LRC 113-2005) para. 6.35.
1219. *See* Kelly, 'Consumer Reform in Ireland and the United Kingdom: Regulatory Divergence Before, After and Without Brexit' (2018) 47(1) *Common Law World Review* 53.

the assignment of life insurance policies and section 50 of the Marine Insurance Act 1906 provides that a marine insurance policy is assignable unless it contains a term expressly prohibiting assignment.

526. Historically, the common law courts would not generally allow the assignment of contractual rights, but the equity courts would allow it. The common law courts and equity courts were fused together in the Supreme Court of Judicature (Ireland) Act 1877, and the equitable rules (i.e., those developed in the equity courts) were said to prevail over the common law rules. The 1877 Act did not abolish these equitable rules on assignment, which can still be relied upon if the conditions for a statutory assignment not met. An assignment of an existing debt does not need valuable consideration to be valid.[1220] There is no need to give notice of the assignment to the debtor, although it is recommended to prevent the debtor paying the assignor, and to give the assignee priority over other assignees.

527. The debtor can rely on any defences he would have had against the assignor at the time when he received notice of the assignment, and an assignee cannot recover more than the assignor could have done if there was no assignment.[1221]

528. The purported assignment of rights under a contract which expressly forbids the assignment of rights will not be effective against the debtor. Nor will the assignment of rights under a contract that involves a personal confidence in the other contracting party be enforceable against the debtor. For example, the holder of a motor insurance policy cannot assign the benefits under the policy, as the insurer relies on the insured's skill and record as a driver. It is not possible to assign a contractual obligation, as opposed to a benefit, to a third party without the consent of all parties involved. In *Cendant Limited and others v Galtee Plant hire Limited and others*[1222] Murphy J stated the applicable principles as follows:

(i) The benefit can be assigned where the consideration has been executed and nothing more remains but to enforce the obligation against the party who has received the consideration;
(ii) The special right of ignoring altogether the consent of the person upon whom the obligation lies to the substitution of one person for another as the recipient of the benefit is confined to cases where it can make no difference to the person on whom the obligation lies to which of the two persons he is to discharge it;
(iii) Contracts where there are mutual obligations still to be enforced and where it is impossible to say that the whole consideration has been executed cannot be assigned.[1223]

1220. *See Law Society of Ireland v O'Malley* [1999] 1 IR 162, 172 per Barron J.
1221. *See Dawson v Great Northern & City Railway Co* [1905] 1 KB 260 (Eng.); *Technotrade Ltd v Larkstore Ltd* [2006] EWCA Civ 1079 (Eng.).
1222. [2016] IEHC 389.
1223. *Ibid.*, para. 119.

529. On the facts of this case, the purported assignment of a charterparty was invalid. The consideration was ongoing and required the performance of obligations, including maintenance, insurance and licensing obligations as well as payment obligations, on a regular basis throughout the term of the agreement. Nor was the contract one where it made no difference on whom the ongoing obligations lie.[1224]

530. In *SPV Osus Limited v HSBC Institutional Trust Services (Ireland) Limited & Ors.*[1225] the Supreme Court held that the assignment of a bare cause of action where the assignee has no commercial interest or connection to the action is void as being against public policy:

> [If] it is offensive to public policy to permit a person to fund a plaintiff's litigation in return for some part of the proceedings, then the same public policy must apply a fortiori where the third party purchases the claim outright, removes the party from his or her proceedings, and converts them into a mere witness at best.[1226]

531. In contrast in *Morrissey v. Irish Bank Resolution Corporation Ltd & ors*[1227] the Court of Appeal held that a loan sale agreement, comprising the assignment of the loans and the associated right to sue in respect of the recovery of the loans, was valid as the assignee had a legitimate interest in the enforcement of the loans.

§3. The Special Case of a 'Subcontract', E.g., the (Nominated) Subcontractor in Building Contracts

532. The privity rule applies to subcontracts in the same way as it would to any other contract. If A contracts with B, and then B subcontracts with C to carry out some of the work, then there are two separate contracts. A cannot sue C if the work done is faulty; their cause of action lies with B, who may then have a cause of action against C. Similarly, C cannot sue A, if for example they are not paid. If A and C wish to have a contractual relationship, they must enter into a separate collateral contract.[1228] Alternatively it might be possible to show that B was acting as an agent (either of A or B) if an agency relationship can be made out.

1224. *Ibid.*, para. 120.
1225. [2018] IESC 44.
1226. *Ibid.*, para. 83 (O'Donnell J). *See* the discussion on champerty and maintenance at paras 387 et seq.
1227. [2017] IECA 162.
1228. *See* Law Reform Commission, *Report on Privity of Contract and Third Party Rights* (LRC 88-2008) paras 1.26–1.29; *Shanklin Pier Ltd v Detel Products Ltd* [1959] 2 KB 854.

Chapter 5. The Termination of the Contract

§1. Performance and Breach

I. Discharge by Performance

533. When a party has completed all of their obligations under the contract, the contract is discharged by performance. The contract may also be discharged where there is a valid *tender* of performance, for example the attempted delivery of goods in accordance with the contract, which is refused without justification.[1229] However, if there is a tender of money, which is refused by the creditor, then the debtor's obligation to pay is not discharged.[1230]

534. Difficulties arise when one party seeks payment for their performance, but it is argued that they have not in fact completed performance in full. If the contract is an 'entire' contract, then they cannot claim payment. A contract is said to be an 'entire' contract where the contract on its true construction requires full and complete performance by one party before the obligation on the other to perform his side of the bargain arises. However, obvious hardship may result, as in the leading case *Cutter v Powell.*[1231] In that case, a seaman died before completion of a voyage. It was held that his widow was not entitled to a proportion of his agreed total payment in respect of his actual service before death as it was an 'entire' contract – the agreed lump sum payment was to be made only on completion of the total voyage. The existence of the express contract further precluded the court from implying a contract to pay a *quantum meruit* for the services provided. The rule on complete performance was applied in *Coughlan v Moloney*[1232] in which the court refused to allow recovery on a *quantum meruit* basis for the uncompleted building of a house.

535. Recovery for part performance may be allowed in the following circumstances:

(i) Where the contract consideration can readily be apportioned
   If a contract consists of a number of separate obligations and performance of the corresponding obligation, such as payment, will become due as each obligation is performed, then payment will not be considered to be dependent on full completion of the work. Each separate payment will fall due as each individual obligation is completed, regardless of whether the rest of the contract is completed. In *Menetone v Athawes,*[1233] for example, a contract for the

1229. The rules as to delivery are set out in the *Sale of Goods Act* 1893, ss 29, 30 and 31.
1230. *See* Clark pp. 658–659.
1231. (1795) 101 ER 573. *See* Stoljar 'The Great Case of *Cutter v Powell*' (1956) 34 Canadian Bar Review 288; Dockray '*Cutter v Powell*: a Trip outside the Text' (2001) 117 Law Quarterly Review 664.
1232. (1905) 39 ILTR 153. *See also Collen v Marum* (1871) 5 Ir CLR 315.
1233. (1764) 97 ER 998. *See also Roberts v Havelock* (1832) 170 ER 145; *Fuller v Patrick* (1849) 18 LJQB 236; *Taylor v Laird* (1856) 25 LJ Ex 329; *Button v Thompson* (1869) LR 4 CP 330; *George v Davies* [1911–13] All ER Rep 914.

repair of a ship provided that work was to be paid for in instalments. Hence, the plaintiff successfully claimed payment under a number of completed instalments for work and labour done even though the repairs as a whole were never completed. In *Brown v Wood* a contract to make and deliver cloth was held to not be entire, as a matter of construction of the contract, meaning that the plaintiff could recover for cloth that was completed (although he was liable to an action for non-delivery for work that was not completed).[1234] In *Verolme Cork Dockyard Ltd v Shannon Atlantic Fisheries Ltd*[1235] Finlay P held that it was an implied term of the contract that a substantial payment on account would be made by the defendants when a reasonably high proportion of the work contracted for was carried out.

However, even where a contract expressly provides for payment in instalments, each instalment or stage could be considered 'entire' in and of itself, so that there could be no remuneration for part performance of an individual stage.[1236]

Legislation has granted jurisdiction to the courts to consider the consideration in types of contracts apportionable. The Apportionment Act 1870[1237] provides for the apportionment of 'all rent, annuities, dividends, and other periodical payments in the nature of income'.[1238] Section 2 of the Act provides that these payments shall 'be considered as accruing from day to day, and shall be apportionable in respect of time accordingly'. However, it is important to note that section 7 provides that the Act does not apply where it is 'expressly stipulated that no apportionment shall take place'. The Merchant Shipping Act 1894, which consolidated previous Merchant Shipping legislation, provides in section 155 that a seaman's right to wages shall be taken to begin at the time at which he commences work, or the time agreed for his commencement of work, whichever should happen first. Section 158 of the Act provides for the apportionment of wages where the seaman is unable to complete the voyage through no fault of his own.[1239] It seems clear that this section would cover a situation like that in *Cutter v Powell* where the seaman dies.

Modern building and engineering contracts will normally be on standard form contracts which provide for various payments related to 'stage' performances. The Construction Contracts Act 2013 provides a mechanism where parties to a construction contract are to fix interim payments and final payment amounts and dates, with default provisions for contracts that fail to do so.

(ii) Where not all of the obligations under the contract can be viewed as entire

---

1234. (1854) 6 Ir Jur 221.

1235. Unreported, High Court, 31 July 1978.

1236. *Stubbs v Holywell Ry Co* (1867) LR 2 Ex 311. Williams 'Partial Performance of Entire Contracts' (1941) 57 Law Quarterly Review 373, 374 distinguishes between contracts which are 'infinitely severable' and those which are 'made up of an agglomeration of entire parts'.

1237. 33 & 34 Vict. c. 35. Matthews 'Salaries in the Apportionment Act 1870' (1982) 2 Legal Studies 302; Williams 'Partial Performance of Entire Contracts' (1941) 57 Law Quarterly Review 373, 382–383.

1238. Section 2.

1239. This was originally to be found in s. 185 of the Merchant Shipping Act 1854, 17 & 18 Vict c.104.

Only some of the obligations in a contract may be entire, in which case the liability of the defendant to pay may depend on which obligation has not been completed. For example, a contract for the carriage of goods by sea, with freight payable on arrival, is generally entire, with respect to delivery at the stipulated port. Thus where a contract for the carriage of goods by sea provides that freight is due on arrival of the goods, the shipowner cannot recover anything even if he is compelled to abandon the voyage by *perils* of the sea and to discharge the cargo at an intermediate port.[1240] However, it is not entire with respect to the quantity of cargo delivered[1241] or the condition/quality of that cargo when it arrives.[1242]

(iii) The doctrine of substantial performance

The doctrine of substantial performance provides a remedy where there is defective performance (as opposed to only partial performance) in relatively minor respects.[1243] The work must be carried out in its essential respects, with the dispute usually referring to whether the work done meets the contract standard, and the other party is still able to claim for damages for any defective performance. However, the courts are wary of allowing this remedy where the party has abandoned the work: *see Kincora Builders Ltd v Cronin* where payment under this rule was refused where a builder refused to insulate an attic.[1244]

(iv) Where a fresh contract can be implied

It is possible to recover for performance rendered if a new contract between the parties can be implied from the conduct of the parties. The most common way in which a new contract is implied is by the defendant's free acceptance or retention of a benefit conferred on him by the plaintiff. For example, if a shipowner contracts to carry goods from A to B, but because of storms or other perils of sea, is forced to travel to an alternative port C, and their owner voluntarily accepts the goods at C, a new contract may be implied to pay a *quantum meruit* for the carriage of the goods to C.[1245] Such a fresh contract between the parties is implied in the context of the sale of goods: section 30 of Sale of Goods Act 1893 provides that where the seller delivers to the buyer a quantity of goods less than he contracted to sell, the buyer may reject them, but if he

---

1240. *Cook v Jennings* (1797) 7 TR 381; 101 ER 1032; *Metcalfe v Britannia Iron Works Company* (1877) 2 QBD 423.

1241. *Ritchie v Atkinson* (1808) 10 East 295; 103 ER 787.

1242. *Dakin v Oxley* (1864) 15 CB (NS) 646; 143 ER 938. In some cases where the contract has provided for a lump sum freight it has been held that the carrier is entitled to the entire freight, less any damages for the failure to perform: *Merchant Shipping Co v Armitage* (1873) LR 9 QB 99; *Thomas v Harrowing SS Co* [1915] AC 58.

1243. *See Hoenig v Isaacs*[1952] 2 All ER 176. *H Dakin & Co v Lee* [1916] 1 KB 566, which was approved by Pringle J in the High Court in *Kincora Builders Ltd v Cronin*, Unreported, 5 March 1973. The law in this area has been rightly criticised by Treitel *The Law of Contract* (11th ed., 2003) pp. 785–788.

1244. *Kincora Builders Ltd v Cronin*, Unreported, 5 March 1973.

1245. *See*, for example, *Luke v Lyde* 2 Burr 883; *Christy v Row* 1 Taunt 300; *St Enoch Co v Phosphate Co* [1916] 2 KB 624 (here no new contract was formed between the parties).

accepts the goods so delivered he must pay for them at the contract rate. However, outside these contexts, the courts are unwilling to find that there is an implied contract.[1246]

(v) Fault of one party preventing performance

In some circumstances, where complete performance is prevented by the act or default of the other party to the contract, the plaintiff can claim *quantum meruit* for part performance.[1247]

II. Discharge by Breach

536. A breach of contract usually gives the innocent party the right to claim damages, but not every breach of contract gives the innocent party a right to treat the contract as at an end. If the breach is one that does give the innocent party the right to treat the contract as at an end, this does not happen automatically; the innocent party has the option to terminate the contract or they may decide to continue with the contract. The right to terminate the contract may be lost if the contract is affirmed or if there is a delay in claiming the right to rescind.[1248] The right to terminate a contract arises: (i) where there is a repudiatory breach; (ii) where there is a breach of condition; (iii) where there is a fundamental breach of contract; or (iv) where there is a contractual right to terminate.

537. The terminology can cause confusion, as phrases such as 'termination' 'discharge' and 'repudiation' can be used interchangeably, but 'what is meant is no more than that the innocent party or, in some cases, both parties, are excused from further performance'.[1249] Although commonplace, it is arguably incorrect to use the word 'rescission' in this context,[1250] but at any rate 'rescission' in relation to breach refers to where a contract is terminated after its formation, and is certainly not the same as 'rescission' for misrepresentation, which is where the contract is treated as never having been in existence.

1246. The court in *Coughlan v Moloney* (1905) 39 ILTR 153 was not satisfied that a new implied contract had been made. *See also* the statement of Pollock CB in *Taylor v Laird* (1856) 25 LJ Ex 329 at 352 'One cleans another's shoe; what can the other do but put them on?'.

1247. *Planché v Colburn* (1831) 8 Bing 14; 131 ER 305; *Arterial Drainage v Rathangan* (1880) 6 LR (Ir) 513.

1248. *Bord Iascaigh Mhara v Scallan*, Unreported, High Court, 8 May 1973.

1249. *Photo Production v Securicor* [1980] AC 827, 844. However, clauses such as arbitration clauses, exclusion clauses and liquidated damages clauses will survive termination, and 'the contract survives for the purpose of measuring the claims out of the breach': *Heyman v Darwins* [1942] AC 356.

1250. *See* https://ipdraughts.wordpress.com/2014/02/09/using-the-right-words-in-contracts-knowing-your-3rs/ and *Heyman v Darwins Ltd* [1942] AC 356, 399.

A. Repudiatory Breach

538. A contract may be terminated for breach where the breach consists of a clear indication by one party that they no longer intend to commence or continue performance of the contract; this is referred to as a repudiatory breach. A repudiatory breach may occur where one party says they no longer wish to accept the performance of the other party as agreed. In *Athlone Rural District Council v AG Campbell & Son (No.2)*[1251] contractors were to excavate wells for a local authority, but the local authority said that it did not require the work to be done. This was held to be a repudiatory breach, discharging the contractors from their obligations under the contract and allowing them to recover damages for breach of contract.

539. Difficulties arise when the party who it is alleged has repudiated the contract has not explicitly stated their intention to abandon the contract, but has acted in a manner that indicates that they do intend to do so. In this situation, the court will ask 'whether the defendants, by their conduct, have shown or made quite plain an intention not to perform the contract, so as to entitle the plaintiffs to treat the refusal by the defendants as a repudiation of the contract'.[1252] For example, a painter who is hired to paint a building but who fails to show up on successive agreed dates may be taken to have abandoned the contract, whereas if the painter merely turns up late on the first day they will (most likely) not have intended to abandon the contract. The difficulty here for the innocent party is that if they regard the conduct of the other party as repudiatory, and purport to 'accept' the termination of the contract, but it subsequently turns out that they were incorrect in this assessment, they might themselves be held to have wrongfully repudiated the contract.[1253] There is an extra difficulty here in that if the innocent party fails to act then they may be held to have affirmed the contract, and lose the right to reject. Hence some allowance is made while the innocent party takes time to assess the situation, although it may be prudent to expressly reserve the right to repudiate during this time.[1254]

540. In some cases the issue of whether the contract has been repudiated by one party is discussed in language that closely resembles the language of 'fundamental breach', discussed below, and the parameters between the two are not always clear. For example in *British Leyland Exports Limited v Britain Group Sales Limited*[1255] there was found to be a repudiatory breach of a lease when breaches were of such frequency and such gravity that they had the effect of depriving the innocent party (temporarily at least) of the whole benefit which it was the intention of the parties that they should obtain from the contract. This case was cited in *Parol Ltd v Carroll*

1251. (1913) 47 ILTR 142.
1252. *House of Spring Gardens Ltd v Point Blank Ltd* [1984] 1 IR 611. *See also Bob Bushell Ltd v Luxel Varese SAS*, Unreported, High Court, 20 February 1998 (repudiatory breach of an exclusivity agreement where one party supplies competitors of the other); *Larkin v Groeger and Eaton*, Unreported, High Court, 26 April 1998 (partnership terminated by conduct).
1253. *See*, for example, *Decro-Wall International SA v Practitioners in Marketing Ltd* [1971] 2 All ER 216.
1254. *See Stocznia Gdanska v Latvian Shipping No3* [2002] 2 All ER (Comm) 768.
1255. [1981] IR 335.

Village Retail (Management) Services[1256] where the defendant company, who had closed a major retail outlet ('Superquinn') in a shopping centre, sought to justify its breach of contract by reference to a series of actions by the plaintiff, arguing that these actions amounted to repudiatory breach. Clarke J stated:

> A landlord who either fails to comply with the landlord's obligations under a lease or acts otherwise in a manner to a sufficient extent so as to substantially prevent a lessee from using the lessee's premises in the manner contemplated by the lease in question, renders the lease open to being regarded as having been repudiated by the landlord concerned. What amounts to such conduct will depend on the facts of each individual case. Some actions on the part of the landlord may be one off but nonetheless so serious as to meet that test. On the other hand, a persistent failure on the part of the landlord (particularly when called upon to desist) might also amount, in principle, to circumstances justifying the lessee as treating the lease as having been repudiated, even though such action for a brief period of time or on a relatively small number of occasions, might not be sufficient.

541. However, on the facts repudiatory breach was not made out, and thus Superquinn was not justified in its closure of the store. Similarly in *Westpark Investments Ltd v Leisureworld Limited*[1257] it was held that a tenant was not entitled to refuse to pay rent to a landlord where there was a breach of contract consisting of the ongoing closure of part of the car park; instead an action would lie for damages for breach (in this case in the form of set-off against the claim for rent).

542. Where a repudiatory breach occurs before the time for performance has arrived, it is described as an anticipatory breach.[1258] The other party in such a case has the option of accepting the repudiation of the contract and suing for damages immediately, or waiting until the time for performance has passed and then suing. In *White & Carter (Councils) Ltd v McGregor*[1259] it was held that if there is an anticipatory breach the injured party can elect to affirm the contract and claim the full contract price (which may be more than could be claimed if only a claim for damages is made). There is, however, the risk that if the option to delay is selected,

1256. [2010] IEHC 498.
1257. [2012] IEHC 343.
1258. *Leeson v North British Oil & Candle Co.* (1874) 8 Ir CLR 309; *Hocester v De La Tour* (1853) 118 ER 922.
1259. [1962] AC 413. *See* Nienaber 'The Effect of Anticipatory Repudiation: Principle and Policy' (1962) 20 Cambridge Law Journal 213; Liu, 'The *White & Carter* Principle: A Restatement' (2011) 74 Modern Law Review 171.

an event may occur which terminates the contract by operation of law, such as frustration, and in that event an action for breach will not be maintainable.[1260] The principle in *White & Carter* means that there is no duty to 'mitigate loss', as would normally arise when claiming damages, and it was recently criticised in the Irish High Court:

> Even if the reasoning [in White and Carter] may be correct as a matter of strict logic, it nonetheless leads to results which are distinctly unpalatable and, in truth, unacceptable. […] For my part, I cannot think that an action for debt is so sacrosanct that the ordinary rules as to mitigation do not apply to a breach of an obligation of the kind at issue in the present case just as much as they do in the case of an action for damages for breach of contract.[1261]

543. However this statement was *obiter* as on the facts the repudiation was accepted by the innocent party.

B. Breach of Condition

544. If a contract term that has been breached is a 'condition' then breach of that term gives the innocent party the right to rescind the contract and sue for damages. If the term is a 'warranty' then there is only a right to damages, and no right to rescind the contract. This distinction reflects the fact that not all terms of a contract are equally important – breach of certain important terms (conditions) might justify the ending of the contract, but the breach of minor terms (warranties) might not. This development of this distinction between conditions and warranties is influenced by the Sale of Goods Act 1893–1980, which applies to contracts for the sale of goods. The Act defines a 'warranty' as a term collateral to the main purpose of the contract, the breach of which gives rise to a claim for damages, but not to a right to reject the goods and treat the contract as repudiated. The Act did not expressly define condition, but it is defined by inference as a term the breach of which gives rise to a right to repudiate the contract.

545. Whether a term is a condition or a warranty is a matter of the intention of the parties themselves. The contract may expressly state that a term is a condition or a warranty, although this will not always be determinative.[1262] Phrases like 'of the essence'[1263] also indicate that a term is intended to be a condition. The court will decide, on all the evidence relating to the contract and the surrounding circumstances, whether the term breached was a warranty or a condition.[1264] In some cases,

1260. *Avery v Bowden* (1855) 119 ER 647 where the outbreak of war rendered performance illegal before the time for performance elapsed. *See also MSC Mediterranean Shipping Co SA v Cottonex Anstalt* [2016] EWCA Civ 789.
1261. *Michael Browne v Iarnród Éireann – Irish Rail (No.2)* [2014] IEHC 117, Hogan J.
1262. *Lombard North Central plc v Butterworth* [1987] QB 527; *Wallis v Pratt* [1911] AC 394; *Schuler AG v Wickman Machine Tool Sales Ltd* [1974] AC 235.
1263. *See Crean v Drinan* [1983] ILRM 82; *Hynes v Independent Newspapers Ltd.* [1980] IR 204.
1264. *Bettini v Gye* (1876) 1 QBD 183 and *Poussard v Spiers and Pond* (1876) 1 QBD 410.

legislation may classify certain terms as conditions or warranties – in particular the Sale of Goods Act 1893–1980, as mentioned above classifies certain implied terms as conditions[1265] and others as warranties,[1266] while others are not classified as either.[1267]

546. In commercial contracts certain terms have acquired a known significance such as 'time' clauses or 'expected to load' clauses in charter parties. These are essentially assumed to be conditions, based on commercial practice. Thus, even if the contract does not expressly state it, breach of such a term goes to the essence of the contract and entitles the injured party to treat the contract as repudiated.[1268]

547. However, sometimes a situation arises where it is still unclear whether a term is a condition or a warranty, or it is an over-simplification to categorise the clause in this manner. The leading case on so-called innominate or intermediate terms is *Hong Kong Fir Shipping Co. Ltd. v Kawasaki Kisen Kaisha Ltd.*[1269] In this case a term in a charterparty contract provided that a ship was to be 'seaworthy'. Treating the term as a condition could result in its termination for a very minor breach, whereas treating it as a warranty could meant that the contract could not be terminated even if there was a very significant breach resulting in the ship being unavailable for most of the duration of the charterparty. In this situation, the court examined the result of the breach to ascertain whether or not it deprived the innocent party of substantially the whole benefit which it was intended that he should obtain from the contract. In other words, is the breach sufficiently serious to justify termination of the contract? On the facts of this case the ship was out of service for twenty weeks out of a two-year charterparty, and it was held that this was not serious enough to terminate the charterparty.

548. This approach was followed in Ireland in *Irish Telephone Rentals Ltd v Irish Civil Service Building Society Ltd.*[1270] In this case the plaintiffs supplied a defective telephone system to the defendants, and it was held that there had been a breach of the implied term in section 39 of the Sale of Goods and Supply of Services Act 1980 as the goods supplied under a service contract were not fit for their purpose. However, the Act does not specify whether this term is a condition or a warranty so the question arose whether the breach entitled the defendants to terminate the contract. It was held that the failure of the telephone system had deprived the defendants of the whole of the benefit which they were intended to receive, and was thus sufficiently serious to justify termination of the contract.

1265. Section 12 (seller must have right to sell), s. 13 (goods must correspond to description), s. 14 (goods must be of merchantable quality and fit for purpose).
1266. Section 12 (goods must be free from encumbrances, right to quiet possession), s. 10(1) (stipulations as to time of payment).
1267. Section 39 (regarding services) and s. 10(2) (stipulations as to time).
1268. *The Mihalis Angelos* [1971] 1 QB 164; *Bunge Corporation v Tradax Export SA* [1981] 2 All ER 513.
1269. [1962] 2 QB 26.
1270. [1991] ILRM 880.

C. Fundamental Breach

549. Some breaches of contract are so serious that they entitled the injured party to repudiate the contract. In assessing whether there has been a fundamental breach the court is essentially asking the question posed in *Hong Kong Firs* – has the innocent party been deprived of substantially the whole benefit that they should obtain from the contract?

550. Fundamental breach differs from repudiatory breach in that questions of the intent of the breaching party are only relevant in the context of repudiatory breach; in fundamental breach the impact of the breach on the innocent party and the contract as a whole is the key factor – does it make performance 'a totally different performance of the contract from that intended by the parties'?[1271] There is no need to show that the breaching party intended to abandon the contract. In *Dundalk Shopping Centre Ltd v Roof Spray Ltd*[1272] for example, there was held to be a fundamental breach when a contractor tried but failed to make a roof watertight, when this is precisely what he was hired to do. In this case there was clearly no 'intention' to abandon the contract, as performance was attempted. In *Uniform Construction Ltd v Cappawhite Contractors Ltd*[1273] it was said that there was a fundamental breach caused by a series of cumulative breaches which were 'confidence shattering'. In *Airscape Ltd v Heaslon Properties Ltd*[1274] the court implied a term into a building contract that each party was to co-operate with the other to secure a performance of the contract and that neither party, by his own act or default, was to prevent performance of the contract. There was said to be a fundamental (serious) breach of this term, meaning that the other party could terminate the contract.[1275] In contrast in *Taylor v Smith*[1276] a delay in the performance of an agreement settlement was not such that termination as justified; the defendants still had a substantial benefit from the initial agreement, and could only claim damages.

D. Contractual Right to Terminate

551. A contract might provide for a right to terminate, either on the occurrence of certain breaches or simply by the giving of notice. However, any conditions and procedures in the contract must be strictly followed. In *ICDL GCC Foundation FZ – LCC v European Computer Driving Licence Foundation Ltd*[1277] the Irish Supreme Court held that a purported termination was invalid, and thus itself amounted to a breach of contract, because the conditions did not exist for valid termination and

---

1271. *Hong Kong Fir Shipping Co. Ltd. v Kawasaki Kisen Kaisha Ltd* [1962] 2 QB 26, 59.
1272. Unreported, High Court, 21 March 1979.
1273. [2007] IEHC 295.
1274. [2008] IEHC 82.
1275. The terminology of the court is unclear here. The term is said to be a 'fundamental term' and a 'condition precedent', yet it is clear that only a significant breach thereof would be considered to terminate the contract.
1276. [1990] ILRM 377.
1277. [2012] IESC 5.

because it wrongly purported to terminate the contract in part only (which was not provided for in the contract). A contract might also provide for a right to suspend performance.[1278]

§2. Impossibility, Frustration and Hardship: 'The Unforeseen'

552. If there is a change in circumstances between formation of contract and time of performance, performance may become more difficult or even impossible, and the person who has agreed to perform may seek to get out of the contract. In this situation, it is not the duty of the courts to rescue either contractual party from the situation in which they find themselves: the contract will not be overturned simply because it turns out that one of the contracting parties entered into a bad bargain. However, the doctrine of frustration recognises that parties cannot provide for every possible future contingency in their contract, and that not all contractual obligations are intended to be absolute, regardless of any change in circumstances in the future. If a contract is frustrated the result is that both parties are discharged from performing any future obligations.

553. The classic definition of frustration is that provided by Lord Radcliffe in *Davis Contractors Ltd v Fareham UDC*:[1279]

> Frustration occurs whenever the law recognises that without default of either party a contractual obligation has become incapable of being performed because the circumstances in which the performance is called for would render it a thing radically different from that which was undertaken in the contract. *Non haec in foedera veni.* It was not this that I promised to do.[1280]

554. Thus, a contract may be frustrated where the subject matter of performance is destroyed,[1281] where performance subsequently becomes illegal[1282] or, in the case of a personal contract, where the promisor dies.[1283] For example, a contract to build an extension on a house may be frustrated if the house burns down, if legislation is enacted prohibiting new building in the area, or if the builder dies or suffers a serious injury. In contrast, if the cost of building materials increases because of a shortage in the market, the builder will still be expected to perform – performance may be more difficult, but it is not something 'radically different' from that undertaken in the contract:

1278. *See*, for example, *ESL Consulting v Verizon (Ireland) Ltd* [2008] IEHC 369.
1279. [1956] AC 696, approved in *Zuphen v Kelly Technical Services* [2000] ELR 277.
1280. [1956] AC 696, 728–729.
1281. *See*, for example, *Taylor v Caldwell* (1863) 3 B&S 826 (destruction of a music hall frustrated a contract to provide the music hall); *Kearney v Saorstát and Continental Shipping* [1943] Ir Jur Rep 8 (ship on which employee serves sinks, frustrating the employment contract).
1282. *See Ross v Shaw* [1917] 2 IR 367.
1283. *See Keane v Hart* (1869) IR 3 CL 388 (death of agent terminated agency agreement); *Hall v Wright* (1858) E B & E 765.

> It is not hardship or inconvenience or a material loss itself which calls the principles of frustration into play. There must have been such a change in the significance of the obligation that the thing undertaken would, if performed, be a different thing from that contracted for.[1284]

555. In *Neville and Sons Ltd v Guardian Builders Ltd*[1285] the Irish Supreme Court held that the mere fact that a contract was more onerous to perform than was originally contemplated did not mean it was frustrated. Blayney J approved the following statement of Lord Simon in *National Carriers Ltd v Panalpina (Northern) Ltd*:[1286]

> Frustration of a contract takes places when there supervenes an event (without default of either party and for which the contract makes no sufficient provision) which so significantly changes the nature *(not merely the expense or onerousness)* of the outstanding contractual rights and / or obligations from what the parties could reasonably have contemplated at the time of its execution that it would be unjust to hold them to the literal sense of its stipulations in the new circumstances; in such case the law declares both parties to be discharged from further performance.

556. Even in cases where performance is impossible or radically different it may be difficult to prove frustration of contract, for example the courts may find that one party or the other took the risk that there would be a change in circumstances, or was at fault for the change, or warranted that a particular result would occur. For example, in *Zuphen v Kelly Technical Services*,[1287] where the plaintiffs were technicians from South Africa who had been recruited by the defendant agency to work in Ireland. The defendant agency had agreed to provide workers to a third party, Eircom, but Eircom later told the agency that it no longer required the workers. The agency told the workers that the contract was frustrated and that they should return to South Africa. It was held that the contract had not been frustrated by the loss of the Eircom contract; the contract was not conditional on the availability of work and the risk of lack of work was on the defendant agency. Similarly in *Mc Guill v Aer Lingus & United Airlines*[1288] an airline was unable to argue that a strike was a frustrating event, where they had been aware of the possibility of a strike at the time the tickets had been issued to the plaintiff. In this case the Court set out the basic principles to be applied to cases of frustration:

> (1) A party may bind himself by an absolute contract to perform something which subsequently becomes impossible.

1284. *Davis Contractors Ltd v Fareham Urban District Council* [1956] AC 696, 728–729, approved in *Zuphen v Kelly Technical Services* [2000] ELR 277, 291.
1285. [1995] 1 ILRM 1, 7.
1286. [1981] AC 675, 700 [author's emphasis].
1287. [2000] ELR 277.
1288. Unreported, High Court, 3 October 1983. *See also Leeson v North British Oil and Candle Ltd* (1874) 2 IRCL 297.

(2) Frustration occurs when without default of either party a contractual obligation has become incapable of being performed.
(3) Thc circumstances alleged to occasion frustration should be strictly scrutinized and the doctrine is not to be lightly applied.
(4) Where the circumstances alleged to cause the frustration have arisen from the act or default of one of the parties, that party cannot rely on the doctrine.[1289]
(5) All the circumstances of the contract should be strictly scrutinized.
(6) The event must be an unexpected event.
(7) If one party anticipated or should have anticipated the possibility of the event which is alleged to cause the frustration and did not incorporate a clause in the contract to deal with it, he should not be permitted to rely on the happening of the event as causing frustration.

557. In addition, if the contract itself deals with the events which are alleged to frustrate the contract, then the contract will not be frustrated.[1290]

558. It is, in general, difficult to prove frustration. For example, in *Drocarne Ltd v Seamus Murphy Properties and Developments Ltd*[1291] the plaintiff argued that an agreement to develop land was frustrated when An Bord Pleanála (the Planning authority) granted planning permission for a retail factory outlet to a third party, as this decision meant that the contracting parties would not now be able to obtain similar planning permission for a retail factory outlet as part of their scheme. However, this argument was rejected in the High Court. The development agreement was for an 'as yet unspecified and undefined form of development' and did not of necessity include a factory retail outlet, and there was not such a fundamental change that the agreement was at an end. The fact that the parties were prevented from developing a scheme which includes a factory retail outlet did not prevent the parties from accomplishing either their joint or separate objectives as recorded in the agreement.

Frustration of purpose

559. A situation can arise where, because of a change of circumstances, the contract will not now result in one contracting party securing a benefit which they expected from the contract. This can be referred to as 'frustration of purpose' and the most famous 'frustration of purpose' cases are undoubtedly the English 'Coronation cases'. These cases arose when the coronation of King Edward VII was postponed because of the illness of the King. For example, in *Krell v Henry*[1292] Mr Henry entered into a contract for the hire of rooms overlooking the route of the

1289. This is sometimes referred to as 'self induced' frustration and, for example, means that a party cannot rely on frustration owing to lack of documentation where it was their own failure to obtain said documentation: *Herman v Owners of SS Vicia* [1942] IR 304; *Byrne v Limerick Steamship Co Ltd* [1946] IR 138.

1290. *Mulligan v Browne*, Unreported, Supreme Court, 23 November 1977; *Ringsend Property Ltd v Donatex Ltd* [2009] IEHC 568.

1291. [2008] IEHC 99.

1292. [1903] 2 KB 740.

coronation procession, for the days of the coronation procession. It was held in the English Court of Appeal that the cancellation of the coronation procession frustrated the contract, not because it was impossible to perform but because room was no longer of any use for the mutually contemplated purpose, i.e., watching the coronation. An alternative way of looking at the case is to say that the foundation or basis of the contract, i.e., the coronation procession, no longer existed and so the contract was frustrated.

560. *Krell v Henry* can be contrasted with the decision in *Herne Bay Steam Co v Hutton*[1293] where a contract for the hire of a steamboat was entered into 'for the purpose of viewing the naval review and for a day's cruise round the fleet'. The naval review was subsquently cancelled, again because of the illness of King Edward VII. The defendant refused to pay the balance owed under the contract, claiming that it had been frustrated. The Court of Appeal disagreed, stating that as the naval review had not been the sole basis or foundation of the contract, the contract was not frustrated and the defendant was still obliged to pay the full contract price. It was still possible to use the boat to cruise around the fleet, even though the defendant would not be able to get the full enjoyment they expected from the contract.[1294]

561. Although the Coronation cases are widely cited, there are actually very few, if any, instances of frustration of purpose being successfully claimed. *Drocarne Ltd v Seamus Murphy Properties and Developments Ltd,*[1295] discussed above, shows the narrow view taken of frustration – the mere fact that a party will not now be able to obtain a certain advantage from a contract does not mean that the contract will be frustrated.

Frustration of leases

562. In *Groome v Fodhla Printing Co*[1296] Black J in the Irish Supreme Court adopted the traditional common law approach of doubting whether the doctrine of frustration could be applied to leases. This is based upon the theoretical argument that a lease grants an estate, or an interest, in land, and that this estate or interest survives physical destruction of the land or property. However, this was before the decision in *National Carriers Ltd v Panalpina (Northern) Ltd*[1297] in which the House of Lords accepted the possibility that a lease could be frustrated. In *Neville & Sons Ltd v Guardian Builders Ltd*[1298] Blayney J in the Supreme Court approved

1293. [1903] 2 KB 683.
1294. The court here also took into account the fact that the hiring of the steamboat was a commercial venture, as the defendant hoped to carry tourists and spectators on the boat for a fee. Hence the court was of the view that the defendant took the risk that the venture might fail because of the cancellation of the review. In contrast, the contract in *Krell v Henry* could be viewed as a consumer contract, although it was not expressly stated to be one.
1295. [2008] IEHC 99.
1296. [1943] IR 380, 414.
1297. [1981] AC 675 (Eng.).
1298. [1995] 1 ILRM 1, 7–8.

significant dicta from *National Carriers Ltd v Panalpina (Northern) Ltd*[1299] and it is thus highly unlikely that there is an absolute ban on the application of the doctrine of frustration to lease. However, it remains very difficult to prove frustration of a lease, as *National Carriers* itself shows.

563. In Ireland, section 40 of the Landlord and Tenant Amendment (Ireland) Act 1860, generally known as 'Deasy's Act',[1300] gave a tenant the right to surrender the tenancy if the subject matter of the lease is destroyed or if it is incapable of beneficial occupation 'by accidental fire or other inevitable accident.' However, the Residential Tenancies Act 2004 has overhauled modern residential tenancies law in Ireland. In particular, section 59 of the Residential Tenancies Act purports to exclude 'any existing rules of law or provisions of enactments relating to termination of tenancies and to notice periods in particular'. It would thus appear that the doctrine of frustration and section 40 of Deasy's Act no longer apply to residential tenancies in Ireland, although it is possible for the tenant to terminate the contract by giving a relatively short period of notice.[1301]

Frustration of employment contracts

564. When an employment contract has been terminated by frustration, rather than by the employer dismissing the employee, the employer may be able to avoid certain statutory obligations owed to the employee. This is because some of the statutory protection offered to employees (e.g., in relation to unfair dismissal or redundancy) is dependent on the existence of a dismissal. Where a contract is frustrated it is terminated by operation of the law, not because the employer has dismissed the employee. Hence, it is inevitably the employer who pleads frustration of contract, in order to avoid their statutory obligations to the employee. This position has been subject to academic[1302] and judicial[1303] criticism.

565. If an employee is absent from work for a long duration his employer may seek to claim that the contract of employment has been frustrated by this absence. One of the main reasons for this absence is the illness or physical incapacity of the employee. In *Donegal County Council v Langan*[1304] the Employment Appeals Tribunal set out a non-exhaustive list of factors to take into account when deciding if a contract of employment is frustrated:

1299. [1981] AC 675 (Eng.).
1300. It is so called because the sponsor of the Act in the House of Commons was Serjeant Rickard Deasy, Attorney General for Ireland and later Lord Justice Deasy. *See* Dowling 'The Genesis of Deasy's Act' (1989) 40 NILQ 53.
1301. Section 36(1).
1302. C Kelly 'Frustrating the Rights Out of You – The Doctrine of Frustration and Employment Contracts' (2004) 4 University College Dublin Law Review 1–36.
1303. *See*, for example, the comment of Murphy J in *Zuphen v Kelly* that it is 'inappropriate … to apply a strict contract law approach to employment disputes' [2000] ELR 277, 288.
1304. UD 143/189. *See also Nolan v Brooks Thomas Ltd.* UD 179/1979; *Mulvaney v Riversdale Concrete Products Ltd* UD 457/1981. Cases are reproduced in Madden and Kerr *Unfair Dismissal Cases and Commentary* (2nd ed., 1996).

(i) the length of the previous employment
(ii) how long it has been expected that the employment would last
(iii) the nature of the job
(iv) the nature, length and effect of the illness or disabling event
(v) the need of the employer for the work to be done
(vi) whether wages have continued to be paid
(vii) the actions of the employer in relation to the employment
(viii) whether consideration was given to retaining the employee on the books if not in employment
(ix) whether the employer discussed with the employee and his trade union the employee's problems and prospects
(x) whether adequate medical investigation was carried out
(xi) whether in all the circumstances a reasonable employer could be expected to wait any longer.

566. The EAT indicated a reluctance to utilise the doctrine of frustration, stating that it has been used 'very selectively'. It pointed out that in most cases the appropriate defence is that of fair dismissal by reason of illness, rather than an outright denial of a dismissal in the first place.

567. There has been some doubt as to whether the imprisonment of an employee can frustrate the employment contract. In *Norris v Southampton City Council*[1305] it was pointed out that the employee was at fault in doing something that led to his imprisonment and his inability to carry out the contract, and thus the contract could not be said to have been frustrated. The doctrine of frustration was considered only to apply where neither party was at fault, and could have no application where one party was at fault. This meant that the employee was able to rely on his own fault in order to avoid a declaration of frustration and so avail of statutory protection. However, in *FC Shepherd & Co Ltd v Jerrom*[1306] it was held that an employee could not rely on his own default and misconduct to defeat an argument for frustration (i.e., the contract was frustrated and the employee could not rely on the statutory protections), and a similar result was seen in Ireland in *Purcell v Carey*[1307] and *Gallagher v Eircom Ltd.*[1308] However, in *McGlinchey v Ryan*[1309] it was commented that the failure of the plaintiff, a teacher, to co-operate with an Inquiry into allegations of sexual abuse did not constitute frustration of the contract of employment or related contracts.

1305. [1982] ICR 177.
1306. [1987] QB 301.
1307. *Purcell v Carey* UD 883/1995, cited in *Redmond on Dismissal Law in Ireland* (1999) p. 397.
1308. UD 955/2004. Clark (p. 704) also cites Anonymous EAT decision UD 181/2007 for authority that even if there is a successful appeal of the conviction, this cannot 'undo' the frustrating event (i.e., the original conviction).
1309. [2010] IEHC 536.

568. Other situations which can result in the frustration of an employment contract include changes in statutory requirements[1310] or the abolition of a statutory post.[1311] In general, events affecting the employer's business or enterprise will not frustrate the contract. Keeping the business solvent and alive is seen as the responsibility of the employer, and the risk of business failure is on him.[1312] However, there are some examples where significant events impacting the employer have resulted in frustration: in *Kearney v Saorstát and Continental Shipping*[1313] the sinking of a vessel on which the employee served frustrated the contract.

The consequences of frustration

569. If a contract is frustrated, it is said to be discharged 'forthwith, without more and automatically'.[1314] This means that discharge occurs without the choice or election of either party but rather by operation of law. There is no need to give notice to the other party to terminate the contract.[1315] This applies to employment contracts also, meaning that 'it is not necessary that the employers should take steps to end the employment for the whole point of frustration is that it operates automatically to discharge the contract as a result of the event bring it about'.[1316] In addition, the entire contract is brought to an end and not merely that part which is now impossible to perform or otherwise affected. There is no general concept of partial discharge in Irish law; in other words, the court does not divide the contract up and enforce that which is possible and ignore that which is not possible.[1317] However, there are certain exceptions to this rule. For example, if performance of a severable part of a contract becomes impossible, that part of the contract alone may be discharged and the rest may be enforceable,[1318] and individual clauses in the contract (e.g., arbitration clauses) might survive the discharge of the contract.[1319]

570. The doctrine of frustration means that both parties are discharged from performing the contract, and neither can bring an action for breach of contract against the other for breach of contract. The doctrine is prospective in its effects; rights that

1310. *See Haugh v Atlanta Nursing Home Ltd* UD 490/1994. Reproduced in Madden and Kerr p. 274.
1311. *O'Cruadhlaoich v Minister for Finance* (1934) 68 ILTR 174.
1312. *See*, for example, *Zuphen v Kelly*, discussed above. *See also Fox v Hession* UD 8/2003 where the increased cost of insuring the employee does not seem to have been considered a frustrating event. Contrast *Duggan v Thomas J O'Brien and Co Ltd* UD 156/1978 where it was stated that an increase in employer's insurance premiums due to an employee's disability may lead to the contract being discharged through frustration, even if the worker is able to perform his duties satisfactorily. Clark (p. 706), has argued that this latter case should be regarded as wrongly decided.
1313. [1943] Ir Jur Rep 8. *See also Ryan v O'Flaherty* UD 354/2003 the resignation of the employer, a general medical practitioner who operated a health centre, was held to terminate the contract of employment of his private secretary.
1314. *Hirji Mulji v Cheong Yue SS Co* [1926] AC 497, 505.
1315. *Flynn v Great Northern Railway Ltd* (1953) 89 ILTR 46; *Byrne v Limerick Steamship Co Ltd* [1946] IR 138.
1316. *Donegal County Council v Langan* UD 143/1989. *See also Boyle v Marathon Petroleum Ltd* [1995] ELR 200.
1317. *Ringsend Property Ltd v Donatex Ltd* [2009] IEHC 568.
1318. Treitel *Frustration and Force Majeure* (1994) p. 525.
1319. *Kruse v Questier Ltd* [1953] All ER 954 (Eng.). *See* now the Arbitration Act 2010.

have already fallen due at the time of discharge of the contract cannot be avoided in the name of frustration.[1320] So, if one party, prior to the frustrating event, was liable to have paid any part of the contract price, it would still be payable, at least according to cases such as *Chandler v Webster,*[1321] an English 'Coronation case'. However, in a later English case, *Fibrosa,*[1322] the House of Lords relied on restitutionary principles to reverse the rule in *Chandler v Webster*. It was held that a court could order the return of money which was paid in advance of discharge, if the payor has received none of the benefit expected by him, i.e., if there was a complete failure of performance. If such money was payable in advance of the frustrating event, it would no longer be payable. In England, the Law Reform (Frustrated Contracts) Act 1943 was enacted shortly after the *Fibrosa* decision. However, in Ireland there is no equivalent of the Law Reform (Frustrated Contracts) Act 1943, and no Irish court has ruled on this point.[1323] However, it is likely that the courts would favour *Fibrosa* to *Chandler v Webster,* as the latter is now viewed as little more than an anomaly in the development of the law of unjust enrichment, and the Irish courts will allow recovery of money paid where there has been a total failure of performance.[1324]

§3. Discharge by Agreement

571. The parties may agree to terminate their contract, but there must be both 'accord' (agreement) and 'satisfaction' (consideration). The agreement to discharge is supported by sufficient consideration if both parties' obligations under their original contract are wholly or partly executory. Each party, by agreeing not to sue for performance of the outstanding obligation(s), supplies sufficient consideration for the new agreement to terminate their original contract. The agreement to terminate is not binding where one party has completely performed, while the other has an outstanding obligation. Thus, under a contract for sale of goods where the seller has delivered all the goods but the buyer has not paid, a promise by the seller not to sue for payment and to regard the contract as discharged is not binding because it is gratuitous.[1325] It may be made binding by the simple expedient of recording the promise under seal, or by the debtor providing a nominal but 'sufficient' consideration, or by the debtor providing a bill of exchange or promissory note in satisfaction of the debt which is then renounced by the creditor, [1326] as no 'satisfaction' or consideration is required in such a case.

1320. *See Herman v SS Vicia* [1942] IR 304.
1321. [1904]1 KB 493 (Eng.).
1322. *Fibrosa Spolka Akcyjna v Fairbairn Lawson Combe Barbour ltd* [1942] 2 All ER 122.
1323. *See* Kelly, 'Drafting an Irish Frustrated Contracts Act: Lessons from British Columbia' in Giliker (ed.) *Re-examining Contract and Unjust Enrichment* (Martinus Nijhoff, 2007).
1324. *See United Dominions Trust (Ireland) Ltd v Shannon Caravans Ltd* [1976] IR 225.
1325. *Drogheda Corporation v Fairtlough* (1858) 8 Ir CLR 98.
1326. *Bills of Exchange Act* 1882 ss 63, 89.

572. Where parties wish to extinguish a contract, they may do so orally. If the original contract is one which must be in writing, or evidenced by writing, to be enforceable, the new oral contract, while effective to extinguish, will not otherwise be enforceable because of lack of the statutory memorandum.[1327]

1327. *Morris v Baron & Co* [1918] AC 1; *Jackson v Hayes* [1939] Ir Jur Rep 59. *See* the discussion in Clark pp. 664–665.

Chapter 6. Remedies

§1. General Provisions

573. If one party is in breach, a number of remedies might be available to the other party. The primary remedy is damages, which is money compensation for loss arising from the breach. Damages aim to put the innocent party in the position they would have been in had the contract been performed as promised. However, the innocent party might not wish to continue with the contract, or to continue in a contractual relationship with the party in breach; in this situation they may wish to terminate the contract. Termination is a strong remedy but it is not always available. As a general principle, any defect in performance must attain a minimum degree of seriousness to entitle the injured party to rescind *or* the parties must have made it clear that that particular breach would give the innocent party the right to get out of the contract and refuse to perform their part of the contract. When the contract is terminated, the innocent party also has the right to damages. Finally, one party might try to obtain specific performance of the contract, but this remedy is particularly limited and is only available where damages would be an inadequate remedy.

§2. Specific Performance and Injunctions

I. Specific Performance

574. Specific performance is an equitable remedy from the court which compels a party to an agreement to fulfil their obligations pursuant to that agreement. Specific performance is available where necessary to do justice in cases where damages are not an adequate remedy;[1328] the corollary of this is that it will not be decreed if damages are an adequate remedy.[1329] The most common situation where specific performance is ordered is in relation to contracts for the sale of land – as land is unique, damages may be an inadequate remedy where a seller of land refuses to perform.[1330] In contrast, in contracts for the sale of goods the provision for specific performance in the Sale of Goods Act 1893 is limited and narrowly construed.[1331] Even in contracts for the sale of land, specific performance may be refused where there

1328. *Wilson v Northampton and Banbury Junction Railway Company* (1874) 9 Ch App 279, 284.
1329. *See*, for example, *Duggan v Allied Irish Building Society*, Unreported, High Court, 4 March 1976.
1330. *Adderley v Dixon* (1824) 1 Sim & St 607. For a recent example, *see JLT Financial Services Limited v Gannon* [2017] IESC 70.
1331. Section 52 of the Sale of Goods Act 1893 provides that specific performance can be granted of a contract to deliver specific ascertained goods. *See*, for example, *Societe des Industrie Mettallurgiques SA v Bronx Engineering Co Ltd* [1975] 1 Lloyd's Rep 465.

has been a mistake or misrepresentation[1332] or where it would cause undue hardship.[1333] Hardship is traditionally judged at the time the contract was entered into[1334] although extreme hardship at the time of performance may result in the order of specific performance being refused.[1335] Recent case law in the wake of the financial crisis has shown that the court will not order specific performance of a contract for the sale of land where to do so would be futile due to lack of adequate funds on the part of a purchaser – specific performance is viewed as impossible in such a case, although damages will still be payable.[1336]

575. Specific performance is not granted to enforce a contract for personal services.[1337] The court does not wish to have trap contracting parties in a hostile relationship or to have to continually supervise contractual performance, particularly where it might be unclear what is required of the contracting party to adhere to the court order.[1338] However, a negative stipulation in a contract for personal services, e.g., not to work for some other employer, may be enforced by injunction,[1339] unless the inevitable result of the prohibitory injunction is that the party is forced to perform the original contract,[1340] and provided that the provision is not prohibited as being in restraint of trade.[1341] In *Marine Port and General Workers Union v Pandoro Ltd*[1342] specific performance was refused when it would have been tantamount to ordering the defendants to employ the plaintiff's workers against their will. However, in *Lift Manufacturers Ltd v Irish Life Assurance Co Ltd*[1343] an injunction to restrain the defendants from terminating a contract to install a lift was granted where it was the plaintiffs who were to perform (i.e., to install the lift) and they wished to perform. In this situation there was no need for the court to oversee the performance as the plaintiffs wished to perform, and the defendants had not lost faith in the plaintiffs' ability to do the work. More recently in *Thomas Thompson Holdings Ltd v Musgrave Group plc*[1344] the plaintiff sought an injunction to enforce a 'keep open' covenant contained in the defendant's lease. The defendant, an anchor tenant

1332. *Smelter Corporation v O'Driscoll* [1977] IR 305; *Grist v Bailey* [1967] Ch 532.
1333. *Lavan v Walsh* [1964] IR 87. Hardship is usually judged at the time the contract was entered into – *see Roberts v O'Neill* [1983] IR 47 – although extreme hardship at the time of performance may result in the order of specific performance being refused: *Patel v Ali* [1984] 1 All ER 978.
1334. *Roberts v O'Neill* [1983] IR 47.
1335. *Patel v Ali* [1984] 1 All ER 978.
1336. *Aranbel Limited v Darcy* [2010] IEHC 272.
1337. *Ryan v Mutual Tontine Westminster Chambers Association* [1893] 1 Ch 116.
1338. *See Coop Insurance Society Ltd v Argyll Stores (Holdings) ltd* [1997] All ER 297 (HL). Contrast the interlocutory injunction granted in *Wanze Properties (Ireland) Ltd v Five Star Supermarket and Tesco (Ireland) Ltd*, Unreported, High Court, 24 October 1997. For criticism of this decision, *see* O Breen (1999) 50 NILQ 102.
1339. *Lumley v Wagner* (1852) 1 De GM and G 604, 42 ER 687; *Dublin Port and Docks Board v Brittania Dredging Co. Ltd.* [1968] IR 136.
1340. *Warner Bros. Pictures Inc. v Nelson* [1937] 1 KB 209.
1341. *See* paras 406 et seq.
1342. Unreported, High Court, 3 June 1994.
1343. [1979] ILRM 277.
1344. [2016] IEHC 28.

in the shopping centre, wanted to close its shop due to financial losses. The High Court refused an order of specific performance, as the effect would be to force a business to keep trading at a loss.[1345]

576. If the order of specific performance decree is not complied with, the innocent party may either apply to the court for enforcement of the order or may apply to dissolve the order and put an end to the contract. If the latter, damages may then be awarded.[1346]

II. Injunction

577. An injunction is an order from a court directing a party to do, or to refrain from doing, a specified act. It is an equitable discretionary remedy and is granted to restrain the commission of a breach of contract where damages would not provide an adequate remedy.[1347]

- A prohibitory injunction may be granted where a contract contains an enforceable negative promise, for example, not to compete with a former employer[1348] or, in an exclusive dealing contract, not to obtain supplies from a rival supplier.[1349]
- A mandatory injunction directs a party to do some act to comply with the contract, if necessary by undoing something which has been done, for example, erecting a building in breach of contract. Under the Judicature Act 1877 section 28(8), an injunction might be granted 'in all cases in which it shall appear to the court to be just or convenient that such order should be made'. It is a potentially drastic remedy, and the courts in numerous cases have emphasised the necessity to consider justice, fairness, and the relative convenience of the parties, before granting an injunction.
- An 'interlocutory' injunction may be granted before the full trial of the action to maintain the *status quo* and to prevent possibly irreparable damage to the plaintiff before the issue can be finally determined.[1350] Before an interlocutory injunction is granted, the court must be satisfied that there is a valid interest of the plaintiff to be protected and that the balance of convenience lies in favour of granting the injunction.[1351]

1345. In addition the contract provided for the possibility of the covenant being breached. Contrast the interlocutory injunction granted in *Wanze Properties (Ireland) Ltd v Five Star Supermarket and Tesco (Ireland) Ltd*, Unreported, High Court, 24 October 1997.
1346. *Vandeluer v Dargan* [1981] ILRM 75.
1347. *Fluid Power Technology Co. Ltd. v Sperry Ltd.*, Unreported, 22 February 1985.
1348. *ECI European Chemical Industries Ltd. v Bell* [1981] ILRM 345.
1349. *Continental Oil Co. of Ireland v Moynihan* (1977) 111 ILTR 5.
1350. *See*, for example, *Wanze Properties (Ireland) Ltd v Five Star Supermarket and Tesco (Ireland) Ltd*, Unreported, High Court, 24 October 1997.
1351. *Campus Oil Ltd. v Minister for Industry and Commerce* (No. 2) [1983] IR 88; *Esso Petroleum Co. (Ireland) Ltd. v Fogarty* [1965] IR 531.

578. If a contract is not specifically enforceable, for example, a contract for personal services, the court will not grant an injunction if the inevitable result of so doing would be equivalent to an order for specific performance.

III. Astreinte

579. In Irish law, the ultimate sanction for failure to comply with an order for specific performance or injunction is imprisonment for contempt of court. The device of the *astreinte* in civil law largely fills the gap which exists in that system by the absence of anything corresponding to the possible common law imprisonment for failure to satisfy a money judgment or to comply with orders of specific performance and injunction.[1352] The *astreinte* is an instrument independent of the remedy of damages whereby a court attaches to a judgment an order that the debtor shall pay to the creditor a specified sum for each period of time that he remains in default.[1353] In Ireland judgments for a liquidated sum attract interest at normal rates from the date of judgment, but there is nothing which corresponds to civil law *astreinte*.

§3. Termination

580. The rules relating to termination of a contract, as a remedy for breach, have been considered earlier.[1354]

§4. *Exceptio Non Adimpleti Contractus*

581. This remedy (defence of unperformed contract) derives from Roman law and is translated in French as *exception d'inexecution.* An essential characteristic of the remedy is that the party exercising it need not go to court, although he may choose to do so.[1355] In Irish law, in the circumstances discussed above, one party to a contract may rescind or repudiate the contract on the grounds of non-performance of the obligation(s) imposed by the contract on the other party.

582. Repudiation of a contract or withholding performance is a 'self-help' remedy which may not be justifiable in a particular case, so that an aggrieved party is usually well advised that it is more prudent to invoke the aid of the court in doubtful cases to ensure that the exercise of the self-help remedy is not, in fact, a breach of contract on his part.

1352. Nicholas, *French Law of Contract*, p. 210.
1353. *Ibid.*
1354. See paras 536 et seq.
1355. Nicholas, *supra*, p. 207.

§5. Faulty Behaviour of the Debtor

583. Breach of contract is not fault based. A contracting party may be in breach of contract even if they have behaved reasonably, or if they did not intend to breach the contract. In *ICDL GCC Foundation FZ-LLC & anor v European Computer Driving Licence Foundation Ltd* this was reiterated in the Supreme Court:

> It should be borne in mind that the plaintiff does not, as a matter of the general law, need to establish negligence at all in order to prove breach of contract, except in cases where the breach of contract alleged consists in breach of a duty of care.[1356]

584. For example, a seller of defective goods may be liable for breach of contract even if the defect was 'one which no reasonable skill or care could discover'.[1357]

§6. Limitation of Actions

585. Section 11(1)(a) of the Statute of Limitations 1957 provides that actions founded on simple contract shall not be brought after the expiration of six years from the date on which the cause of action accrued. The same limitation period applies to an action in quasi-contract.[1358] Section 11(5)(a) provides that no action shall be brought on an instrument under seal (a deed) after the expiration of twelve years after the cause of action has accrued.[1359] These limitation periods mentioned above do not apply to a claim for specific performance of a contract or for an injunction or for other equitable relief,[1360] but equitable remedies are subject to the doctrine of laches and may be refused if there is delay in seeking relief.

586. Different limitation periods may apply in specific situations. For example, section 13 of the Sale of Goods and Supply of Services Act 1980 provides for damages where a motor vehicle is sold in an unsafe condition, and any cause of action expires two years from the date on which the cause of action accrued.[1361] Employment protection legislation, such as the Unfair Dismissals Act 1977, also lays down specific limitation periods for claims.

1356. [2012] IESC 55.
1357. *Randall v Newsom* (1876) 45 LJQB 364. *See also Clegg v Andersson* [2003] EWCA Civ 320 where it was stated that 'the real issues in the English law of sale of goods … are not whether either party has behaved reasonably … '.
1358. Section 11(1)(b))
1359. This is subject to some exceptions, e.g., any principal sum of money secured by a mortgage or other charge.
1360. Sections 11 and 9(a).
1361. Sale of Goods and supply of Services Act 1980, s. 13(8), which amends the Statute of Limitations Act 1957, s. 11(2)(d).

587. A cause of action in contract accrues when the breach of the contract occurs, not when damage caused thereby arises. The date of the breach will of course depend on the particular contract involved, for example, in a sale of goods it is when defective goods are delivered, not when the defect is discovered. In general, the fact that a plaintiff was not aware that he had a cause of action will not prevent time running against him. However, if his ignorance was due to fraud concealing the right of action on the part of the defendant, or his agent, section 71(1) provides that time shall not begin to run until the plaintiff has discovered the fraud, or could, with reasonable diligence, have discovered it. In addition, as a general rule, mistake does not prevent time running, but section 72(1) provides that where the action is for relief from the consequences of mistake, time does not begin to run until the plaintiff has discovered his mistake or could, with reasonable diligence, have discovered it.

588. Where any right of action has accrued to recover a contractual debt section 56 of the Act provides that where there is an acknowledgement of the debt, the right of action shall be deemed to have accrued on and not before the date of the acknowledgement. The acknowledgement which must be in writing and signed by the person making it.[1362] An acknowledgement thus may extend the period of limitation which would otherwise apply.

§7. Damages for Breach of Contract

I. Nature of Remedy of Damages

589. The principal remedy for breach of a contract is damages. The object of damages is to place the injured party, so far as money can do it, in the same situation as if the contract had been performed.[1363] This can be contrasted with damages in tort, where the object is to restore the injured party into the position they would have been in had the tort not occurred.

II. Remoteness of Damage

590. The principle of remoteness of damage sets out the limits of what the party in breach is liable to pay compensation. The basic principle on remoteness of damage was set out in 1854 in *Hadley v Baxendale*, in which a delay in the delivery of a broken shaft resulted in the plaintiff's mill being entirely shut down. The court stated:

> Where two parties have made a contract which one of them has broken, the damages which the other party ought to receive in respect of such breach of

1362. Section 58.
1363. *Robinson v Harman* (1848) 1 Exch 850.

contract should be such as may fairly and reasonably be considered either arising naturally, i.e., according to the usual course of things, from such breach of contract or such as may reasonably be supposed to have been in the contemplation of both parties, at the time they made the contract, as the probable result of the breach of it.[1364]

591. The first part of the rule in *Hadley v Baxendale* concerns consequences from the breach which arise in the ordinary course of things. Even if neither party actually contemplated the loss or degree of loss which occurred, the loss which may fairly and reasonably be considered as arising in the usual course of things from such breach will be recoverable. The state of knowledge of the parties is irrelevant. For example animal feed containing lead pellets will, in the ordinary course of events, injure animals that eat it;[1365] and a diseased animal may make land on which it grazes unsuitable for farming.[1366]

592. The second part of the rule concerns special circumstances, or an unusual loss which would not occur in the ordinary course of things; such unusual losses only result in an award of damages where both parties are aware of the possibility of this loss or aware of any special facts which could reasonably give rise to this loss. This principle is well illustrated by the oft-cited decision of the English Court of Appeal in *Victoria Laundry (Windsor) Ltd. v Newman Industries Ltd.*[1367] In this case the plaintiffs, who ran a laundry business, ordered a boiler which was due to be delivered in June, but was only delivered in November. The plaintiffs claimed their lost profits incurred as a result of this late delivery. It was held that while they could claim the lost profits which they suffered as a result of lost business, being a reasonably foreseeable loss in the normal course of events, they could not claim a higher level of lost profits for a particularly lucrative government contract which they also lost out on, as the defendant was not aware of this contract and it was not a 'normal' or foreseeable loss. The Court emphasised that what was at the time of contracting reasonably foreseeable depends on the knowledge then possessed by both parties.[1368] Similarly in *Waller v The Great Western Railway (Ir) Co*[1369] it was held that the failure to supply horses boxes to transport horses to a sale would naturally result in slight deterioration and fatigue of horses fit to make the trip, but would not usually result in serious injury or damage to the horses. The plaintiff could not therefore claim damages for serious injury caused to the horses when this was owing to the particularly delicate condition of the horses, of which the defendant was unaware. In *Lee and Donoghue v Rowan*[1370] it was held that a failure to complete a shed in time for harvest could require the farmer to have to transport his

1364. [1854] 9 Exch. 341, 354. The Irish courts accepted the principle as laid down in *Hadley v Baxendale* in *Boyd v Fitt* (1863) 14 ICLR 43.
1365. *Wilson v Dunville* (1879) 6 LR (Ir) 210.
1366. *Stoney v Foley* (1897) 31 ILT 163.
1367. [1949] 2 KB 528.
1368. [1949] 2 KB 528, 539.
1369. (1879) 4 LR (Ir) 326.
1370. Unreported, High Court, 17 November 1981.

crops to another shed, but it was not foreseeable that it would result in the farmer losing his entire crop. Hence, damages were recoverable for transport and storage costs, but not for loss of the crop itself.

593. The rule in *Hadley v Baxendale* was applied recently by the Irish Supreme Court in *Leahy v Rawson.*[1371] In this case, there was breach of a contract to build an extension onto a house when the resulting building had various defects and was unfit to live in. The plaintiff claimed that she had planned on using the renovated house as a B&B, and had suffered lost profits when she was unable to do this. Although damages of €20,000 were initially awarded for this loss by the High Court, this was overturned in the Supreme Court. It was held that the defendant builders did not know that the plaintiff intended to run a B&B in her house, and damages for the loss of profits suffered were thus not recoverable.

III. Measure of Damages

594. Contract damages aim to put the injured party in the position they would have been in had the contract been performed as promised. However, applying this broad principle in different contexts can be difficult.

A. *Expectation Loss*

595. Damages awarded to compensate the plaintiff's 'expectation loss' are intended to protect the plaintiff's expectation that the contract will be performed, and provide the plaintiff with that which they intended to obtain from the contract. A common example of expectation loss is the lost profit which would have been made by the plaintiff if the contract had been duly performed. In the sale of goods, damages for non-delivery of goods are awarded on the basis of how much it would cost the buyer to go into the market to buy replacement goods.[1372]

596. It is not always clear what outcomes would have arisen from proper performance of the contract. However, the courts will attempt to calculate damages even if the exercise is speculative, such as ascertaining the possible performance of a racehorse in a number of races from which it was wrongfully removed.[1373] It has been stated that a court 'should be alert, energetic and if necessary ingenious to assess damages where it is satisfied that a significant injury has flowed from the breach'.[1374] In *O'Keefe v Ryanair*[1375] for example, the High Court had to calculate the value of the plaintiff's loss of the right to free flights with Ryanair for life. This

1371. Reported in *The Irish Times* 30 November 2006.
1372. Sale of Goods Act 1893, section 51(3). *See Williams v Agius* [1914] AC 510; *Melachrino v Nickoll & Knight* [1920] 1 KB 693.
1373. *Hawkins v Rogers* [1951] 85 ILTR 129.
1374. *Grafton Court Ltd. v Wadson Sales Ltd.*, Unreported, High Court, 17 February 1975.
1375. [2003] 1 ILRM 14.

included speculation as to future events in the plaintiff's life, but the court nonetheless carried out a detailed assessment and arrived at an estimated figure of damages.

597. In cases of defective building work, putting the plaintiff in the position they would have been in had the contract been performed may involve substantial costs, for example the demolition of and rebuilding of a building. This is referred to as 'cost of cure', or the 'performance interest', and in building contracts this level of damages will usually be chosen,[1376] as opposed to the alternative measure of awarding the reduction in the value of the building or land. For example, in *Leahy v Rawson*[1377] when an extension to a house was so defective that the house was unfit to live in, the damages awarded included the cost of demolishing the extension to slab level and rebuilding it. In other cases, however, the courts may have difficulty in choosing between the reduction in value of work and the cost of repairing defective performance, particularly where cost of cure is disproportionately high and the plaintiff has no legitimate interest in actually repairing the work done.[1378]

B. Reliance Loss

598. Reliance loss is the loss which a plaintiff suffers in incurring expenditure in reliance on the contract. Reliance loss will be recovered usually where the expectation loss is too difficult to assess, or where no expectation loss can be proved, for example where a buyer can buy the same goods at the contract price or less, or where it is inherently uncertain whether any profit will be made.[1379] If a defendant can show that the expenditure would have been wasted because it would not have been recouped even if the contract had been performed, reliance loss will not be awarded.[1380] In addition, the court will not overcompensate the injured party by awarding both expectation loss and reliance loss. Expenditure which would in any case have to be incurred to realise a profit should not be awarded if the loss of profits is awarded.[1381]

1376. *Kincora Builders v Cronin*, Unreported, High Court, 5 March 1973.
1377. Unreported, High Court, 14 January 2003.
1378. *See Ruxley Electronics Ltd v Forsyth* [1995] 3 All ER 268, in which damages were awarded for 'loss of amenity' when damages for 'cost of cure' would have over-compensated the plaintiffs, but damages for loss of value to the property would have been merely nominal.
1379. *See*, for example, *Anglia Television Ltd. v Reed* [1972] 1 QB 60; *Afton v Film Studios of Ireland*, Unreported, High Court, 12 July 1971.
1380. *C. & P. Haulage v Middleton* [1983] 3 All ER 94; *Bowlay Logging v Domtar* (1978) 87 DLR (3d) 325; (1982) 135 DLR (3d) 179.
1381. *Waterford Harbour Commissioners v British Rail Board*, Unreported, Supreme Court, 18 February 1981; *Mahon v Dawson & O'Connor* [2006] IEHC 331.

C. Restitution Loss

599. A party who has breached a contract, for example, a seller who has failed to deliver goods as promised, and who has received the consideration for his promise (the price) is liable to restore at least what he has received. Here the defendant has received a benefit from the plaintiff which must be restored.

D. Account of Profits

600. Another type of restitutionary interest may need to be protected where the defendant acquires a benefit from a third party as a result of breaching an obligation owed to the claimant. The defendant may be required to disgorge his wrongfully obtained gain, i.e., to account for the profits made. A claim for an account of profits is based on the gain to the defendant rather than the loss suffered by the plaintiff (as in expectation loss or reliance loss). Claims such as this are rare, such as the English case of *Attorney General v Blake*[1382] in which the House of Lords ordered an account of profits made by a former spy turned double agent from the publication of a memoir which was in breach of a confidentiality agreement. It was said that this remedy would only be used in exceptional circumstances where usual remedies are inadequate and the plaintiff had a legitimate interest in preventing the defendant's profit-making activity. Such damages are unlikely to be awarded in a commercial context, although the courts have awarded 'hypothetical release damages', in which gains-based damages are awarded based on the licence fee that might reasonably have been agreed by the parties.[1383] In *One Step (Support) Limited v Morris-Garner* it was stated that this 'might be considered to be simply one form of compensatory damages, in the form of the sum the claimant should have received from the defendant for giving consent'.[1384]

601. The traditional compensatory approach to damages allows parties to breach a contract where they calculate that this is more economically efficient for them, even after paying damages to the injured party. A claim for an account of profits, however, can have the result of deterring parties from breaching a contract, by making them hand over the profits which they make as a result of the breach. Although unusual (and arguably undesirable) the Irish case of *Hickey v Roches Stores (No1)*[1385] indicates that this approach might on occasion be taken. In this case, a department store breached a contract with a drapery outlet by evicting it from the store. The store had calculated that it would make a profit even after paying expectation damages. It was held that if there was mala fide conduct the defendant would

1382. [2000] 4 All ER 385.
1383. *See*, for example, *Wrotham Park Estate Co Ltd v Parkside Homes Ltd* [1974] 1 WLR 798; *Experience Hendrix LLC v PPX Enterprises Inc* [2003] EWCA Civ 323; *WWF-World Wide Fund for Nature v World Wrestling Federation Entertainment Inc* [2008] 1 WLR 445; *Pell Frischmann Engineering Ltd v Bow Valey Iran Lt* [2009] UKPC 45.
1384. [2014] EWHC 2213 (QB). *See* [2016] EWCA Civ 180.
1385. Unreported, High Court, 14 July 1976. *See* Clark, 'Damages and Unjust Enrichment' (1978) 29 NILQ 128.

have had to pay the profits it made and hand them over to the defendant, but mala fide conduct was not proved on the facts.

E. Punitive or Exemplary Damages

602. In general, damages are designed to compensate rather than to punish, and punitive or exemplary damages are not awarded for breach of contract.[1386] However, if there is a claim in tort then damages may be awarded for aggravated loss. The Supreme Court stated that aggravated damages are compensatory damages increased by reason of: (a) the manner in which the wrong was committed, involving such elements as oppressiveness, arrogance or outrage; or (b) the conduct of the wrongdoer after the commission of the wrong such as a refusal to apologise or to ameliorate the harm done or the making of threats to repeat the wrong; or (c) conduct of the wrongdoer and/or his representatives in the defence of the claim of the wronged plaintiff, up to and including the trial of the action.[1387]

603. In *Garvey v Ireland*[1388] the dismissal of a Garda Commissioner from his post was held to be unconstitutional and exemplary damages were awarded against the State.[1389] However, the Law Reform Commission has made the point that while this 'suggests that exemplary damages may be available in some contract cases … the issue was not specifically addressed'.[1390] However, if the breach of contract also constitutes a tort, exemplary damages may be available,[1391] and Clark has suggested that 'punitive damages may be awarded by placing stress on the tortious aspect of the defendant's conduct'.[1392] In its report, the Law Reform Commission did not recommend extending exemplary damages to contract law cases; however nor did it recommend prohibiting exemplary damages for breach of contract by legislation, preferring to leave 'any possible development of the law on this matter … to the courts where it can be judged on a case by case basis'.[1393]

1386. Law Reform Commission, *Report on Aggravated, Exemplary and Restitutionary Damages* (LRC 60-2000) states at para. 1.01: 'The aim of exemplary damages is two-fold: to punish the defendant and to deter both the defendant and others from engaging in conduct that is extremely malicious or socially harmful with the additional, incidental effect of providing compensation and satisfaction to the plaintiff. In the context of the Constitution, the particular purpose of exemplary damages is to vindicate and defend individual constitutional rights, to punish the defendant's disregard of them and to deter their breach.'

1387. *Conway v Irish National Teachers Organisation* [1991] 2 IR 305 and *Swain v Commissioners for Public Works* [2003] 2 ILRM 252. *See also Gary Simpson v The Governor of Mountjoy Prison & others* [2019] IESC 81, para. 125.

1388. [1979] ILRM 266.

1389. *See also Conway v Irish National Teachers Organisation* [1991] 2 IR 305. A claim for punitive damages was rejected in *Swain v Commissioners for Public Works* [2003] 2 ILRM 252.

1390. Law Reform Commission, *Report on Aggravated, Exemplary and Restitutionary Damages* (LRC 60-2000) para. 1.48.

1391. *Ibid.*, para. 1.49, citing *Kennedy v Allied Irish Banks Ltd*, Unreported, Supreme Court, 29 October 1996.

1392. Clark p. 724.

1393. Law Reform Commission, *Report on Aggravated, Exemplary and Restitutionary Damages* (LRC 60-2000) paras 1.55–1.56.

F. Damages for Stress and Inconvenience

604. Traditionally damages for stress, worry and upset could not be awarded.[1394] This general rule was recently confirmed by the Supreme Court in *Murray v Budds*[1395] where it was held, following *Addis v Gramaphone Co. Ltd,*[1396] that the contract-breaker cannot be liable for damages for injured feelings or distress.

605. However, there is an exception to this rule where relaxation or enjoyment was an objective of the contract[1397] or where the loss suffered is a 'loss of amenity' suffered by a consumer. In these cases, the injured party often did not expect to make a 'profit' from the contract, so protecting the consumer's 'expectation interest' requires the award of damages for the stress and inconvenience suffered as a result of breach. In *Murray* the Supreme Court agreed with the following statement of Bingham LJ:

> A contract-breaker is not in general liable for any distress, frustration, anxiety, displeasure, vexation, tension or aggravation which his breach of contract may cause to the innocent party. This rule is not, I think, founded on the assumption that such reactions are not foreseeable, which they surely are or may be, but on considerations of policy. But the rule is not absolute. Where the very object of a contract is to provide pleasure, relaxation, peace of mind, or freedom from molestation, damages will be awarded if the fruit of the contract is not provided or if the contrary result is procured instead.[1398]

606. In assessing whether a contract may be an exception to the rule in *Addis* the Court considered it 'useful to consider the analysis' in *Baltic Shipping Co. v Dillon:*[1399]

> To ascertain whether the obtaining of peace of mind is the object of a contract or, more accurately, an object of a contract, reference is made to its terms, express or implied, construed in the context of facts which the parties know or are taken to have known. Thus, if peaceful and comfortable accommodation is promised to holidaymakers and the accommodation tendered does not answer the description, there is a breach which directly causes the loss of the promised peacefulness and comfort and damages are recoverable accordingly. In cases of this kind, a statement of the promisor commending a service or facility to be provided under the contract is frequently a term of the contract, not a mere representation.

1394. *Kinlan v Ulster Bank* [1928] IR 171; *Addis v Gramaphone Co Ltd* [1909] AC 488.
1395. [2017] IESC 4.
1396. [1909] AC 488.
1397. *Jarvis v Swan Tours Ltd* [1973] QB 233.
1398. *Watts v Morrow* [1991] 1 WLR 1421.
1399. (1993) 111 ALR 289, cited at [2017] IESC 4, para. 45.

607. Cases were damages have been awarded for stress and inconvenience include cases where a honeymoon on a luxury cruise was cancelled,[1400] where building work for consumers failed to meet contractual standards[1401] and where distress and humiliation was caused when a contract for provision of a buffet after a wedding was breached, with guests being asked to leave the premises.[1402] In *O'Keefe v Ryanair,* discussed above, damages were awarded for disappointment, frustration and upset suffered by the plaintiff 'arising from the unpleasant and shabby treatment which she suffered' on one holiday weekend.[1403] Damages of this type have also arisen where there was a wrongful adjudication as a bankrupt[1404] or where insufficient measures have been taken to prevent an abduction of children[1405] or molestation.[1406] However, it is clear that in commercial breach of contract cases, damages for mental distress caused by the breach will not be awarded.[1407]

608. In the employment context, *Addis v Gramaphone Co Ltd*[1408] is authority for the principle that an employee could not recover damages for injury to reputation or injured feelings on wrongful dismissal. In *Johnson v Unisys*[1409] the House of Lords confirmed that damages would not be available for mental distress caused by the manner of dismissal, and this has been followed in a number of Irish cases.[1410] However damages may be available where there is an injury going beyond normal levels of mental distress.[1411] In addition, in a slightly different context, in *Browne v Iarnród Eireann (No.2)*[1412] damages for inconvenience and loss of employment were awarded when the defendants wrongfully refused to allow Mr Browne early retirement.

IV. Mitigation of Loss

609. A party who is injured by a breach of contract has a duty to mitigate his loss or damage.[1413] This means that a plaintiff cannot recover loss that could have

1400. *Circuit court case, Irish Times*, 2 July 1997 cited in Clark p. 751. *See also Peacock case*, *Irish Times* 25 April 2006.
1401. *Johnson v Longleat Property*, Unreported, High Court, 19 May 1976; *Leahy v Rawson*, Unreported, High Court, 14 January 2003; *Mitchell v Mulvey* [2014] IEHC 37.
1402. *Dinnegan v Ryan* [2002] 3 IR 178.
1403. *O'Keefe v Ryanair* [2003] 1 ILRM 14.
1404. *Hussey v Dillon [*1995] 1 IR 111.
1405. *Hamilton Jones v David & Snape* [2004] 1 WLR 924. Approved in *Murray v Budd* [2017] IESC 4.
1406. *Heywood v Wellers* [1976] 2 WLR 101.
1407. *Kelly v Crowley*, Unreported, High Court, 5 March 1985.
1408. [1909] AC 488.
1409. [2001] 2 All ER 801. *See*, however, *Malik v Bank of Credit and Commerce International* [1997] 3 All ER 1 where there was said to be a breach of an implied duty of trust and confidence, and the loss suffered was categorised as financial loss, not injured feelings.
1410. *Orr v Zomax Ltd* [2004] IEHC 47, *McGrath v Trintech* [2004] IEHC 342.
1411. *Berber v Dunnes Stores* [2009] IESC 10 (damages not awarded on facts); *Pickering v Microsoft*, Unreported, High Court, 21 December 2005.
1412. [2014] IEHC 117.
1413. This is also found in statutory form in the Civil Liability Act 1961, s. 34(2)(b).

been avoided had they acted reasonably in the prevailing circumstances. For example, the owners of property must take steps to prevent continuing damage to their property where a hirer has wrongfully repudiated the contract and abandoned the property,[1414] a disappointed buyer of goods must seek out replacement goods,[1415] and a wrongfully dismissed employee must seek and accept an offer of reasonable alternative employment.[1416] What is to be considered reasonable in any case is a question of fact and the trial judge's decision will not be lightly interfered with.[1417]

610. It must be remembered that the party in breach is not always well placed to criticise the plaintiff's actions, and it might be held that the plaintiff acted reasonably, even if with hindsight the plaintiff might have acted differently. For example, in *Rosbeg Partners Ltd v LK Shields (a firm)*[1418] it was held that a failure to accept lower offers to purchase a property did not constitute an unreasonable failure to mitigate loss, even if with hindsight this would have been an appropriate measure. In this case, owing to negligence and breach of contract[1419] by LK Shields in not registering certain land, Rosbeg Partners lost out on a subsequent sale of land for €10 million. The prospective purchaser later offered €6 million for the same land, but this offer was rejected. By the time the action was heard in 2013, the property had a value of €1.5 million. It was held that with the benefit of hindsight, the offer to buy for €6 million should have been accepted, but 'would not be appropriate to impute to the [plaintiff] a degree of foresight regarding the collapse of the market in September, 2008, which many others did not foresee'. The decision was appealed to the Supreme Court, where the case was decided on the basis of causation issues rather than mitigation, and it was held that the damages awarded should be reduced on the basis that LK Shields could not be held liable for losses that occurred after they obtained actual registration of the title to the property in October 2008.[1420]

611. One controversial situation that can arise is where it is argued that the plaintiff failed to mitigate their loss because they did not accept an offer or new contractual arrangement from the defendant themselves. In *Payzu v Saunders*[1421] the defendant had agreed to supply silk to the plaintiff on monthly credit terms, but then refused to deliver, repudiating the contract. The defendant then offered to deliver the silk if the plaintiff paid cash on delivery, but the plaintiff refused. When the plaintiff sued for damages, it was held that they had not mitigated their loss, and that in the context of a market where there was no alternative supply they should have

1414. *Bord Iascaigh Mara v Scallan*, Unreported, High Court, 8 May 1973.
1415. *Cullen v Horgan* [1925] 2 IR 1.
1416. *Herman v Owners of SS Vicia* [1942] IR 305; *Irvine v Midland and Great Western Railway* (1879) 6 LR Ir 55.
1417. *Hay v O'Grady* [1992] 1 IR 210; *Kelly v Hennessy* [1995] 3 IR 253.
1418. [2016] IECA 161.
1419. It was stated in the Supreme Court that 'nothing, for present purposes, turns on whether it is viewed as a claim for breach of a contractual duty or a parallel duty in tort arising out of the parties' professional relationship' [2018] IESC 23, para. 2.
1420. [2018] IESC 23.
1421. [1919] 2 KB 581.

accepted the defendant's offer. Although this decision has been criticised, it was applied in the recent Irish case of *Hyland & Ors v Dundalk Racing (1999) Limited*[1422] where it was cited as authority for the proposition that 'a claimant's obligation to mitigate loss may require him to enter into contractual obligations with those who have earlier been in breach of their contractual terms, even if those terms are less favourable than those previously enjoyed'.[1423] This case concerned a dispute between bookmakers and the Dundalk racing course concerning changes in the relationship between the parties. The bookmakers alleged Dundalk Racing was in breach of contract, and sought damages for lost profits suffered as a result of their inability to set up business at the race grounds. However, Dundalk Racing had offered to supply the bookmakers with space for their business on payment of an €8,000 per person capital contribution. It was held that by rejecting this offer, the bookmakers had failed to mitigate their losses. They should have paid the contribution sought on a without prejudice basis while simultaneously commencing proceedings seeking a declaration that the demand for that payment was in breach of contract. The court emphasised that in this situation there was 'no other avenue available to the bookmakers to mitigate their potential losses',[1424] and the terms offered were favourable.

§8. Restitution

612. Restitution arises in contract where one party to a contract has either fully or partially performed his obligations under a contract while the other party has failed to perform his corresponding obligations. Restitution seeks to return the value of the performance so given, be that money or work undertaken.[1425] A simple example of restitution is in a contract for the sale of goods, when a right to 'reject the goods' would be useless if not accompanied by the right to a refund of the price paid. The Sale of Goods Act 1893–1980 does not in fact refer to the right to a refund,[1426] but it is provided for under the law of restitution.

613. The basis of restitution in these cases is that there has been a total failure of consideration. 'Consideration' here refers to failure of performance rather than a failure of consideration in the formation of the contract.[1427] In general therefore, a total failure of consideration is said to occur where a promisor has failed to perform any obligations owed under the contract. For example, in *Hayes v Stirling*[1428] a payment was made to purchase shares in a company which was supposed to be formed

1422. [2017] IECA 172.
1423. *Ibid.*, para. 105.
1424. *Ibid.*
1425. *See* paras 63 et seq. and paras 819 et seq.
1426. It is mentioned in s. 11 of the 1980 Act, which provides makes it a penalty for a business to have a notice stating that 'money will not be refunded'.
1427. *See Fibrosa Spolka Akcyjna v Fairbairn Lawson Combe Barbour Ltd* [1943] AC 32.
1428. (1863) Ir CLR 277 (Ex.).

at a later date. In fact no such company was ever formed. The court held that there had been a total failure of consideration and permitted restitution of the money so paid.[1429]

614. The courts will look at whether the promisor has performed any obligations owed under the contract, and not at whether the promise has received any benefit under the contract. In *Lecky v Walter*[1430] the plaintiff had purchased shares which it subsequently transpired were worthless. He sued, claiming in effect that he had contracted for valuable shares and he had not received what he had contracted for. The court held that there had not been a total failure of consideration since he had obtained shares: it was irrelevant that the said shares were not as valuable as had been hoped for. Similarly in *Stapleton v Prudential Insurance*[1431] premiums paid under a voidable contract of insurance were not recoverable since during the validity of the contract, a claim could have been made under the policy of insurance; hence the plaintiff obtained a benefit from the contract. If the contract had been void the result would, of course, have been different.

615. However, the mere fact that the payor has received some benefit will not prevent a finding of total failure of consideration if that benefit was not a benefit for which the payor contracted. Perhaps the best known application of this principle is in *Rowland v Divall.*[1432] There the plaintiff bought a car from the defendant and used it for several months. It emerged that the defendant had no title to the car and the plaintiff had to return the car to its true owner. The plaintiff sued the defendant to recover back the purchase money he had paid. It was held that the consideration had totally failed and the plaintiff could recover back the purchase money, even though the plaintiff had had the use of the car. Bankes LJ stated:

> [I]t cannot possibly be said that the plaintiff received any portion of what he had agreed to buy. It is true that a motor car was delivered to him, but the person who sold it to him had no right to sell it, and therefore he did not get what he paid for – namely a car to which he would have title.[1433]

616. Rowland v Divall was applied by the Irish Supreme Court in *United Dominions Trust (Ireland) Ltd v Shannon Caravans Ltd.*[1434] There, T wished to obtain £3k to pay for a caravan which had been delivered to him. A junior employee of the plaintiff company suggested that X should purport to sell the caravan to the plaintiff for £3k and give the £3k to T. T would then 'purchase' the caravan from the plaintiff under a hire-purchase scheme, paying the hire-purchase instalments. In other words, the plaintiff would pay X £3k, X would give this money to T and T

1429. Such cases should be distinguished from those where the parties are contracting over an event that is uncertain in outcome, or is an adventure. *See*, for example, *Griffen v Caddell* (1875) IR 9 CL 488.
1430. [1914] IR 378.
1431. (1928) 62 ILTR 56.
1432. [1923] 2 KB 500.
1433. [1932] 2 KB 500, 504.
1434. [1976] IR 225.

would pay the hire-purchase instalments. T became insolvent after 8 out of 36 payments and it was only then that the plaintiff executives became aware of the facts. The plaintiffs brought an action against X for recovery of the £3k paid for the caravan, claiming it had been paid on the basis of a consideration which had wholly failed: it was argued that the money should be returned as the plaintiff had paid X £3k for a caravan which was never the property of X and therefore never became the property of the plaintiff. It was held in the Supreme Court, applying *Rowland v Divall,* that there had been a total failure of consideration for the £3,000 paid by the plaintiff.

617. Similarly in *Chartered Trust Ireland Ltd. v Healy and Commins*[1435] a finance company hired a vehicle on hire purchase to the defendant who used the vehicle for a year before discovering that it had in fact been illegally imported into the State. Barron J held that the defendant had not benefitted from the contract, since the essence of a hire-purchase contract is the right to purchase at the end of the hire period, something which the defendant was unable to do. Since the defendant had not benefitted under the contract there was a total failure of consideration and Barron J ordered the repayment of the instalments paid to date.

1435. Unreported, High Court, 10 December 1985 per Barron J.

Part II. Specific Contracts

Chapter 1. Agency

§1. The Nature of Agency

618. In a contract of agency, an agent is given authority to act on behalf of another, the principal. The contract so made will be binding on both the principal and the third party. As Fridman states:

> Agency is the relationship which exists between two persons when one, called the agent, is considered in law to represent the other, called the principal, in such a way as to be able to affect the principal's legal position in respect of strangers to the relationship by the making of contracts or the disposition of property.[1436]

619. If an agent (A) acting on behalf of a principal (P) negotiates and concludes a contract with a third party (T) the parties to that contract are P and T. P and T can sue each other for breach of contract. Agency is thus a long established exception to the doctrine of privity of contract.

620. In as much as the relationship between the agent and their principal depends on a contract, the normal rules of the law of contract apply, including such matters as implied terms.[1437] However, the relationship is regarded also as one which raises fiduciary obligations, so that an agent, for example, must avoid conflicts of interest, make disclosure of all relevant matters to his principal, and account for any moneys received from, or for the account of, his principal. The obligation to act in good faith which applies to an agent forbids the making of all secret profits (including taking bribes) from the agency and any such profits are recoverable by the principal. In return, the agent is given certain rights at common law, most notably a right to be indemnified against expenses incurred while acting on the principal's behalf.

1436. Fridman *The Law of Agency* (London, Butterworths, 7th ed., 1996) p. 11.
1437. *Ward v Spwack* [1957] IR 40.

621. 'Commercial agents' are a particular category of agents with duties and rights under the EU Commercial Agents Directive.[1438] A commercial agent is a self-employed intermediary who has continuing authority to negotiate and/or conclude the sale or the purchase of goods on behalf of another person, the 'principal'. Specific rules govern the relationship between a commercial agent and their principal, and these are dealt with below.

§2. The Creation of an Agency

622. An agent has the power to bind their principal where they have 'authority' to act on P's behalf and a distinction is drawn between the various types of authority.

I. Actual Authority

623. Actual authority is where P consents in advance to A's actions, giving A actual authority to act in a certain manner and bind P:

> An 'actual' authority is a legal relationship between principal and agent created by a consensual agreement to which they alone are parties. Its scope is to be ascertained by applying ordinary principles of construction of contracts, including any proper implications from the express words used, the usages of the trade, or the course of business between the parties. To this agreement the contractor is a stranger; he may be totally ignorant of the existence of any authority on the part of the agent. Nevertheless, if the agent does enter into a contract pursuant to the 'actual' authority, it does create contractual rights and liabilities between the principal and the contractor.[1439]

624. The agreement defines the scope of the agent's authority. Thus, where a vendor of property expressly in the contract of agency merely authorises his agent to receive offers and pass them on to him, the agent does not have authority to accept offers and conclude a contract of sale on behalf of his principal.[1440] Actual authority may also be implied from the circumstances.[1441]

625. Where an express authority is given to an agent, the court may find that there is also an implied authority to do acts which are necessary to achieve the purpose or purposes of the agency. What these 'implied' powers are will depend on the particular circumstances of the case including especially the trade or business involved, the nature of the agent, and any consistent course of dealing which may

1438. Directive 86/653/EEC on the co-ordination of the laws of the Member States relating to self-employed commercial agents.
1439. *Freeman and Lockyer v Brockhurst Park Properties (Mangal) Ltd* [1964] 2 QB 480, 502–503 per Diplock LJ.
1440. *Brennan v O'Connell* [1980] IR 13.
1441. *Hely-Hutchinson v Brayhead Ltd* [1968] 1 QB 549.

have existed between the parties concerned. It is accepted, for example, that an auctioneer, having been authorised to sell property by auction, has implied authority to sign the memorandum of the contract of sale on behalf of the vendor and the purchaser.[1442] This is sometimes referred to as 'usual' or 'customary' authority.[1443]

626. Implied authority in connection with an express agency authority is governed by the ordinary rules of the law of contract dealing with implied terms, and the Irish courts have considered this matter in a number of modern cases. These cases show that a term will not be implied lightly. In *Brennan v O'Connell*,[1444] the Supreme Court refused to imply a term that an agent must disclose information or inquiries which, according to ordinary (objective) business standards, could not be said to be material to a principal's decision to accept or reject a particular offer for property.

II. Ostensible Authority

627. Where a principal conveys an impression that an agent has authority to act on his behalf, the principal will not be permitted to deny the agent's authority so as to avoid liability on a contract apparently made on his behalf with a third party. He will be estopped from doing so. This type of agency may be described as an agency by estoppel, and it is said that the agent has ostensible authority or apparent authority. The estoppel will operate whether the principal has allowed his apparent agent to act when in fact he had no authority at all or (which is more usual) when his admitted agent exceeds a limitation imposed on his actual authority and this limitation was not made known to the third party.[1445]

628. To prove apparent authority:

(i) There must be a representation to the third party that the agent had authority. The representation can be express or implied, through words or conduct.[1446]
(ii) The representation must have been made by the alleged principal or someone with authority to do so acting on his behalf.
(iii) The representation must have been relied on by the third party and induced him to enter the transaction.

1442. *Sheridan v Higgins* [1971] IR 291.
1443. On the unusual example of *Watteau v Fenwick* [1893] 1 QB 346, *see* Tettenborn 'Agents, Business Owners and Estoppel' (1998) 2 Cambridge Law Journal 274.
1444. [1980] IR 13. *See also Galvin (Estates) Ltd. v Hedigan* [1985] ILRM 295.
1445. *Hely-Hutchinson v Brayhead Ltd* [1968] 1 QB 549; *Freeman and Lockyer v Brockhurst Park Properties (Mangal) Ltd* [1964] 2 QB 480.
1446. *Summers v Saloman* (1857) 7 E&B 879; *Todd v Robinson* (1825) Ry&M 217.

III. Authority by Ratification

629. Where an agent expressly contracts as agent for an existing named or identifiable principal, without the authority to do so, the principal may subsequently adopt or ratify the contract. The contract will then take effect retrospectively as if they had authorised it when the agent entered into it. An undisclosed principal cannot ratify; thus if an agent purports to contract on his own behalf, the principal cannot ratify.[1447] If a principal does not ratify the unauthorised act or contract of the agent, the agent will be personally liable to the third party.[1448]

630. Before a principal can be held to have validly ratified it is well established that he must have been made aware of all the material facts on which the contract was founded.[1449] This was discussed in the Irish Supreme Court in *Brennan v O'Connell*.[1450] In this case the defendants appointed an agent to procure for them a purchaser who was willing to buy one of the defendants' farms for £25,000. The agent then concluded an agreement without the authority of the defendants, but when the agent informed the defendants, the defendants approved the action. However, when the defendants expressed their approval they did not know that, on the day after the agent had contracted on their behalf, another person had inquired of the agent whether the particular farm and another of the defendants' farms could be sold as a single lot and, if so, the price that would be demanded for both properties. The Court held:

> In the instance of a vendor and an estate agent, the vendor should not be held to have ratified a contract for sale which the estate agent has purported to make on his behalf unless the vendor is made aware of all facts in the knowledge of the estate agent which, in the particular circumstances and without the benefit of hindsight, could *objectively* be said to have been necessary to enable the vendor to decide if he should assent to the sale.

631. The Court justified the objective approach to this issue as follows:

> If information which, merely by the subjective standards of a particular vendor, is thought necessary to be disclosed before a sale can be approved, the contract of agency should provide for such disclosure. If that were not the law, a vendor could avoid an otherwise valid ratification, on which the estate agent may have acted, by claiming that the estate agent had withheld from him information which he (the vendor), for private and unpredictable reasons, considered necessary – such as the identity of the purchaser; or the nature of his race,

1447. *Keighley Maxsted and Co. v Durant* [1901] AC 240. The principal does not have to have been named, but must have existed and been capable of being ascertained at the time when the agent purported to act on his behalf: *Watson v Swann* (1862) 11 CB (NS) 756.
1448. Under an action for breach of warranty of authority: *Collen v Wright* (1857) 8 E&B 647; *Firbank's Executors v Humphreys* (1887) LR 18 QBD 54.
1449. *Marsh v Joseph* [1897] 1 Ch 213.
1450. *Brennan v O'Connell* [1980] IR 13.

> religion or politics; or the way in which the property is to be used by the purchaser; or other purely personal or idiosyncratic considerations which would not reasonably be expected to be material to a decision to reject or to accept an offer to purchase.

632. Here, the fact that at the time of their approval the defendants were not aware of a mere inquiry of the nature described did not invalidate their approval, as this was not objectively a material fact of which the defendants should have been aware.

633. There are some further restrictions on ratification. A principal cannot ratify a void contract or a nullity,[1451] but may ratify a voidable contract before it has been avoided. The transaction must be one which the principal himself might have legally made both at the time of the contract and the time of ratification.[1452] Ratification must not unfairly prejudice third parties and must take place within a reasonable time.[1453]

634. If the contract is ratified, the ratification operates retroactively, so it is as if the principal authorised it at the time the agent entered into it.[1454] The principal can sue or be sued by the third party on the contract made by the agent.

IV. Agency by Operation of Law (Agency of Necessity)

635. Agency might also arise by operation of law in emergency situations, and this is referred to as 'agency of necessity'. Bowstead on Agency states:

> A person may have authority to act on behalf of another in certain cases where he is faced with an emergency in which the property or interests of that other person are in imminent jeopardy and it becomes necessary, in order to preserve the property or interests, so to act.[1455]

636. This type of agency would typically arise in the context of carriage by sea, for example, when cargo on a ship would have to be sold in an emergency situation. For this type of agency to arise: (i) there must have been an emergency, (ii) as a result it must have been impossible to get instructions from the principal, (iii) the agent must have acted bona fide and in the interests of the principal and (iv) the agent must have acted reasonably in all the circumstances.[1456] In modern times of

1451. *Brook v Hook* (1871) LR 6 Ex 89.
1452. *Boston Deep Sea Fishing and Ice Co Ltd v Farnham* [1957] 1 WLR 1051; *Grover and Grover v Mathews* [1910] 2 KB 40.
1453. *Metropolitan Asylums Board Managers v Kingham & Sons* (1890) 6 TLR 217; *Bird v Brown* (1850) 4 Exch 786.
1454. *Bolton Partners v Lambert* (1889) 41 Ch D 295; *Brennan v O'Connell* [1980] IR 13, 15.
1455. *Bowstead on Agency* (16th ed., 1996, Article 35).
1456. *Gunn v Roberts* (1874) LR 9 CP 331; *Notora v Henderson* (1872) LR 7 QB 225.

almost instantaneous communications, the circumstances giving rise to an agency of necessity in commercial situations of emergency will rarely arise.

§3. The Main Rights and Duties of Parties in an Agency Situation

637. The principal and agent have certain rights against each other as a result of the agency arrangement. If there is an agreement, this will be the primary source of rights and obligations of the parties. However, many of the rights and liabilities of the principal and agent do not depend on any contract but are imposed by the law because of the fiduciary relationship between them.

638. The common law traditionally took the view that the agent had a *stronger* position than the principal, and that the principal therefore needed to be protected by the imposition of fiduciary duties on the agent:

> The position of principal and agent gives rise to particular and onerous duties on the part of the agent, and the high standard of conduct required from him springs from the fiduciary relationship between his employer and himself. His position is confidential. It readily lends itself to abuse. A strict and salutary rule is required to meet the special situation. The rules of English law as they now exist spring from the strictness originally required by Courts of Equity in cases where the fiduciary relationship exists. Those requirements are superadded to the common law obligations of diligence and skill.[1457]

639. As a result the agent is given only basic rights and is subject to numerous duties.

640. This can be contrasted with the approach of civil law countries which regard the agent as having an interest in the principal's business, potentially spending years generating business for the principal, spreading goodwill and obtaining clients. Under this approach, the agent needs protection from the possibility that the principal could exploit their position. One category of agents in particular, self-employed agents known as commercial agents, has extensive rights and similar protection to that afforded to an employee. Although this category of agents was relatively unknown in Ireland, it was introduced to the legal system with the transposition of the EU Commercial Agents Directive[1458] by means of the European Communities (Commercial Agents) Regulations 1994, as amended in 1997. Commercial agents covered by the Regulations now have more extensive rights than they enjoy at common law, including rights to commission, rights on termination and protection against dismissal. However, the Regulations do not apply to all agencies, so it is necessary to look at the common law rules which apply to agents before turning to the Regulations.

1457. *Armstrong v Jackson* [1917] 2 KB 822, 826.

1458. Directive 86/653/EEC on the coordination of the laws of the Member States relating to self-employed commercial agents.

I. Agent's Duties Arising from the Agreement with the Principal

641. The agent is under a general duty to comply with the contract and obey the principal's lawful instructions.[1459] If the instructions are ambiguous, the agent will not be liable if they act on a reasonable interpretation of them, although there may be a duty to seek clarification of the instructions.[1460] Connected to this is the principle that the agent must not exceed their authority.[1461] The agent must also act with due skill and care,[1462] although this can be limited by a term in the contract.[1463] Where the agency is non-contractual this duty of care arises only in tort.[1464] Where an agent holds themselves out as possessing some special skill and contracts to exercise that skill on behalf of a principal, they will be held to such higher standard.

II. The Agent's Fiduciary Duties to the Principal

642. The fiduciary duties of the agent depend on the context, but include:

- The duty not to delegate
  The agent must personally perform the contract unless delegation is authorised or delegation is inherent in the nature of the agency (e.g., by trade custom or reasonably necessary to achieve the objective of the agency.)[1465]
- The duty to avoid a conflict of interest
  An agent must not allow their personal interests to conflict with those of the principal.[1466] This duty is strictly applied. A breach may arise even if there is in fact no conflict; it is enough that there is the possibility of conflict.
- The duty not to take advantage of their position
  An agent cannot make use of the principal's property or exploit confidential information unless the agent has the principal's consent.[1467] This obligation may continue even after the agency terminates.[1468] The remedy is usually an account of profits.
- The agent must not make a secret profit or accept a bribe
  The agent must account to the principal for all profits made from their position.[1469] They may only keep a profit if it is disclosed to the principal, who, with full knowledge, consents to their retaining it.[1470] This duty is strict and liability

---

1459. *Turpin v Bilton* (1843) 5 Man & G 455.
1460. *Ireland v Livingstone* (1872) LR 5 HL 395.
1461. *Dufrene v Hutchinson* (1810) 3 Taunt 117; *Williams v Evans* (1866) LR 1 QB 352.
1462. *Solomon v Barker* (1862) 2 F&F 726; *Keppel v Wheeler* [1927] 1 KB 577.
1463. *Henderson v Merrett Syndicates Ltd* [1994] 3 All ER 506.
1464. *Wilkinson v Coverdale* (1793) 1 Esp 74; *Chaudhry v Prabhakar* [1988] 3 ALL ER 718.
1465. *De Bussche v Alt* (1878) 8 Ch D 286; *Chariot Inns Ltd. v Assicurazioni Generali SPA* [1981] ILRM 173,178.
1466. *Armstrong v Jackson* [1917] 2 KB 822.
1467. *Keech v Sandford* (1726); *Reid Newfoundland Co v Anglo-American Telegraph Co Ltd* [1910] AC 555.
1468. *House of Spring Gardens Ltd. v Point Blank Ltd.* [1984] IR 611.
1469. *Boston Deep Sea Fishing Co. v Ansell* (1888) 39 ChD 339.
1470. *Rhodes v Macalister* (1923) 29 Com Cas 19; *Hurtsanger Ltd v Wilson* [2007] 1 WLR 2351.

arises from the mere fact of a profit having been made by an agent from their position – there is no need to show corruption or motive.[1471]

If an agent accepts from a third party any secret commission or reward as an inducement to make the contract, it is considered to be a bribe.[1472] In this situation the agent is acting in their own interest, and not the interest of the principal.

Where an agent has accepted a bribe, they must account for the profits made. In *Reid v AG for Hong Kong*[1473] it was held in the Privy Council that the fiduciary held the bribe on a constructive trust for the person injured. This means in effect that where the fiduciary has invested the bribe or secret commission the beneficiary may be able to trace those funds in equity. It also means that in the event of the fiduciary's insolvency, the beneficiary's property rights will trump the personal rights of the fiduciary's other creditors. This was doubted in subsequent UK cases[1474] but in *FHR European Ventures LLP and others (Respondents) v Cedar Capital Partners LLC (Appellant)*[1475] the UK Supreme Court confirmed that a secret commission or bribe received by a fiduciary is held on constructive trust for the beneficiary, thus giving the beneficiary property rights in the secret commission or bribe.

– The duty to account

The agent must account for all sums received him on behalf of the principal[1476] and is under a duty to keep his own property separate from that of P.[1477]

III. The Agent's Rights at Common Law

643. The agent has limited rights at common law. The agent is entitled to remuneration if that has been agreed with the principal, or if the court implies such a right. The court will normally imply such a right where the agent is acting in a professional capacity or in the course of his normal business.[1478] The agent is only entitled to commission if the event has happened on which the contract provided for payment, and if the agent was the effective cause of that event. Estate agents or auctioneers agency agreements have given rise to much litigation on this point, and the precise wording of the relevant agreement is crucial in such cases.

644. Estate agents (as distinct from auctioneers) are usually employed 'to find a purchaser' or 'to introduce a purchaser willing and able to purchase', and in the usual situation will not be entitled to payment unless they are the effective cause of a completed sale. A claim for commission where there has been no completed sale

1471. *Boardman v Phipps* [1967] 2 AC 46.
1472. *Andrews v Ramsay & Co.* [1903] 2 KB 63; *Rhodes v Macalister* (1923) 29 Com Cas 19.
1473. [1993] 3 WLR 1143.
1474. *Sinclair Investments (UK) Ltd v Versailles Trade Finance Ltd (In Administration)* [2011] EWCA Civ 347, [2012] Ch. 453.
1475. [2014] UKSC 45.
1476. *Edgell v Day* (1865) LRICP 80.
1477. *Henry v Hammond* [1913] 2 KB 515.
1478. *Way v Latilla* [1937] 3 All ER 759.

will normally not succeed unless the agency agreement clearly provides for it.[1479] In *Murphy Buckley and Keogh v Pye (Ireland) Ltd*[1480] the plaintiff were contracted 'as sole selling agents' for the sale of property, the contract expressly providing for payment of commission on completion of a sale to a purchaser introduced by the plaintiffs. Henchy J held that the sole agency did not prevent the defendants from selling the property to a purchaser found by themselves and no commission was payable. A similar 'sole selling agency' agreement was entered into in *Galvin (Estates) Ltd. v Hedigan* [1481] but in that case the agents were also employed to act as lobbyists to assist in an effort to persuade Dublin County Council to rezone the land for industrial purposes. Costello J held that the parties must have intended that if the rezoning occurred, the agents would be entitled to commission if they introduced a purchaser, and their entitlement to remuneration could not be defeated by the defendants themselves directly negotiating with, and selling the land to, a purchaser. If the sole agent is appointed with exclusive selling rights, such an agent will normally be entitled to commission on the sale even if the principal, or another agent, effects the sale.[1482]

645. If an agent incurs liability or is forced to spend money in the performance of the agency, the general rule is that they are entitled to an indemnity from their principal unless the contract excludes this right. If the agency contract does not expressly contain a term providing for an indemnity the court may imply such a term.[1483] However this right can be lost, for example of the agent acts are unauthorised or they are in breach of their duties.

646. In order to protect his rights to indemnity and remuneration, an A may be entitled to a lien over property belonging to the P which is in his possession. A lien is a right to retain goods or possessions of the principal by way of security until some debt is paid. A lien is generally founded on possession, and the agent can therefore only claim the lien if they have lawful possession of the goods. The right is one of retention of property until payment; it does not entitle the agent to sell the property of his principal to realise the sums owed to him. The contract of agency may exclude the right to a lien.

IV. Commercial Agency

647. The EU Commercial Agents Directive[1484] was implemented in Ireland by means of the European Communities (Commercial Agents) Regulations 1994, as

1479. *Luxor (Eastbourne) Ltd. v Cooper* [1941] AC 108; *James H. North Ltd. v Dinan* [1931] IR 486.
1480. [1971] IR 57.
1481. [1985] ILRM 295.
1482. *Ibid.*
1483. *Henehan v Courtney and Hanley* (1966) 101 ILTR 25.
1484. Directive 86/653/EEC on the coordination of the laws of the Member States relating to self-employed commercial agents.

amended in 1997.[1485] The Directive applies to commercial agents only, and provide for rights for commercial agents, particularly on termination.[1486]

648. A commercial agent is a 'self-employed intermediary who has continuing authority to negotiate the sale or the purchase of goods on behalf of another person, hereinafter called the 'principal', or to negotiate and conclude such transactions on behalf of and in the name of that principal.'[1487] The Directive provides that Member States have the right to provide that the Directive shall not apply to those persons whose activities as commercial agents are considered 'secondary',[1488] but the Irish Regulations have applied this only in relation to 'a consumer credit agent or a mail order catalogue agent for consumer goods', whose activities are presumed to be secondary unless the contrary is established.[1489]

649. The commercial agent is self-employed, and therefore employees are not commercial agents.[1490] An agent must be involved in the buying or selling of *goods.*[1491] Agents dealing in services or land are therefore excluded. Nor do the regulations apply to other distribution arrangements such as distributorship or franchising nor to agents acting in one off transactions. Moreover, where a contract is concluded, the Regulations only apply where the contract is made in the name of the principal, thus excluding agents who act for undisclosed principals. In addition, the Regulations provide that 'The agency contract shall not be valid unless it is evidenced in writing'.[1492]

650. An agent can be a commercial agent even if they just negotiate the sale or purchase of goods on behalf of the principal. In *Kenny v Ireland ROC Ltd.* [1493] the plaintiff ran a series of petrol stations trading under the Esso name, and the question arose whether they were a commercial agent for the purposes of the Regulations.

1485. The European Communities (Commercial Agents) Regulations 1994 which transposed the Commercial Agents Directive did not outline the rights and obligations of commercial agents and their principals in any detail whatsoever, instead simply providing that the directive 'shall, subject to these Regulations, apply to the relations between commercial agents and their principals from 1 January 1994' and selecting some of the options where Member States had a right to choose. The references below are thus mostly to the Directive rather than to the Regulations.

1486. *See* generally P. Fogarty and C. Bergin-Cross, 'Commercial Agents Directive and Liability' (2014) 32(13) Irish Law Times 195–200; (2014) 32(14) Irish Law Times 209–212.

1487. Regulation 2(1). There are some exceptions, including a commercial agent who is unpaid.

1488. Article 2(2).

1489. Regulation 2(1)(f), Regulation 2(2).

1490. *See John Sheridan v Fairco Limited* [2006] 17 ELR 246.

1491. It is unclear whether this includes software: *see Computer Associates UK Ltd v Software Incubator* [2018] EWCA Civ 518 where the Court of Appeal of England and Wales held that for the purposes of the Directive software sold and delivered by digital download is not a sale of 'goods'. The question has been referred to the CJEU.

1492. Regulation 4. *See Bushell Interiors Ltd v Liecht Küchen A.G.* [2014] IEHC 3 where it was held *obiter* that the purported agency contract, if it existed, would be invalid for the purposes of the Commercial Agents Regulations as not having been adequately evidenced in writing. *See also Aranwell Limited v Pura Food Products Limited and Qualifry Limited*, Unreported, High Court, 23 April 2004.

1493. [2005] IEHC 241. *See also Cooney & Company and Another v Murphy Brewery Sales Limited*, Unreported, High Court, 30 July 1997.

Could they be said to have 'negotiated' sales where they simply present goods to customers? The court stated that 'negotiate' does not require 'what may be termed active negotiation or bargain by bid and counter bid'. Instead the correct approach is to consider whether the person who may be said to be negotiating has to 'deal with, manage or conduct' the sale or purchase concerned and in so doing to use some skill or consideration. This can be a skill in bargaining, or, as in this case, skill in marketing and promotion, or presenting the goods in a way to make it attractive to the public. Hence, the plaintiff was held to be a commercial agent for the purpose of the regulations.[1494]

651. A commercial agent has obligations under the Directive. Under Article 3 of the Directive, a commercial agent must look after his principal's interests and act dutifully and in good faith.[1495] In particular, a commercial agent must:

(a) make proper efforts to negotiate and, where appropriate, conclude the transactions he is instructed to take care of;
(b) communicate to his principal all the necessary information available to him;
(c) comply with reasonable instructions given by his principal.[1496]

652. This is not particularly different to the position at common law, although the Directive specifies that these duties cannot be contracted out of.[1497] However, the Directive provides for significant new obligations on the principal. Article 4 provides that a *principal* must act dutifully and in good faith. In particular, a principal must:

(a) provide his commercial agent with the necessary documentation relating to the goods concerned;
(b) obtain for his commercial agent the information necessary for the performance of the agency contract, and in particular notify the commercial agent within a reasonable period once he anticipates that the volume of commercial transactions will be significantly lower than that which the commercial agent could normally have expected.[1498]

653. In addition, a principal must inform the commercial agent within a reasonable period of his acceptance, refusal and of any non-execution of a commercial transaction which the commercial agent has procured for the principal.[1499]

654. The Directive also sets out the agent's right to commission, providing that in the absence of any agreement between the parties, a commercial agent is entitled

---

1494. *See* Gardiner 'The EC (Commercial Agents) Directive: Twenty Years After Its Introduction, Significant Approaches still Emerge from Irish and UK Courts' (2007) Journal of Business Law 412.
1495. *See Rossetti Marketing Ltd v Diamond Sofa Company Ltd* [2011] EWHC 2482.
1496. Article 3(2).
1497. Article 5.
1498. Article 4(2).
1499. Article 4(3).

to the remuneration customarily allowed in the region, or a reasonable remuneration.[1500] If the remuneration varies with the number or value of business transactions it is deemed to be commission. The commercial agent is entitled to commission on commercial transactions concluded during the period covered by the agency contract where the transaction has been concluded as a result of his action; or where the transaction is concluded with a third party whom he has previously acquired as a customer for transactions of the same kind.[1501] A commercial agent is also entitled to commission on transactions concluded during the period covered by the agency contract where the agent has an exclusive right to a specific geographical area or group of customers and where the transaction has been entered into with a customer belonging to that area or group.[1502] The European Court of Justice has held that a commercial agent who is responsible for a particular geographical territory has a right to commission even in circumstances where the contract(s) was concluded without the agent's involvement.[1503] The Directive further sets out when the commission falls due and is to be paid,[1504] and rights of the agent to information about commission due and calculations used.[1505]

655. One of the most important aspects of the Directive is the rights of the commercial agent on termination of the agency. In relation to commission, the Directive provides that a commercial agent shall be entitled to commission on commercial transactions concluded after the agency contract has terminated:

(a) if the transaction is mainly attributable to the commercial agent's efforts during the period covered by the agency contract and if the transaction was entered into within a reasonable period after that contract terminated; or
(b) if, in accordance with the conditions mentioned in Article 7, the order of the third party reached the principal or the commercial agent before the agency contract terminated.[1506]

656. Further rights of the agent on termination are discussed below.

§4. Termination of Agency

I. Termination at Common Law

657. An agency relationship may be terminated by mutual agreement, or terminated unilaterally by the principal. In the latter case the required contractual notice

1500. Article 6(1).
1501. Article 7.
1502. Regulation 4, applying Article 7(2) of the Directive.
1503. Case C-104/95, *Georgios Kontogeorgas v Kartonpak AE* [1997] 1 CMLR 1093.
1504. Article 10.
1505. Article 12.
1506. Article 8.

must be given, or if none is provided for, reasonable notice.[1507] The principal's right to terminate by notice will be subject to an implied term such as that he will not without justification, interfere with the agent's ability to complete the task required and thereby earn the agreed commission.[1508] An agent may terminate the agency contract in accordance with its express or implied terms. An agency might also be terminated by operation of law, for example by complete performance or frustration. Some grants of agency authority are legally irrevocable. This occurs where the agent's authority is said to be 'coupled with an interest', for example, where a principal owes money to the agent and the agent is given authority to sell the principal's property to discharge the debt. This applies only where the agency is created specifically to protect the agent's interest already existing before the agency was created.

658. If the agency is over it will terminate the agent's actual authority, but the agent may continue to have apparent authority.[1509] Therefore the principal may need to publicise the termination of the agent's authority in order to draw it to the attention of those who have dealt with the agent in the past.

II. Termination under the Commercial Agents Directive

659. Where a commercial agency agreement is for an indefinite duration, the Commercial Agents Directive sets out minimum periods of notice for termination of the agency contract, and provides that the parties cannot provide for shorter periods of notice.[1510] To bolster this right, an agency contract for a fixed period which continues to be performed by both parties after that period has expired shall be deemed to be converted into an agency contract for an indefinite period.[1511]

660. As noted above, the agent has a right to commission even after the agency agreement is terminated.[1512] However, a potentially even more important right is found in Article 17, which provides that on termination of the agency contract the commercial agent is entitled to be either 'indemnified' (as defined in Article 17(2)) or 'compensated for damage' (as defined in Article 17(3)). Member States were expected to choose between these two options, although Ireland did not choose in its initial transposition of the Directive. The Commission decided to open proceedings against Ireland for non-implementation of the Directive,[1513] and the omission

---

1507. *Irish Welding Co. Ltd. v Philips Electrical (Ireland) Ltd.*, Unreported, High Court, 8 October 1976.

1508. *O'Hanlon, Another and Robinson v Belfast Inns Ltd.* (1962) Ir Jur Rep 25.

1509. *Drew v Nunn* (1879) 4 QBD 661.

1510. Article 15. The Directive allows for immediate termination in exceptional circumstances or because of the failure of one party to carry out all or part of his obligations: Article 16.

1511. Article 14.

1512. Article 8.

1513. In addition, despite being given until 1 January 1994 to implement the directive (as opposed to 1 January 1990, which applied to all other member states except the UK and Italy), Ireland failed to do so until 21 February 1994.

was eventually remedied in the European Communities (Commercial Agents) Regulations 1997,[1514] with the State opting to choose the remedy of compensation. This can be contrasted with the UK's mixed approach of opting for a 'default' remedy of compensation unless the parties provide for compensation.[1515]

661. Article 17(3) of the Directive sets out the 'compensation' alternative:

> The commercial agent is entitled to compensation for the damage he suffers as a result of the termination of his relations with the principal.
>
> Such damage shall be deemed to occur particularly when the termination takes place in circumstances:
>
> – depriving the commercial agent of the commission which proper performance of the agency contract would have procured him whilst providing the principal with substantial benefits linked to the commercial agent's activities,
> – and/or which have not enabled the commercial agent to amortize the costs and expenses that he had incurred for the performance of the agency contract on the principal's advice.

662. Compensation is not payable under certain circumstances,[1516] but otherwise the parties may not derogate from this provision.[1517] The main difference between this concept of compensation, and that found at common law, is that compensation here is not fault based or based on any breach of contract; it is payable even if the termination was lawful, and may be payable even if the agent is in breach, provided the breach is not repudiatory in nature.[1518] It is thus a new concept of 'compensation', which raises the question of how it is to be interpreted and calculated. This has resulted in a series of cases in the UK outline the approach to be taken, and factors to be examined when assessing compensation.[1519] The European Court of Justice has stated that Member States enjoy a margin of discretion when applying these concepts,[1520] although there are limits to this discretion.[1521] However, there do not appear to be any Irish cases applying this principle.

1514. S.I. No. 31 of 1997.
1515. Regulation 17(2) Commercial Agents (Council Directive) Regulations 1993.
1516. Article 18.
1517. Article 19. *See Ingmar GB Ltd v Eaton Leonard Technologies Inc* [2001] 1 CMLR 9.
1518. *Crocs Europe BV v Craig Lee Anderson & Anor (T/A Spectrum Agencies)* [2012] EWCA Civ 1400.
1519. *See* for example *Tigana Ltd. v Decoro Ltd.* [2003] EWCA Civ 375; *Lonsdale (t/a Lonsdale Agencies) v Howard & Hallam Ltd* [2007] UKHL 32. *See* Saintier 'The interpretation of Directives to suit commercial needs: a further threat to coherence' (2012) *Journal of Business Law* 128; Saintier 'Final guidelines on compensation of commercial agents' (2008) 124 Law Quarterly Review 31; Saintier 'The principles behind the assessment of the compensation option under the Agency Regulations: clarity at last?' (2007) Journal of Business Law 90.
1520. *Honeyvem Informazioni Commerciali Sri v Mariella De Zotti* [2006] ECR I-02879 (regarding indemnities).

Chapter 2. Bailment

§1. The Nature of Bailment

663. 'Bailment' is a general term originating in the early common law to describe a large range of circumstances where goods are delivered by one party (the bailor) to another (the bailee) on the express or implied condition that they shall be returned to the bailor or dealt with according to his directions, as soon as the purpose for which they are delivered has been achieved.

664. Bailment normally, but not invariably, is associated with a contract involving reward or consideration. In such a case, the rights and duties of the bailor and bailee are determined primarily by the particular contract concerned, including any variation of liability which would otherwise arise simply by virtue of the existence of the bailment. However, a bailment may be entirely gratuitous or even involuntary, so clearly it is not necessary that it should depend on contract with requirements of agreement and consideration. Gratuitous bailments may arise from a delivery of goods to a bailee to be looked after without reward, or simply loaned gratuitously for the bailee's use, or with instructions to do something to the goods such as transporting them, without any reward for the services rendered. An involuntary bailment arises where the bailee acquires legal possession of goods without having sought this.[1522]

665. A bailment of goods for reward arises in a wide and increasing range of commercial transactions such as hire purchase, rental or hiring of goods, sale of goods with a reservation of title, goods delivered 'on approval' for sale or return, as well as transactions involving carriage of goods, goods delivered for cleaning or repair, goods pledged or pawned as security, goods delivered for storage, etc. Because most such transactions nowadays are governed to a greater or lesser extent by statute, the modern rules on bailment are largely to be found interspersed in the rules of statute and case law dealing with specific transactions and relationships.

§2. Rights and Duties of a Bailor

666. A bailor has the right to have the goods bailed returned to them, or disposed of in accordance with their instructions, when the purpose of the bailment is achieved. They may sue the bailee to enforce these and any other obligations which the bailment imposes on the bailee. The bailor may sue third parties for loss or damage to the goods in certain circumstances, such as when the bailee has wrongfully terminated the bailment and a third party has the goods or has converted them to his

1521. *Semen v Deutsche Tamoil GmbH* (C-348/07) [2009] E.C.R. I-2341 '[T]he discretion that Member States have to adjust, where necessary, the indemnity payable … in order to make it equitable cannot be construed to the effect that the indemnity can only be adjusted downwards.'

1522. The Sale of Goods and Supply of Services Act 1980, designed to deal with the practice of 'inertia-selling', enables the bailee of unsolicited goods to treat the goods as an unconditional gift: s. 47.

own use,[1523] or for example where a third party is responsible for an accident to a vehicle owned by a leasing company and bailed 'on lease' to the bailee.[1524]

667. The bailor has a duty to ensure that he has a title to the goods bailed for reward which enable him to give undisturbed possession to the bailee.[1525] Goods bailed for reward must be fit and suitable for the purpose for which they are bailed. This implied duty must be considered in light of the normal rules on implied terms which apply in the general law of contract and in light of statutes such as the Consumer Credit Act 1995 which imply other terms such as merchantable quality.[1526] These statutes are relevant in the law of bailment insofar as hire purchase and leasing of goods ('consumer hire') involve bailment for reward. In the case of a gratuitous bailment, as in the simple case of lending an article without payment, there is a duty on the bailor to disclose any dangerous defect in the goods of which they are aware.[1527]

§3. RIGHTS AND DUTIES OF A BAILEE

668. The bailee has the right to possess the goods bailed, and the right to sue third parties in respect of loss or damage to the bailed goods. The third party cannot raise the defence of *jus tertii*, i.e., that the bailee is not entitled to possession because he is not the true owner of the goods.[1528]

669. The bailee may, with the consent of the bailor, deliver the bailed goods to another party to hold them as bailee. This 'bailment by attornment' commonly arises in situations such as where a bailor instructs a warehouseman holding goods as a bailee to deliver them to another, or to hold them for another.[1529] In a 'bailment by attornment', the 'replacement' bailee is substituted for the original bailee. However, the original bailee may also, with the express or implied consent of the bailor, transfer possession of the bailed goods to a sub-bailee. In that case, the bailment relationship between the bailor and the original bailee continues in the normal way, but a new bailment relationship also comes into existence between the original bailee and the sub-bailee.

670. There are a number of duties that are imposed on the bailee. The bailee must return the bailed goods, or to deal with them in accordance with the instructions of the bailor, when the purpose of the bailment is completed. The bailee must

1523. *British Wagon Co. Ltd. v Shorn* [1961] IR 164.
1524. *Mears v London and South Western Rail Co.* (1862) 11 CBNS.
1525. *See* s. 74 and s. 88 of the Consumer Credit Act 1995, concerning hire purchase and consumer hire respectively.
1526. Sections 76 and 88 Consumer Credit Act 1995 which imply such a term into hire purchase and consumer hire agreements.
1527. *Campbell v O'Donnell* [1967] IR 226.
1528. *Webb and Webb v Ireland* [1988] IR 353.
1529. *See also* s. 29(3) Sale of Goods Act 1893.

not deviate from the terms of the contract by, for example, changing the route specified in a contract of carriage, or storing goods in a place or manner differently from that specified.

671. A bailee must exercise the degree of care and skill in relation to the bailment which might be reasonably expected of a bailee in that particular situation.[1530] A specific example of this can be found in the Consumer Credit Act 1995, which provides in section 67 that where a hire-purchase agreement has been terminated before the final payment is made, the hirer shall, if he has failed to take reasonable care of the goods, be liable to pay damages for the failure. In addition, section 90 provides that in a consumer hire, a hirer shall take all reasonable care of goods which are let to them and shall be liable to the owner if they fail to take such care.

672. Bailees, in principle, are liable for negligence, whether the bailment is gratuitous or not, but the standard of care required of a gratuitous bailee is less than that of a bailee for reward.[1531] An involuntary bailee will not be liable in negligence for the loss of, or damage to the goods, but may be liable for wilful or intentional damage and for wilfully preventing the owner from recovering the goods.

1530. *Keenan v Mulcahy* (1953) Ir Jur Rep 74.
1531. *Doorman v Jenkins* (1834) 2 Ad. & El. 256; 111 ER 99.

Chapter 3. Gaming and Wagering

§1. Gaming and Lotteries

673. Gaming and wagering agreements, and lotteries, have a long history of legislative regulation,[1532] judicial interpretation of the relevant statutes, and a mass of case law generally in both England and Ireland. Public policy was to discourage gambling by declaring wagering and gaming contracts and lotteries either illegal or unenforceable. The Gaming and Lotteries Act 1956 and the National Lottery Act 1986 are now the principal governing Acts in Ireland, but these have been amended several times, in particular by the Gaming and Lotteries Act 1970 and the Gaming and Lotteries (Amendment) Act 2019. This legislation is now cited together as the Gaming and Lotteries Acts 1956–2019 and is to be construed together as one.[1533] The 2019 Act was an attempt to modernise the legislation in this area, and changes introduced included changes (increases) to the maximum stake and maximum prize limits for gaming machines, and set the legal age for all gambling activities at 18 years. However, this is seen as an interim reform measure, pending the introduction of a comprehensive Gambling Control Bill.[1534] These reforms are likely to include the possibility of a regulator for gaming activities.

674. Gaming is defined in the 1956 Act as 'playing a game (whether of skill or chance or partly of skill and partly of chance) for stakes hazarded by the players'.[1535] Although the original Act provided for various situations under which gaming was unlawful,[1536] this was substituted in 2019 as follows:

> A person shall not promote gaming unless he or she is, or is the employee or agent acting as such of, a person who is the holder of a gaming permit or a gaming licence that is for the time being in force and the gaming is in accordance with the permit or licence.[1537]

675. Contravention of this provision is an offence.[1538] Gaming permits are to be issued by the Gardai,[1539] and the Acts set out the criteria and procedures for obtaining a gaming permit or licence. For example, a gaming permit cannot be issued 'for

1532. For example, the Irish Gaming Act 1712 and the Gaming Acts 1835, 1845 and 1892.
1533. Gaming and Lotteries (Amendment) Act 2019, s. 27(2).
1534. *See* the Report of the Inter-Departmental Working Group on Future Licensing and Regulation of Gambling, March 2019, available at: http://www.justice.ie/en/JELR/Inter-Departmental_Working_Group_on_Future_Licensing_and_Regulation_of_Gambling.pdf/.
1535. Section 2.
1536. Under the old version of s. 4, gaming is unlawful if the chances of all the players, including the banker, are not equal, or if a portion of the stakes are retained by the banker otherwise than as winnings, or the gaming is conducted by way of slot machines. The 2019 Act also repealed several provisions of the 1956 Act which governed gaming at events and places such as a circus, carnival, or funfair: *see* s. 24(1) of the 2019 Act which repealed ss 5, 6, 7, 8, 9, (and 21, 22, 22A, 23, 24, 25, 27, 28A, 29, 31, 34, and 45) of the Principal Act.
1537. Section 4(1) as amended.
1538. Section 4(2).
1539. Section 9A.

any kind of gaming in which by reason of the nature of the game, the chances of all the players, including the banker, are not equal'.[1540] The stake in each game shall not be more than €10 for each player,[1541] and no player may win more than the value of €3,000 in each game.[1542] Gaming machines can only be operated in licensed amusement halls or funfairs under a gaming licence, and only in areas where the local authority allows licensed amusement halls or funfairs.[1543]

676. Similarly, section 26 of the Act now states that 'a person shall not promote a lottery unless he or she is, or is the employee or agent acting as such of, a person who is the holder of a lottery permit or a lottery licence that is for the time being in force and the lottery is conducted in accordance with the permit or licence'. Exceptions are made where lotteries held for charitable or philanthropic purposes[1544] or where the lotteries are conducted in conjunction with the selling or marketing of a particular product,[1545] provided certain criteria are met.

§2. Wagering

677. Wagering is not defined in the *Gaming and Lotteries Acts* 1956 (and was not defined in the earlier legislation) and reference must be made to the older cases in which attempts were made to define a wager. In *Carlill v Carbolic Smoke Ball Co.* Hawkins J suggested that:

> A wagering contract is one by which two persons professing to hold opposite views touching the issue of a future uncertain event, mutually agree that, dependent upon the determination of that event, one shall win from the other, and that other shall pay or hand over to him, a sum of money or other stake, neither of the contracting parties having any other interest in that contract than the sum or stake he will so win, or lose, there being no other real consideration for the making of such contract by either of the parties.[1546]

678. There may be a wager on a past or present fact or event also. In *Duff v Racing Board*[1547] Pringle J in the Irish High Court held that a bet placed with the Totaliser ('Tote') organised under statute by the Irish Racing Board was not a wager because it lacked the essential requirement for a wager that one party is to win and the other is to lose on the outcome of the matter. Under the 'Tote' system, the Board is required to pay all the receipts from bets placed to the winners and the Board can neither win nor lose.

1540. Section 9A(6).
1541. Section 9A(11)(a).
1542. Section 9A(11)(b).
1543. *See* Part III of the 1956 Act, as amended.
1544. Section 26A.
1545. Section 27A.
1546. (1892) 2 QB 484, 490–491.
1547. Unreported, High Court, 19 November 1971.

679. The element that neither of the parties in a wager-like situation must have any interest in the contract other than the sum staked explains why insurance contracts and genuine contracts for buying and selling stocks and shares are not classified as wagers. Despite the speculative nature of these and similar contracts, the intention of both parties must point to a gambling transaction. If the assured has an insurable interest in the subject matter (e.g., a ship's cargo in a marine insurance contract) or if a person actually contracts to buy shares rather than agrees to pay the difference between the market price of these shares as between different dates, it is not a wager.

§3. Gaming and Wagering Contracts

680. Section 36 of the *Gaming and Lotteries Act* 1956 provides:

(1) Every contract by way of gaming and wagering is void.
(2) No action shall lie for the recovery of any money or thing which is alleged to be won or have been paid upon a wager or which has been deposited to abide the event on which a wager is made.
(3) A promise, express or implied, to pay any person any money paid by him under or in respect of a contract to which this section applies or to pay any money by way of commission, fee, reward or otherwise in respect of the contract or of any services connected with the contract is void and no action shall lie for the recovery of any such money.

681. The section substantially re-enacts section 18 of the Gaming Act 1845 which is now repealed, and decisions given on section 18 of the earlier Act are still largely relevant.

682. Contracts of gaming and wagering are *void*, not illegal. The practical consequences of this context is that the loser on a betting contract has a privilege. They may and, if a 'professional' like a bookmaker, normally will pay out the winner, but they can elect not to do so and cannot be sued.[1548] If they pay by cheque and subsequently cancel it, they cannot be sued on the stopped cheque. If, however, they do pay, they cannot sue to recover the money paid. However, it has been held that if the loser claims their stake back before it has been paid by an agent to the winner, thus revoking the authority of his agent to pay it out, the stakeholder must return it in an action for money had and received.[1549]

1548. *Crean v Deane* [1959] IR 347.
1549. *Graham v Thompson* (1867) IR 2 CL 64.

Chapter 4. Sale of goods

§1. Introduction

683. By the end of the nineteenth century, there was a substantial body of case law on contracts for the sale of goods. These decisions were 'codified' in the Sale of Goods Act 1893,[1550] which sets out the rules applicable to contracts for the sale of goods. However, the general rules of the law of contract continued to apply, once not inconsistent with the Act.[1551] The Sale of Goods Act 1893 applies to both commercial and consumer sales transactions.

684. The Sale of Goods Act 1893 still applies in Ireland, but has been amended by the Sale of Goods and Supply of Services Act 1980, which, as its name suggests, also sets out rules on the provision of services. The main changes introduced by the 1980 Act included making the implied terms regarding the quality of goods mandatory in consumer contracts,[1552] providing for additional consumer remedies of repair and replacement,[1553] and adding a new set of rules on the provision of services.[1554] In addition, the sale of goods to consumers is subject to consumer protection legislation emanating from the European Union, in particular the Consumer Sales Directive 1999/44/EC.[1555] This Directive was implemented by means of a stand-alone statutory instrument, the European Communities (Certain Aspects of the Sale of Consumer Goods and Associated Guarantees) Regulations 2003, without any attempt at consolidation. Although in theory Irish consumers are not harmed by this method of transposition—the 2003 Regulations are stated to be 'in addition to, and not in substitution for' *inter alia* the Sale of Goods Act – it has resulted in 'a confusing and, in some respects, contradictory legislative framework.'[1556] In practical terms, it has meant that Irish consumers have continued to rely on the rights found in the Sale of Goods Act, with the Consumer Sales Directive having relatively little impact.

685. More recently, there has been acknowledgement that sales law is somewhat incoherent and outdated. In 2011, the Sales Law Review Group published its *Report on Legislation governing the Sale of Goods and Supply of Services,* and made recommendations for a scheme of legislation capable of providing a statutory

1550. Chalmers, 'An Experiment in Codification', 2 Law Quarterly Review 125; Ferguson 'Legal Ideology and commercial Interests: The social origins of the Commercial Law Codes' (1977) 4 British Journal of Law & Society 18; Rodger 'The codification of commercial law in Victorian Britain' (1992) 108 Law Quarterly Review 570.
1551. Section 61(2).
1552. Section 22 of the Sale of Goods and Supply of Services Act 1980, amending s. 55 of the Sale of Goods Act 1893.
1553. Section 21 of the Sale of Goods and Supply of Services Act 1980, amending s. 53 of the Sale of Goods Act 1893.
1554. Sections 39 and 40 of the Sale of Goods and Supply of Services Act 1980.
1555. Other relevant legislation would include Council Directive 85/374/EC on Products Liability, implemented in Ireland by the Liability for Defective Products Act 1991 and the European Communities (Liability for Defective Products) Regulations 2000.
1556. Sales Law Review Group, 2011: 10.

sales law framework appropriate to modern-day conditions and needs. This included a significant reform of consumer sales, and the consolidation of domestic and European measures. As a result of this Report, and a Consultation Paper issued in 2014 by the Department of Jobs, Enterprise and Innovation, an Irish Consumer Rights Bill was published in May 2015. However, that same month the European Commission produced its Digital Single Market strategy,[1557] and this was followed up with *inter alia* a proposal for a Directive on sales of goods. Due to the overlap between these proposals and the Scheme of the Consumer Rights Bill, the Bill was stalled pending the finalisation of the European measures. The only major section of the Bill which was eventually enacted concerned gift vouchers, as this was not included in the European proposals.[1558]

686. Only the principal features of the Act can be considered here. Specialist and more detailed works are available, and should be consulted to obtain the complete picture on sales law.

§2. The Sale of Goods Acts 1893–1980

I. Definition of a Contract for Sale of Goods

687. The Sale of Goods Act applies to a contract for the sale of goods, which is defined in the Act as 'a contract whereby the seller transfers or agrees to transfer the property in goods to the buyer for a money consideration, called the price'.[1559] No distinction at this stage is made between consumer and commercial sales transactions – the Act applies to both. However, certain provisions within the Act apply only to consumer sales.

688. This definition requires that the property in goods (i.e., ownership) is transferred to the buyer; thus contracts of hire would not be included within the scope of the definition. In addition, section 61(4) explicitly excludes 'any transaction in the form of a contract of sale which is intended to operate by way or mortgage, pledge, charge or other security'.

689. The requirement of a money consideration (price) means that other transactions concerning goods such as barters or gifts are not included in the Act. A part-barter, i.e., transaction where goods are bought for cash plus goods, such as in the common transaction of buying a new car with a trade-in of a used car, may satisfy

1557. European Commission Communication, 2015.
1558. The Consumer Protection (Gift Vouchers) Act 2019, which provides, inter alia, that gift vouchers must remain valid for five years from the date on which they were purchased.
1559. Section 1(1), Sale of Goods Act 1893.

the definition if the contract establishes 'the price' of the goods, with the seller willing to take the used car in lieu of part of the agreed price.[1560] However, if no price is set, then it is a barter and the Act will not apply.[1561]

690. The contract must be for the sale of 'goods', defined in section 62 as including 'all chattels personal other than things in action and money'. Contracts for the sale of land or interests in land are excluded, as are intangible property rights like shares in a company or intellectual property rights. A contract for the supply of a service is not a sale of goods, even if the contract also involves the provision of some materials. If the essential subject matter of the contract predominantly requires the exercise of skill and labour, it is for the supply of a service, not a sale of goods, but the case law is not always clear.[1562] This distinction was of greater significance in the past, but even today differences remain between the regime applicable to the sale of goods and that applicable to services, for example with regard to the extent of the seller/supplier's obligations, and their ability to exclude liability.

691. More recently, the restriction of the Act to the sale of 'goods' has caused particular difficulties in the context of computer software and digital content. In *St Albans City and District Council v International Computers Ltd*[1563] it was stated obiter in the English Court of Appeal that while a computer disk was goods, the program or software was not, meaning that contracts for the sale of digital content fall outside the scope of the Act. Despite the lacuna this left in the law, the Sales Law Review Group did not recommend expanding the definition of 'goods' in the Act to include digital content, arguing instead that regulation should be specific to digital content.[1564] Consequent to this, the Consumer Rights Bill 2015 introduced specific rules regarding digital content; [1565] however as mentioned this Bill was abandoned due to developments at a European level. Directive 2019/770 on certain aspects concerning contracts for the supply of digital content and digital services now governs this area, and is due to be implemented in Ireland by July 2021.[1566]

1560. *Aldridge v Johnson* (1857) 7 E & B 885.

1561. *Flynn v Mackin* [1974] IR 101. *See* EM Clare Canton 'Sale of Goods and Barter' (1976) 39 Modern Law Review 589.

1562. *See* for example *Clay v Yates* (1858) 1 H&N 73; *Lee v Griffin* (1861) 1 B & S 272; *Robinson v Graves* [1935] 1 KB 579; *Lockett v A & M Charles Ltd* [1938] 4 All ER 170; *Dodd v Wilson* [1946] 2 All ER 691; *Cammell Laird v Manganese Bronze* [1934] AC 402; *Hyundai Heavy Industries Co Ltd v Papadopoulos* [1980] 1 WLR 1129; *Carroll v An Post National Lottery Co* [1996] 1 IR 443.

1563. [1996] 4 All ER 481.

1564. Sales Law Review Group paras 2.25–2.29.

1565. *See* Caterina Gardiner 'Scheme of Consumer Rights Bill 2015: Paving the way for Digital Consumers. Part 1: Background and Scope' (2015) 22(9) *Commercial Law Practitioner* 222; Caterina Gardiner, 'Scheme of Consumer Rights Bill 2015: Paving the way for Digital Consumers. Part 2: Rights and Remedies' (2015) 22(10) Commercial Law Practitioner 243.

1566. Article 24(1). *See* generally Paula Giliker 'Regulating Contracts for the Supply of Digital Content: The EU and UK Response' in Synodinou T, Jougleux P, Markou C (eds) *EU Internet Law* (2017) Switzerland: Springer International Publishing AG, Switzerland, pp. 101–124.

II. Formation of a Contract of Sale: Certainty of Price and Formalities

692. A contract for the sale of goods is generally subject to the normal rules of contract, including the rules on formation of contract; however some specialized rules apply.

693. Usually, if the consideration in a contract is not fixed or ascertainable, the contract may be void for uncertainty. However, in contracts for the sale of goods, if the price of the goods is not fixed or determinable by the contract, or determined by the course of dealing between the parties, section 8(2) states that the buyer must pay 'a reasonable price'. What is a reasonable price is a question of fact dependent upon the circumstances of each particular case.[1567]

694. No special formalities are required to make a valid contract for the sale of goods,[1568] and the contract may be oral. However, section 4 of the 1893 Act provides that a contract for the sale of goods of the value of £10 (€12.70) or more is not enforceable unless:

(i) the buyer accepts, and actually receives, part of the goods sold; or
(ii) the buyer gives something in earnest to bind the contract; or
(iii) the buyer has made part payment; or
(iv) there is a note or memorandum in writing of the contract, signed by the party 'to be charged'.

695. In assessing whether there is a note or memorandum in writing of the contract, the courts are more lenient with regard to goods than they are with respect to the sale of land. In *Tradax (Ireland) v Irish Grain Board*[1569] the court found that there was a memorandum in writing for the purposes of the Act, even though the price was not included. Even if there had not been a memorandum, it was held that partial receipt of the goods (acceptance of 1,871 tonnes of grain out of a total of 25,000 tonnes) would also be sufficient to evidence the contract. However, delivery to a third party such as a carrier will not suffice, as there is no actual receipt of the goods.[1570] Similarly, part payment or full payment will make the contract enforceable, but payment must be accepted and not merely tendered.[1571] The reference to giving 'something in earnest' to bind the contract is unclear, and it has been suggested that giving credit card details over the phone might suffice here.

696. This section is outdated, as inflation clearly means that contracts which were never intended to be subject to an evidentiary requirement now fall within its scope. This has been resolved to a certain extent by judicial flexibility which means

1567. Section 8.
1568. *See* however the special rules on auctions in s. 58.
1569. [1984] IR 1.
1570. *Hopton v McCarthy* (1882) 10 LR (Ir) 266.
1571. *Kirwan v Price* [1958] Ir Jur 56.

that it is usually not difficult to satisfy, but nonetheless the abolition of this requirement has been recommended by the Sales Law Review Group.[1572]

III. The Obligations of the Seller

697. A major feature of the Sale of Goods Act 1893–1980 is that the Act implies certain terms (conditions or warranties) into every contract for sale of goods. Sections 12–14, in particular, imply a series of obligations on the seller of goods as follows:

Section 12: The seller should have the right to sell the goods.[1573]
Section 13: Where the goods are sold by description, they should correspond with that description.
Section 14(2): The goods should be of merchantable quality and fit for their purpose.
Section 14(4): The goods should be fit for the buyer's purpose where he makes that known to the seller.

698. It is not possible to exclude any of these implied terms in a consumer contract,[1574] and even in a commercial contract it is not possible to exclude section 12,[1575] and it is only possible to exclude sections 13 and 14 if it is 'fair and reasonable' to do so.[1576] These implied terms are said to be 'conditions', meaning that breach gives rise to a right to reject the goods and damages. However this right to reject the goods may be lost in certain circumstances (*see below*), and additional rights of repair and replacement apply to consumers.

A. *Section 12: The Seller Must Have the Right to Sell the Goods*

699. Although section 12 is sometimes referred to containing a right to 'good title', in fact section 12(1)(a) refers to the seller having 'the right to sell' the goods. Thus, although it clearly gives a cause of action to a buyer who has been sold stolen goods,[1577] with or without the knowledge of the seller,[1578] it also covers situations where the seller is the true owner of the goods, but nonetheless does not have the 'right' to sell them. This might occur where the sale infringes intellectual property

1572. Sales Law Review Group para. 13. *See also* M Ní Shúilleabháin, 'Formalities of Contracting: A Cost-Benefit Analysis of Requirements that Contracts be Evidenced in Writing', (2005) Dublin University Law Journal 113.
1573. Section 12 also states that the goods should be free from encumbrances and the buyer should enjoy quiet possession of them. These are warranties, giving rise to an action in damages but not a right to reject the goods.
1574. Section 55(4).
1575. Section 55(3).
1576. Section 55(4).
1577. As in *Mallett and Sons (Antiques) Ltd v Rogers* [2005] IEHC 131 – breach of s. 12 where an antique bookcase was in fact stolen.
1578. *Rowland v Divall* [1923] 2 KB 500.

rights,[1579] or where, for example, the goods sold have been brought across the border into the jurisdiction without the appropriate customs duty being paid.[1580]

700. The implied term in section 12(1)(a) is a condition so that breach allows a buyer to reject the goods and terminate the contract, and sue for damages for any loss caused. As discussed below, usually this right to reject the goods can be lost where the goods have been 'accepted'; however these rules do not apply when a breach of section 12(1)(a) has occurred. There is said to have been a total failure of performance in this situation, meaning that the buyer is entitled to a full refund of the price paid, even if they have had the benefit of the use of the goods for a period of time.[1581]

B. Section 13: The Goods Must Match the Description

701. Section 13 of the Sale of Goods Act 1893–1980 provides that where goods are sold by description they will correspond with the description. For example, in *Fogarty v Dickson*[1582] there was a breach of section 13 when winter wheat was supplied under a contract for 'spring wheat'. Unlike section 14 (below), this section applies to all sales of goods regardless of whether or not it is in the course of business, so would apply to example to private sales.[1583]

702. Section 13 was initially intended to protect buyers of future or unascertained goods, who do not get a chance to inspect the goods and would thus rely heavily on the description given of the goods. It was then held that it would apply to all types of unseen goods,[1584] and its scope was later extended further to include goods which the buyer could actually see before them.[1585] Section 13, as amended, now states:

> 13 (2) A sale of goods shall not be prevented from being a sale by description by reason only that being exposed for sale, they are selected by the buyer.
> 13 (3) A reference to goods on a label or other descriptive matter accompanying goods exposed for sale may constitute or form part of a description.

703. Section 13 is, in some ways, a strange provision. It only applies to a 'sale by description', which refers to a term of the contract describing the goods. Not all 'descriptions' given in relation to the goods are said to be terms – they might be

1579. *Niblett v Confectioners Materials Co. Ltd.* [1921] 3 KB 387.
1580. *Stock v Urey* [1955] NI 71.
1581. *Rowland v Divall* [1923] 2 KB 500, approved in Ireland in *United Dominion Trust (Ireland) Ltd. v Shannon Caravans Ltd.* [1976] IR 225.
1582. (1913) ILTR 281.
1583. *See* for example *Beale v Taylor* [1967] 3 All ER 253.
1584. *Varley v Whipp* [1900] 1 QB 513 (s. 13 applies to 'specific goods').
1585. *Grant v Australian Knitting Mills Ltd* [1936] AC 85; *Beale v Taylor* [1967] 3 All ER 253.

representations,[1586] or puffery, or not be incorporated into the contract.[1587] Moreover, not all terms of the contract form part of the description – they may relate, for example, to the quality of the goods rather than its description,[1588] or may be used to simply identify the goods in question.[1589] It could be asked, then, what section 13 *adds* to the position at common law, and whether it makes any sense to have an 'implied' term that only applies if there is already an express term? The answer relates to the remedies available for breach of the term. Section 13 makes any descriptive term of the contract a condition, i.e., it gives the buyer the right to reject the goods for *any* breach of the term. This provides certainty and a very strong remedy for the buyer. Once the description is a term of the contract, there must be strict compliance with the description or the buyer will be able to reject the goods.[1590] This is stronger than the position would be at common law (unless the parties specifically stated that the term was a condition). However, this remedy in itself has posed problems for the courts. Sometimes buyers would claim a breach of section 13 where the difference in description was very slight, in an attempt to escape their bargain through a technicality.[1591] This resulted in the English courts attempting to *restrict* the application of section 13 or opining that basic contract law principles and freedom of contract should take priority over provisions such as section 13.[1592] In the UK, statutory reform means that a non-consumer buyer may no longer reject goods on the basis of breach of implied term where the breach is so slight that rejection would be unreasonable.[1593] No such reform has occurred in Ireland.

C. Section 14(2): Goods Should Be of Merchantable Quality

704. Section 14(2) states that where the seller sells goods in the course of a business[1594] there is an implied condition that the goods supplied[1595] under the contract are of merchantable quality. Section 14(3) states goods are of merchantable quality if they are as fit for the purpose or purposes for which goods of that kind are commonly bought and as durable as it is reasonable to expect having regard to any

1586. *Oscar Chess Ltd v Williams* [1957] 1 WLR 370.
1587. Whether or not there was reliance on the description may be a factor here: *Harlingdon and Leinster Enterprises v Christopher Hull Fine Art Ltd.* [1990] 1 All ER 737.
1588. *Ashington Piggeries Ltd. v Christopher Hill Ltd.* [1972] AC 441. Contrast *Pinnock Bros v Lewis and Peat Ltd* [1923] 1 KB 690.
1589. *Reardon Smith Line Ltd. v Yngvar Hansen Tangen* [1976] 3 All ER 570.
1590. *See Arcos Ltd. v EA Ronaasen & Son* [1933] AC 470; *Re Moore & Co Ltd and Launder & Co's Arbitration* [1921] 2 KB 519.
1591. *Arcos Ltd. v EA Ronaasen & Son* [1933] AC 470.
1592. *See Ashington Piggeries Ltd. v Christopher Hill Ltd.* [1972] AC 441.
1593. Section 4 of the Sale and Supply of Goods Act 1994, which introduced s. 15A into the Sale of Goods Act1979.
1594. *Stevenson v Rogers* [1999] QB 1028.
1595. The s. 14 condition applies not only to the goods sold under the contract, but also the goods 'supplied', which includes the packaging in which they were delivered. A defect in the packaging might therefore render the goods unmerchantable, even if the packaging remains the property of the seller and is returnable: *Geddling v Marsh* [1920] 1 KB 668.

description applied to them, the price (if relevant) and all the other relevant circumstances. In *O'Regan & Sons Ltd. v. Micro-Bio (Ireland) Ltd & Intervet Laboratories Ltd.*[1596] for example, a faulty batch of vaccine bought for chickens resulted in a high proportion of the chickens dying. It was held that the purpose of the vaccine was to vaccinate chickens, and it was clearly not fit for this purpose.

705. One difficulty with this provision is whether it is sufficient that the goods are fit for *any* of their common purposes. Although older English cases suggest that goods will be of merchantable quality if fit for any one of their common purposes,[1597] the recent Irish Supreme Court decision in *James Elliot Construction Ltd v Irish Asphalt Ltd*[1598] has stated that the goods must be fit for *all* their common purposes. In this case, rock from a quarry was contaminated with pyrite, and thus unsuitable for laying down foundations under buildings. It was, however, still suitable for other purposes such as use in the hardcore of carparks. The Supreme Court held that goods will not be considered of merchantable quality if they are merely fit for one of their common purposes.

706. An objective standard still applies, however. The goods do not have to be suitable for *every* purpose, including the buyer's particular or individual purpose for the goods. For example, the common purpose of ballet shoes is to use them for dancing. A buyer who buys them and uses them for mountain climbing would not be able to claim that they are not fit for their 'common' purpose. Any claim that the goods are not suitable for the buyer's particular purpose should be taken under section 14(4) (*see below*). Section 14(2) is primarily concerned with the *quality* of the goods; section 14(4) is concerned with whether they are suitable for the buyer's *particular* purpose.

707. In addition, the goods must be as 'durable as is reasonable to expect'. This can be difficult to define with any precision, but again it is an objective standard of quality. The description applied to the goods will affect the standard that can reasonably be expected of them. For example, a higher standard will be expected from goods described as 'brand new' or 'deluxe' than those described as 'second hand'.

708. One issue that may arise is whether it is possible to bring an action for 'non-functional' defects, such as defects relating to appearance and finish, even if the goods are still technically fit for their common purpose. The English case of *Rogers v Parish (Scarborough) Ltd*[1599] established that goods (in this case a car) could be technically functional, but still not of merchantable quality owing to non-functional defects. Mustill LJ stated that the purpose for which cars are bought would include 'not merely the driver's purpose of driving the car from one place to another but of doing so with the appropriate degree of comfort, ease of handling and

---

1596. Unreported High Court, 26 February 1980.

1597. *Henry Kendall & sons v William Lillico & Sons* [1969] 2 AC 31. *See also Aswan Engineering Establishment Co. v Lupdine Ltd.* [1987] 1 All ER 135.

1598. [2014] IESC 74.

1599. [1987] QB 933.

reliability and, pride in the vehicle's outward and interior appearance'. This was applied in the Irish case of *Marah v Kellehers Ltd*[1600] in which a defect in the paintwork of a car meant that it was not of merchantable quality. However, again the standard is objective – what is it reasonable to expect? Thus, if you buy a second hand car, you might not be entitled to as high a standard as you would be if you were to buy a new car, although it must as a minimum requirement be safe.[1601]

709. It is not possible to exclude section 14(2) in a consumer contract, although it is possible to do so in a commercial contract provided the exclusion is fair and reasonable. However, it should be noted that section 14(2) is said not to apply where the defect is bought to the buyer's attention, or, where the product has been examined, to defects which ought to have been apparent by that examination.[1602]

710. Thus, if you buy an item in a shop and it is pointed out to you that it is damaged (e.g., 'zip broken') then you cannot later claim that it is not of merchantable quality because of this. However, items which are reduced in a price in a sale are still covered by section 14.

711. Section 14(2) is a condition, breach of which gives a right to reject the goods and claim a refund, or possibly damages. It is not possible to exclude section 14 in a consumer contract, but it can be excluded in a commercial contract where it is fair and reasonable to do so.

D. Section 14(4): Goods Must Be Fit for Any Particular Stated Purpose

712. It is perhaps unfortunate that section 14(4) is included as a sub-section of section 14, as it deals not with a general quality standard, but rather with whether the question of whether the goods are fit for any particular stated purpose. Section 14(4) states:

> Where the seller sells goods in the course of a business and the buyer, expressly or by implication, makes known to the seller any particular purpose for which the goods are being bought, there is an implied condition that the goods supplied under the contract are reasonably fit for that purpose, whether or not that is a purpose for which such goods are commonly supplied, except where the circumstances show that the buyer does not rely, or that it is unreasonable for him to rely, on the seller's skill or judgement.

713. The first question to ask is whether the buyer made known to the seller 'any particular purpose' for which the goods were being bought? In some early cases, the purpose for which the goods are to be used was implied from the circumstances,

---

1600. Unreported, High Court, Quirke J, 3 December 1998.
1601. Section 13 of the Sale of Goods and Supply of Services Act 1980 also deals with the issue of car safety (*see below*).
1602. *Thornett & Fehr v Beer and Son* [1919] 1 KB 486; *Wren v Holt* [1903] 1 KB 610.

e.g., the 'particular purpose' of milk was said to drink it.[1603] It could be argued that in these cases the 'particular purpose' for which the goods are used is really just their common purpose, e.g., clearly the common purpose of milk is to drink it. However, at this time (i.e., in the original version of the 1893 Act) there were restrictions on the operation of section 14(2) which reduced the protection available under it; hence some plaintiffs relied on a broad description of 'particular purpose' to try to bring their case under section 14(4) instead. Today these cases would probably be dealt with under section 14(2); there would be no need to rely on section 14(4). These older cases are not particularly helpful when interpreting the existing provisions.

714. The main purpose of section 14(4) is to impose liability on a seller *who has assumed a certain responsibility to the buyer.* Where the buyer has a particular or special need, the seller is not liable unless they are aware of it. Thus, in *Griffiths v Peter Conway*[1604] the seller was not liable for selling a coat where the buyer had particularly sensitive skin and suffered a reaction. The coat was fit for its common purpose; it just was not fit for this buyer's particular purpose (i.e., a coat for sensitive skin), of which the seller was unaware. Cases such as *Griffith v Conway* can be explained on the basis that the seller could not possibly have exercised his skill and judgment when he did not know the special requirements of the buyer.

715. Section 14(4) does not apply if 'the circumstances show that the buyer did not rely, or that it is unreasonable for him to rely, on the skill or judgment of the seller'. In general, reliance will most likely be present where there is a straightforward purchase of an item and the seller has the skill and knowledge, e.g., in a situation such as *Grant* where goods are bought by a consumer from a retailer. It could be rebutted in a situation where the buyer exercises skill and judgment, e.g., where the buyer is an expert in a particular area or where the buyer produces specifications for the seller to work with, or where it is unreasonable for the buyer to rely on the skill and judgment of the seller.[1605]

716. Section 14(4) is a condition, breach of which gives a right to reject the goods and claim a refund, or possibly damages. It is not possible to exclude section 14 in a consumer contract but it can be excluded in a commercial contract where it is fair and reasonable to do so.

E. Additional Obligations on the Seller

717. Section 15 provides that where the goods are sold by sample, the goods should correspond with that sample. It is not possible to exclude section 15 in a consumer contract, and it can only be excluded in a commercial contract where it is fair and reasonable to do so.

1603. *See Frost v Aylesbury Dairy Co Ltd* [1905] 1 KB 608.
1604. [1939] 1 All ER 685.
1605. *See*, for example, the English case *Jewson Ltd v Boyhan* [2003] EWCA Civ 1030.

718. Section 13 of the 1980 Act provides that in every sale of a motor vehicles there is an implied condition that at the time of delivery of the vehicle under the contract it is free from any defect which would render it a danger to the public, including persons travelling in the vehicle. It applies to private sales, i.e., even if seller is a private individual, although it does not apply where the buyer is a motor dealer. Section 13(7) also provides an important exception to the privity rule, in that it gives a cause of action to any person 'using a motor vehicle with the consent of the buyer of the vehicle who suffers loss as the result of a breach' of section 13.

719. This is an important provision to ensure that only safe cars and vehicles are sold. In *Glorney v O'Brien*[1606] for example, there was a breach of section 13 when a car went of control on a public road and crashed because of defective suspension. Lynch J stated:

> No matter how old or cheap a motor vehicle may be, it must not be sold to an ordinary member of the public not in the motor trade in a condition which would render it a danger to the public, including the occupants of the vehicle, if driven on the road.

720. Section 12 of the 1980 Act provides for an implied warranty that where a seller gives a promise of spare parts or after-sales service that these will be available for the period promised or for a reasonable period. However, it is important to note that this only applies if the seller has promised to provide spare parts or after-sales services; it is not a general obligation to provide these.

721. The seller also has certain obligations regarding the time and quantity of delivery, and these are dealt with below.

IV. Remedies Available to the Buyer

722. The terms implied by sections 12, 13, 14 and 15 are said to be conditions, breach of which means that the buyer can reject the goods and claim a refund, and claim damages in an appropriate case. However this right is not as clear as it might seem. Under section 11(3) a buyer may lose the right to reject where he is deemed to have 'accepted' the goods. Section 35 then provides that a buyer will be deemed to have accepted the goods where:

(i) he intimates acceptance;
(ii) he does an act inconsistent with ownership of seller; or
(iii) he keeps the goods without good and sufficient reason, without rejecting them.

1606. Unreported, High Court, Lynch J, 14 November 1988.

723. Some cases have taken a harsh approach to this, meaning the consumer has lost their right to reject within a short timeframe.[1607] Goods might be 'accepted' before any latent defect has been discovered, meaning that the right to reject is lost and the buyer is limited to a remedy in damages. The lack of certainty concerning this provision has been criticised, and it has been suggested that a thirty-day return period might be more appropriate.

724. The Sale of Goods Act also outlines some remedies which are specifically available for consumers.[1608] Section 53 of the 1980 Act provides that the buyer 'promptly upon discovering the breach' can request to the seller that they either repair or replace the goods. If the seller refuses to do so, or fails to do so with a reasonable time, then the buyer is entitled either to have the goods repaired elsewhere and to claim the cost incurred, or to simply reject the goods at this stage and claim a full refund. This is sometimes referred to as the buyer's 'long-term' right to reject the goods, as it is not lost in the same way as the initial 'short-term' right to reject might be.

725. In addition, the buyer has a right to damages. Damages can be awarded for a breach of warranty under section 53. This can arise where there has been a breach of condition (e.g., the goods are not of merchantable quality) but the buyer has either opted not to reject the goods or has lost the right to reject the goods, and thus the condition is treated as a warranty. Section 53 reflects general contract law principles, and provides that the 'measure of damages for breach of warranty is the estimated loss directly and naturally resulting, in the ordinary course of events, from the breach of warranty'.[1609] This is 'prima facie the difference between the value of the goods at the time of delivery to the buyer and the value they would have had if they had answered to the warranty'.[1610] Damages may also be awarded for non-delivery, and this includes a situation where the buyer has a right to reject the goods. Again, the basic rule reflects general contract law principles: the measure of damages is 'the estimated loss directly and naturally resulting, in the ordinary course of events, from the seller's breach of contract'. However, a specific rule, known as the 'market price rule' applies to cases of non-delivery of goods. Section 51(3) states:

1607. *See Bernstein v Pamson Motors Ltd* [1987] 2 All ER 220. Contrast the UK decision in [2003] EWCA Civ 320.

1608. Section 3 defines consumers as following:

> 3.—(1) In the Act of 1893 and this Act, a party to a contract is said to deal as consumer in relation to another party if—(*a*) he neither makes the contract in the course of a business nor holds himself out as doing so, and (*b*) the other party does make the contract in the course of a business, and (*c*) the goods or services supplied under or in pursuance of the contract are of a type ordinarily supplied for private use or consumption.

1609. Section 53(2).

1610. Section 53(3).

> Where there is an available market for the goods in question the measure of damages is prima facie to be ascertained by the difference between the contract price and the market or current price of the goods at the time or times when they ought to have been delivered, or, if no time was fixed, then at the time of the refusal to deliver.

726. The buyer will thus receive the difference between the contract price and the market price on the date the goods ought to have been delivered, i.e., the date of the breach.[1611] The buyer is expected to have mitigated their losses by going into the market immediately and making a replacement purchase.[1612] Whether or not they actually did so is irrelevant for the purpose of assessing damages. This also means that if it is a falling market, the buyer would not receive damages (although in this situation they would have essentially escaped a bad bargain so it is unlikely they would pursue damages). The court will not take into account the fact that the buyer might have agreed to sell the goods on at a lower/higher price than the market price; what matters is the cost of replacement goods.[1613]

V. Seller's Duty to Deliver the Goods

727. Section 27 of the Sale of Goods Act states that it 'is the duty of the seller to deliver the goods, and of the buyer to accept and pay for them, in accordance with the terms of the contract of sale'. Delivery is the voluntary transfer of possession (as opposed to transfer of ownership), and it can be a physical transfer of the goods themselves, handing over the means of control of the goods,[1614] or a document of title, or delivery to an agent of the buyer.[1615] The duty to 'deliver' the goods does not mean a duty to bring the goods to the buyer (in the sense that 'delivery' is often understood) – in fact, unless a contrary intention is shown, the place of delivery is the *seller's* place of business.[1616]

728. Where under the contract of sale the seller is bound to send the goods to the buyer, but no time for sending them is fixed, the seller is bound to send them within a reasonable time.[1617] If the goods are delivered late (i.e., after a fixed time if time for delivery is fixed, or after a reasonable time if it is not) the seller is in

---

1611. However, if the seller rescinds before the due date for delivery, the market price is still ascertained as of date of delivery, and not the earlier date of rejection. Otherwise the seller would have control over the date at which damages were to be ascertained. *See Melachrino v Nickoll & Knight* [1920] 1 KB 693; *Tai Hing Cotton Mill ltd v Kamsing Knitting Factory* [1979] AC 91.

1612. *Cullen v Horgan* [1925] 2 IR 1.

1613. *Williams v Agius* [1914] AC 510.

1614. *Wrightson v McArthur* [1921] 2 KB 807. Contrast *Dublin City Distillery v Doherty* [1914] AC 823.

1615. Section 32(1). *See Michel Freres v Kilkenny Woollen Mills (1929) Ltd.* [1969] IR 157.

1616. Section 29(1). If the seller does not have a place of business, then it is their residence. In the case of 'specific goods' the location of the goods is the place of delivery.

1617. Section 29(2).

breach of contract and the buyer can sue for damages.[1618] Whether or not the buyer can also reject the goods for late delivery depends on the contract[1619] but in ordinary commercial contracts for the sale of goods, the presumption is usually that the time for delivery is 'of the essence', meaning it is treated as a condition, breach of which gives rise to the right to reject the goods.[1620] This rule does not apply to consumer contracts, however. In addition, where time is of the essence, the buyer may lose their right to terminate the contract for late delivery by acting in such a manner as to lead the seller to believe they intend to continue to perform the contract. In other words, a buyer who presses the seller for delivery for several months cannot suddenly terminate the contract, but must give reasonable notice to the seller that this is their 'last chance' to deliver.[1621]

729. The seller must also deliver the right quantity of goods. Section 30 states:

(1) Where the seller delivers to the buyer a quantity of goods less than he contracted to sell, the buyer may reject them, but if the buyer accepts the goods so delivered he must pay for them at the contract rate.[1622]
(2) Where the seller delivers to the buyer a quantity of goods larger than he contracted to sell, the buyer may accept the goods included in the contract and reject the rest, or he may reject the whole. If the buyer accepts the whole of the goods so delivered he must pay for them at the contract rate.
(3) Where the seller delivers to the buyer the goods he contracted to sell mixed with goods of a different description not included in the contract, the buyer may accept the goods which are in accordance with the contract and reject the rest, or he may reject the whole.

730. The buyer also retains the right to sue for damages for any shortfall in delivery, which is treated as a non-delivery.

731. The law is very strict in its insistence on the correct quantity; however, a *de minimis* principle applies and can be invoked to avoid termination of the contract for what would otherwise be a technical breach, particularly where the seller has delivered a minor excess of goods and is not seeking payment for that excess.[1623] This principle has not been placed on a statutory footing, however, unlike in the UK.[1624]

732. Finally it should be noted that in cases of non-delivery, it is very difficult to obtain an order of specific performance of the contract. This is only available, at

1618. Damages for late delivery are governed by general contract principles: *see Victoria Laundry (Windsor) Ltd. v Newman Industries Ltd.* [1949] 2 KB 528.
1619. Section 10.
1620. *Hartley v Hymans* [1920] KB 475.
1621. *Ibid.*
1622. In addition, the buyer does not have to accept delivery in instalments unless agreed in the contract: s. 31 and *Behrend & Co. Ltd. v Produce Brokers Ltd.* [1920] 3 KB 530.
1623. *Shipton Anderson v Weil Brothers* [1912] 1 KB 574; *Harland v Burstall* (1901) 6 Com. Cas. 113.
1624. Sale and Supply of Goods Act 1994 added in s. 30(2A) and (2B).

the court's discretion, for 'specific' goods,[1625] and in reality only available for unique goods where damages would be an inappropriate remedy.

VI. Buyer's Obligations and Seller's Remedies

733. The buyer's obligations under the contract of sale are to take delivery of the goods and pay for the goods.[1626] Section 49 allows the seller to bring an action for the price only where the property in the goods has passed to the buyer and the buyer has wrongfully neglected or refused to pay for the goods according to the terms of the contract, or the price is payable 'on a day certain irrespective of delivery' and the buyer has wrongfully neglected or refused to pay the price. A seller may be entitled to damages under section 50 if the buyer refuses to accept and pay for the goods. Where the property has not passed, this is the only claim available to the buyer. Even if the property has passed, and the buyer can claim under section 49, they may choose to claim damages instead. Where there is an available market for the goods, the measure of damages is prima facie the difference between the contract price and the market price of the goods on the date when they should have been accepted.[1627]

734. In addition to these personal remedies (an action for the price or for damages), an unpaid seller is given certain 'real' rights over the goods. Real remedies allow the seller to look to the goods as a form of security for the payment of price. This is particularly important where a personal claim against the buyer for money is of little use, e.g., because the buyer is insolvent. However, the remedies provided for in the Act (lien/stoppage in transit/right of resale[1628]) are of limited value in modern commercial sales because the conditions of their operation[1629] are not normally met. Sellers have developed other mechanisms to protect themselves, such as retention of title clauses.

VII. Retention of Title

735. A seller may attempt to retain property in the goods until he is paid, by means of a retention of title clause. These clauses are sometimes called 'Romalpa' clauses, after the leading case of *Romalpa.*[1630] The major advantage of a retention of title clause is that if the buyer becomes insolvent before paying the seller, the seller can claim back the goods as their own, and prevent the goods from becoming part of the assets of the insolvent buyer and used to satisfy the claims of the other

1625. Section 52. *See Behnke v Bede Shipping* [1927] 1 KB 649; *Re Wait* [1927] 1 Ch 606.
1626. Sections 27 and 37.
1627. Section 50(3).
1628. Section 39.
1629. As set out in ss 41–48.
1630. *Aluminium Industrie Vaassen BV v Romalpa Aluminium Ltd.* [1976] 1 WLR 676.

creditors. Reservation of title is not expressly dealt with in the Sale of Goods Act, but the basic principle of retention of property in the goods is to be found in section 17(1) of the Act, which states:

> Where there is a contract for the sale of specific or ascertained goods the property in them is transferred to the buyer at such time as the parties to the contract intend it to be transferred.[1631]

736. However, liquidators and other creditors will often object to retention of title clauses, as they take away from the resources of the insolvent company and reduce the amount that is left for other creditors. Liquidators argue that the clause is essentially a charge, which, as is it unregistered, is void against a liquidator or creditor. This argument has succeeded in some instances and not in others.

737. A simple retention of title clause, which reserves title to the goods in their original form, will tend to be successful, but it is only useful in so far as the goods remain in their original form.[1632] A claim to goods which undergo any form of alteration or manufacturing process by the buyer will generally fail, as the courts will not imply an intention that the parties had intended the buyer to retain ownership in the goods, but where the clause specifically covers manufactured goods the matter is less clear.[1633] In the Irish case of *Kruppstahl AG v Quitmann products Ltd*[1634] steel was supplied for a manufacturing process, subject to a retention of title clause which claimed 'joint title to the new goods in accordance with the ratio of the invoice value of the reserved goods to the invoice value of the other goods used'. The buyer went into liquidation and the seller claimed ownership of some unworked steel and some original steel. It was held that the original steel remained the property of the seller but the seller's interest in the steel used in the manufacturing process amount to a charge, which was unenforceable because it had not been registered.

738. The seller may include a term in the contract that the goods supplied remain their property until *all* sums due (not just those due under the particular sales contract) have been paid for. However, once all sums owing are paid, property in any goods supplied up to that point will pass to the buyer.[1635]

739. If the buyer resells the goods before paying for them, the seller's rights over the goods will normally be extinguished because the sub-buyer will take a good title to the goods.[1636] In order to overcome this problem, the seller may try to claim an

1631. *See also* s. 19.
1632. *See*, for example, *Somers v J. Allen Ltd* [1985] IR 340.
1633. *Borden (UK) Ltd. v Scottish Timber Products Ltd.* [1981] Ch 25; *Re Peachdart Ltd.* [1984] Ch 131. Contrast *Hendy Lennox (Industrial Engines) Ltd. v Grahame Puttick Ltd.* [1984] 1 WLR 485 (title retained where goods underwent reversible physical changes).
1634. [1982] ILRM 551.
1635. *Armour v Thyssen* [1990] 3 All ER 481. For criticism, *see* Bradgate 'Retention of Title in the House of Lords: Unanswered Questions' (1991) 54 Modern Law Review 726.
1636. Normally by virtue of s. 25(2) of the 1893 Act.

interest in ('trace'[1637]) the proceeds of the resale by the inclusion of a stipulation that the buyer will hold the proceeds of any sub-sale in trust for the original seller. Essentially the seller is attempting to claim a proprietary interest in the money made by the sale rather than bringing a personal action against the buyer. This claim was successful in the *Romalpa* case itself,[1638] where the seller successfully claimed the existence of a fiduciary relationship, but in subsequent UK decisions the courts have been very reluctant to recognise a fiduciary relationship between a buyer and seller when in truth the relationship is one of debtor and creditor.[1639] Initially Irish courts seemed willing to follow the *Romalpa* case. For example in *Re Sugar Distributors Ltd.*,[1640] Carroll J held that the proceeds of a sub-sale were to be held in trust even if there is no express stipulation in the reservation of title clause to that effect or to the segregation of the proceeds of the sub-sale into separate funds.[1641] However, not all claims succeeded – in *Re Interview Ltd.* [1642] Kenny J held that the effect of the stipulation on resale in the clause in that case was that the proceeds of sub-sales were only subject to a charge. A claim also failed in *Carroll Group Distributors v G & JF Burke*.[1643]

740. More recently in *Unitherm Heating Systems Ltd v Kieran Wallace as official Liquidator of BTH Group Ltd*[1644] the Court of Appeal emphasised that retention of title clauses in such contracts do not establish a relationship of principal/agent or any other fiduciary relationship from which a trust might be inferred. Irvine J stated:

> However, there is now a significant body of case law in support of the proposition that, if the buyer ... is permitted to resell the goods, it is usual for it to do so on its own account unless there is very clear evidence to the contrary. ... Accordingly, regardless of the use of words such as 'trustee' or 'fiduciary' in the conditions of sale, no fiduciary duty will be deemed to exist with the parties being considered to be in a relationship of debtor and creditor.
>
> In general, most recent authorities have tended to treat 'proceeds of sale' clauses as giving rise to charges which require registration and the courts have been reluctant to infer the existence of a fiduciary relationship between parties who, as Murphy J. described in *Carroll*, appear to be engaged in arm's length commercial transactions as vendors and purchasers.[1645]

1637. *In re Hallett's Estate* (1880) 13 Ch D 696.
1638. *Aluminium Industrie Vaassen BV v Romalpa Aluminium Ltd.* [1976] 1 WLR 676.
1639. *See*, for example, *Re Andrabell Ltd.* [1984] 3 All ER 407; *Compaq Computers Ltd. v Abercorn Group Ltd.* [1991] BCC 484.
1640. [1982] ILRM 399.
1641. *See also* the successful claims in *Re W. J. Hickey Ltd* [1988] IR 126; *SA Foundries Du Lion v International Factors Ltd* [1985] ILRM 66; *Frigoscandia (Contracting) Ltd. v Continental Irish Meat Ltd.* [1982] ILRM 396.
1642. [1975] IR 382.
1643. [1990] ILRM 285.
1644. [2015] IECA 19.
1645. *Ibid.*, paras 72–73.

741. The clause in this case offered potential security to the seller by way of charge over the proceeds of sale. This charge would be have to be registered to be enforceable. This was applied recently in the case of *Comans Wholesale v Donohue Beverages Ltd*[1646] where it was held that the clause in question created a charge and not a trust.

742. Reform of the law on retention of title clauses was considered by the Law Reform Commission in 1989, including a system of registration for this form of security, but these recommendations have not been implemented.[1647] The Sales Law Review Group declined to recommend any substantial reform of provisions of the Sale of Goods Act concerning retention of title. This was not to say that it considered the current state of the law satisfactory, but rather that it should be done within the broader context of personal property security reform, and not as part of a review of sales law.[1648]

VIII. Passing of Property in Goods

743. The Sale of Goods Act contains several provisions dealing with the passing of property in the goods from seller to buyer. In this context, property means *ownership* of the goods as opposed to mere possession of them. There is no necessary connection between the passing of property and physical possession of the goods, or between the passing of property and payment. The Sale of Goods Act uses the concept of property to deal with a number of issues:

(a) The basic rule as to risk is that risk of damage or destruction of goods passes with property, not with delivery or possession.[1649] For example, in *Clarke v Reilly*[1650] a car was damaged while in the possession of the seller, but as property in the car had passed to the buyer, the risk of the damage was also passed to the buyer. Certain exceptions to this rule apply, including where the parties intend for the risk to pass at a different time,[1651] or where delivery is delayed.[1652] And more recently it has been provided that where the buyer is a consumer, the risk passes on physical delivery of the goods.[1653]

(b) If the property in goods passes to a buyer who has not paid for them, who then becomes insolvent, the goods belong to the buyer's estate leaving the seller to claim as an unsecured creditor in the bankruptcy. If the buyer becomes insolvent and the property has not passed to the buyer, e.g., because of a retention of title clause, the seller can recover the goods back from the buyer by asserting

1646. [2019] IEHC 657.
1647. Law Reform Commission, *Report on Debt Collection (2): Retention of Title* (LRC 28) (1989).
1648. Sales Law Review Group para. 6.47.
1649. Section 20(1). *See Tarling v Baxter* (1827) 6 B&C 360; 108 ER 484.
1650. (1962) 96 ILTR 96.
1651. *Sterns v Vickers Ltd* [1923] 1 KB 78. *See also* ss 32 and 33.
1652. Section 20(2).
1653. European Union (Consumer Information, Cancellation and Other Rights) Regulations 2013, Regulation 20, which amended s. 20 of the 1893 Act.

his proprietary right and gaining priority over the buyer's creditors. If the property has passed to the buyer and the seller becomes insolvent, the goods belong to the buyer and they are entitled against the liquidator or assignee to have the goods delivered up to them. If the seller becomes insolvent and the property has not passed to the buyer, although he has paid for the goods, all he has is a claim for damages for breach of contract against the estate of the insolvent. This claim would rank alongside all other claims in the insolvency.

(c) Under section 49(1) the passing of property to the buyer means that the seller is entitled to sue the buyer for the price of the goods but, if the property in the goods has not passed, the seller can only maintain an action for damages for non-delivery of the goods.

744. Hence it is important to know when property passes from one party to the other and there are several rules governing this. The key factor is generally the intention of the parties – section 17 provides that where there is a contract for the sale of specific or ascertained goods the property in them is transferred to the buyer at such time as the parties to the contract intend it to be transferred. For example in *Anderson v Ryan*[1654] in relation to an agreement to sell a car, the High Court found that it was the intention of the parties that the property would not pass until certain repairs were done and paid for.[1655]

745. Section 18 then sets out prima facie rules or presumptions as to the intentions of the parties in different situations. These rules apply 'unless a different intention appears', i.e., they only apply if the parties' intention is not clear. One such rule is that the property in specific goods[1656] passes when the contract is made – hence in *Clarke v Reilly,*[1657] mentioned above, the property passed to the buyer of a car when the contract was made.

746. Section 16 sets out a mandatory rule that property in unascertained goods cannot pass unless and until the goods are 'ascertained'. Unascertained goods become ascertained by being identified and appropriated to the contract. This usually requires that the goods be physically identified and if selling goods in bulk, they need to be physically separated from the bulk.[1658] When goods become ascertained, sections 17 applies, i.e., property passes when the parties intend for it to pass. Where the terms of the contract do not deal with passing of property, it is governed by section 18 Rule 5, which provides that property will pass once the goods are 'unconditionally appropriated' to the contract. In *Healy v Howlett & Sons*[1659] the

1654. [1967] IR 34.
1655. This would also fall under s. 18 Rule 2 which states 'Where there is a contract for the sale of specific goods and the seller is bound to do something to the goods for the purpose of putting them into a deliverable state, the property does not pass until the thing is done and the buyer has notice thereof.'
1656. Specific goods are goods which are fully identified and agreed upon at the time the contract was made (s. 62).
1657. (1962) 96 ILTR 96.
1658. *Re Wait* [1927] 1 Ch 606.
1659. [1917] 1 KB 337.

defendant, based in London, ordered 20 boxes of mackerel from the plaintiff who was Co. Kerry. The plaintiff dispatched 190 boxes to go to Holyhead and instructed the railway officials at Holyhead to earmark 20 boxes for the defendant and the rest for two other buyers. The train was delayed before the defendant's boxes were earmarked and by the time this was done, they had deteriorated and were not merchantable. The defendant fishmonger refused to pay. It was held that no property in the goods had passed to the defendant buyer, as the goods had not been ascertained or unconditionally appropriated to the contract, and hence the deterioration of the goods was the seller's loss and not the buyer's:

> Suppose that in the present case twenty boxes only had become bad, it is quite impossible on the evidence to say which of the various purchasers would have been bound to take the twenty bad boxes when they were at Holyhead. If it was impossible to determine which of the purchasers was bound to take the twenty bad boxes, it follows that no particular twenty boxes were the property of any particular purchaser at that time.

747. The rules on passing of property have been criticised, particularly as can be very harsh on a buyer who has pre-paid for goods in bulk, where the seller becomes insolvent before the goods have been separated from the bulk.[1660] These rules have undergone reform in other jurisdictions.[1661] Similar reform was recommended by the Sales Law Review Group,[1662] but this has not yet been implemented.

IX. Transfer of Title: *Nemo dat quod non habet*

748. The section above is concerned with the passing of property from the seller to the buyer. However, even if property has passed from the seller to the buyer, it is possible that a third party may also attempt to claim ownership of the goods. As Atiyah states, 'the mere fact that the property in the goods has passed to the buyer does not confer on him a title good against the whole world'.[1663] The principle *nemo dat quod non habet* essentially translates as 'no one can give a better title to goods than he has himself', and this principle is contained in Section 21 of the *Sale of Goods Act* 1893:

> Subject to the provisions of this Act, where goods are sold by a person who is not the owner thereof, and who does not sell them under the authority or with the consent of the owner, the buyer acquires no better title to the goods than the seller had, unless the owner of the goods is by his conduct precluded from denying the seller's authority to sell.

1660. As in *Re Wait* [1927] 1 Ch 606.
1661. *See*, for example, the Sale of Goods (Amendment) Act 1995 in the UK.
1662. Sales Law Review Group para. 31.
1663. Atiyah, Adams & McQueen *Sale of Goods* (Pearson Longman, 12th ed., 2010) p. 305.

749. A number of exceptions to this rule are set out in section 21 itself (where the owner is 'precluded by his conduct from denying the seller's authority to sell'), and in sections 22–26. A detailed discussion of these provisions, and the need to reform these provisions, is available in the Report of the Sales Law Review Group.[1664]

§3. The Consumer Sales Directive: Directive 1999/44/EC on Certain Aspects of the Sale of Consumer Goods and Associated Guarantees

750. The Consumer Sales Directive 1999 introduced a minimum standard of protection in consumer sales. The Directive was implemented in Ireland by the European Communities (Certain Aspects of the Sale of Consumer Goods and Associated Guarantees) Regulations 2003.[1665] Regulation 3 provides that the Regulations are *in addition to* and not in substitution for any other enactment relating to the sale of goods or the terms of contracts concluded with consumers, including the Sale of Goods Act 1893–1980.

751. Under this Directive, sellers of consumer goods within the EU are obliged to guarantee the 'conformity of the goods with the contract' for a (minimum) period of two years after the delivery of the goods. Although the language used is different to that in the Sale of Goods Acts (e.g., there is no mention of 'merchantable quality', or 'sale by description' or implied terms) there is in fact a significant overlap between the two. Regulation 5(2) provides that goods are in conformity with the contract if they meet four requirements specified:

(a) comply with the description given by the seller and possess the qualities of the goods which the seller has held out to the consumer as a sample or model,
(b) are fit for any particular purpose for which the consumer requires them and which he or she made known to the seller at the time of conclusion of the contract and which the seller has accepted,
(c) are fit for the purposes for which goods of the same type are normally used,
(d) show the quality and performance which are normal in goods of the same type and which the consumer can reasonably expect, given the nature of the goods and taking into account any public statements on the specific characteristics of the goods made about them by the seller, the producer, or his representative, particularly in labelling or advertising
  (d) Regulation 5(3) provides a safeguard for the seller in that there will not be deemed to be a lack of conformity for the purposes of the Regulations if either —

1664. Sales Law Review Group paras 7.12–7.40. *See also* Kelly 'Losing Nemo: Reform of the Nemo Dat Rule in Ireland' in *Law and Practice: Essays on Reform* (Editors Shannon G and O'Dell E), Clarus Press (2008).
1665. SI No 11/2003.

(a) at the time the contract was concluded, the consumer was aware or ought reasonably to have been aware of the lack of conformity or

(b) the lack of conformity has its origin in materials supplied by the consumer.

752. At first sight, these provisions seem very similar to the quality provisions in the Sale of Goods Acts. However, there are some differences. For example, there is no requirement in the Regulations that there be a 'sale by description'. Regulation 5(2)(d) is a new type of provision. In assessing the quality which the consumer can reasonably expect, account must be taken of any 'public statements on the specific characteristics of the goods made about them by the seller, the producer, or his representative, particularly in advertising or on labelling'. This Regulation appears to be directed particularly at advertisements. The new provision will allow a consumer to rely on advertising produced by a *manufacturer* of the goods when seeking to render the *seller* liable where those goods are not in conformity with the contract of sale. However, the seller can avoid liability for a manufacturer's statements in certain circumstances.[1666]

753. Regulation 7(1) provides that the seller is liable for lack of conformity which exists at the time the goods are delivered, and the remedies are set out in Regulation 7(2). If the goods are not delivered in conformity with the sales contract, consumers can ask for the goods to be repaired or replaced. If this is not possible, or is disproportionate, the consumer can ask for a price reduction or for the contract to be rescinded. The consumer is not entitled to have the contract rescinded if the lack of conformity is minor.

754. Regulation 8(1) introduces an important new right for consumers. It provides that any lack of conformity which becomes apparent within six months of delivery of the goods shall be presumed to have existed at the time of delivery unless this presumption is incompatible with the nature of the goods or the nature of the lack of conformity.

755. Regulation 10 is an important provision which states that any contractual terms or agreements purporting to waive or restrict the rights resulting from the Regulations shall not be binding on the consumer.

1666. Regulation 6(1).

Chapter 5. Building Contracts, Hire of Work and Skills

756. In general, building contracts must conform to the same requirements as any contract. Building contracts and contracts for the labour and skill would also fall under the 'services' provision of the Sale of Goods and Supply of Services Act 1980, and a construction contract entered into a consumer would additionally be subject to consumer protection legislation such as the Unfair Contract Terms Regulations.[1667] However, in addition, the Construction Contracts Act 2013 has recently introduced a statutory scheme for dispute resolution in construction contracts, and sets out rules relating to prompt payment for contractors.

§1. The Construction Contracts Act 2013

757. The Construction Contracts Act 2013 aims to regulate payment under construction contracts, and it is not possible to exclude the provisions of the Act by contractual provision.[1668]

758. The Act applies to construction contracts entered into after 25 July 2016, which are worth more than €10,000.[1669] The Act applies to a long list of activities including temporary to permanent construction, alteration, repair, maintenance, extension, or demolition of works including buildings, road-works, utilities, scaffolding, landscaping, painting and even the installation of sculptures or murals.[1670] The Act also applies to agreements to provide services ancillary to construction, including architectural, design, surveying, engineering or project management services.[1671] It does not apply to construction contracts relating to residential dwellings of less than 200 square metres, where one of the parties to the contract occupies or intends to occupy the dwelling.[1672]

759. Construction contracts are to provide for the amount of each interim payment, and the final payment, to be made under the contract,[1673] as well as the payment claim date and the date on which the amounts fall due.[1674] If they fail to do so then standard default provisions set out in the Schedule will apply,[1675] and these provide for payment claims every thirty days. This Schedule also applies automatically to subcontractors, unless the contract provides for more advantageous arrangements

1667. For example, in R*e Application by the Director of Consumer Affairs*, Unreported, High Court, 5 December 2001, Kearns J in the High Court declared fifteen sample terms in consumer construction contracts in breach of the 1995 Unfair Contract Terms Regulations.
1668. Section 2(5).
1669. Section 2(1)(a).
1670. Section 1(1)
1671. Section 1(2).
1672. Section 2(1)(b).
1673. Section 3(1).
1674. Section 3(2).
1675. Section 3(3).

for the subcontractors.[1676] This means that, irrespective of the provisions of the subcontract, subcontractors are entitled to be paid the full value of work completed every thirty days. In addition, 'pay when paid' provisions are no longer permitted – in other words, it is not possible to make payment of an amount due under the construction contract, or the timing of such a payment, conditional on the making of a payment by a third party.[1677]

760. The Act sets out procedures to resolve disputes between the parties.[1678] Where any amount due under a construction contract is not paid in full by the day on which the amount is due, the executing party may suspend work under the construction contract by giving notice in writing.[1679] A party to a construction contract has the right to refer disputes relating to payment to adjudication.[1680] The adjudicator must give a decision within twenty-eight days, and the amount awarded by the adjudicator is payable immediately, even if dispute may then be the subject matter of arbitration or litigation.[1681]

§2. The Sale of Goods and Supply of Services Act 1980

761. Building contracts, and other contracts for labour or services, fall under the Part IV of the Sale of Goods and Supply of Services Act 1980.[1682] Section 39 implies the following terms into every contract for the supply of a service where the supplier is acting in the course of business:

(a) that the supplier has the necessary skill to render the service;
(b) that he will supply the service with due skill, care and diligence;
(c) that, where materials are used, they will be sound and reasonably fit for the purpose for which they are required; and
(d) that, where goods are supplied under the contract, they will be of merchantable quality.

762. There is no useful statutory definition of 'services'[1683] although there is a series of decisions on the difference between contracts for the sale of goods and contracts of service.[1684] Provisions are intended to be of general application and contract of service would include construction contracts, repairs, car maintenance,

---

1676. Section 3(4).
1677. Section 3(5).
1678. *See* ss 4(3) and 5.
1679. Section 5(1).
1680. Section 6(1).
1681. *See* ss 6 and 7 of the Act for details of the adjudication process.
1682. *See* Donnelly and White, *Consumer Law Rights and Regulation* (Round Hall, 2014) pp. 149–161.
1683. Section 2(2) states 'A reference in this Act to the supply of a service includes reference to the rendering or provision of a service or facility and to an offer to supply.'
1684. *See* para. 690.

travel, leisure, holidays, house repairs, consultation with a solicitor and so on. A limited number of services are expressly excluded, including meteorological services,[1685] contract for the carriage of passengers or goods by land, sea, air or inland waterway from one place to another within the State[1686] and the postal service.[1687]

763. The supplier of a service does not promise a particular result, although this may be expressly undertaken or possibly implied. Instead it is asked whether the service was provided with 'due skill, care and diligence' – i.e., a reasonableness requirement. For example in *McKenna v Best Travel*[1688] the plaintiff purchased a holiday, which included a visit to Bethlehem. A stone was thrown at the bus and she sustained physical injuries. She argued there was breach of contract in that she received no warning as to the possible danger inherent in travelling in certain parts of Israel. The High Court held that there was no breach of section 39.

764. Section 39 is an implied term, but it is not expressly defined as a condition (which would allow termination of the contract and damages) or a warranty (which would allow damages only). The effect of breach will generally depend on how serious the breach is. For example, in *Irish Telephone Rentals v ICS Building Society*[1689] a breach of section 39 was said to be serious enough to allow termination of the contract. This case concerned the hire of a telephone system. However owing to a defect in the system, it was unable to cope with an increased volume of calls. It was held that there was a breach of section 39 because the goods supplied were not fit for purpose of providing a reasonably efficient telephone system and not of merchantable quality. This was a serious breach which justified the termination of the contract.

765. Section 40 provides that it is possible to exclude section 39 but if the recipient of the service is a consumer any such exclusion must be fair and reasonable and brought to the attention of the consumer. Schedule 2 lists factors to be taken into account when assessing if an exclusion is fair and reasonable, e.g., bargaining strength.

1685. Section 2(1).
1686. Section 40(6).
1687. The Communications Regulation (Postal Services) Act 2011, s. 26(3).
1688. [1998] 3 IR 57.
1689. [1991] 1 ILRM 880.

Chapter 6. Lease

766. A contract of lease can be defined as an agreement by one party, known as the lessor, to grant possession of their property to another party, known as the lessee, for a certain period of time during which a rent is payable by the lessee to the lessor. In a lease the ownership of the property remains at all times with the lessor. A contract for a lease can be for real property or personal property and slight differences arise for both.

§1. LEASE OF REAL PROPERTY

767. The law related to leases of real property, including the law on landlord and tenant, is complex and cannot be dealt with in a significant manner here. Readers are referred to the leading texts on Land Law in Ireland for a full discussion of these issues.[1690]

I. Statutory Framework

768. The basis of modern landlord and tenant relations is the Landlord and Tenant Law (Amendment) Act (Ireland) 1860, commonly known as 'Deasy's Act'. Section 3 of that Act provides that the relationship of landlord and tenant is 'founded on the express or implied contract of the parties'. More recently the Law Reform Commission recommended reforms to the landlord/tenant relationship,[1691] and the Draft General Scheme of Landlord and Tenant Law Reform Bill 2011 purports to amend significantly the existing legislative framework governing the relationship between landlords and tenants, although the relationship will still be based on the express or implied agreement of the parties. In addition, a plethora of legislative provisions regulate different aspects of different types of landlord and tenant relationship, including the Landlord and Tenant Acts 1967–1980 and the Residential Tenancies Acts 2004–2016,[1692] as well as the provision and regulation of social housing.[1693] The Residential Tenancies Acts have radically transformed the landlord-tenant relationship in relation to dwellings, providing much more extensive protection for residential tenants, particularly as regards protection from increased rent, and improved notice periods for termination of the tenancy.

1690. *See* Howlin and McGrath, *Lyall's Land Law in Ireland* (4th ed., Round Hall, 2018), Chapters 20, 21.

1691. Law Reform Commission, *Report on the Law of Landlord and Tenant Law* (LRC 85-2007).

1692. A consolidated version of the Residential Tenancies Acts, and relevant related statutory orders, is available on the website of the Law Reform Commission, including, at the time of writing, the Emergency Measures in the Public Interest (Covid-19) Act 2020 (2/2020) and Planning and Development Act 2000 (s. 181) Regulations 2020 (S.I. No. 93 of 2020): http://revisedacts.lawreform.ie/eli/2004/act/27/revised/en/html.

1693. *See*, for example, the Housing Acts 1966–2015.

II. Formalities

769. Section 4 of Deasy's Act provides that leases to last longer than a year are to be 'by deed executed or note in writing signed by the landlord or his agent'.[1694] In addition, the parties must have agreed upon essential terms, including the parties, premises, term, commencement date and rent.[1695]

770. Under the Residential Tenancies Acts 2004–2016, a landlord must register details of a tenancy with the Residential Tenancies Board apply no later than one month from the commencement of the tenancy.[1696]

III. Obligations of Lessor and Lessee

General Obligations

771. The lessor and lessee both have implied obligations under the lease. The lessor must have good title to the leased property,[1697] and the lessee should have quiet and peaceable enjoyment of the premises without interruption by the landlord.[1698] The right of exclusive occupation is 'an essential component of a lease or tenancy',[1699] although the landlord may reserve the right to inspect the property or carry out repairs. The lessee must pay the rent stated in the agreement when due.[1700] The lessee must give up peaceable possession of the property in good and substantial repair on the ending of the lease.[1701] A tenant under a covenant to repair does not have to rebuild or carry out works to improve the premises beyond the state of repair enjoyed at the date of the demise.[1702] Indeed, on quitting the tenement at the expiration of the tenancy, a tenant may be entitled to compensation for improvements made by him to the leased property which have added to the value of the property.[1703] In addition, section 87 of the 1980 Act provides that where a landlord 'refuses or fails to execute repairs to a tenement which he is bound by covenant or otherwise by law to execute and has been called upon by the tenant to execute, and the tenant executes the repairs at his own expense, the tenant may set off the expenditure against any subsequent [rent] until it is recouped'.

1694. Section 4 states: 'Every lease or contract with respect to lands whereby the relation of landlord and tenant is intended to be created for any freehold estate or interest, or for any definite period of time not being from year to year or any lesser period, shall be by deed executed or note in writing signed by the landlord or his agent thereunto lawfully authorized in writing.'

1695. *Cosmoline Trading Ltd v DH Burke and Company Ltd and DHB Holdings Ltd* [2006] IEHC 38; Howlin and McGrath, *Lyall's Land Law in Ireland* (4th ed., Round Hall, 2018), paras 2.70–2.71.

1696. Section 134.

1697. *Knight v Smith* [1947] Ir Jur Rep. 17; s. 41, Deasy's Act.

1698. *Bowes v Dublin Corporation* [1965] IR 476; s. 41, Deasy's Act.

1699. Howlin and McGrath, *Lyall's Land Law in Ireland* (4th ed., Round Hall, 2018), para. 20.14.

1700. *Wycherly v Flynn* [1922] 2 IR 28; s. 42 Deasy's Act.

1701. *Rushbrooke v O'Sullivan* [1908] 1 IR 232. Deasy's Act s. 42, the tenant must keep the property 'in good and substantial repair and condition'.

1702. *See Udarás na Gaeltachta v Uisce Glan Teoranta* [2007] IEHC 95.

1703. Sections 48–52.

772. Regarding the condition of the premises, if the lease is of furnished accommodation, such accommodation must be fit for habitation at the beginning of the tenancy.[1704] In *Siney v Dublin Corporation*[1705] the Irish Supreme Court held that where the landlord was a local authority providing housing under the Housing Acts, there was an implied warranty that the flat was fit for human habitation at the date of the letting. This obligation has now been supplemented in the case of residential tenancies, as discussed below.

Obligations of Landlord and Tenant under the Residential Tenancies Acts

773. Under the Residential Tenancies Acts, a landlord is obliged to:[1706]

- allow the tenant to have peaceful and exclusive occupation;
- carry out repairs to ensure certain standards are met (unless the tenant has caused damage beyond normal wear and tear);
- provide bins outside the dwelling;
- insure the structure of the dwelling against destruction and damage, and obtain landlord's liability insurance;
- return any deposit paid by the tenant upon agreeing to enter the lease or tenancy, (subject to the right to retain a deposit to cover any arrears of rent or the cost of repairs for damage caused by the tenant beyond normal wear and tear);
- notify the tenant of the identity of the landlord's agent and of the contact details of either the landlord or the agent;
- reimburse the tenant vouched expenses reasonably incurred by the tenant in undertaking repairs for which the Act ascribes responsibility to the landlord, where the landlord has failed to carry out the repairs at the tenant's request and a postponement of them would have caused a health or safety risk or a significant reduction in the quality of the living environment;
- where the dwelling is in an apartment complex, notify the management company of any complaint about the performance by it of its duties, in relation to the apartment complex, made by the tenant, and forward to the tenant any response by the management company, including a statement of any steps that the management company may already have taken to deal with the matter; and
- where the tenancy is of a dwelling in a rent pressure zone, furnish the tenant with a written statement of the amount of rent that was last set for the dwelling, the date at which this was set, and a statement as to how the rent has been calculated.[1707]

1704. *Wilson v Finch Hatton* (1877) 2 ExD 36; *Sarson v Roberts* [1895] 2 QB 395.

1705. [1980] IR 400. *See also Burke v Dublin Corporation* [1991] 1 IR 341.

1706. This list is modified from the list in Howlin and McGrath, *Lyall's Land Law in Ireland* (4th ed., Round Hall, 2018), para. 20.220, which is drawn from the detailed requirements set out in s. 12 of the Act. *See also* https://onestopshop.rtb.ie/beginning-a-tenancy/rights-and-responsibilities/

1707. Rent pressure zones were introduced in the Planning and Development (Housing) and Residential Tenancies Act 2016, s. 36 of which inserted s. 24A into the Residential Tenancies Act 2004.

774. Under the Residential Tenancies Acts, a tenant is obliged:[1708]

- to pay the rent and any charges or taxes which may lawfully be required of a tenant;
- to ensure that no act or omission of the tenant causes the dwelling to fall below the standard required in the relevant regulations;
- to allow the landlord or his or her agent access upon reasonable request, for the purpose of inspection, on a date and at a time agreed in advance;
- to notify the landlord of any defects arising which it is the landlord's responsibility at law to repair;
- not to cause any deterioration to the dwelling beyond such wear and tear as is reasonable;
- not to act, or allow other occupiers or visitors to act, in such a way as would invalidate the landlord's insurance;
- not to assign or sub-let the tenancy without the written consent of the landlord (which consent the landlord may, in his or her discretion, withhold); but in the event of such consent being withheld, regardless of whether the tenancy is for a fixed or periodic term, the tenant can give notice to terminate the tenancy;
- not to alter or improve the dwelling without the consent of the landlord, which the landlord in his or her discretion may withhold, except in the case of repairing or repainting or decorating where the landlord's consent cannot be unreasonably withheld;
- not to use the dwelling for any purpose except as a dwelling without the landlord's consent, which consent the landlord in his or her discretion may withhold;
- to notify the landlord in writing of the identity of each person ordinarily resident in the dwelling;
- not to behave within the dwelling, or within the vicinity of it, in a way that is anti-social or allow other occupiers of, or visitors to, the dwelling to behave within it, or in the vicinity of it, in such a way.

IV. Sub-letting and Restricted Uses

775. Section 66 of the Landlord and Tenant Amendment Act 1980 allows for sub-letting subject to the landlord's consent, such consent not to be unreasonably withheld.[1709] In contrast, section 16(k) of the Residential Tenancies Act 2004 requires the tenant not to 'assign or sub-let the tenancy without the written consent of the landlord (which consent the landlord may, in his or her discretion, withhold)'. There is no express restriction that the landlord shall not unreasonably withhold consent.[1710]

1708. This list is modified from the list in Howlin and McGrath, *Lyall's Land Law in Ireland* (4th ed., Round Hall, 2018), para. 20.254, which is based on RdTA 2004 ss 16–18, as amended. *See also* https://onestopshop.rtb.ie/beginning-a-tenancy/rights-and-responsibilities/.

1709. *Meagher v Luke J. Healy Pharmacy Ltd* [2010] IESC 40.

1710. Howlin and McGrath, *Lyall's Land Law in Ireland* (4th ed., Round Hall, 2018), para. 20.141–20.149.

776. Similarly, any covenant restricting use of the premises (e.g., not for trade or to sell alcohol) 'takes effect as if it were a covenant prohibiting a change of user without the landlord's consent, with the stipulation that the landlord's consent shall not be unreasonably withheld'.[1711] In *Dunnes Stores (ILAC Centre) Ltd v Irish Life Assurance plc and O'Reilly*[1712] the plaintiff was refused consent by the landlords for change of use or part of a retail outlet to a 'high quality food hall'. Consent was refused on the standard ground of 'good estate management' as the plaintiff's proposed use was inconsistent with the defendants' overall 'vision and image' for the relevant part of the centre, primarily as a retail fashion area. It was held that the landlord was unreasonable in withholding consent, and refusal of consent based upon an improper consideration, or one not contemplated by the lease, would not be permissible.[1713] In the more recent case of in *Perfect Pies Ltd and Farrell v Chupn Ltd*[1714] it was noted that 'a practice of refusing or declining consent for an improper motive, and then later attempting to rely on a 'good' reason, is something that the courts should not encourage or permit'.

777. In contrast, section 16(m) of the Residential Tenancies Act 2004 obliges a tenant not to use the dwelling for any purpose except as a dwelling without the landlord's consent, which consent the landlord in his or her discretion may withhold.

V. Determination of the Lease

778. A lease may be determined by expiry of the term;[1715] notice to quit served by the lessor giving the requisite notice;[1716] surrender of the lease by the tenant;[1717] forfeiture for breach of covenant (term) of the lease;[1718] ejectment for non-payment of rent;[1719] merger with another interest in the property;[1720] or frustration of the agreement.[1721]

779. In the case of a tenancy to which the Residential Tenancies Acts 2004–2016 apply, the landlord or the tenant can terminate the tenancy only in accordance with the procedures set out in Part 5 of the Acts and subject to giving the requisite notice. The amount of notice required to end a tenancy depends on how long the tenant has

1711. *Ibid.*, para. 20.151; s. 67 of the 1980 Act.
1712. [2008] IEHC 114.
1713. *See* the discussion at Howlin and McGrath, *Lyall's Land Law in Ireland* (4th ed., Round Hall, 2018), paras 20.162–20.165.
1714. [2015] IEHC 692.
1715. *O'Farrell v Woods* [1975] Ir. Jur. Rep. 26.
1716. *Wilkinson v Morris* (1883) J I.L.T. 153.
1717. *Deasy's Act* 1860, s. 7; *Trench v Duffy* [1899] 2 I.R. 41.
1718. *Doe d Henniker v Watt* (1828) 8 B.&C. 308.
1719. *Deasy's Act* 1860, s. 52; ejectment proceedings may be brought when the rent is in arrears for more than one year: *Chester v Beary* (1852) ICLR 120; *O'Sullivan v Ambrose* (1893) 32 LR Ir. 102.
1720. *Lennon v Mark* [1899] 1 IR 416; merger is the merging of two or more interests in land.
1721. *Neville & Sons Ltd v Guardian Builders Ltd* [1995] 1 ILRM 1.

lived in the property.[1722] If the tenancy has lasted for six months or more, the landlord needs need to use one of six permitted grounds under section 34 of the Act to end the tenancy. These include selling the property or the landlord or a family member wishing to move back in. In addition, rent can only be increased every telve months,[1723] and tenants must be notified in writing and provided with a minimum of ninety days' notice where a landlord is seeking a new rent amount.[1724]

§2. Lease of Personal Property

780. The crucial element in a lease is the fact that during the period of the lease, the lessor retains the full ownership of the property and the lessee accrues no rights to the property. Lease contracts between a business and a consumer are regulated under the Consumer Credit Act 1995. Lease contracts are dealt with in Part VII, and are referred to in the Act as 'consumer hire agreements'.

781. A lease can be contrasted with a hire-purchase agreement. Under a hire-purchase agreement, the hirer gains possession of the goods, paying a sum of money in instalments, and obtains ownership of the goods on the payment of the last instalment. Under statutory provisions, the hirer accrues a certain interest in the property with the payment of each instalment. Hire-purchase agreements are now regulated under Part VI of the Consumer Credit Act.

I. Formalities for the Creation of a Consumer Hire Agreement

782. A consumer hire agreement must be in writing and signed by the hirer and all the parties to the agreement.[1725] A copy of this agreement should be handed over personally to the hirer on signing the agreement or posted to their address within ten days.[1726] The agreement should contain the following information:[1727]

- the total cash price of the goods to be hired;
- the amount of each instalment and the date on which each instalment is due;
- where the agreement is for a fixed duration, the total amount payable and the number of instalments;
- the cost of terminating the agreement before the final payment;
- the names and addresses of all the parties to the agreement and the supplier of the goods;
- any costs or penalties to which the hirer will become liable for any failure by the hirer to comply with the terms of the agreement;
- a description of the goods subject to the agreement;

1722. Section 66, Table 1 and Table 2.
1723. Section 20.
1724. Section 22(2).
1725. Section 84(1).
1726. *Ibid.*
1727. Section 84(2) (unless otherwise noted).

- a prominent notice to the effect that the goods remain the property of the owner during the entire period of the agreement;
- that a cooling off period of ten days from the receipt by the hirer of a copy of the agreement shall apply enabling the hirer to withdraw from the agreement without penalty, though the hirer may sign a waiver to such right of withdrawal separate and additional to his signature to the agreement;[1728]
- the words 'Consumer Hire Agreement' shall appear in a prominent position on the agreement;[1729]
- the agreement must include a term requiring the owner to give information as to the whereabouts of the property which is the subject matter of the agreement.[1730]

783. Failure to comply with these requirements renders the agreement unenforceable unless a court considers that: (a) the failure to comply was not deliberate, (b) the rights of the hirer have not been prejudiced, and (c) that it would be just and equitable to enforce the agreement subject to such orders as the court deems fit.[1731]

II. Obligations of the Parties to the Agreement

784. The hirer of the property must comply with any contract terms, subject to the normal consumer protections regarding unfair terms. In addition, the hirer must take reasonable care of the property which is the subject matter of the agreement and to be liable for any failure to take such care,[1732] and must inform the owner of the property the whereabouts of such property within ten days of a written request by the owner.[1733]

785. The hirer of the property has certain statutory rights in addition to those contained within the agreement itself. The hirer may terminate a consumer hire agreement at any time by giving notice to the owner of the property, such termination to take effect either in accordance with the agreement or after three months, whichever is the earlier.[1734] There is an implied warranty that the property which is the subject matter of the consumer hire agreement is free, and will remain free, from any encumbrances or charges not disclosed and that the hirer is entitled to the quiet and peaceable possession of the property subject to the rights of any disclosed charge or encumbrance.[1735] Goods must correspond with any description given, and be of merchantable quality – in essence, the provisions regarding sales contracts are

1728. Section 84(5).
1729. Section 84(7).
1730. Section 84(6).
1731. Section 85.
1732. Section 90.
1733. Section 91.
1734. Section 89.
1735. Section 88.

also implied into consumer hire agreements.[1736] Any attempt to exclude these provisions is void unless fair and reasonable.[1737] Sections 12 (implied warranty regarding spare parts and after-sales service), 13 (safety of motor vehicles) and 15–19 (enforceability of commercial guarantees) of the sale of goods and Supply of Services Act 1980 also apply to consumer hires.[1738]

1736. *Ibid.* importing ss 75–83 of the Act which deal with hire-purchase agreements.
1737. Section 79.
1738. Sections 81–82.

Chapter 7. Compromise Settlement

§1. Compromise of a Debt

786. As has already been shown,[1739] an agreement to accept a lesser sum in settlement of a legally valid debt is enforceable only when either executed under seal or where fresh consideration has been given. A principal exception to this rule arises under a composition with creditors. Here each creditor agrees to forego his or her strict legal entitlements to enforce their individual debts in return for part payment by the debtor. Strictly speaking such composition is unenforceable as, according to the rule in *Pinnel's Case*,[1740] it is unsupported by consideration between the debtor and his creditors. However, the courts have adopted the longstanding commercial practice and will enforce such an agreement.[1741]

§2. Compromise of a Claim

787. Where a legal claim has been initiated or threatened against an individual, a promise made in return for the cessation of proceedings under such claim is valid,[1742] provided that:

- such claim is reasonable, and not vexatious or frivolous;[1743]
- the claimant had an honest belief in his chances of success;
- there must have been no withholding of facts or evidence that would have shown the claim in its true context.[1744]

788. Where both parties know that the claim is not valid then the agreement is not enforceable. In *O'Donnell v O'Sullivan*[1745] the compromise agreement concerned a gambling debt which both parties knew could not be legally enforced; hence the court refused to enforce the agreement.

789. It is not necessary for parties to make a formal agreement not to sue or prosecute a claim. It is sufficient if there is a request, express or implied, to forbear from bringing proceedings which induces some forbearance.[1746]

1739. *See* paras 164 et seq.
1740. (1602) 77 ER 237.
1741. *Morans v Armstrong* (1840) Arm Mac. Og. 25 (Exch.).
1742. *Taylor v Smyth* [1990] ILRM 377.
1743. *See*, however, *Miles v New Zealand Alford Estate* (1886) 32 Ch D 266 (valid compromise agreement even though original claim could not have been successful).
1744. *Leonard v Leonard* (1812) 2 Ball & B. 171.
1745. [1913] 47 ILTR 253.
1746. *Barry v Barry* (1891) 28 LR (Ir) 45; *Commodity Broking Co. v Meehan* [1985] IR 12.

Chapter 8. Suretyship

790. A contract of guarantee (suretyship) is a promise to answer for 'the debt, default or miscarriage of another person'. It is essentially a collateral undertaking, whereby the guarantor (or surety) becomes contractually bound to 'another' (the creditor) to be responsible for the obligation of a third party (the debtor).[1747]

791. The normal general rules of the law of contract apply also to guarantees. Agreement, consideration (or a deed) and intention to create legal relations are required for a valid contract of guarantee. The consideration will often consist of a promise by the creditor to grant a loan or overdraft, or further advances, to the debtor. In *ACC Bank Plc v Dillon*[1748] Charleton J stated that what is relevant is whether any money was actually advanced and 'the mere recitation in a document of guarantee that the guarantee was given for consideration for 'advances to be made' by the person to whom the guarantee was given will not, by itself be sufficient to support the guarantee if the evidence demonstrates that no such advances were, or were intended to be, made'.[1749]

792. Under section 2 of the Statute of Frauds 1695, a contract of guarantee must be evidenced in writing, and signed by the party 'to be charged', to be enforceable. In contrast a contract of indemnity is enforceable even if purely oral. In an indemnity, the promisor undertakes a primary or original liability for the debt of another, not a collateral liability.[1750] Judicial interpretation of the Statute of Frauds confined the Statute's provisions on guarantees to cases where the main purpose of the contract consisted of the guarantee itself. If the guarantee was merely incidental to the main purpose, for example, the promise in a *del credere* agency contract to be answerable for the debts of third parties introduced by the agent to the principal, the Statute did not apply. In *Danske Bank v RQB Ltd,*[1751] it was stated that the guarantee must be strictly construed with ambiguities being resolved in the guarantor's favour.

793. The guarantor can demand that the creditor seek payment from the debtor on the primary obligation when payment becomes due but, unless the guarantee contract expressly provides for it, he cannot compel the creditor to first sue the debtor. However, when the guarantor has discharged his own obligation on the guarantee, he can compel the creditor to assign the benefit of the primary obligation so that he himself can sue the debtor or he can join the creditor in an action against the

1747. This is not to be confused with a commercial guarantee, which is essentially an undertaking or warranty provided by a manufacturer or retailer to the recipient of goods or services. *See* the Sale of Goods and Supply of Services Act 1980 ss 15–19.

1748. [2012] IEHC 474.

1749. Quoting the Supreme Court of Victoria in *McKay and Another v National Australia Bank Ltd* [1998] 1 VR 173.

1750. *See Commodity Broking Co. Ltd. v Meehan* [1985] IR 12.

1751. *Danske Bank a/s trading as National Irish Bank v RQB Ltd (formerly known as Redquartz Boundary Ltd)* [2010] IEHC 347.

debtor. Under section 3 of the Mercantile Law Amendment Act 1856, the guarantor becomes subrogated to all the rights of the creditor after he has paid off the creditor.

794. Any defences available under the normal law of contract to the debtor on the primary obligation are also available to the guarantor. If for some reason (e.g., lack of capacity) the primary liability is void or unenforceable there is no 'primary' debtor liable, so the guarantor cannot be secondarily or collaterally liable on his guarantee. As regards the guarantor and the contract of guarantee, the normal defence pleas such as duress and undue influence, mistake, misrepresentation and *non est factum* are available.

795. Conduct on the part of the creditor may have the effect of releasing the guarantor from his guarantee. If the creditor is negligent in respect of the primary obligation, or releases the primary obligation or securities given therefor, or varies the primary obligation in some way detrimental to the interests of the guarantor, the guarantee may be wholly or partially discharged.

Chapter 9. Pledge

796. A pledge is a bailment of goods, or the document of title to goods, to a creditor as security for a debt. A pledge is created by contract, and if the debt is not paid the creditor can sell the goods. A pledge can be contrasted with a lien, which is a personal right to retain goods,[1752] but without a right to sell the goods, although statute might provide such a right.[1753] In a lien and a pledge, possession of the goods remains with or is given to the creditor, but not so in the case of a mortgage or charge, in which a proprietary interest in the goods is transferred to the mortgagee-creditor, but possession remains with the debtor.

797. Delivery of possession of the goods is essential for a pledge. It may be actual, symbolic (a key to a warehouse or store), or constructive delivery (by a document of title such as a bill of lading). Goods in the possession of a third party, such as a warehousekeeper, may be pledged by appropriate instructions to the third party.

798. In a pledge, the pledgee has the right to take possession of the pledged property; to sell the property in order to realise their security; to sue in trespass or conversion in respect of the pledged goods; and to transfer or sub-pledge their interest in the pledged goods. The right to sell arises when the time for payment of the debt has expired or, if no time was fixed, after a reasonable time following an unsuccessful demand for payment. Any surplus on the sale must be paid over to the pledgor.

799. The pledgor has the right to redeem the goods pledged at any time before they have been sold by the pledgee; to recover any surplus over the debt realised by the sale of the goods, which must be conducted in a bona fide manner; to transfer their title in the goods to a third party who thereupon acquires all the rights of the pledgor; and to sue in detinue or conversion in respect of their ownership of the pledged goods.

800. In Ireland pledges of goods as security for small private loan transactions as distinct from commercial securities were formerly commonly made with pawnbrokers. The business of pawnbroking is regulated in Ireland by the Pawnbrokers' Act 1964, as amended in particular by Part XV of the Consumer Credit Act 1995, under which pawnbrokers must operate under licence and comply with the formalities regulating pawnbroking as set out in the Act. The regulations cover matters like

1752. For example, Sale of Goods Act 1893, s. 41(3) (unpaid seller's lien); Hotel Proprietors Act 1963, s. 8. A lien can be lost if possession of the goods is lost.
1753. *See*, for example, Hotel Proprietors Act 1963, s. 8(3): 'The proprietor may sell by public auction any property to which his lien extends if, after six weeks, the debt remains unsatisfied.'

record-keeping, maximum charges and interest, redemption and sale of pledges, prohibition on pledges of certain goods, etc. The Act applies to loans not exceeding €6,348[1754] on pledges. There are currently three pawnbrokers licensed in Ireland.[1755]

1754. Consumer Credit Act 1995, Eighth Schedule, amending sections 2 and 3 of the Pawnbrokers' Act 1964 to increase the scope of the Act to loans exceeding £5,000, which is €6,348 on conversion to Euro.

1755. https://www.ccpc.ie/business/help-for-business/pawnbrokers/.

Chapter 10. Loans

801. Whether a contract of loan exists is assessed according to ordinary contract principles; there is no requirement that a contract of loan be evidenced in writing.[1756] Moreover, other general contract principles apply to loan agreements, including defences such as misrepresentation or undue influence. The economic crisis starting in 2008 resulted in a deluge of cases before the courts concerning the enforcement of loan agreements, (and guarantees related to loans) with defences such as *non est factum* and undue influence being pleaded, even where there was no arguable basis for the defence. The court is understandably sceptical of such claims,[1757] but in rare cases a defence such as *non est factum* will be made out.[1758]

802. Financial services are now heavily regulated by legislation, including general consumer protection directives, such as the Unfair Contract Terms Directive,[1759] and others which are specific to credit or the financial sector – *see*, for example, the Consumer Credit Act[1760] or the Directive on the distance marketing of financial services.[1761] Gaps in the legislative schemes are filled by the Central Bank codes of practice, such as the Consumer Protection Code 2006, as revised in 2012 and 2016, the Code of Conduct on Mortgage Arrears (2013) and the Consumer Protection Code for Licensed Moneylenders (2009). These codes of practice are drawn up by the Central Bank, but they have a statutory basis[1762] and are binding on financial institutions.

803. The Consumer Protection Code applies to financial services providers authorised, registered or licensed by the Central Bank or in another EU or EEA Member State when providing services in Ireland on a branch or cross-border basis. Provision 4 of the Code provides for general information transparency requirements. Prior to providing a product, such as a loan, information must be provided about the main features and restrictions of the product,[1763] as well as the terms and conditions attaching to any such product or service.[1764] Where a loan is offered for the purpose of consolidating other loans, information must be provided comparing

---

1756. Breslin, *Banking Law* (3rd ed., Round Hall, 2013) at paras 4–13, as cited in *Bank of Ireland Mortgage Bank v Murray* [2019] IEHC 234, para. 141. *See ACC Bank v Deacon* [2013] IEHC 427 where the fact that the first defendant had used the money to buy land was 'substantial confirmation' that a loan agreement existed, in the light of the stated purpose of the loans.
1757. *Irish Bank Resolution Corporation Ltd v Quinn & Another* [2011] IEHC 470.
1758. *Friends First Finance v Lavelle* [2013] IEHC 201.
1759. *See* Mary Donnelly, 'Loan Contracts and the Unfair Terms Regulations' 2010) 17(6) Commercial Law Practitioner 107. *See also* the cases discussed at para. 468 above.
1760. *See* Donnelly and White *Consumer Law Rights and Regulation* pp. 411–437 on credit agreements and the Consumer Credit Act 1995, as amended.
1761. Directive 2002/65.
1762. Section 117(1) of the Central Bank Act 1989.
1763. Consumer Protection Code para. 4.21. In fact this information must be provided before offering or recommending such product.
1764. Consumer Protection Code para. 4.22.

the total interest to be paid under the new loan structure, as compared with the existing facilities.[1765] In light of the recent financial crisis in Ireland, regulated entities are now also obliged to conduct a suitability assessment to ensure that the product in question is suitable for that consumer's needs.[1766] In particular, a credit institution should not offer credit or a mortgage without ensuring that it is appropriate and the consumer has the capability to pay off the debt. The consumer is then entitled to a written 'suitability statement' setting out the reasons why the product or service offered to a consumer is considered to be suitable to that consumer. This aims to help ensure that consumers are protected, and (in theory) would take into account the needs of vulnerable consumers.[1767]

804. The Code of Conduct on Mortgage Arrears (2013) sets out how mortgage lenders must treat borrowers in or facing mortgage arrears, 'with due regard to the fact that each case of mortgage arrears is unique and needs to be considered on its own merits'.[1768] The Code 'sets out the framework that lenders must use when dealing with borrowers in mortgage arrears or in pre-arrears' and states that 'all such cases must be handled sympathetically and positively by the lender, with the objective at all times of assisting the borrower to meet his/her mortgage obligations'.[1769]

805. There is also a specific Code of Conduct for Business Lending to Small and Medium Enterprises.[1770] Guidelines issued by the Central Bank state that when dealing with SMEs,[1771] lenders must:

- give SME borrowers transparency around the application process;
- provide SME borrowers with reasons for declining credit, in writing, that are specific to their application;
- provide protections for guarantors;
- contact SME borrowers who have been in arrears for fifteen working days;
- warn SME borrowers if they are in danger of being classified as not co-operating and provide SME borrowers with the right of appeal.[1772]

1765. Consumer Protection Code para. 4.27.
1766. Chapter 5.
1767. Provision 3.
1768. Code of conduct on mortgage arrears (2013) p. 1.
1769. *Ibid.*
1770. The current version is found in the Central Bank (Supervision and Enforcement) Act 2013 (s. 48) (Lending to Small and Medium-Sized Enterprises) Regulations 2015 (S.I. No. 585 of 2015), as amended by the 2016 and 2018 Regulations.
1771. A micro and small enterprise means an enterprise which employs fewer than 50 persons and which has either or both of the following: (a) an annual turnover which does not exceed €10 million, (b) an annual balance sheet total which does not exceed €10 million.
1772. Central Bank *A Guide for Micro and Small Enterprises and Guarantors: Regulations on Lending to Small and Medium-Sized Enterprises* (2016), https://www.centralbank.ie/docs/default-source/consumer-hub-library/2016-06-03-a-guide-for-micro-and-small-enterprises-and-guarantors-final.pdf?sfvrsn=8.

806. The Codes are enforced by the Central Bank, which monitors advertising, and carries out reviews and themed inspections to ensure and encourage compliance with the Code.[1773] It takes a 'risk and evidence-based approach' in prioritising its work, focusing resources on areas where there is 'a significant threat' to consumer protection objectives.[1774] The Codes are also utilised by the Financial Service Ombudsman, who deals independently with unresolved complaints from consumers about financial service providers.[1775] A failure to comply with the Code may be the basis of a finding against the service provider.[1776] Most decisions of the FSO remain confidential and unpublished; however some information about how the Ombudsman operates can be gleaned from sample case studies, and from cases which are appealed to the courts. In one decision, the High Court stated that the Code 'is a significant feature of the landscape within which the [FSO] operates and it is probably expected by many complainants that they can rely on it'; it would thus be 'desirable' that the FSO should refer to it in his decisions.[1777] The issue of whether non-compliance with the Code can be relied upon in private litigation before the courts is more complex. It has been said that failure to comply the Codes is a 'factor that can be relevant in exercising any judicial discretion'.[1778] However, the Supreme Court has stated that on relation to the Code of Conduct for mortgage arrears a lender who seeks an order for possession without observing the moratorium provision in the code may be denied such an order.[1779]

1773. *See* https://www.centralbank.ie/regulation/consumer-protection/compliance-monitoring.
1774. Central Bank *Consumer Protection Outlook Report 2017* p. 5.
1775. *See* https://www.financialombudsman.ie/.
1776. White and Donnelly (2011) p. 382.
1777. *Carr v Financial Services Ombudsman* [2013] IEHC 182, para. 84.
1778. Clark p. 290 referring to *Zurich Bank v McConnon* [2011] IEHC 75; *Stepstone Mortgage Funding Ltd v Fitzell* [2012] IEHC 142; *Irish life and Permanent plc v Duff* [2013] IEHC 43. *See*, however, *ACC Bank Plc v Deacon* [2013] IEHC 427 'It seems clear that compliance with the SME code is not a prerequisite of establishing liability – failure to comply with the code does not wipe out the loan or furnish a defence.' In this case, however, the failure to comply was arguably technical.
1779. *Irish Life and Permanent plc v Dunne and Dunphy* [2015] IESC 46.

Chapter 11. Contracts with the Government and Other Public Administrations

807. The Government and other public administrations may sue or be sued in contract or tort like any other defendant and such a case is heard in the normal way in the normal courts. There is no separate set of contract rules governing these contracts. The doctrine of legitimate expectation has been developed to deal with particular situations where a representation is made by a public authority to an identified person or group of persons, in such a way as to create an expectation, reasonably entertained, that the public authority will abide by the representation such that it would be unjust to permit the public authority to resile from it.[1780] Legitimate expectation has its origins in contractual doctrines such as estoppel,[1781] and indeed the Supreme Court has spoken of the 'difficulties posed by cross-fertilisation of concepts such as proprietary estoppel, promissory estoppel and legitimate expectation'.[1782] However, it is usually considered in the context of administrative actions, rather than traditional contract law cases, and is often limited on public policy grounds.[1783]

808. The other major difference between private contracts and contracts with the government and other public administrations concerns national and EU rules governing public procurement. The National Public Procurement Policy Framework sets out the procurement procedures to be followed by Government Departments and State Bodies when awarding contracts for works, goods and services.[1784] Full details of the procurement system are outside the scope of this work but can be found elsewhere.[1785]

1780. *Glencar Exploration plc v Mayo County Council (No. 2)* [2002] 1 IR 84, 130.
1781. *See Webb v Ireland* [1988] IR 353. For a discussion of the complexities of the conceptual basis of the doctrine, *see* Redmond Arigho 'Legitimate Expectations in Irish and EU Law – Lessons for Ireland?' (2016) 19 Irish Journal of European Law 76.
1782. *Lett & Company Limited v Wexford Borough Council & others* [2012] 2 IR 198.
1783. *See* for example *Atlantic Marine Supplies Limited & another v Minister for Transport & others* [2016] IESC 43, *Cromane Seafoods Limited & another v Minister for Agriculture, Fisheries and Food & others* [2016] IESC 6.
1784. National Public Procurement Policy Framework (November 2019), available at https://ogp.gov.ie/national-public-procurement-policy-framework/
1785. *See* Browne and McGovern, *Procurement Law in Ireland* (Round Hall, 2018).

Chapter 12. Contract of Partnership

809. Under the Partnership Act 1890 a partnership[1786] is 'the relation which subsists between persons carrying on a business in common with a view of profit'.[1787] Persons who have entered into partnership with one another are called collectively a firm.[1788] The Partnership Act 1890, as amended,[1789] sets out the rules governing partnerships. Every partner is an agent of the firm and his other partners for the purpose of the business of the partnership, and any acts done by the partner will bind the firm.[1790] Every partner in a firm is liable jointly with the other partners for all debts and obligations of the firm incurred while he is a partner.[1791]

810. The Act sets out the rights of the partners as regards each other, although these can be varied by the consent of all partners.[1792] Unless the contrary intention appears, property bought with money belonging to the firm is deemed to have been bought on account of the firm.[1793] All property and rights and interests in property originally brought into the partnership stock or acquired on account of the firm, or for the purposes and in the course of the partnership business, must be held and applied by the partners exclusively for the purposes of the partnership and in accordance with the partnership agreement.[1794] All the partners are entitled to share equally in the capital and profits of the business, and must contribute equally towards the losses sustained by the firm.[1795]

811. It is a fiduciary relationship, so there is a duty to act in good faith, to disclosure information[1796] and to account for profits made without the consent of the other partners,[1797] or in competition with the partnership.[1798]

812. No person may be introduced as a partner without the consent of all existing partners,[1799] and no majority of the partners can expel any partner unless a power to do so has been conferred by express agreement between the partners.[1800]

1786. The law of partnership is comprehensively discussed in Twomey and Clancy, *Twomey on Partnership* (2nd ed., Bloomsbury, 2019).
1787. Section 1(1).
1788. Partnership Act 1890, s. 4(1).
1789. *See*, for example, Investment Limited Partnerships Act 1994.
1790. Section 5.
1791. Section 9. However, the Limited Partnership Act 1907 made it possible for a person 'to become a partner in a firm while at the same time limiting his liability to the creditors of the firm to the amount of capital contributed by him'. *See* Twomey, 'The Limited Partnership Act 1907' (1996) 3(8) Commercial Law Practitioner 211.
1792. Section 19.
1793. Section 21.
1794. Section 20.
1795. Section 24(1).
1796. Section 28: Partners are bound to render true accounts and full information of all things affecting the partnership to any partner or his legal representatives.
1797. Section 29.
1798. Section 30.
1799. Section 24(7).
1800. Section 25.

Where no fixed term has been agreed upon for the duration of the partnership, any partner may determine the partnership at any time on giving notice of his intention so to do to all the other partners. The partnership may also be dissolved by expiration of a fixed term,[1801] by termination of an undertaking for which it was entered into,[1802] by giving notice to other partners,[1803] or subject to an agreement between the parties, on the death or bankruptcy of a partner,[1804] or because of illegality,[1805] or in certain circumstances by order of the Court.[1806]

813. The Legal Services Regulation Act 2015 provides for the establishment of three new types of business structure for the legal profession, including legal partnerships (a partnership between practising barristers, or between one or more practising barristers and one or more practising solicitors); multi-disciplinary practices (a partnership between one or more practising lawyers (solicitors and/or barristers) with non-lawyers; and the Limited Liability Partnership (LLP).[1807]

1801. Section 32(1).
1802. Section 32(2).
1803. Section 26.
1804. Section 33.
1805. Section 34.
1806. Section 35.
1807. Maedhbh Clancy 'Irish Limited Liability Partnerships: the State of Play' (2019) 26(2) *Commercial Law Practitioner* 19.

Chapter 13. Quasi-contracts

814. Quasi-contracts are a group of actions falling between contract and tort, which could be resolved by the fictional implication of consent or agreement, thus giving the name, quasi-contract. It is now recognised that the principle of unjust enrichment is the true rationale of cases traditionally dealt with under the heading of quasi-contract:

> It is clear that, under our law, a person can, in certain circumstances, be obliged to effect restitution of money or other property to another where it would be unjust for him to retain the money. Moreover, a Henchy J noted in *East Cork Foods Ltd v O'Dwyer Steel Co Ltd* this principle no longer rests on the fiction of an implied promise to return the property which, in the days when the forms of action still ruled English law, led to its tortuous rationalisation as being quasi-contractual in nature.[1808]

815. The general approach to restitution and quasi-contracts is outlined elsewhere in this book.[1809] The following outlines some actions falling under this heading. In situations where plaintiff is seeking to recover the return of money paid, the action is known as an action for money had and received. In *Bank of Ireland Mortgage Bank v Murray*[1810] a bank sought repayment of money advanced to a joint bank account, with the action being brought as an action for money had and received as there was no contractual relationship with one of the parties. It was held that this was unjust enrichment at the expense of the plaintiff and ordered restitution.[1811] In situations where the plaintiff is seeking a sum to compensate for work done or services rendered, the action is known as *quantum meruit.*

§1. Money Paid under a Mistake

816. The general rule that recovery of a payment can be made where a mistake[1812] is fundamental and relates to the terms of a contract was stated in *Kelly v Solari*[1813] and endorsed in Ireland in *National Banks Ltd. v O'Connor and Bowmaker Ireland Ltd.*[1814]

1808. *Lord Mayor, Aldermen and Burgesses of the City of Dublin v Building and Allied Trade Union* [1996] 1 IR 468, 483. *See also East Cork Foods Ltd v O'Dwyer Steel Company* [1978] 1 IR 103; *Murphy v Attorney General* [1982] IR 241 and more recently *Bank of Ireland Mortgage Bank v Murray* [2019] IEHC 234.
1809. *See* paras 63 et seq.
1810. [2019] IEHC 234. *See also ACC Bank v Fahey* [2010] IEHC 41.
1811. A defence based on change of position was rejected, as the court stated that the defendant would have to show that 'he entered a transaction he would not have entered but for the enrichment, and that the balance of fairness means that the money is not to be restored', and he had not done this.
1812. *See* Cleary 'Restitution of Mistake of Law in Ireland' (2016) 55 Irish Jurist 25; Clark pp. 787–795; the discussion of mistake of law in *Vanguard Auto Finances Ltd v Browne* [2014] IEHC 465.
1813. (1841) 9 M and W 54.
1814. (1966) 103 ILTR 73.

817. Thus, although there is a general rule that payments made voluntarily are not recoverable, if the money was paid because the plaintiff mistakenly thought they were liable to pay it, or because the mistake is 'fundamental', then it will be recoverable.[1815] Thus if a bank makes a payment to the defendant as in *National Banks Ltd v O'Connor and Bowmaker Ireland Ltd*[1816] in circumstances where the payment was gratuitous, recovery is possible if the mistake is a fundamental one.

818. In 1937 the Irish Supreme Court has confirmed and applied the rule that the mistake must be a mistake of fact not law,[1817] and despite changes of approach in other jurisdictions,[1818] in the absence of a reversal of this decision by the Supreme Court this remains the law.[1819] However, Clark notes that the Supreme Court has hinted that it 'will be prepared to formally overrule the earlier line of authority when the opportunity presents itself'.[1820] However, it is possible to circumvent the rule – so, for example, where one person is in a better position to ascertain the truth or is primarily responsible for the mistake the court may order restitution,[1821] and wherever the boundary between fact and law become relevant, the courts endeavour to classify it as one of fact.[1822]

§2. Total Failure of Consideration

819. If the plaintiff has paid money to the defendant in pursuance of a valid contract and the defendant fails to completely carry out his part of it, the plaintiff can sue for the return of the money on the basis of total failure of consideration.[1823] This applies even if the defendant was unable to complete performance through no fault of their own, i.e., if the contract is frustrated.[1824] A classic example of a total failure of consideration is to be found in the case of *Hayes v Stirling*.[1825] A payment was made in order to secure shares in a future company, but the company was never formed. The money was recoverable as money had and received to the use of the plaintiff on the basis of a total failure of consideration. In the recent case of *Vanguard Auto Finances Ltd v Browne*[1826] there was said to be a total failure of consideration when money was advanced on the basis of invoices which were a 'fiction', relating to goods which had never been purchased. In *Mallett and Sons*

1815. Cleary 'Restitution of Mistake of Law in Ireland' (2016) 55 Irish Jurist 25.
1816. (1966) 103 ILTR 73.
1817. *Casey v The Irish Sailors and Soldiers Land Trust* [1937] IR 208. *See also O'Loughlin v O'Callaghan* (1874) IR 8 CL 116.
1818. *Kleinwort Benson Ltd v Lincoln City Council* [1999] 2 AC 349.
1819. For example, *see O'Callaghan v Ballincollig Holdings*, Unreported, High Court, 31 March 1993, Blayney J.
1820. Clark p. 789, citing *Harris v Quigley and Irwin* [2006] ILRM 401.
1821. *Roger v Louth County Council* [1981] ILRM 144; *Dolan v Nelligan* [1967] IR 247; *Dublin Corp v Trinity College Dublin* [1985] ILRM 283.
1822. *Piatt v Casey's Drogheda Brewery Co* [1912] 1 IR 271.
1823. *Wilkinson v Lloyd* (1845) 7 QB 27.
1824. *Fibrosa Spolka Akcyjna v Fairbairn Lawson Combe Barbour Ltd* [1943] AC 32.
1825. (1863) Ir CLR 277.
1826. [2014] IEHC 465.

(Antiques) Ltd v Rogers[1827] restitution was ordered on the purchase price when the plaintiff purchased an antique bookcase which had in fact been stolen:

> The consideration for the sale was the title to the bookcase (in return for the sum of STG80,000). The title to the bookcase never passed from the defendant to the plaintiff. The consideration for the sale failed wholly and the plaintiff is entitled to the return of the sum of STG£80,000.

820. However, there needs to be a *total* failure of consideration. Hence in *Stapleton v Prudential Assurance*[1828] restitution of insurance premiums paid by the plaintiff on foot of a voidable contract was denied because the plaintiff was covered by the policy during the time that the contract was valid. However, it is possible to recover money paid even if *some* benefit was received, where it is not in fact the benefit one was supposed to receive from the contract. Thus money will be recoverable under a hire-purchase contract which is null and void, even if the hirer had some use of the item hired, as the consideration under this contract is seen as the option to purchase.[1829] Similarly, in a contract of the sale of goods, the transfer of ownership is the consideration; hence a breach of section 12 of the Sale of Goods Act 1893 (seller must have the right to sell) gives the buyer the right to reject the goods and gain a full refund, even if the buyer has had the use of the goods for a period of time.[1830]

§3. Money Paid in Pursuance of an Ineffective Contract

821. In general, money paid under a contract which is void *ab initio*, or which has been vitiated for some reason, is recoverable under an action in restitution. This money might be recoverable on the basis of a mistake of fact, or because of a total failure of consideration, or even just because of the fact that the contract is void,[1831] although where a contract is void under statute the result will depend on the wording of the statute.[1832] Money paid can also be recovered where a contract is conditional on an event occurring, which does not then occur, provided that the contract does not provide otherwise.[1833]

822. Where the contract is void *ab initio* because of illegality, money paid may be recovered only if the plaintiff does not have to disclose the illegality in order to sustain the action.[1834] However, if the parties are not *in pari delicto* or if one party

1827. [2005] IEHC 131.
1828. (1928) 62 ILTR 56.
1829. *UDT (Ireland) v Shannon Caravans Ltd* [1976] IR 225; *Chartered Trust Ireland Ltd v Healy & Commins*, Unreported, High Court, 10 December 1985.
1830. *Rowland v Divall* [1923] 2 KB 500.
1831. *Kleinwort Benson Ltd v Lincoln City Council* [1999] 2 AC 349.
1832. *See* the discussion at paras 378 et seq.
1833. *Lowis v Wilson* [1949] IR 347. *See* s. 59 of the Land and Conveyancing Law Reform Act 2009, regarding the return of deposits.
1834. *Collins v Blastein* (1767) 2 Wils 341.

has perpetrated a fraud on the other, then restitution might be possible.[1835] If the source of illegality is a statutory provision, then the statute may declare the restitutionary implications.[1836]

§4. Money Paid by Plaintiff to Defendant's Use

823. If the plaintiff has been compelled to pay money for which the defendant is liable, he may sue the defendant for the amount so paid. There is no right to recover unless (1) there is an obligation in law on the defendant to pay the money due[1837] and (2) the plaintiff paid the money under some form of compulsion or constraint.[1838] The most direct form of constraint is the pressure of legal action. In *Beresford v Kennedy*[1839] both plaintiff and defendant owned adjoining farmland. Some of the plaintiff's cattle had strayed onto the defendant's land. The defendant had failed to pay a local tax, and accordingly a number of his cattle were seized in satisfaction of the delinquent taxes. The plaintiff's cattle were among those seized. The plaintiff paid the back taxes in order to release his cattle, and the court held that the plaintiff could recover this money from the defendant. In *Midland Great Western Railway v Benson*,[1840] the defendant transferred a consignment of butter to Kelly via the plaintiff. The defendant was dissatisfied with the financial arrangements between himself and Kelly and wrongfully secured the return of the butter before it reached Kelly. Kelly had paid £40 on account for the butter, and under threat of legal action, the plaintiff paid the £40 to Kelly. It was held that the plaintiff could recover this £40 from the defendant as money paid to the defendant's use.

§5. Claims Against Wrongdoers

824. A plaintiff who has suffered a loss through a wrongful act committed against him by a defendant may, in certain circumstances, be entitled to sue the defendant in quasi-contract for money had and received to his use.[1841] Wrongful acts here can include misrepresentations or economic duress.

1835. *Byrne v Rudd* [1920] 2 IR 12.
1836. *See* the discussion at paras 366 et seq.
1837. *Brooks Wharf v Goodman Brothers* [1937] 1 KB 534; *Irish National Insurance Co v Scannell* [1959] Ir Jur Rep 41.
1838. One notable exception to this occurs in salvage at sea, where the owner of a ship is bound to compensate a plaintiff who rescues his property from imminent peril: *Five Steel Barges* (1890) 15 PD 142.
1839. (1887) 21 ILTR 17.
1840. (1875) Ir CL Rep. 52.
1841. *Meskell v Horner* [1915] 3 KB 106; *Great Southern and Western Railway Co v Robertson* (1878) 2 LR (Ir) 548.

§6. Quantum Meruit

825. If the plaintiff has transferred some property or performed some services for the defendant, the plaintiff can seek a reasonable remuneration for the services rendered or property transferred under the action is known as *quantum meruit.*

826. A claim in quasi-contract cannot override the terms of an existing contract. Thus where a contract has been voluntarily terminated by the agreement of both parties, one party cannot seek to recover on *quantum meruit.*[1842] Similarly a claim for *quantum meruit* will not succeed where the plaintiff fails to complete an entire contract.[1843] However, it may be possible to recover under *quantum meruit* where the contract has been wrongfully discharged by the defendant.[1844]

827. Where no contract exists, an award to compensate the plaintiff for the amount of work undertaken is readily made.[1845] In *O'Connor v Listowel UDC*[1846] the plaintiff had been employed for six months by the defendant before it was discovered that he had been invalidly appointed. Dismissing a claim by the plaintiff to recover in contract, the court awarded reasonable remuneration for services rendered. Similarly in *Fanning v Wicklow County Council*[1847] a builder was entitled to recover the value of work done on a *quantum meruit* basis where it transpired that there was in fact no underlying contract. As Goff J stated in *British Steel Corporation v Cleveland Bridge & Engineering*:[1848]

> the law simply imposes an obligation on the party who made the request to pay a reasonable sum for such work as has been done pursuant to that request, such an obligation sounding in quasi contract, or as we now say, in restitution.

828. Restitution on a quantum meruit basis is available for work undertaken during preparatory negotiations which it was intended would lead to a contract but which did not. In *British Steel Corporation v Cleveland Bridge & Engineering Co.*[1849] restitution was ordered for goods delivered on foot of a letter of intent indicating that the defendants would like performance to begin pending the formal adoption of a contract, which was never adopted. Further, it does not appear that the

---

1842. *Travers Construction Ltd v Lismore Homes Ltd*, Unreported, High Court, 9 March 1990.
1843. *Creagh v Sheedy* [1955–1956] Ir Jur Rep 85.
1844. *Lawlor v Alton* (1873) IR 8 CL 160.
1845. In *Rover International v Canon Film Sales* (No. 3) [1989] 3 All ER 423 the court held that this was not limited to the maximum that would have been payable under the contract. *See also McCabe Builders (Dublin) Limited v Sagamu Developments Limited & ors* [2009] IESC 31, para. 41.
1846. [1957] Ir Jur Rep 43.
1847. Unreported, High Court, 30 April 1984.
1848. [1984] 1 All ER 504.
1849. *Ibid.*

person who has requested the work need obtain any benefit, so that in *Folens v Minister for Education*[1850] the plaintiff was compensated for preparatory work undertaken during negotiations with the Minister for Education for the publication of a children's encyclopaedia, when the Department of Education decided not to proceed with the publication.

829. However, where work is done under an apparent agreement after protracted negotiations, the court will be reluctant to find that there was no contract, thus leaving the parties to the uncertainty of a quantum meruit claim. Instead, it will be assumed that commercial parties intended to enter into contractual relations, and work will be paid for in accordance with the contract.[1851]

1850. [1984] ILRM 265.
1851. *See McCabe Builders (Dublin) Limited v Sagamu Developments Limited & ors* [2009] IESC 31.

Selected Bibliography

Arran Dowling-Hussey and Derek Dunne, *Arbitration Law* (2nd ed., Round Hall, 2014)

Barry Mansfield, *Arbitration Act 2010 and Model Law: A Commentary* (Clarus Press, 2012)

Bryan McMahon and William Binchy, *Law of Torts* (4th ed., Bloomsbury, 2013)

David Browne and Patrick McGovern, *Procurement Law in Ireland* (Round Hall, 2018)

Declan Madden and Anthony Kerr, *Unfair Dismissal Cases and Commentary* (2nd ed., FIE: Federation of Irish Employers, 1996)

Desmond Ryan, *Redmond on Dismissal Law* (3rd ed., Bloomsbury, 2017)

Fidelma White and Mary Donnelly, *Consumer Law: Rights and Regulation* (Round Hall, 2014)

Fidelma White, *Commercial Law* (2nd ed., Round Hall, 2012)

Gerard Hogan, Gerry Whyte, David Kenny and Rachel Walsh, *Kelly: The Irish Constitution* (5th ed., Bloomsbury, 2018)

Hilary Biehler, *Equity and the Law of Trusts* (7th ed., Round Hall, 2020)

John Breslin, *Banking Law* (3rd ed., Round Hall, 2013)

Mairead Enright, *Principles of Irish Contract Law* (Clarus, 2007)

Ronan Keane, *Equity and the Law of Trusts in Ireland* (3rd ed., Bloomsbury, 2017)

Michael Twomey and Maedhbh Clancy, *Twomey on Partnership* (2nd ed., Bloomsbury, 2019)

Níamh Howlin and Noel McGrath, *Lyall's Land Law in Ireland* (4th ed., Round Hall, 2018)

Paul A. McDermott and James McDermott, *Contract Law* (2nd ed., Bloomsbury, 2017)

Raymond Byrne, Paul McCutcheon, Claire Bruton and Gerard Coffey, *The Irish Legal System* (6th ed., Bloomsbury, 2014).

Robert Clark, *Contract Law in Ireland* (8th ed., Round Hall, 2016)

Tanya Ní Mhuirthile, Catherine O'Sullivan and Liam Thornton, *Fundamentals of the Irish Legal System: Law, Policy and Politics* (Round Hall, 2016)

Index

The numbers here refer to paragraph numbers.

Index